(MULTI) MEDIA TRANSLATION

BENJAMINS TRANSLATION LIBRARY

The Benjamins Translation Library aims to stimulate academic research and training in translation studies, lexicography and terminology. The Library provides a forum for a variety of approaches (which may sometimes be conflicting) in a historical, theoretical, applied and pedagogical context. The Library includes scholarly works, reference books, post-graduate text books and readers in the English language.

Volume 34

Yves Gambier and Henrik Gottlieb (eds.)

(Multi) Media Translation

Concepts, practices, and research

(MULTI) MEDIA TRANSLATION

CONCEPTS, PRACTICES, AND RESEARCH

Edited by

YVES GAMBIER
University of Turku

HENRIK GOTTLIEB
University of Copenhagen

JOHN BENJAMINS PUBLISHING COMPANY
AMSTERDAM/PHILADELPHIA

The paper used in this publication meets the minimum requirements of American National Standard for Information Sciences — Permanence of Paper for Printed Library Materials, ANSI Z39.48-1984.

Library of Congress Cataloging-in-Publication Data

(Multi)media translation : concepts, practices, and research / edited by Yves Gambier, Henrik Gottlieb.

p. cm. -- (Benjamins translation library, ISSN 0929-7316 ; v. 34)

Papers presented at two conferences held Sept. 26-27, 1997, near Rimini, Italy and Oct. 15-16, 1998, Berlin, Ger.

Includes bibliographical references and index.

1. Translating and interpreting--Congresses. 2. Multimedia systems--Congresses. I. Title. Multimedia translation. II. Gambier, Yves, 1949- III. Gottlieb, Henrik. IV. Series.

P306.93 M85 2001
418'.02--dc21 2001035865
ISBN 90 272 1639 8 (Eur.) / 1 58811 088 5 (US)

John Benjamins Publishing Co. • P.O.Box 36224 • 1020 ME Amsterdam • The Netherlands
John Benjamins North America • P.O.Box 27519 • Philadelphia PA 19118-0519 • USA

Table of Contents

Part III: Empirical Research

MULTIMEDIA, MULTILINGUA: MULTIPLE CHALLENGES

1. Language and the Screen

Globalization, in many ways a cliché, does have some pretty direct implications for us all, as modern Information and Communication Technology (ICT) is changing a large part of our daily lives. At the same time, communication itself becomes a product in the international marketplace. For these two reasons, language practices – and, most of all, those related to language transfer – are gaining importance these years and increasingly affect the circulation of knowledge, the development of cultural identities, etc. We see it in the mass media, in business, wherever people work and interact. Language competence plays a more and more important role through reading text on TV/video/computer screens, through the reception of online (Internet) and offline (CD-ROM) products. Computerized work stations, production based on data processing, dissemination of information on the Web, identification of groups (firms, associations) use both verbal language and other semiotic systems. Convergence between media, telecommunications and ICT keeps increasing the multimedial, or polysemiotic, nature of electronic communication.

A great many studies have been done about the impact of technology on democratic decisions, public administration, work, business, services (educational and training services, social and health care, access to information and culture). But very few have considered the impact of technology on our command of (foreign) languages, or the effects that our (lack of) linguistic skills have on technology, even though modern communications technology implies multilingualism, yet at the same time paves the way for the development of a *lingua franca*.

The challenges are not only industrial, political, social, administrative, juridical, ethical; they are also cultural and linguistic. Change in technology is always faster than change in our behaviour, as supply in technology is often ahead of consumer demand.

With all these concerns in mind, two international forums were recently organized. This volume is a collection of selected contributions from these two events. The Misano Seminar on *Multimedia & Translation*, held near

Rimini (September 26-27, 1997) was structured around four thematic sessions, with contributions from more than 20 specialists. The two-day Berlin conference (October 15-16, 1998) presented parallel sessions and two panel discussions, the key issue being *Quality and Standards in Audiovisual Language Transfer*.

The present volume contains the edited results of some of the presentations and debates. Altogether the two events had nearly 350 participants from both private and public sectors, including scholars, professional translators and interpreters, postgraduate students, decision-makers on language adaptation from the media, producers, manufacturers of language technology and tools, distributors, etc.

The 26 contributions are arranged in order to constitute, as far as possible, a structured and cohesive whole, yet some overlapping could not be avoided. In what follows, we would like to present a general perspective.

2. Concepts

Thoughts on language in the media are of quite recent origin. Since 1995, the number of conferences and other fora dealing with language transfer in TV, radio, cinema and video has increased, and yet, if you consult Journals like *Communication and the Media Studies*, *Gazette – The International Journal for Communication Studies, Communication Research, Discourse and Society, European Journal of Communication, Media, Culture and Society, Theory, Culture and Society, New Media & Society*, and catalogues of different collections focusing on the media from publishing houses like Sage, John Libbey / University of Luton Press, etc., the feeling is that specialized studies are rather restricted. There are many monographs, essays, directories about media production in a free market economy, media distribution, media effects on children, stereotypes, violence, etc., the audience, history and future of the media, rights and their regulation and control authorities, media policy, but practically nothing about the media as one of the essential elements in forming cultural and linguistic identities. Multimedia localization also seems to be out of the hands of professional and academic circles usually dealing with translation.

In addition, audiovisual and multimedia translation do not rule out terminological misunderstanding. As a case in point, even a simple term as 'subtitler' may be ambiguous. This is due to the different division of labour found at different subtitling companies and TV channels: the tasks of translating, editing and subtitle cueing might be done by two people (translator + technician) or by just one (translator = subtitler).

It is also easy to notice the great diversity of expectations and representations related to the concept of translation, hence the different labels existing today in some professional fields: localization, language transfer, adaptation, editing, revision, documentation management, co-authoring, technical writing, multilingual text creation and design, versioning, language mediation, language-service provision, language management, proofreading, copywriting, language consultancy, etc. There are at least two reasons for this: "translation" remains synonymous with transcoding, word for word, while the concept of "text" is no longer seen as a string of sentences, partly because language is seen as being integrated with images, sounds, graphics, etc. (see section 5). This double explanation shows how the concepts of translation and the translator's world are generally considered archaic.

Whatever the label, it is realized that translation is not a simple transfer from one language to another, but a complex process, a set of activities including at least such basics as review, layout, respect for writing and punctuation conventions, converting currencies and ways of giving time, dates and addresses, minding legal, fiscal and security regulations, etc. In short, the new labels for translation jobs make explicit why clients have to pay what they are asked to pay.

In connection with these designations, several important questions have to be raised. Two at least have to be borne in mind: how to get a better idea of the translation market and predict the needs of tomorrow if we do not have reliable data due to lack of consensus on the definition of supply and demand? What competencies must future translators be trained in, and how can curricula be adapted accordingly? These questions were implicit at the Misano and Berlin conferences.

The last terminological hesitation: how do we define "media"? In professional and academic contexts, the notion of screen translation has for a long time been synonymous with subtitling and dubbing; but it also covers voice-over, narration, simultaneous interpreting and surtitling. To what extent can we integrate the discussion concerning radio, TV, DVD (Digital versatile disk) and the Internet?

Is convergence a problem in the perspective of translation and Translation Studies? Is surtitling an opera similar to localizing software? Is interpreting in a TV studio like translating a CD-ROM?

In Translation Studies, texts with pictures have for a long time been ignored. K.Reiss (1971: *Möglichkeiten und Grenzen der Übersetzungskritik*. München: Hueber, p. 34) was the first to our knowledge to draw attention to the "audio-medial" texts which have been written to be spoken or sung, for instance, political speeches, lectures, songs, opera libretti. Later in 1984 (with H.Vermeer: *Grundlegung einer allgemeinen Translationstheorie*. Tübingen: Niemeyer, p. 211), Reiss replaced the term by "multi-medial" in order to include texts such as comics which have visual but not acoustic elements.

"Multimedia", nowadays a buzzword, was first associated with teaching (slides, TV, video) and underground art forms, but then its importance increased with computers and the Internet. In the same way, "audiovisual" has for a long time been limited to training and education, for methods using pictures and sounds. Its meaning has gradually changed, more and more often referring to cinema and TV screens. In fact, multimedia communication is ubiquitous in daily life. We exploit multiple sensory systems or modes of communication including vision, audition, and touch. Aren't all "texts" such polysemiotic multi-signs? Booklets, prospectuses, magazines, children's books, ads, all combine verbal utterances, images, drawings; they play with typography and layout. Hence, the new ambiguity: sometimes drama and opera translation are placed together with the translation of films and TV programmes, while translation or localization for Web or CD-ROM media is forgotten; sometimes all polysemiotic documents (including spoken and written natural language, graphics, non-speech audio, maps, animation, etc.) are considered to be multimedia. Without a doubt there is a certain confusion here between media in a *stricto sensu* meaning (TV, cinema, computer) and codes such as verbal and visual codes. However, screen translation (film, domestic and corporate video, TV programmes), translation for and on the Net, translation of offline products and services might come under the same umbrella of "multimedia translation". Indeed, with audiovisual and multimedia texts, the borders are blurred between centre and periphery in terms of production and reception, between public and private sectors in terms of organization, between distance and proximity in terms of space, between live and pre-recorded in terms of broadcasting, between reality and fiction in terms of reference, between written and oral in terms of code, between verbal and non-verbal in terms of systems of signs. The new media literacy results from ubiquity, portability, flexibility, and interconnection of the media. Interactivity is also a key word, with various degrees depending on whether you are dealing with TV, CD-ROM, or the Internet: the consumers' behaviour is not really the same in front of each type of screen. The use of TV is rather family-oriented, while the use of the computer is rather individual.

In addition to their multimodal dimension, audiovisual and multimedia translation typically have these four features in common:

(1) Teamwork is crucial, whether simultaneous and non-linear, or cumulative, as for instance in drama translation, in which the commissioner, the publisher, the translator, the director and the actors take the floor successively.

(2) Translators often work with intermediate "texts" (scenarios, scripts, drafts), which tends to defy the traditional dichotomy between source and target text. The work is mostly done in order to produce and broadcast products with a limited lifespan. In this case, translators do not refine a static text to be used or distributed over many years for a local market.

(3) Criteria applied to audiovisual and multimedia translation are comprehensibility (the logic of structuring and reading hypertexts is not the logic of a conventional "text"), accessibility and usability. The function of these texts

prevails over the quality of their legibility, over their acceptability, too often limited to language norms. The new media compel us to review the roles of written and oral language as well as the established view on translation, where error analysis is no longer the only relevant criterion for evaluation.

(4) Finally, the above characteristics have implications for training, as the gap between universities and professional life is becoming more and more pronounced.

In their own way and from their own experiences, the seven authors of the contributions in Part I (P. Cattrysse, A. Remael, S. Viaggio, D. Sánchez-Mesa Martínez, J. Ritter Werner, G. Goethals and K. Wehn) ponder the relationship between media and multimedia, verbal translation and multimedia translation, the links between text, images and sounds, the new models of communication inferred by ICT, the new elements and parameters of translating for the cinema, video, CD-ROM, the Web, etc.

They all point to the necessity of interdisciplinarity. Translation Studies must open up to Communication Studies, Media and Film Studies, Cultural Studies, as well as to Semiotics, Sociology, Anthropology, Information Sciences and Computer Sciences. It is not certain, however, that multimedia translation will become a specialized object of study; to date, we cannot speak of a uniform field of audiovisual and multimedia Translation Studies (see A. Pym).

3. Changing Landscapes

3.1 Transformation of the Audiovisual Market

Different factors are influencing the multilingual AV landscape. Among them, we can consider (I) distribution, (II) digitization and (III) supply of programmes.

(I) The rapid internationalization of distribution alters the trade strategies concerning films and TV programmes. At the same time, majors American film companies (Columbia, Fox, Warner, Disney, MCA/Universal, Paramount, Metro-Goldwyn-Mayer) have a stronger hold over distribution circuits, either directly in every country, or through mergers and alliances with local distributors. The financial integration between TV broadcasting companies and the film industry, as well as the synergy between broadcasting, cinema releases and video & DVD rentals and sales, make transnational management of AV products and services more and more dependant on communication.

A feature-length film generally follows a rather linear chronology in its distribution: it may be paid for in advance by a television channel, released in cinemas, marketed on VHS and DVD, broadcast on scrambled TV, then on pay-per-view TV, and finally on public TV channels. This chronology in various distribution circuits is still the subject of hard negotiations between producers, distributors, broadcasters, TV owners, and European authorities (cf. the directive "TV without borders").

(II) Digitization is changing production and broadcasting and speeding up convergence between media, telecommunication and ICT. The volume of programming will increase accordingly. The competitive advantage already lies in ownership of the rights to quality programming. This is changing the relationship between the owners of rights and distributors and leading to vertical integration of the broadcasting industry. Commercial and technical convergence of networks and equipment (PC, TV sets, telephones) does not yet imply convergence of copyrights and regulations. But to what extent are TV viewers and computer users interchangeable? Is the digitized cultural industry leading to language standardization?

(III) A few other technological innovations are worth mentioning here because they are also changing the relationship between cinema, TV and viewers:

* The Internet with large capacities for storing and showing films and TV programmes. But, for all that, do we have to dream of digitopia?

* The DVD format is capable of storing up to 8 different soundtracks (the original plus max. seven dubbed versions) plus 32 different sets of subtitles for the same film (*interlingual* subtitles in number of different languages as well as *intralingual* subtitles for different audiences: the deaf and hard of hearing, young viewers, etc.).

Until now, TV production and distribution have very often been seen as simply mass media communication, understood as unilateral, one-way communication – from a single transmitter to all the TV sets receiving the same programme at the same hour. These patterns are frequently also in agreement with the homology taken for granted between a country (territory), a language and a mode of language transfer. Today, AV is more and more marked by relay and networking, with pay-TV, transfrontier television, thematic TV channels, local TV, ethnic TV programmes, all of which have increased thanks to cable and satellite television.

This development towards more precise targets has linguistic consequences: by watching a channel on e.g. history, sports, cartoons or financial affairs, the viewer expects to hear a certain register and terminology, a certain style and rhetoric. Will the fragmentation of audience, analogous to the division between the 'inforich' and the 'infopoor', be defined in sociological and linguistic terms, leading to or reproducing inequalities between age groups, natives and migrants, urban dwellers and rural dwellers? Maybe the development only indicates the end of a centralized model, in challenging the language standard – the viewers changing habits from watching non-specialized channels to favoring specialized ones. The AV media seem to be both a factor of differentiation and a factor of homogenization. They cease to be exclusively mass communication, hence the difference between broadcasting and narrowcasting because audiences have varying sociolinguistic and terminological expectations.

The effects of the three factors briefly outlined above are enough to show the tensions and contradictions on the AV market, the challenge represented by linguistic and cultural diversity.

Some of the contributions in this volume discuss the current transformations in AV media policy (A. Jäckel, R. Meylaerts) and the alternatives in the different modes of language transfer (P. Zabalbeascoa et al., F. Karamitroglou).

3.2 Some Language Complexities in Multimedia

In a very limited period of time, the World Wide Web has grown into a standard communication medium. Since the first prototype in 1991, the Web has come into use at an amazing pace. But simply having a Web presence does not guarantee that a site will attract visitors. The multitude of available websites decreases the chances of reaching the interested audiences and of achieving the intended communicative effects. The web presence should no longer be the responsibility of only the computer people: it should be treated as an essential and integrated part of a (internal and external) communication policy.

There are quite a lot of books on the technical aspects of website design, but very few have a communications perspective. As if producing communication were not an interactive process, involving designers and users, in which one seeks the best possible solution to a particular communication problem, in order to present information in concise and well-organized terms, according to certain rhetorical conventions and cultural habits. Hardly a webpage goes by without announcing a new language-enabled product or service for business, international communication, or the home-user. Decades of language-processing development are finally maturing, especially in such areas as speech interfaces, smarter search engines, more extensive product multilingualism and Machine Translation (MT). Data and information on the Internet reflect more and more the language diversity of the Net, even if English remains the dominant language.

Along with this increased multilingualism there is an increased need for translation of webpages – to say nothing about auctions of translations on the Net, a way to get better prices with new providers. On the Hyperkoran server, for instance, there are different possibilities: the written illuminated version of the Koran, the sung version, translations in several languages, the phonetic transcript in Latin (in order to sing the Arabic text). A number of firms are ready to transfer their documentation onto Intranets: their information is thus centralized, quickly updated and instantly disseminated. If there is a need for foreign versions, translating must be equally quick without the translator getting instructions on what needs changing. She/he uses a translation memory system; she/he has to check the coherence between key words to be translated and the related documents; with a new webpage, she/he has to insert the text among vignettes, pictures, icons. The use of free services of online MT is inevitable to speed up the production of contents. World Community Forum, Systran, Easy Translator, Web Translator, Auto Translate and Babelfish are examples of such a service. E-mails and advertisements are being translated in a few minutes.

The language quality of MT text often makes people smile, to put it mildly. However, in spite of the obvious limits of the output, the permanent access and the speed of the work are qualities worth considering.

To easily monitor, identify and align all the content and changes in multilingual websites is an asset: it would be a real pity if localization were taken out of translators' hand for good because of a terminological misunderstanding and because their training would not have been adapted.

What about online software products with their help files and their manuals, and offline products like CD-ROM? The production of the latter is diversified: you have cultural and educational products, encyclopedias, dictionaries and games. The localization/translation of all these products aims to adapt to the linguistic and cultural characteristics of the addressees, of the contents dealing with information, arts, training, etc. Contents are both verbal and iconic (a letter box on the roadside, the head of a baseball coach, a drawing of a smiling face, an apple, etc.).

In the case of CD-ROMs, translation also has to respect the norms, conventions and values of the receivers. This includes dubbing, text adaptation, sometimes changes in the pictures and addition of sounds, etc. To localize a CD-ROM with English nursery rhymes implies finding texts consistent with the new context, and recordings if possible without copyrights to be paid. Translating, editing, selecting voices, sound mixing, management of different contracts are all various steps that are better developed together with the "original" and arranged in different files. In all cases, the translator is part of a team made up of technical, artistic, legal, business and field experts. With multimedia, any topic is possible: cooking, Peruvian Indians, biology, heart troubles, Impressionism, Andersen's fairy tales, European children in traffic, etc.

The dichotomy media/multimedia is no longer a sustainable one. It is a pity that this convergence was outside the focus of both the Misano seminar (1997) and the Berlin conference (1998) in discussions of translators' perspectives, their skills, attitudes, routines and training. Hence the brackets around (Multi) in the title of this book: they signal an absence and provide the incentive to examine both entities together.

4. Language Transfer

4.1 Practices

To the three factors already mentioned in section 3.1, we could add the changes in the working conditions of screen translators – changes connected with privatization of TV channels, relocation, development of subcontracting and the emergence of multinational companies in subtitling and dubbing. These conditions are such that nowadays some TV channels prefer to hire freelancers; they are cheaper and not always aware of reruns.

What about quality in language transfer? On the one hand, changes at work tend to deskill specialists, and on the other hand, audiovisual media (especially television) are given a more important role in keeping, transforming and spreading sociolinguistic norms.

Yesterday, language standards were defined by literature, school, the press. Is this the case today with the audiovisual media? Screens have changed the hierarchy between genres (comics, programme for children, documentary, science fiction, horror) which are no longer "minor". But are they really the place and power source of linguistic standardization? True, because of their omnipresence, they do help bring about certain linguistic changes.

In this perspective, quality has to be defined in the transfer process, in relation to translators' rights and duties, and in the final product. Several papers, especially in Berlin 1998, have emphasized this problem. E. Gummerus and C. Paro have stressed that quality in subtitling has an organizational aspect which implies strong cooperation between various decision-makers and employees. This conception has consequences for the recruiting of freelance subtitlers, on-the-job training and work results. We share the concern of F. Mueller: wherever we are, in Finland or in Australia, the way we select translators has implications for what is written on the screen, what the editor and reviewer will have to do. H. James wonders about quality control when you have to meet a client's expectations. Obviously this control should be linked with the linguistic role the TV channel is willing to play. Subtitling might be done in a conventional way (H.R. Morgan), or in real time (C. den Boer), or in special conditions like during a public performance (see surtitling opera by L. Dewolf); the fact remains that several quality parameters can be defined. The translator aims to make subtitling or surtitling legible, acceptable and as precise as possible. This means that she/he has to take into consideration her/his working situation, the available tools (is there access to the dialogue list? Cf. J. Diaz Cintas), the functions of language in the audiovisual media (for instance, according to the genre) and the conditions of reception (age, level of education, reading habits of the viewers).

Among the features of an optimum quality in subtitling worth mentioning are spatiotemporal features (fonts, position and the length of the two lines on the screen) and textual features (division into semantic and syntactic coherent units; language register; etc.). Between these sets of features, (good) subtitle punctuation establishes a certain rhythm in reading and makes immediate processing and comprehension of the subtitles easier (cf. C. Cerón). The viewer's comfort is the result of the legibility and readability of the subtitles.

Quality requirements for simultaneous interpreting in a TV studio have different criteria, partly because the communication situation and the audience expectations are different (cf. B. Alexieva, G. Mack).

4.2 Empirical Research

Subtitling has been under systematic investigation for rather a short time. Research methodology is still uncertain; problems are sometimes difficult to work out; explanations are groped for in the dark. A. Assis Rosa shares her original thoughts on the role of oral code and oralization in writing subtitles. It is not only a difference of register; more radically, the question is how to represent an oral code within the written one and to find out why in subtitling there is a reluctance to insert oral features. Here one might raise the question of standard vs. non-standard varieties in subtitles and, implicitly, the question of the translator's and the commissioner's attitudes towards the language to be used on the screen. The same has to be asked about foreign-language influence (cf. H. Gottlieb on Anglicisms in Danish).

Subtitling *La haine* forces one to take a stand on how young people talk, their slang, since such or such a translation decision will have socio-political and socio-linguistic implications (cf. A. Jäckel). To better understand these implications, we must know the financial effects of a film, the reactions from different audiences with their own values. Nor can the cultural references be transferred in a mechanical way, even though the time-and-space constraints limit the strategies available to the subtitler (as demonstrated between Polish and French by T. Tomaszkiewicz).

One last effect of subtitling that we want to mention here has been largely neglected so far: its impact on language acquisition (cf. M. van den Poel & G. d'Ydewalle) and on maintaining language competence. A survey conducted in 1997 has shown that 75% of TV viewers of BBC World watch the channel to improve their English. Those responsible for broadcasting at F3 and TV5 (in French), and TV4 (in Swedish), to give just a few examples, have understood this function of intralingual subtitles. Intra- and interlingual subtitling does play a major role in strengthening reading skills. We are reading TV!

5. (Multi)Media Translation and Translation Studies

The electronic media with their polysemiotic codes somehow disturb the established world of translation and the discipline of Translation Studies. How should translators' organizations, for instance, classify subtitlers? They hardly belong in the field of "technical translation", "literary translation", or "conference interpreting"? In (subtitling) countries like Holland and Denmark, screen translators now have their own organizations. But what about localizers of computer games and technical software? This question may already be irrelevant since localizers tend to identify with the computer industry rather than with their role as language professionals.

Within Translation Studies, the media force us to reformulate certain questions and to redefine certain concepts which have for a long time been taken for granted. For instance, the concepts of "text" and "meaning". With a film or a webpage, "meaning" is not generated by verbal signs only: it is based on the totality of verbal utterances and non-verbal signs (pictures, sounds, music, non-verbal elements, graphics, graphic design, colours, etc.). "Text" usually calls for a well-ordered sequence of sentences, a regular structure, referring to a specific genre; sometimes the "text" comes with a certain language standard: you don't write the way you speak. On TV and computer screens, there are dialogue lines or fluid discourse (hypertext), fragmented on the surface, the coherence being established through the context: visual and sound elements are not cosmetic features of embellishment but constitutive parts of the meaning. Hyperlinks on the webpage are there so that verbal utterances function with pictures, maps, tables, dictionaries and other websites. The organization of data, information, sentences, in relation to users' assumed knowledge, and to other parts of the film or the site, compels the reader to question the role of language in the media, and urges the translator to wonder about translating strategies (expansion, substitution, omission, explication, etc.) Instead of the term "text" one may prefer "document" in these situations where various semiotic systems subordinated to each other in different ways are combined: the verbal (written or oral) sometimes dominates, sometimes plays a minor role. The media communication therefore alters a number of representations, a number of well-established norms, most of them coming from the literary tradition.

Ways of reading are changing as well. Reading with constant monitoring gives way to fragmented reading: the viewer jumps from the subtitles to the picture, from one subtitle to another, both running at a different speed. The Netsurfer jumps from one part of the website to another, without caring about the possible linear order of elements. Thus, the effort to understand is no longer focused on only one system of signs, on only one logic. These performative and multimodal dimensions affect translating (multi)media. For this type of translation, Reception Studies are not only to be understood as in literary theory; they have to include such neuro-physiological and psycho-linguistic components as perception and comprehension of image-sound-word compounds. Reading subtitles on a screen is not identical to reading plain text. Another transformation: (multi)media translation working with "intermediate texts" (see section 2) alters not only the usual central position of "text", but also the central position of the interpretive authorities. Making a video or a website of a part of the Bible (cf. G. Goethals, J.R. Werner) is to displace the central authority of the written text as the source of biblical truth, to challenge the conventional concept of Scriptural authority (Sacred texts) and to give rise to a new set of interpretive authorities.

The different modes of language transfer in audiovisual media and localization in multimedia make it clear that translation does not end with "text" but with delivery. This dynamic view of translation forces us to consider the multisemiotic dimension of multinational communication of today, to take into consideration the various parameters and constraints which determine the (multi)media production.

To what extent is the concept of (multi)media translation relevant to Translation Studies?

* It reveals the complexities and challenges of all types of communication and highlights the necessary functions of any translation.

* It establishes certain ways of viewing language, of dealing with verbal code, of considering the relationship between verbal and other semiotic systems in order to focus more on cultural and communicative aspects rather than solely on language and text.

* It forces us to rethink concepts like "original" "meaning", "faithfulness", "acceptability", "readability", "usability" – concepts which involve consideration of source text/culture(s), the medium, communication models, distribution channels, the ability of the audience to participate in the reconstruction of meaning. The different shifts of paradigm brought about by new media involve the interpretive process, the authority of a written text, the role of functional equivalence, and the addressing of an audience – to give just some examples.

* It shatters the very notion of translation, to which a consensual definition has never been tied. Translation has now come into contact with other activities such as technical writing, editing and so on (see section 2).

* It changes the work of translating and revising, for a long time submitted to written language standards, "textual" conventions.

* It leads us to take a fresh look at the translator's competencies and practices, at the ways of recruiting and testing, and hence at training methodology.

In spite of the many contributions presented in this volume, research in (multi)media translation remains difficult (cf. A. Pym), for lack of appropriate theoretical frames and methodological tools. Until today, this research has not been confronted, for instance, by relevance theory, polysystemic approach, critical discourse analysis (so useful in Media Studies) or cognitive psychology. Does it cover too many different modes (subtitling, dubbing, voice-over, interpreting, localization, etc.)? Does it call for too many disciplines, like Film and Media Studies, Semiotics, Cultural Studies? Is it a new field of study with a new profile of experts or an umbrella framework for scholars from various specialized disciplines? Is it a trick to surpass the absence or the loss of prestige in translation research?

These questions remain open. But we trust that the 26 contributions will give a fair picture of what is going on.

6. Acknowledgements

Many thanks are due to all the participants who have contributed to the debate. Those present in Misano will remember the Assisi earthquake at the beginning of our seminar – maybe a sign that in the near future (multi)media will shake up the work of all translators and the field of Translation Studies.

We would also like to warmly thank Bob Hodgson, Irena Kovačič and José Lambert for their advice and fruitful assistance before and during the Misano seminar, and Mary Carroll for her efficient help before and in Berlin.

Finally special thanks to Jane Lindell and Jonna Ristolainen for their patience in preparing the manuscript for publication.

November 2000

Yves Gambier, University of Turku (Finland)
Henrik Gottlieb, University of Copenhagen (Denmark)

PART I: CONCEPTS

MULTIMEDIA & TRANSLATION: METHODOLOGICAL CONSIDERATIONS

Patrick Cattrysse
Flanders Script Academy
Brussels, Belgium

1. Concepts & Terminology

There are many definitions of *multimedia* (MM) just as there are many types of multimedia projects: electronic books, electronic magazines, multimedia databases, interactive education, interactive games, interactive music, interactive art and performance, interactive sales and marketing, presentations and communications, desktop and videoconferencing, productivity and authoring tools, etc. Multimedia has become a buzzword that is used in so many senses and contexts that its meaning has started to wear away.

Multimedia can be defined in a very wide sense as 'the processing and presentation of information in two or more media simultaneously. In a more narrow, and gradually more usual sense, however, multimedia is referred to when speaking of the processing and presentation of text, graphics and pictures, if not animation and motion video. Another important parameter that is generally required is interactivity.

Translation studies have evolved from linguistic and literary translation into audio-visual (AV) and so-called media translation, and now into *multimedia* (MM) *translation*. MM translation, like media translation, is often understood as the (verbal) translation of the linguistic part of MM messages. This approach is problematic because it isolates the linguistic part from the rest of the MM message[1]. Questions concerning the relations between the linguistic part and the rest of the MM message are not often raised. If one wants to analyse how the translation of the linguistic elements of a MM message affects its global MM effect, one has to integrate the analysis of the verbal part within the global MM communication.

Progressively, scholars have learned that even so-called *verbal translation* is never purely verbal. Through the words, other codes such as cultural (e.g. politeness codes), political, and economic codes are translated at the same time. Let us agree that for the comfort of the reader, this complementary aspect of *verbal translation* is understood when it remains implicit hereafter.

Audio-visual or multimedia translation can also be defined as *the translation of a message into an AV or MM message*. Traditionally, however, these translational phenomena are called *adaptations*. Elsewhere, however, I have explained that translations and adaptations show important resemblances (cf. Cattrysse 1992: 11-19). This second definition of AV or MM translation offers several important advantages: the analysis is able to integrate the linguistic translational aspects into the global AV or MM communication. Furthermore, an integrated approach permits to analyse what is common and what is specific to verbal and nonverbal translation. One practical drawback however, might be that this implies a truly interdisciplinary approach integrating scholars, research methods and terminology coming from different disciplines and faculties.

2. The Multimedia production process

MM production combines business models from different industries: the print industry, the software and telecommunications industry and more recently the film and TV industry. As technologies keep on changing, combined skills and working methods change with them, and the search for better management of the production process continues. Consequently, the MM production process is not fixed as of yet. The very idea of starting every production with a plan or *scenario* is quite new in MM production, and the phases that MM producers distinguish, vary from one company to another. Following the AV-paradigm, one can distinguish a pre-production phase from a production and post-production phase. The pre-production phase concerns all preparatory activities. Although standardisation is still in progress, one can generally distinguish four steps:

- concept development and planning
- design (and sometimes prototyping)
- screenplay
- flow chart[2]

The concept and development phase gathers information about the approach (e.g. CD-ROM, DVD, on-line application), the content, the target audience, the objectives, the use of the programme (e.g. stand-alone vs. guided application), the evaluation criteria, budget, deadlines, technical requirements, etc. The design phase deals with the design of the information, the interactivity and the graphic or interface or still screen design. The screenplay is a text-based document that describes in a chronological way what is seen and heard in the programme, and how users can interact with the programme. The flow chart offers a graphical presentation of the successive screens to be seen, sounds to be heard, and summarises the (type of) content (e.g. titles of chapters to choose, pictures, moving images, sounds fragments, etc.).

This is followed by the production phase where the different media elements such as text, graphics, photographs and moving images, animation and sound, speech and music are produced.

During the post-production phase, these media elements are digitised (if necessary) and integrated with interactivity through programming. Then, the product is tested and (if meant for the consumer market) marketed and distributed.

3. Multimedia and translational phenomena

3.1 Different types of verbal translation

Multimedia production encounters many types of translational behaviour, even if we restrict the concept to the translation from one natural language to another. Verbal translation often turns into copywriting or copyfitting, matching spatial restrictions. These restrictions resemble those traditionally known in the print industry: text has to fit within a specific space on the printed page. A similar restriction occurs in multimedia production: text strings take up a certain amount of space, not only on the screen, but also within resources or other internal storage areas in a system, authoring tool or programming resource. Text written in one language may take twice or thrice as much space in another language. This implies that translators working in MM translation ought to know the basics of MM production and that they must collaborate closely with the graphic designer and the programmer. The better their collaboration is, the better the graphic surrounding will fit the different translated versions.

MM translation also means dubbing existing voice-overs or speaking characters. This presents time-related restrictions, also known in traditional AV-production.

Next to copywriting or copyfitting, verbal translation can imply adapting content to different target culture conventions and customs: what may look familiar to one audience may be offensive to another.

Since new technologies install new genres, verbal translation can also mean translating text from one genre into a new genre, installing or removing hyperlinks for example, or translating linear or flatland novels into hypernovels, etc.[3]

We have seen how the coming of computers and word-processing software has brought about a multiplication of the number of versions of texts, and consequently the amount of paper used or spoiled. With the coming of on-line texts, evolution takes us one step further: on-line texts get published earlier, but change quicker also. As a consequence, the nature of texts becomes more 'fluid'. Concepts like original, subsequent version, translation or adaptation shift consequently. A text may exist in one form or another one day, but change considerably the next day. No traces are left of the first version. Whereas printed texts are spatially fixed in their publication, electronic texts can move around and change places, servers or web addresses. As a consequence, it may be harder to retrieve a text, and traditional bibliographical references become inadequate if they can not be updated on a regular basis.

As AV and MM production becomes more expensive, the need for international production increases, and new types of translation are required: e.g. where international financing has to be found on the basis of pre-production documents, or where a project concerns an international production crew, translation may deal with synopses, design reports, screenplays, flow charts, etc., targeted either at several producer-financiers in different countries or cultures, or at the international production crew. According to the targeted reader, the translations will be written in a different style since they focus on different objectives: a purely informative, neutral style if intended for the production crew; a more promotional style if addressed to potential financiers. In these cases, it might be important for translators to acquire some knowledge about the type of documents they are translating.

3.2 Translation occurs at different times

In MM production, translational phenomena occur at different times. Translation decisions often occur as an afterthought when the project has been successful on a local or national basis. Only then does the client think it could be interesting to produce translations or versions in other languages. Needless to say, in MM production, this way of proceeding creates many problems. Verbal text has been stored with nonverbal material in identical files, and to translate or to change the textual parts, one has to adapt and reprogram the entire files. This is a time-consuming and thus costly process. More often than not, the result is unsatisfactory. Consequently, production managers should plan international distribution of their products as early as possible in the pre-production process, so as to permit the designers and programmers to prepare the translation possibilities from the very start.

Exceptions confirm the rule, and it happens that a multilingual market is considered early in the planning phase. However, since the production process – and especially the pre-production process – is not yet standardised in MM production, the exact moment where translation actually occurs, varies from one company to another. In some cases, MM producers might even decide to produce (parts of the) scripts in different languages simultaneously, for example if the information that has to be given differs considerably from one country to another in terms of content and volume, or when the different language versions have to look as 'originals' to the respective target audiences. An old question that pops up again then is: When does translation become simultaneous multilingual production?[4]

3.3 Verbal and nonverbal translation

Language is the most obvious element that must be changed in order to reach several native audiences, but it is not the only one. Although imagery and icons usually cross borders more easily than the printed or spoken word, not all visuals function in a universal way.

In some cases, verbal translation goes hand in hand with the translation/adaptation of the nonverbal material. When translating graphic material, it might be wise (if possible) to check with graphic designers in the respective target culture(s), to learn whether the visuals are offensive or not, and whether they are well-understood. Here, one interesting question araises: What are the relations between the verbal and the nonverbal translation? For example, if an icon has to be changed, it might well be that its description has to change, too. What if certain verbal information in one culture is better rendered nonverbally in another or vice versa? These simple questions show how crucial it is for any verbal translator to keep a close eye at all times on the global MM message. As stated above, it implies, again, that the translator is familiar with the reading of and working with the different MM pre-production documents: e.g. that he/she can read a flow chart or screenplay, that it is clear how the verbal information fits into the global MM message, and what its partial function is with respect to the communicational whole.

4. Multimedia Translation: a specific discipline?

Should we develop a new MM Translation methodology? Is MM Translation a specialised object of study? Can we speak of a uniform field of MM Translation studies?

4.1 Translation and Intertextuality

If one accepts verbal translation as one out of many forms of intertextual relationships, studies in translational behaviour fit within the larger field of *Intertextuality studies*. This is actually old news since early in intertextuality studies of the 1970's, translations are set next to other types of intertextual relations such as the quotation, the parody, the summary, the adaptation, etc. Analysing verbal translation next to other types of intertextual relations is an interesting first step because a comparative or contrastive scope is the only way to pinpoint the specifics vs. the common features of translational relations and other types of intertextual relations.

Also, the concepts of *text* and *intertextuality* have broken out of the 'verbal text' corset since the early 1970's, in film studies in particular and semiotics in general[5]. Elsewhere[6], I have explained how some analytical tools for studying verbal intertextual relations (cf. Genette's *Palimpsestes*) can be used to study audio-visual translation or adaptation. Studying verbal translations next to nonverbal translations (e.g. AV or MM translations) represents a second interesting step since it permits the analysis to pinpoint the specifics vs. common features of verbal translation compared to nonverbal types of translation or adaptation.

4.2 Translation and Comparative Communication Studies

In Cattrysse (1997: 79ff.), I already suggested how a polysystem approach of film adaptation naturally evolves into what, by analogy to comparative literature, could be called *comparative film studies*. Film adaptations of novels for example do not only adapt the written literary material. At the same time, musical conventions, photographic and acting styles, but also target audience AV competence, and many other contextual factors co-determine the way the film adaptation is produced and the way it functions within a specific spatio-temporal context. In this way, comparative film studies actually continues the traditional intertextuality studies, but opens its perspectives – traditionally closed to linguistic or literary phenomena – onto AV and MM horizons. Applying the multilateral model as explained in Cattrysse (1997: 79ff.) to a historical functional analysis of all forms of communication, one could expand the concept even further and outline one common field of study called *comparative communication studies*[7] or *comparative semiotics* (including *comparative semantics* and *comparative pragmatics*). Every name will have disadvantages due to hereditary ballast. One practical procedure might be to apply state-of-the-art knowledge from various disciplines, in order to:

- Develop, try out, adapt methods (plural!) for descriptive (= historical) research
- Execute descriptive research
- Develop, try out, adapt methods (plural!) for education and training
- Execute training

On the level of research, this implies that on a meta-level, one determines one's object of study and then proceeds by describing:

1. How and why it was made the way it was made
2. How and why this object of study functions the way it does within its specific spatio-temporal context.

More concretely, it seems that using this model (cf. Figure 1), (Cattrysse 1997: 79ff.) may work on MM Translation just as well as it did in film adaptation studies. The different sources (modeling semiotic devices) refer to many different types of modeling source material: narrative, acting style, setting, photography, music and sound as well as the surrounding cultural, political, and social norms and conventions.

The object of study is one particular aspect of what is called *MM*

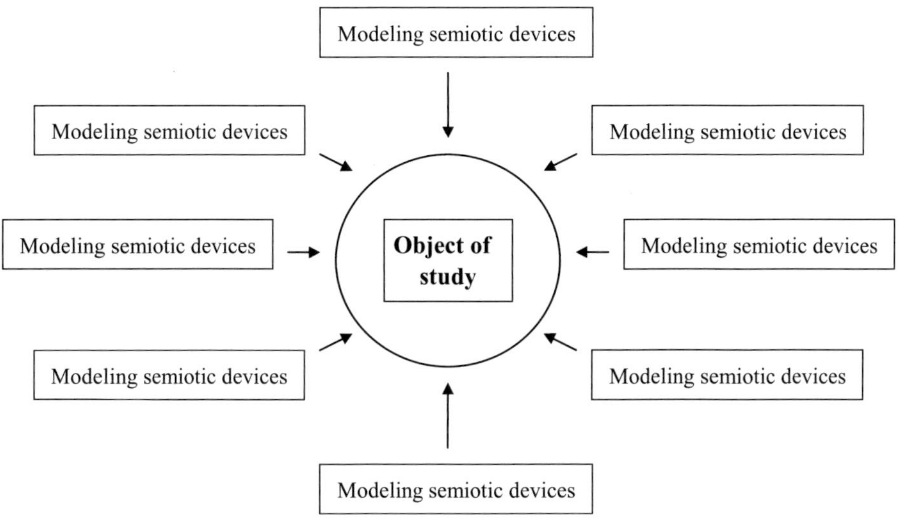

Figure 1. *Star diagram of translation*

Translation. The fact that scholars do not agree on what the words *multimedia* and *multimedia translation* mean, represents nothing new. One has only to check the many definitions that are used for what is called *translation*. This situation, however, does imply a number of consequences: it might be interesting to make a historical-functional analysis of the phenomena that have or have not functioned as *multimedia* or *multimedia translation*. Such an analysis might indicate possible similarities and differences among phenomena that in a specific spatio-temporal context have or have not functioned as such. On a meta-level, however, scholars still have to agree on terminology and objects of study. Considerations of social relevance may or may not be part of an argument to decide upon one object of study rather than another. Since the concept of multimedia translation can cover a large field of work, any scholar will necessarily have to limit the scope of her or his analysis. The only but necessary condition will be to make this limitation as explicit as possible.

The selected object of study can than be described as it functions or has functioned within a particular spatio-temporal context. Following the approach of Descriptive Translation Studies (cf. Toury 1995), the approach is descriptive and target-oriented. This does not imply that the target side is considered dominant a priori. Neither does it mean that the approach is binary, that is that it takes into account only one target text and one source text or model. A target-oriented approach only implies that the research starts with its object of study functioning within its proper context(s). Norms and models that function within this target context are studied next to norms and models that function outside this target context, and they may reveal to have been/be less important, equally important or more important.

As explained in Cattrysse (1997: 79ff.), Figure 1 presupposes only one target text which represents the object of study. If more than one object of study is analysed at the same time, one has only to multiply the circle with the objects of studies 2, 3, 4, and so on, and to multiply the respective boxes with modeling semiotic devices. Since only one object of study is presupposed in the scheme above, the arrows go in only one direction. Needless to say that if one (aspect) of the rectangular boxes with modeling semiotic devices is turned into an object of study, the arrows can/must be returned in the other direction. If a polysystem approach of MM Translation Studies is applied, then research can start with questions such as:

- How can we compare messages expressed in different semiotic systems?
- How can we establish tertia comparationes?
- How can we describe and explain the different translational processes in a systematic way?

- How can we describe and explain the final results of the translational processes?
- How can we describe and explain the functioning of these results within their respective target contexts?
- How can we translate research results into relevant information with an eye on MM Translation training and education?

On the level of training and education, questions to be asked include:

- What can we learn from research results?
- What are efficient MM Translations?
- How can we make efficient MM translations?
- How can we set up efficient training for making efficient MM translations?

Since MM translation touches many disciplines, the approaches will necessarily be highly interdisciplinary. Therefore, what is equally important is the willingness to recognise that multimedia translation studies goes beyond the immediate interest of each of us (= separate traditional disciplines), and the willingness to recognise as relevant also approaches and findings from other disciplines.

Reflecting the problems of the interdisciplinary MM production team, where collaboration goes through an often painful learning process, it is interesting to notice how academics and scholars will have to go through a similar learning process, probably even more painful, if they want to keep up with this new reality and be able to study this new object of study in an adequate way.

5. To translate or not to translate: Localisation vs. globalisation

5.1 Globalisation vs. localisation in the film industry

The question concerning localising vs. globalising communication represents a huge field of discussion. I pick up only one partial topic: *When is a message suitable/liable to be translated? What genres of French film are suitable for subtitling and thus for export?*

If it is possible to answer this question in general at all, a first reaction would be that:

1. for a message to appeal to an international audience, it must *function in an efficient way* in an international context. Generally speaking, this has nothing to do with genre. A very local genre such as the American Western has proven its

international success for many decades.
2. international appeal is not directly linked with the use of widely known languages as opposed to languages covering only a limited geographical space, such as Dutch. This has generally been the excuse for Belgian filmmakers to ask for ever more subsidies from the national and European authorities, who end up by actually paying the audience to come and see their movies. Phenomena like *Gaston & Leo*, *Max*, *Kamiel Spiessens* are Belgian television successes that are afterwards exploited in cinema. They all fail on the international market, not because of linguistic obstructions, but because the whole concept has never been developed with an international distribution in mind. Of course, the translation of humour is already a very special matter but stories can be successful or fail for many reasons. Since some European scholars and critics do not like to admit that we could learn from American film production, let us turn back to our European roots: Aristotle and his *Ars Poetika*, written somewhere between 335 and 323 B.C. Aristotle speaks mostly about the tragedy, but his principles apply just as well to audio-visual drama. This, the American cinema has proven more than extensively. Aristotle distinguishes six levels of audience appeal: plot, character, language, theme, spectacle and song (or music). A story can appeal on the level of plot because of efficient use of rhetoric, narrative or communicational devices. The crucial question here is: how does the communicator/narrator influence the empathy of the international audience? Empathy will also be the key word when dealing with character: what kind of characters are appealing to an international audience? Here we talk about physical, psychological, social, politico-economical and cultural features and values. The spectacle (joining the Latin 'speculum') refers to what is seen: the setting, the landscapes, the general atmosphere created through photography, editing, and eventually the special effects. The other elements speak for themselves: the themes and the way they are dealt with, the language (in aesthetic terms) that is used, the music and the sound.

So if Anne Jäckel in this volume asks *what genres (...) are suitable for (...) export*, this question does not so much relate to genre as to the elements mentioned by Aristotle. And language is clearly only one aspect of a communicational whole. As for genre, the concept is, if possible, even less clear than the concept of *multimedia*. Still genres have been in and out of fashion, but whatever made them fail or succeed has to pass through the communicational devices exposed above.

5.2 American or European universals?

If, in spite of the warnings of wise men, we nevertheless look at how American cinema has proceeded and managed to cover about 85% of the European market by now, we see that they attach a lot of importance not only to *character* and *spectacle* (sometimes but not always in a very literal sense), but also and especially to *plot*: which have become the universal communicative, narrative and rhetoric devices to enhance maximal empathy from an international audience? These communicative devices have been described extensively in (mostly) American manuals on screenwriting. Because of the mechanical nature of most of these writings, European scholars and writers alike have largely ignored this empirical knowledge or discarded it as not relevant. They did not understand that the mechanical nature was in the learning process, not in the application when properly assimilated.[8] Because of the apparent and at the same time misleading simplicity of the devices, many Europeans have not seen the underlying fundamental communicational mechanisms. Looking superficially at the manuals, they have thought that the limited number of communicational devices implied a limited number of formulas or even stories. They did not realise that, just as a limited number of phonemes permits an unlimited number of expressions, a limited number of communicational devices permits an unlimited number of communicative products. When communicational devices were badly applied, they blamed the communicational devices, whereas the limited skills of the communicator were to blame. Americans have been looking for universals ever since the beginning of cinema. Especially after World War II, they seem to have been successful in 'inventing' what Europeans often disdainfully call the American formula, as if there was only one formula, and as if this formula were American. After having read the preceding paragraph, it will come to no one as a surprise that most of the rhetorical devices were already exposed some 300 years before Christ in Aristotle's *Ars Poetika*.

Conclusion

To me, the largest challenge for multimedia translation seems to be the new types of colla-bo-ra-tion. Such new types of collaboration will be necessary on three levels: on the level of scientific research, on the level of education and training, and on the level of MM production. It is only when terminological and methodological barriers, as well as those related to power and money, are broken down, that research, training and production will find a way to efficiency and success. As has been said: 'Tout le reste n'est que littérature' (it's a lot of waffle).

Notes

1. Cf. Some of the studies on subtitling and dubbing.

2. See for example *Multimedia Demystified* (1994) by Apple Computer, Inc. (ed. Random House, New York)

3. On hypermedia and new forms of translation, see (a.o.) Landow 1992, Balasubramanian 1994 Deemer (1994), Moulthrop 1995, etc. See also Cattrysse (1997: 86).

4. About translation, adaptation and simultaneous multilingual production, see (a.o.) Vincendeau 1989.

5. Metz (1971: 66), for instance, defines text as *Tout déroulement sémiotique qu'il soit linguistique, non linguistique ou mixte*, that is *any chain of signs, linguistic, non-linguistic or mixed.*

6. See Cattrysse (1991 and 1992).

7. See also Cattrysse (1998: 8).

8. Think of the drill exercises in language courses: how mechanical it looked to speak sentences, ask questions, conjugating verbs, etc. Once the grammatical and other rules were assimilated though, speaking became natural.

SOME THOUGIITS ON THE STUDY OF MULTIMODAL AND MULTIMEDIA TRANSLATION

Aline Remael
Hoger Instituut voor Vertalers en Tolken
Hogeschool Antwerpen, Belgium

In this brief essay, I will attempt the beginning of an answer to some of he questions confronting anyone with a background in translation studies, wishing to venture into the new world of "Translation and Multimedia".

Multimedia has become somewhat of a catch-all phrase for a large array of new communication technologies. On the one hand, it is used to refer to an array of hi-tech features of our time such as interactive television, virtual reality, digital video discs and the like, one the other, audiovisual translation for film or television, i.e. subtitling, dubbing, voice-over etc. could also be seen to involve multimedia activities.

The first and main question I would therefore like to propose for consideration is: "What are the semiotic and pragmatic specificities of multimedia translation?"

To analyze the usefulness of this concept, I will be drawing on my research into screenwriting and dialogue writing and their function in film adaptation, as well as on my research into film subtitling, but also on inspiration found elsewhere; that is, in the work of Gunther Kress and Theo Van Leeuwen (1996 and 1997) in Social Semiotics. Their research applies the essential concepts of 'meaning making' from Michael Halliday's systemic-functional linguistics to all kinds of texts.

1. A working field

First of all, I wish to stress that in multimedia translation, we are not really dealing with intersemiotic translation, i.e., translation from one semiotic system to another, but with the translation of texts and intertextuality. These texts can, however, involve the use of signs from different semiotic systems, which is why some of the concepts used by Kress and Van Leeuwen prove to be very useful.

The three central concepts are: sign, mode, and medium. *Signs* are defined as "[...J *motivated* conjunctions of signifiers (forms) and signifiers (meanings)". In other words, signs are never arbitrary: sign-makers always use the form they find appropriate for the meaning they wish to express (Kress & Van Leeuwen 1996: 7). Such signs can therefore be made of different materials, or *modes,* and they can be communicated through different media, (the latter being the manner of dissemination chosen by a sign-maker. Kress gives the following example: if I write someone a letter, my *letter* will he the *medium* of communication, my *writing*, the graphic material, its mode (Kress 1997: 6-7).

Transferring these concepts to, for instance, a TV movie, the medium would in this case be television, and it would disseminate a text that makes use of various aural and visual modes to construct aural-verbal, aural non-verbal, visual-verbal and visual non-verbal messages. According to this definition, multimodal texts also include any simple written text without additional pictorial elements, since all texts consist of both verbal and visual elements: all texts have a layout. Indeed, as Kress (1997) points out, under the influence of, for instance, laptop publishing and the use of computers generally, layout has come to acquire greater prominence in writing. It influences the shape, including the sentence structure of the written text.

To return to the combined concept of multimedia translation: how can the above concepts be put to use within this framework? They provide us with a way out of the aimless discussions that would inevitably be the result of any attempt to formulate an all-inclusive definition of what a new multimedia branch of translation studies would need to study; the more so since new forms of communication keep appearing.

In order to group research with a common interest and encourage indispensable (interdisciplinary) interaction, we need to define a working field instead, and one that is capable of accommodating change. Since our roots lie in translation studies, I would propose the study of (translated) texts that do have a verbal constituent, but in the study of which special attention is paid to their multimodal functioning, and to the transformations this might undergo due to the transfer from a source to a target context. In using the concept of multimodal texts, a link with translation studies generally can be maintained (which can hence continue to provide an umbrella field) but the inclusion of texts other than purely verbal or written ones is made possible. In other words, useful distinctions can be incorporated, such as that between spoken and written verbal texts, a distinction that has been undergoing major shifts lately, and that is crucial in many forms of audiovisual translation. Specific research projects would have to delineate more specific working fields, defining the multimodal texts they are dealing with, as well as the medium/media of their dissemination and the possible influence exerted by these on the modes used in the text. This would allow the constitution of working fields covering the study of multimodal texts and their translations within a single medium (with or without international variants), or the study of multimodal (translated) texts disseminated by various media, or the study of texts translated from one medium of dissemination into another. The influence of this medium on a particular mode could be considered; for instance, the influence of the medium of television on the written mode of subtitles.

Returning once again to our initial, but somewhat reformulated question "What are the semiotic and pragmatic specificities of multimodal and multimedia translation?" I would like to have a look at the role of language in this type of text production, since I have proposed to include only multimodal texts with a verbal constituent in our working field. This topic will be linked to what are seen to be "the semiotic and pragmatic specificities" of multimodal, and multimedia translation.

2. The role of language

A question that is often heard with reference to translation in a multimedia context is: "What is the role of language in these source and target texts?", or "Has the role of language changed?" Formulated in this way, these questions are unanswerable. First of all, the role of language will be determined by the use to which the text is put. My research in screenwriting has shown that which particular mode comes to dominate the others in a certain text, or what balance is achieved, will be determined by the sign-maker's purpose and background, and by how and where, and in what medium, the text is to be used. Secondly, when dealing with either the creation or the translation of multimodal texts, it is often extremely difficult to make the distinction between the influence of purely semiotic and more pragmatic differences in the use of these modes.

I shall take an example from film studies. Film is usually considered to be a visual medium, and part of its history and the history of film studies have been devoted to establishing this visual film medium as an art in its own right. In order to do so, film scholars and teachers have often consciously focused on what they term the *filmic* aspect of the art form, and neglected its ties with literature, or even the determining influence of screenwriting. Studies in film adaptation are often carried out by scholars from the field of literary studies. Whenever film scholars have devoted some attention to less film-specific aspects of their object of study, it has often been with a view to incorporating them in, or subjecting them to the truly filmic. In mainstream narrative cinema, however, some characteristics that have come to be appropriated as filmic, such as e.g. a tight dramatic structure and clearly delineated characters, are not filmic in the sense that they are semiotically bound to the visual medium: they have their sources in literature and/or the theatre and are determined by a filmic tradition, not by film as a medium[1]. Film dialogues constitute another example. Most if not all mainstream screenwriting courses[2] prescribe that film dialogues should be concise, i.e., that they should consist of short sentences and exchanges. The manuals and courses I have read all point out that film dialogues need to fulfil a number of functions: they must contribute to the evolution of the narrative, typify the characters and/or make them more realistic, and supply comments on the action. At the same time, they must fit into the dramatic context and never be too verbose or carry obvious messages from the filmmaker to the viewer. Some will grant that whether certain features are dominant will largely depend on genre, but generally speaking the verbal mode should be subservient to the visual mode in film. My study of seven British New Wave films, traditionally grouped as a movement, shows that there is significant variation in their dialogue functions and features, reflecting the influence of various models in varying degrees.[3] The final shape the dialogues took in each film was to some extent determined by so-called generic film dialogue features, following the generally accepted – if then never explicitly acknowledged – views of what film dialogues should look like, but also by the influence of other models and by the particular concerns of each individual screenwriter. As a result, the influence and dominance of the verbal mode in the films mentioned varies considerably. Today, more films, even explicitly mainstream American ones, are less afraid of foregoing the absolute dominance of image over word, which traditional screenwriting manuals promote as being *filmic*. They have incorporated some features from a different model, from so-called 'art house' cinema, and have started upgrading the importance of (sometimes lengthy) dialogues. One obvious example is Quentin Tarantino's *Reservoir Dogs*. Screen and dialogue writing, and the models they use, change with the type of film which directors and screenwriters want to make; they are not that strictly bound to the film medium as such.

If the above holds for screenplays and films as texts, there is no reason why it should not do so for other types of multimodal texts, created for today's multimedia technology. Some initial, tentative conclusions can hence be drawn.

3. Multimodal texts

Firstly, even though the present communication explosion may be tempting research into the study of current evolutions and trends, diachronic and contrastive studies will reveal that in the use of different modes within a text what is seen to be semiotic and what is seen as pragmatic changes with the times. Secondly, to return to the role of language in today's multimodal text production: the shape it takes is not just semiotically, but also pragmatically determined, and influenced by various models. As a result, the prominence or subservience of its role (or that of any of the models) cannot be presupposed. Thirdly, and this brings us back to translation, in film adaptation, and probably to different degrees in other forms of multimodal translation, there is not just one source and one target text; instead, various other source texts or models impose themselves or are consciously imposed by the sign-maker on (the translation process, and contribute to the eventual shape of the target text and all its modes.

If we take a look at film subtitling instead of film adaptation, this last point may seem less clear.[4] The source text is now a clearly finished film, the target text is 'the same' film with subtitles added. Still, what determines the shape of the subtitles? Not the source text's verbal mode only, nor simply the technicalities of space and time imposed on the translator. Subtitlers also minimally bring to bear their (and the TV channel's) concept of subtitle-language, linked to their concept of the intended viewer. Moreover, if the film is a documentary, it is usually adapted to the documentary concept of the channel that will be broadcasting the translated version. This may involve cutting scenes, rewriting and speaking in adapted commentaries (based on varying norms of adequacy versus acceptability), and subtitling some passages (for instance, interviews). All these interventions will determine the role of verbal mode in the target text: both quantitatively and qualitatively, dominance of one model over another will be determined by the overall purpose of whoever is responsible for the project.

Still, not all can be reduced to pragmatics. Some parts of a message will – I suppose – be carried more efficiently by images, others by words, but the borderline of the division should not be taken for granted. Nowadays, images seem to have become dominant in communication, and their interaction with language needs to be studied, but in studying the interaction, language should not be considered to be subservient as a matter of fact. It may no longer have the same responsibility in some types of multimodal texts, but is it not paradoxical that in film, the quintessential visual medium, dialogue is now gaining some ground with the development of particular sub-genres?

Having more or less concluded the discussion of the different components constituting our modified initial question, i.e, "What are the semiotic and pragmatic specificities of multimodal and multimedia translation?", I will now turn to a number of related questions.

4. Reading pictures

A few problems regularly confronting anyone involved in audiovisual translation are these: "To what extent is linguistic translation incorporated into the picture? To what extent does it interpret it? Does the picture need language to pinpoint its semantic dimensions? How does this affect traditional translation strategies?"

Again, rather than attempting to answer these questions generally, one should incorporate them into specific research projects operating within a clearly delineated working field. The degree of incorporation of language in the other textual modes, the relation between the semantic dimensions of language and those of other textual modes, first needs to be determined for each type of text to be translated or researched. In some of the British New Wave films discussed above, dialogue is more prominent than in others: in some it is very theatrical, in others it imitates natural conversation. Subtitlers need to recognize these differences, which are functional, and base their translation strategies on the source texts' different modal features in combination with the linguistic, technical and cultural-political constraints they themselves may be subjected to because they are, for instance, translating for the medium of television.

It will not do to start from the idea that film dialogue is *spoken language* that needs to be rendered in *written language,* taking the images into account. Even film dialogue that masquerades as everyday speech is determined by underlying structures that may more closely resemble those of writing. Film dialogue may have much less of a linear structure than ordinary conversation. The length of the sentences is not simply determined by the demands of planning an utterance on the spot, but also by dramatic considerations. In other words, in the case of feature films, the subtitler needs to consider to what extent the film dialogue remains the apparent sequentiality of spoken language, but is also dictated by other, hierarchic, concerns, which are determined by the story as told dramatically through a structure underlying its pictures. To contrast feature film and documentary once again, even a cursory look at some TV documentaries, or newscasts in particular, shows that the relation between word and image is not always close. Indeed, in many such programmes, verbal and visual modes are largely dissociated from one another, the pictures being almost merely illustrative.[5]

On the other hand, some pictures do not need language at all to pinpoint their semantic dimensions. One example, given by Kress and Van Leeuwen (1996), are those children's books in which the story is simply told visually. Still, even such pictures presuppose a common culture and knowledge of, in our case, the Western "grammar of visual design", a type of grammar today's translators had best familiarize themselves with. Due to today's globalization I believe that the common knowledge required for reading pictures is expanding, if only through a widening knowledge of other cultures, most certainly within Europe. In films too, the increasing amount of co-productions may be homogenizing the pictorial messages conveyed, besides making them more widely known across borders. However, major problems remain for the translator who is trying to help films (and other texts) cross continents. In such cases, language may have to take over part of the source text's pictorial message, but this depends greatly on the kind of translation the producers of the new text have in mind, on what models are brought into the transformation, and what kind of equivalence is aimed at, if any. All the same, this does not necessarily mean that traditional translation strategies such as expansion, explication, substitution etc. can no longer applied.

The degree of common cultural knowledge required for reading pictures and the concomitant need for more or less explanatory translations, brings us to the target audience. What are they supposed to get out of the translated text? What do they actually get out of the translated text? More research is no doubt needed into how images (both static and filmic) are read, and into how texts with mixed modes are read, not just for the sake of translation but for the benefit of all those involved in drawing up multimodal texts. Others are no doubt better placed than I am to expand on which course such research should take, but it should obviously be linked to how multimodal texts are read in a particular culture. To what extent do our verbal reading habits influence the way we look at pictures, and what does this imply for the way in which e.g. Arabs look at a picture? What kind of texts have audiences come to expect and accept? In this respect, I believe research into the acceptability of (translated) texts may need to receive greater prominence than research into their adequacy, since it has in some cases of audiovisual translation, for instance, become almost impracticable to trace a particular text's supposedly original audience. It might therefore - indeed in some fields it already has - become increasingly important for translators, as for TV producers, to focus more on the audience they aim to reach, rather than on the one a supposed source text may have wanted to reach. This would in its turn influence the translators' concern with how their readers/viewers interpret the target text's visual mode.

Still, research into how multimodal texts are read is not only complicated by the quickly changing relations between different modes, but also by the intrinsic changes that these modes are, themselves, undergoing. Right now, the dominance of the image in many fields of communication goes hand in hand with a change in the media for the dissemination of texts, and has one of its most visible effects in a gradient transition from what constitutes spoken and what constitutes written language. Another, sometimes related result, is the restructuring of language into smaller units (e.g. for CD-ROM publications). Referring, again, to a socio-semiotic approach to meaning-making, and more in particular Gunther Kress's book (1997), I concur with him, and no doubt many others, that we do not *use* language, but *make* it. Social factors lead people to *remake* language and to *remake* images. Anyone involved in writing or translating multimodal texts will remake the language they use, just as on a higher level (e.g. in the case of a documentary that will eventually require subtitling) the re-producers will *remake* the programme or film (to varying degrees, of course). As the dialogue writer is writing (s)he *remakes* language using language forms from different models. While translating, the subtitler will do the same.

This brings me to the question whether all these shifts might eventually lead to changes in now generally accepted communicational norms in society at large. Will they influence people's use of language in other situations? Will they influence what language is acceptable in what circumstances? I believe they will. Going back to my 50's - 60's film adaptations, once again, it is clear that these films changed the norms of what was linguistically acceptable in films at the time, by drawing on literary models in which apparently more was permitted. Indeed, very different censorship laws applied to literature, theatre and film at the time, and the change in the film dialogues went together with a loosening up of film censorship. Whether the success of (some) of the films forced the censorship to change, or whether a changed censorship in fact stimulated the production and critical appreciation of the films is not such a simple matter to resolve. I do not believe that language changes simply because the material conditions for change are present; there must be a reason (or there are reasons/causes) for material conditions to change. To return to Britain in the late 50's, the then secretary of the British Board of Film Censors,[6] John Trevelyan, consciously promoted *quality adult films* and used the newly introduced X-certificate, limiting viewing to persons of over 16 years of age, in order to do so. While thus allowing and even promoting the exhibition of previously risqué films, he simultaneously ensured the persistence of film censorship, which the absence of an X-category would have made impossible. Theatre censorship was, indeed, abolished in 1968.

Whatever changes a shift in textual modes in text creation and translation may bring about, I believe it will be co-determined by power-relations between the source and target cultures or systems. In my research multimodal translation, of course, also involved a transition from the medium of literature to the medium of film, but within one culture. This means that the target audience for the films may (and probably will) have been a different one from the target audience for the novels and plays, but that both were still part of the same national culture. The situation was special because the New Wave films were to a great extent meant for a specifically British audience, whereas today's films aim at international or sufficiently Americanized audiences. Still, the study of cross-cultural influences and power struggles are different aspects of a similar mechanism.

5. An interdisciplinary approach

To conclude, a word on the methodological approaches which are open to a new branch of translation studies concerned with research into multimodal and multimedia translation. In my opinion, the nature of multimodal or even multimedia texts need not require translation scholars to abandon all their trusted methods. On the other hand, the study of such texts and translations will require interdisciplinary approaches, in which the know-how of the other disciplines is brought to bear. I have demonstrated the usefulness of the simple application of a few concepts from a branch of socio-semiotics concerned with the production of multimodal texts which can easily be incorporated into existing methods in translation studies. Joint projects with specialists from different fields are required, allowing all participants to draw on their specific methodology. Besides, my research has also shown the importance of diachronic as well as synchronic studies in order to moderate the impression of permanence which some dominant synchronic trends might convey.

Whereas in my research I try to work descriptively, discovering the norms and models underlying text production and translation, when I am teaching subtitling my concern is with normative rules: how do I teach my students to write better subtitles, and what indeed are "better subtitles"? What do I tell them about the influence of the institutions within which they will have to work? How much do they need to know about other disciplines in order to become competitive translators?

It is to supply answers to these questions, and because of the increasing complexity of both textual concepts and text production today, that I think the focus of multimodal and multimedia translation studies should first be on descriptive approaches. Some of the concepts and methods from 'standard' descriptive translation studies will have to be adapted, but not necessarily discarded. One tendency I have already referred to is that translation and text production are at times becoming almost indistinguishable, which will increase the emphasis of research on text analysis and different forms of intertextuality, rather than on translation in the strictest sense. To replace the binary source text – target text approach from descriptive translation studies, Patrick Cattrysse (1995 and in this volume) has suggested a star-like constellation in which one target text is seen to derive from various source texts of varying influence. This seems a useful construct to start from, but the various source texts exerting an influence on the target text,- should also be studied in their socio-political context, i.e. as, to some degree, institutionally determined. The interdisciplinary approach required will therefore have to make use not only of the insights gained from various branches of linguistics, but also, at least, of those of media studies and sociology.

Notes

1. This has been commented on in greater detail by David Bordwell (1985).

2. In the course of my research I have looked mainly at screenwriting manuals from the 1980's and early 90's (a boom-period in the publication of such manuals), but also at much earlier ones from the 1940's and 50's. In the 1960's the interest in screenwriting rules appears to subside for some time, possibly under the influence of auteur theories. The later manuals are much more specific in their instructions.

3. These films are *Room at the Top* (1959), *Look Back in Anger* (1959), *The Entertainer* (1960), *Saturday Night and Sunday Morning* (1960), *A Taste of Honey* (1961), *The Loneliness of the Long-Distance Runner* (1962) and *This Sporting Life* (1963). They are all adaptations from novels, plays or short stories, but also reflect the influence of filmic models, such as The French nouvelle vague, and The British Free Cinema documentaries.

4. The relevance of the comparison is demonstrated in my article "From the BBC's Voices from *the Island* to the BRTN's *De President van Robbeneiland*. A Case Study in TV translation." (1995-96), which applies the methodological model proposed by Patrick Cattrysse (1995), discussed briefly at the end of this paper as well.

5. This is discussed extensively by Michel Chion (1988 and 1990).

6. Today BBFC stands for the British Board of Film Classification.

SIMULTANEOUS INTERPRETING FOR TELEVISION AND OTHER MEDIA: TRANSLATION DOUBLY CONSTRAINED

Sergio Viaggio,
United Nations
Vienna, Austria

1. Introduction

Simultaneous interpreting for the media (SMI) is a relatively new phenomenon that has radically altered several key factors in interlingual intercultural mediation. Over the last few years, several papers have been published by practitioners (see Kurz & Bros-Brann 1996 for a comprehensive bibliography), all of them stressing its distinctive peculiarities vis-a-vis traditional conference interpreting. In this one I shall limit myself to pointing out what I deem to be the most salient features at the communicative, translational, neurophysiological, psychomotor, pedagogical, deontological, social and financial levels.

I shall be referring to the expanded models of verbal communication and mediation that I have developed on the basis of García Landa's 1990 models of the speech act and prototypical translation as initially presented in Viaggio 1998 (and specifically applied to interpretation in Viaggio 1999), and to relevance as defined by Sperber & Wilson 1986/1995.

2. García Landa's model of verbal communication as expanded by Viaggio

According to García Landa, every successful act of verbal communication is an exchange of mental perceptions articulated in linguistic signs. In any written or oral speech act what is communicated is what he calls a *linguistic percept intended* (*LPI*)[1] – a mental representation that is the result of perceiving that which one wishes to convey as a synthesis of propositional and perhaps pragmatic content and speech. Communication is achieved as long as the receiver manages to generate in his mind a *linguistic percept comprehended* (*LPC*) that holds a relevant identity relationship to the one intended.[2] It is worth stressing that such perceptual identity, as a *socially relevant commonality of features* between intended and comprehended *LP*s, is at a higher level than equivalences or similarities at the utterance or textual levels – including the level of semantic representations. On the basis of García Landa's general model of the speech act[3] and in close cooperation with him, I have developed an "applied" model taking into account all relevant factors intervening in communication.

Let me briefly describe the model's latest version here published for the first time:

1) Every *successful speech act D* (whether oral *V*, written *T*, or interiorised *I*) in a given language *o* is a social transaction whereby someone (the subject of production), out of a *conscious motivation W*, governed by *an unconscious predisposition to cooperate Z*, with a *main pragmatic intention Y* and *secondary pragmatic intentions y*, communicates *a linguistic percept intended LPI* which is a function of a given *set of pre-comprehension schemes, knowledge base* or *passing theories K.*

2) To that effect, the speaker sets in motion a complex mental operation which involves mainly constructing and presenting to his interlocutor(s) a finished social product which is a *sign chain F* in that language *o*. Such a chain consists of a) a *phono-morpho-syntactic structure X* (actualising a certain *phono-morpho-semantic system L*); b) a *semantic potential S* (actualising a *semantic system H*); c) a *rhythmic-prosodic structure V* (actualising a *rhythmic-prosodic system R*); and d) a *register J* (from a *register series Q*). This chain is also necessarily accompanied by a series of *suprasegmental (paralinguistic or typographical) features C*, and *kinetic or graphic* features *E* that reinforce, nuance or modify its sense. (In face-to-face and written communication, then, the stimulus triggering the comprehension process consists of three components: *F*, *C* and *E*, although the latter one is lost in strictly acoustic communications such as radio, telephone, etc., often making comprehension more difficult).

3) The speech act is carried out in a given *social situation* or *socio-historical field G* governed by a *shared system of beliefs, norms and practices*, or a certain *shared life and personal experience P*, within a given *relevant world M*, at a *historic moment VH*, and, within that moment, at a *specific time t*. (All components are characterised by specific sets of features *m*, *n*, etc.).

4) The interlocutor is listening and understanding in a complex mental operation which results in his producing in turn a *linguistic percept comprehended LPCo*, itself a function of the same knowledge base *K*. In order to do so, he must resort to or overcome his *conscious motivation or resistance*

U and be governed in turn by an *unconscious predisposition to cooperate Z*. We should stress the active nature of comprehension, whereby the comprehender (re-)constructs his speech perception of the speaker's intended meaning applying his own filters *U*, *Z* and *K* to the acoustic/visual stimulus *FCE*. Comprehension produces, moreover, *main* and *secondary pragmatic effects Aa*, which may or may not correspond to the speaker's pragmatic intentions.

Regardless of its pragmatic success, communication will have succeeded in so far as, in a given social situation, relevant perceptual identity (*[=]*) is achieved between what the speaker wants to convey (*LPI*) and what the comprehender has understood (*LPC*) – otherwise it will have failed to a greater or lesser degree. Since neither perception is open to observation, such identity is often impossible to verify empirically: it can only be postulated. What is crucial to retain is that, in the end, this identity is a function of the relevant linguistic (*LHRQ*) and cognitive (*KPM*) baggage – what García Landa calls the *hermeneutic package* – shared by both parties and partly determined by how predisposed they are to communicate with each other (*Z*) – what Toolan 1996 calls *mutual-orientedness.*

3. The model of interlingual intercultural mediation

García Landa defines translation as a language game consisting in reproducing an *LPI* in a new language by means of a new speech act. In actual practice, of course, the sheer "transparent" reverbalisation of an original *LPIo* in the new language *i* – i.e. zero mediation – is impossible and, more often than not, ill-advised: *Vouloir dire* and understanding are not symmetrical, in that they pursue different aims. This same asymmetry obtains, often to an even greater degree, between the original speaker and the translation's addressee.

The truly expert interpreter (or translator), then, does more than merely re-produce an *LP*: He *mediates*, modifying or altogether disregarding certain formal or content elements as a function of his own *skopos*. In this liberty lies the heuristic nature of his activity. As has often been said, the translator does not find equivalences, he creates them each time he comes up with a verbalisation – an *Fi* which, besides his relevant rhetoric competence, is the product of a) his comprehension of the *LPIo* – his *LPCo* (the hermeneutic part of his task), plus b) his assessment of the new communicative situation (*K*, *G*, *P*, *M*, *VHtm+n*), and c) his assessment of the new addressees' expectations U^Z. Such analyses may well lead him to modify even the intention or function of the original speech act. His aim is *relevant* identity, which implies a relevant correlation of the speaker's and the mediator's pragmatic intentions and the contextual or pragmatic effects achieved by the latter. Between what he has understood as comprehender of the *LPIo* and what he decides to convey as verbaliser of his *LPIi* lies the essence of the interpreter's mediating activity: by transmuting the one into the other he exercises both his deontologically responsible freedom and his loyalty. (There is, of course, a *continuum* from prototypical “transparent” translation to non-translation – which may be a legitimate mediating choice. It is impossible strictly to circumscribe what are essentially fluid phenomena – in this case, what is still a translation from that which can no longer be deemed to be one.)

Resorting to the symbols alone (where > indicates determination, → production, and ← retro-projection, while the mantissas represent the events and phenomena taking place in real space/time and the exponents the virtual systems or structures gravitating upon them) interlingual intercultural mediation (which can be heterofunctional and heteroscopic) is then formulated as:

$$\text{Do: } W^{Z} > Yy > LPIo^{K} \rightarrow [Fo(Xm^{L},Sm^{H},Vm^{R},Jm^{Q})CmEm]G^{PM}VHtm \leftrightarrow U^{Z} > LPCo^{K} \rightarrow Aa\ [\rightarrow]$$

$$[\rightarrow]\ \text{Di: } W^{Z} > Yy > LPIi^{K} \rightarrow [Fi(Xn^{L},Sn^{H},Vn^{R},Jn^{Q})CnEn]G^{PM}VHtm{+}n \leftrightarrow U^{Z} > LPCi^{K} \rightarrow Aa$$

Here the symbol *[→]* stands for the adaptation that the mediator operates between *LPCo* and *LPIi*. As monolingual communication, mediated communication succeeds when, in the new social situation, relevant perceptual identity is established between what the original speaker wishes to convey and what the new interlocutor understands in the specific situation:

$$G^{PM}\ (LPIo\ [=]\ LPCi)$$

The subtype of homoscopic, homofunctional mediation will have been successful if:

$$G^{PM}\ (Yy > LPIo\ [=]\ LPCi \rightarrow Aa)$$

This means that, besides relevant perceptual identity between intended meaning and meaning understood, there is also a relevant correspondence between the original speaker’s pragmatic intentions and the pragmatic effects on the mediator’s addressee(s).

Mediation, moreover, can aim exclusively at pragmatic success, even at the expense of perceptual identity (i.e. of translation), in whose case the felicity condition is:

$$G^{PM}(Yy > (LPIo[\neq/=]LPCi) \rightarrow Aa)$$

This insight allows for a simple definition of quality in any kind of mediation. Any mediation that ensures sufficient pragmatic correspondence and perceptual identity (and such correspondence or identity may be zero), i.e. relevant identity, is, by definition, successful. The closer it gets to ensuring optimum relevant identity, the better it is.

To my mind, what makes this proposal unique is its dialectic assimilation and development of all modern attempts at defining translation, while encompassing and accounting for all factors identified so far as pertinent to the phenomenon. Another salient feature is its symbolic notation, which allows for a direct graphic representation of the different concepts. Also, it is a model that can be easily adapted to sign-language interpreting (both oral-to-sign or sign-to-oral, and sign-to-sign) - a decisive advantage when it comes to SMI, for which it is ideally suited.

4. Simultaneous interpretation for the media as twice-constrained translation

Interlingual intercultural mediation is always confronted with epiphenomena that can limit and, at times, distort communication. In view of its neurophysiological component, simultaneous interpretation falls within what Mayoral *et al.* (1988) call *constrained translation*. It is precisely this psycho-motor constraint that lays bare the communicative essence of translation. SMI adds a further series of constraints both at social and cognitive levels: When his job is exposed to an audience of millions, especially if his voice becomes for all practical purposes the essential part of a video's soundtrack, the interpreter has a torrent of additional factors to attend to that cannot but add to the already complex set of competing efforts he is simultaneously engaged in (Gile 1995: 159-190). The interpreter's success thus depends on a more efficient neurophysiological, psychological and motor support. But it depends crucially on an adequate assessment of the communicative priorities: on what, under the circumstances, will be the optimum communicative vehicle (the *right* kind of verbalisation) required to help produce a relevantly identical *LPC* in the target audience. Such assessment clearly requires its own effort. This particular effort, moreover, is the one that is more difficult to automatise.

5. Specific constraints

The key question, then, is the kind of *LPI*/*LPC* identity deemed relevant under the specific circumstances; i.e. what kind of functionality is the interpreter's speech act to pursue. Whatever such functionality, the media can ill afford less-than-optimum relevance – except that, in many cases, such relevance cannot be directly controlled by them. Specifically, they cannot help a rambling, obscure or otherwise un-perspicuous speaker, save through *post facto* editing or, at best, well managed interviewing techniques. If the speaker is to be interpreted live, however, there is much that the media interpreter can do to increase relevance. I submit that this very ability ought to be his main distinctive asset vis-a-vis a conference interpreter. As already pointed out, the foremost constraint is immediate intelligibility of content and immediate acceptability of form coupled to an optimum synchronisation with the relevant images (in other words, *Fi* must fit *En*). Next comes the consequent need to weed out any basically irrelevant or, worse, parasitic information. Information may be parasitic in two overlapping senses: details demanding a processing effort incommensurate with the cognitive effects that may be derived by a mass audience in real time, and details that force the interpreter into inordinate speed, therefore impeding both immediate intelligibility and acceptability by conspiring against the overall quality of delivery (which in turn increases the processing effort on the part of the audience and reduces relevance).

Thus, in our notation, the interpreter's chain *Fi*, acquires particular autonomy with a view to optimising the addressees' processing effort as a function of their presumed knowledge base *K* and expectations U^Z, and culture and personal experience *P*, within the relevant world *M*, in the new given socio-historical field *G*, epoch *VH*, and specific time *tm+n*. As a direct consequence of the other factors' increased importance, then, equivalence at the morpho-syntactic Xn^L and semantic Sm^H levels tends to weigh less heavily in SMI than in normal conference conditions, where, on the other hand, it can be assumed that all participants share the extralinguistic hermeneutic package and social setting. This means, in fact, that the media interpreter is called upon a) to bridge a potentially much wider cultural and psychological disparity between the producer of the original speech act and the addressees of the new one, and b) consciously to adapt his own speech act so that it will be immediately intelligible and acceptable to a heterogeneous mass of addressees (often more so than the one originally intended, and certainly incommensurably more so than the audience targeted at a conference).

There are, besides, several *ad hoc* constraints adding to stress. Among the most prominent we can list the following:

a) Although in some instances the interpreter is in the same room as both the interviewee(s) and the interviewer(s), very often he is nowhere near either of them.
b) Even when he is sharing in the socio-communicative situation, the mediator's task is totally asymmetric: whilst his performance into the interviewee's language is private, his interpretation into the broadcast language is public, which faces him with as many as three potentially different sets of expectations and, therefore, norms: the interviewer's, the originator's, and the virtual audience's.
c) In most cases, the interpretation is taped and re-broadcast, which opens it to repeated mass consumption and scrutiny at an ever greater distance in time

– to boot, by a massive audience of consumers as strict and demanding as they are ignorant of the workings of interpretation.

d) If he is to be seen, then his “presence” (*E*) must be impeccably unobtrusive.

e) As Kurz and Bros-Brann point out, the media interpreter can seldom prepare for a specific job: he must be able to tackle any subject and any speaker at any time – he must boast a most comprehensive set *K*.

f) The interpreter's physical environment may be less than ideal (cramped space, poor insulation, unholy hours, etc.).

g) Sound quality can be less than optimal: the speaker may be in an environment with lots of background noise, the microphone awkwardly placed (especially if several interviewers are vying with each other), etc.

h) Many difficult speakers get to be interpreted over the media who would seldom make it to a conference room (the man in the street, semi-verbal adolescents, illiterate peasants, distraught victims, incoherent junkies, or, at the more sophisticated end of the spectrum, philosophers, scientists, artists, writers, actors, etc.).

i) Elocution (*C*) being much more decisive an intelligibility and acceptability factor than in non-media interpreting, it demands a larger amount of attention.

j) It is normally essential that the interpreter complete his utterance not later than the speaker – and at times even before him (so that the value of *n* in *tm*+*n* is negative).[4]

k) Indeed, the media interpreter takes on the heavy burden of incarnating the profession before the general public, who witness and judge it and its practitioners exclusively by him. All efforts tend, therefore, to become more demanding, whereby no alleviating tradeoff is realistically possible among them - which, especially when in unfavourable physical conditions, cannot but tremendously add to stress.

All this stress bears directly upon the interpreter's conscious and, above all, unconscious motivation or resistance as either listener or speaker (U^Z and W^Z) filtering his specific mediating task. Unconscious resistance may well transpire paralinguistically or kinetically, i.e. it may “spill over” into *C* and/or *E*: the interpreter can sound or look nervous, ill at ease, irritated, despondent or bored. All of this he is normally keenly aware of - which in turn cannot but complicate even further an already most stressful activity.

6. The specific expectancy and professional norms

As mentioned, the distinctiveness of SMI gives rise to specific expectancy norms (see Viaggio 1997 and 1999). Whilst the expectancy norms in conference interpreting are basically those of the mediator's users, in SMI the more immediate expectancy norms are those set by an elusive and in many cases naive initiator (perhaps the most curious of these norms is that many – mostly American – newscasters will not tolerate an interpreter who does not suffer from the relevant foreign accent). Yet, as I have tried to prove, it is acceptability to the intended audience that must be the guiding professional norm – and nobody that I know of has really cared to determine it. As I have argued above, in most cases, the speaker's thick accent, inordinate speed, or gruesome inarticulateness (all detracting from relevance) ought not to stand in the way of the interpreter's clarity: He must strive, come what may, to adapt his own verbalisation for maximum intelligibility and acceptability by the presumed audience. Thus, the constant tug-of-war between expectancy and professional norms becomes, if anything, more intense. This may add yet another layer of stress: that of the uneasy relationship between the piper and whoever pays him and calls the wrong tune, or, at best, calls it to be played the wrong communicative way.

7. Media interpreting: a new, particularly sophisticated specialisation

Unlike the conference interpreter, then, the media interpreter has to be in a position to tackle any subject and any speaker, any dialect, any sociolect and any idiolect, at any time. Except that his competence must go far beyond that, since, ideally, he is expected to be a consummate mediator, with the psychomotor reflexes of the conference interpreter, the cultural sensitivity of the community interpreter, the analytical keenness and background knowledge of the journalist, and the rhetorical prowess of the seasoned communicator. Indeed, indispensable as the skills and resilience normally required at an international conference are, they are not nearly enough; so much so that most conference interpreters that I know – at least in the US – charge considerably more when called upon to work for the media. Both understandably and unfortunately, interpreting schools do not provide specific training to this day, so that practitioners working for the media have to find their bearings on their haphazard isolated own. With the emergence of systematic multilingual broadcasts such as the Euronews or Arte TV channels, the time has surely come to fill this gap.[5]

8. Remote conference interpreting

Somewhere between regular SI and SMI will eventually stand remote conference interpretation in its four basic "geographic" configurations:

a) a speaker tele-interpreted to an audience co-present with the interpreter;
b) a co-present speaker interpreted for an absent audience;
c) an absent interpreter interpreting a speaker co-present with his audience;

d) speaker, audience and interpreter scattered over the globe – all of this combined with the different communicative modalities characteristic of regular conference interpreting: monologue/dialogue, formal/informal, political/technical, informative/negotiating, etc.

A particularly important issue is whether remote interpreting is equally suited – or at least well suited enough – to all the communicative modalities mentioned above. Common sense tells us that formal monologic plenary debates, with mostly prepared speeches and mostly non-functional kinesics, would lend themselves better than informal, unstructured negotiations, but the fact remains to be empirically proven.

9. Conclusions

To my mind, these new modalities of SI face the mediator with a complex array of hitherto unsuspected challenges. As was the case with the emergence of traditional conference SI half a century ago, the new constraints cannot but reveal different aspects of translation's essence as a particular kind of mediated interlingual intercultural communication. But the consequences go well beyond, reaching into all nooks of professional practice, i.e. of translation as it actually exists. They deserve, therefore, most careful research in all their aspects, to wit, from the standpoints of: *communication* (all relevant aspects of mass-communication theory enter now more evidently into play); *translation theory* (given the decisiveness of instant acceptability and intelligibility, new definitions of content identity and formal equivalence, or at least new parameters to assess them, may be required); *neurophysiology* (the way in which the new conditions affect the interpreter's mental and physical health and resilience must be determined); *didactics* (the necessary additions to interpreting curricula must be contemplated); *professional practice* (the new forms of contradiction between professional and expectancy norms, and the special status of loyalty to speaker, audience, and, most particularly, client is to be weighted); *deontology* (in view of the interpreter's new social – and professional – role and visibility); and, last but by no means least, *economics* (the levels of remuneration relative to non-media interpreting must be established).

Appendix

THE SYMBOLS AND THEIR DEFINITIONS

W	Conscious motivation governing elocution.
Z	Unconscious mutual-orientedness governing both interlocutors.
Y	Main pragmatic intention.
y	Secondary pragmatic intentions.
U	Conscious motivation or resistance governing comprehension.
A	Main pragmatic (or contextual) effect.
a	Secondary pragmatic (or contextual) effects.
LP	Speech perception - articulation of the propositional and affective content through speech.
LPI	Intended speech perception - what the speaker means to convey.
LPC	Comprehended speech perception - what is perceived by the comprehender.
K	Relevant knowledge and pre-comprehension schemes.
D	Speech act - *V* oral, *T* written, *I* inner, *L* reading).
F	Chain of linguistic signs (utterance).
o	Source language.
i	Target language
X	Phono-morpho-syntactic structure.
L	Phono-morpho-syntactic system.
S	Semantic potential.
H	Semantic system.
V	Rhythmic-prosodic structure.
R	Rhythmic-prosodic system.
J	Register.
Q	Possible registers (it is moot whether registers constitute a system).
C	Paralinguistic (elocutional) or perilinguistic (typographic) configuration.
E	Kinetic or graphic configuration.
G	Socio-historic field.
P	System of beliefs, experiences, norms and practices (culture or background knowledge).
M	Relevant geographical setting.
VH	Historical time.
t	Moment.
n, *m*	Specific characteristics.
>	Determination.
→	Production.
↔	Retro-projection by the comprehender on the sensorial stimulus of his motivation/knowledge on the speech perception).
=	Perceptual identity.
[=]	Relevant perceptual identity.
[→]	Transmutation by the mediator of the comprehended perception into intended perception the basis of relevant identity.

Notes

1. Following García Landa's latest unpublished work, in previous versions I used the symbol *EPH* (acronym of *espacio perceptual hablístico*). I am now reverting to *LP*.

2. This identity is analogous to that obtaining in natural perception between the perception and the object perceived: You and I both see the pencil you have in front of you from different angles and distances; maybe you are colour blind and cannot make out its colour; but both you and I see the same pencil. In this sense and despite their differences, our perceptions are, nevertheless, relevantly identical. On the other hand, If I ask you for the red pencil – which you cannot tell from the green one next to it – our perceptions are no longer relevantly identical, and communication cannot prosper. In order for it to succeed, we must find perceptual identity through some other means (viz. that I ask you for the long pencil, or the one on your right, etc.). This is what normally happens in everyday communication: little by little we correct our aiming until we finally hit that target which is *LPI[=]LPC.*

3. $LPIo^{K} \rightarrow Fo(Xm^{L},Sm^{H},Vm^{R})G^{PM}VHtm \leftrightarrow LPCo^{K}$. (See the appendix for the definitions of the symbols).

4. At the AIIC meeting with Chief Interpreters in 1998, the Chief Interpreter of ARTE complained about the inability evinced by most interpreters in this respect.

5. As a case in point, as far as I have been subject to it, Euronews' interpretation into Spanish is nothing short of excruciating, especially when compared to interpretation into English, French and German.

HYPERTEXT AND CYBERSPACE: NEW CHALLENGES TO TRANSLATION STUDIES

Domingo Sánchez-Mesa Martínez
Universidad de Granada, Spain

1. Between reality and fiction

At the very beginning the concept of multimedia should be clarified a little in order to suggest some pertinent distinctions between the kind of communicative practices which are being considered within the emergent field of *Multimedia Translation*.

Since audiovisual transfer started to deserve a systematic attention on behalf of Translation Studies, major shifts have been occurring with regard to the technological development, the internationalization and globalization processes, and the human communicative and social patterns. The underlying idea is that, although we may have been dealing yesterday with certain kind of cultural practices (opera, theatre, cinema, documentaries, etc.) where the multisemiotic aspect of translation is evident enough, there is still a difference between the kind of communication conveyed in multisemiotic texts distributed by mass media or other more traditional cultural spectacles (theater, opera), and that one emerging in the new multimedia communication (interactive CD-ROMs, digital & on-demand TV, Internet, virtual reality).

The fact is that we witness a shift in our perception of reality and communication (perhaps a new kind of symbolic interchange is gradually more visible), also in our understanding of collectivity, identity (including our physical one), mainly due to an increasing mobility of human and material resources as well as of data and information. This mobility, linked to an outstanding growth of both computer and informatics industries and markets, involves a new perception of time and space (space turning into time). Finally, the confluence of these factors results in the rise of the looseness and vagueness of the borders between reality and fiction, precisely because of the power of immersion that new media are developing. It is true that in a modern context, fiction has had little to do with the notions of *true* or *false*, as long as it has been a pragmatic agreement accepted by the reader (depending on his *willing suspension of disbelief*). It has been a question of credibility, instead of accommodation to reality. However, simulation becomes a predominant symbolic interchange mode when people's perception of the non-fictitious world starts to be principally mediated by so powerful audiovisual devices (from TV onwards) which take the place of reality as guarantors of truth.

To put it in simple terms, I think that the new Information Technology (IT) can influence decisively the way we deal with reality as long as we accept the communicative behavior prevailing in the net as a natural one (immateriality, constant interchange and gathering of information, an isolated sense of belonging to a community, etc.). This creation of simulacrum clearly started with the power of TV to *substitute reality* (the *live* effect is crucial in this) and multiplies in new immersive media. All these epistemological, sociological and political issues must be taken into consideration when trying to outline the role and new functions of multimedia translators.

2. Multilingualism on-line?

The *hypertext* is a sort of non-sequential writing, a text which bifurcates, thus constantly allowing the reader to choose his reading path on the interactive support of a computer screen. In short, a hypertext is a series of fragments – what Barthes would have called *lexias* – and the electronic links connecting them. The Internet itself would stand for a perfect illustration of a *mega-hypertext.*

Confronting this "new" kind of textuality we might felt impelled to consider a new kind of translation:

a) Firstly, from texts in the form of books (maybe literary classics) to hypertext ones. Even though being intralinguistic, is this not a mode of transfer which conveys a significant number of implications attached to new conceptualizations of the activity of writing/reading and of the object *text* in itself?

Take the example of Borges' well known text *The Garden of Forking Paths*, one of the classical "prehypertextual" ones, as it is versioned electronically by Stuart Moulthrop in *Forking Paths: An Interaction after Jorge Luis Borges* (1987).[1] This operation was somehow prefigured in Barthes' fragmentation and interpretation of Balzac's *Sarrasine* in *S/Z.* (1970. Paris: Le Seuil.)

b) Related to this challenging mode of transfer there lies the translation within the hypertextual domain, as a technological support which eventually breaks some constraints of previous attempts to produce bilingual or multilingual texts (poetry mainly, but also the lyrics of a CD-ROM,[2] or TV programs).

Teaching through hypertext is another issue, which deserves at least to be quoted here. Apart from the availability of a number of materials which could be difficult to find in universities, the system raises the level of flexibility and empowers the role of learners in their own process of learning. This new kind of organizations or pseudoacademic networks confronts similar problems of communication and linguistic management as those found in other multinational organizations, such as multinational companies or international institutions. The level of success of this system of learning, as the efficiency of communication in multinational enterprises, strongly depends on culture and language (Sels & Van den Branden 1995, Van den Branden & Lambert 1999). Although the resource of a lingua franca has pervaded in the experiments carried out so far there are powerful reasons to expect than multilingual designs will enter into the Open and Distance Learning (ODL) panorama in a short time (Sánchez-Mesa 1997). The perspectives opened by *automatic translation* seem at first sight quite promising. However, the substantial investment in financial and human resources made in the last years has been awarded with an uneven level of results (let us remember the failure of the program *Eurotra).* When talking about *automatic translation* we must differentiate between the *aided* or *assisted translation*, namely the resources of glossaries and dictionaries available on-line, and what is called *machine translation*, e.g. specific software for automatic on-line linguistic transfer.

Anyway, whatever possibilities might be discovered in the immediate development of these tools, the fact is that there is a strong resistance among professionals to tackle and confront this promising market, even though, paradoxically, it appears to be *the future* of translation (an approximate idea of this market is grasped when we consider the amount of text liable to be translated in the World Wide Web environment and the need for multilingual on-line services).

Those announcing the so-called hypertextual revolution find in this "new" type of electronic text (hypertext) a sort of communitarian space shared along large interwoven networks, a situation which would have been prefigured by some poststructuralist critics: Barthes and his notion of the reader's text Foucault, considering the text as a node interconnected with many others in a net of crossed references; Derrida, insisting in the irrelevance of the "hors-texte", intertextuality and dissemination and Bakhtin himself, as we will see immediately. Hypertext is meant to reconfigure literary creation, consumption, education (Landow 1992). Moreover, hypertext becomes the paradigm from which a pre-hypertextual literature is identified (Borges, Cortezar, Calvino, Queneau, etc.). Following a more accurate (contextualized) historical view, we should better analyse the so-called pre-hypertextual (modern or post-modern) literature as the consequence of some contemporary conceptual or aesthetical shifts instead of rewriting retrospectively, that means teleologically, the recent developments in literary textuality taking hypertext as its end. Multiperspectivism, heterogeneity, fragmentation, polyphony, metareflection, collage, all these cultural and artistic notions have been floating in the air of the twentieth century.

Hypertexts are considered to be *polyphonic*, in a Bakhtinian sense, as long as the relative independence of his characters' voices resembles the deconstruction of the former authority of the author. In this sense it seems like hypertext was gifted with some sort of musical quality, as a contrapunctual space where a plurality of voices were put together to be conducted by the will of the formerly called spectator. The impact of hypertext and electronic digital media on the cultural system has to be looked into in order to draw conclusions as far as translation is concerned. That impact could roughly be summarized in the debate on the interchange between author and reader (user) roles in literary activity. All this revolutionary modality of writing and interacting with texts (navigation substitutes the concept of linear reading) is considered to be *essentially democratic* (no predominance of author over readers; collective creation; bi-directional communication; non-hierarchical relationships; non-economic restriction to cultural production and consumption). This leads us to another important issue I just can mention here: the politics of cyberspace (Poster 1995, 1997, Talens 1995). Is the role of the translator, as agent of transculturation, meant to be more widely recognized in this *dissolution* of authorship?

3. Virtual Reality

New electronic media have the power to produce an increasing effect of dematerialization in the perception of our bodies. Virtual reality (VR) is probably the most powerful device in terms of immersion of the subject into the virtual world.[3]

Although to many of us it might still sound as something belonging to science fiction, the fact is that this technology is being applied in research within disciplines like architecture, medicine, movie production and military activities (flight simulators, war action simulations), whereas a presumably extraordinary entertainment market is just waiting for it to be developed. The implications that this technology may convey for our future ways of communication are just being grasped (Shreve 1997).

What is the feedback provided by proprioception when acting in a VR simulation compared with the current use of objects? The dematerialization of the body (Hayles 1992). On the other hand, the immersive effect of this technology could be compared to that traditionally encountered when entering narrative fiction (literature). Rooting in the theory of fiction as a process of making up possible worlds by literary imagination (author/reader), Marie-Laure Ryan praises the possibilities embedded in VR to push immersion further while combining it with interactivity, thus erasing that major pitfall she also identifies in the effacement of semiotic mediation, that is, the naturalization of the representation or simulation (Ryan 1994).

What are the features of virtual reality experience which we should bear in mind in our inquiry for possible implications for translation matters:

a) We are dealing with multisensory experience,

b) It is a space where different subjects can meet (jack in) in an artificially *realistic* environment which the subject can easily "live in" as if he or she were interacting in real empirical life,

c) The user controls the simulation.

Cyberspace is a term coined by the fiction novelist William Gibson. This concept expands virtual reality to a vast second-order reality which could be experienced hypothetically by thousands of people worldwide. To realize the range of this second-order reality we only have to imagine the possibility of entering a four-dimension Internet. The qualitative change that this technology is announcing when being compared with wired communication (e-mail) rests on the chance of summing up the instantaneous nature of the latter with a much more sophisticated simulation of a physical (face-to-face) real encounter.

It makes sense to think in virtual reality as a potential new medium for human communication. Which kind of communication will be attached to this incoming medium? Anwers to this question still lay in a partly hypothetical domain. Although I do not want to fall into the trap of turning from theory into prophecy, it is pertinent to foresee at this embryonic stage of VR technology the fact that cyberspace is meant to be a place where translation is going to be much needed, either when interacting with other individuals or with the computer-generated characters, whose dialogue could eventually be listened to in each user's language.

4. Towards a new aesthetics and new regulations

Transculturality and *networked electronic communication* also find another confluence in some proposals launched from the perspective opened by what Jaishree Odin calls *net aesthetic* for postcolonial discourse (Odin 1996). Here, hypertext is given a more consistent political potential, far from other exaggerated claims concerning its liberating powers. In postcolonial discourse the politics of embodiment shows that bodies do not exist in transparent space, nor do languages, we might add. According to Odin, although

> Technology might claim to have made possible a clean virtual space where categories of race, gender and class are said to be irrelevant and where humans can experience the freedom of total disembodiment, we know better, that since humans are half of the interaction of the real with the virtual, if our society is not changed at a fundamental level, no leaps into virtual space can bring us freedom from the inequality and injustices of social reality. (Odin 1996)

Communication, Odin is right, is not revolutionary in itself, as well as information is not equal to knowledge.

Consequently, through hypertext the postcolonial critic accomplishes the avoidance of the cartography as a territorialized knowledge which deals with colonizing and mastering the unknown by setting it as *the other* in order to appropiate him. Moving instead to the model of the *itinerary* provided by hypertext, it is possible to represent spaces as *practiced places* (as Michel de Certeau would put it) which brings out the richness of the cultural matrix without crystallizing into any fixed form. According to Odin again, the orality of ethnics narratives resembles the multiple possibilities of textual mutation in hypertext environment.

The reshifting of subjectivity led by postcolonial critics finds in the emergence of hypertext a new field to reinforce peripheral subjects' positions while recording the cracking of the centered, autonomous and self-sufficient western subject into a "nomadic", hybrid, border one. This discourse introduces a major correction in the monotopic hermeneutic tradition of the West, calling our attention to the urgent need to interpret history (including that of West) from other sites which are two-faced (and multilingual) in themselves. The political relevance of this argument does not hide, however, any reductionism, not only of the different functions of books in history (also liberating in many circumstances) but also when that hypertext will materialize that *net aesthetics* by its own sake.

In favour of hypertext and Internet as a multidirectional environment in which to communicate we must perceive the heavy struggle among the big companies and telecommunication holdings, together with central governments, to normalize the net legally. Internet is a space where it is still not possible to silence many critical voices and small actions calling for a more socialist political consciousness. The web is a financially appealing, growing market and the increasing pressure against it confirms this. At this moment the number of voices raised in favour of a regulation of information traffic and access to data through the Internet is worthy of consideration. Noble principles support these claims in many cases (neo-nazi propaganda, child pornography, etc.) but the point here is to realize the interests which actually rest beside those principles. Big communication holdings do not like overpopulated electronic networks annoying the smooth universality of their marketing chant. They need clean spaces where the newly arrived will get the same security that we feel when entering a commercial mall. Actually we are facing one of the most interesting debates in these years, a debate where two different concepts of freedom collide. On the one side, the financial neoliberalism with the values of market at its core (competence, productivity, economic expansion, liberalization, interest, profits) vehemently fighting the suppression of any regulation over freedom, except from that regulating competence. At present national states have started to play the same game with more or less intensity.

On the other side, and beyond state interventionism, there has been a social action willing to reinstall cooperation at the core of social practice. Not everything was competence for this electronic community (virtual society) who openly discarded commercial publicity as something exterior to their environment.

While the Internet was a minority phenomenon, users had a sense of solidarity and cooperation quite alien to current social life. I do not want to depict a romantic image of this phenomenon. The truth is that at least there has been some moment, which somehow is not over, when users have managed to subvert the purposes of those agents behind the production and functioning of informatics (states and big enterprises), that is, moving from control and financial profit to cooperation.

5. The relevance of Bakhtin's concepts

Bakhtin's translinguistics and poetics grant an outstanding relevance to "the other's word". Every single *utterance* (the word functioning in the communicative chain; language in motion, the word as history) is overlapping with the others' utterances in a everlasting chain of embedded discourses (intertextuality, or better, interdiscursivity) which we could consider as one manifestation of translation, understood as a general phenomenon (present in everyday communication). Accordingly, based on Bakhtin Circle's discourse theory I would like to bring in some theoretical insights to be worked out when dealing with multimedia translation.

5.1 Language as heteroglossia

The notion of language as *heteroglossia* (in order to get rid of the so often constrained notion of national language) is much more functional than the sociolinguistic concept of *sociolect.* Language functions as a discursive plurality (*heteroglossia).* Its stratification and the coexistence of many socially different languages makes it hardly advisable to talk only in terms of national languages as there is always tension among the manifold discourses coexisting in a particular time. Therefore, *heteroglossia* means the coexistence of social and ideological contradictions between present and past discourses, between different past discourses, those of different social groups, geographical variants, between theoretical or academic schools, etc. This has to do with the very fact that the communities participating from one single pole within an international virtual network should not be considered as an homogeneous unit from a linguistic point of view.

Furthermore, the concept of heteroglossia has the advantage of presenting dynamically (in their dialogic/conflictive interrelation) a series of linguistic (discursive) differentiating factors (gender, sociolect, professional register, dialect, reception anticipating strategies...) that could become a dead discoursive catalogue once it is isolated from their specific socio-ideological (contextual) implications.

5.2 Discourse genres

Whenever we speak we select our utterance not from the abstract system of our language but from some relatively fixed types of utterance – ones that are relatively stable regarding topic, style and composition. We learn how to handle those registers during the social communication process. These genres function as "conveyor belts" between social heterogeneity and verbal utterances. They are, to put it that way, an institutionalized form of discursive mediation, that is, one way to explain the intrinsic interconnection of the social and the individual, or else, between language and ideology. In a virtual forum we will interact through these discoursive genres (shuffling from one to another) which should enable different interest coming from opposing collectivities.

5.3 Dialogic comprehension

An authentic/coherent dialogic communication requires
a) Awareness of one's own *locus enuntiationis* (within a given cultural tradition and social context), that is - in Bakhtinian terms - *dialogic inclusion.*
b) Extraposition: I can't approach and interact with some "other" (a person, a text or a film) unless I occupy some different position and thereby represent a potentially critical locus. This is crucial to understanding in transnational/ crosscultural virtual communication through IT. The immateriality of the medium might provoke or ease the feeling that we are somewhere else when entering into the forum.
c) Answerability: in the double sense implied by this neologism (= ethical responsibility + answer). Every real interaction demands an answer which is at the same time supported by somebody's responsibility.

Dialogics (a certain sort of understanding and practise of dialogue in cultural interaction) aims to assure authentical interaction through a real act of comprehension. We are not talking here about ideal – Gadamer – or abstract understanding – Saussure, Jakobson – but rather about comprehension as an answer to a question which raises new questions (this also could be another characterization of translation).

5.4 The moveless traveller

Which of these entities would be, on the basis of dialogics, the *chronotope* of this virtual subject (virtual for a while) who interacts though the screen (via e-mail, videoconference, satellite sessions, etc.), either synchronically or asynchronically? I would suggest calling it *the itinerary of the moveless traveller* (again that forking paths garden of Borges), fighting in the time of the absolute present. By *fighting* I mean escaping from the empire of rhetoric over meaning to go beyond the vanishing rumour of immediately consumable flickering signs.

6. Conclusion

As a consequence of what been said, I would conclude that one of the main aims in international multimedia communication management should be to provide a real *comprehensive environment to multilingual (heteroglossic) and multicultural interaction*.This strategy would increase the awareness of the importance of an *active reception in virtual interaction*, taking into account the weight of traditions in every comprehensive deed as well as the need to assume the position of virtual interaction within the global intercultural framework in time, that is, within a wide concept of history, what Bakhtin called *great time.*

Notes

1. The program used in this case is called *Storyspace.* The first window of this electronic version resembles the usual cover of a book. At the bottom of the window the user finds several clickable frames (Yes, No, Up, Down, Back, Left, Right) with which he/she can either answer the questions posed by the program or progress/change the sense of the navigation within the works' hyperspace. The open frame at the right of the buttoms allows the introduction of one or more words which will make the system open a lexia where that word is present. Under the text's window the general map of the reading is displayed by Storyspace.

2. Nowadays one can be working on his/her computer while listening to Verdi's Aida. Wouldn't it be equally nice to open another window and take a look at the script translated in different languages? Multilingual TV programs are already a well-known reality although the possibilities of augmenting the number of versions available thanks to digitization have not been fully exploited yet.

3. VR is a sophisticated computer technology which puts the body into an intense and direct feedback loop with a simulation. In one version, the user wears a stereovision helmet and a body glove that senses the position of both head and hand. When turning the head the computer adjusts the simulation in a way that the scene changes as if the user would be inside the screen looking around. A representation of the user´s hands appears in the simulation so that it is possible to manipulate objects by moving the hand and even change one's position by making certain codified hand movements. *Proprioception* creates a link between the body extensions and habitually used objects (the baton of a conductor, the racket of a professional tennis player or the keys of a secretary's typewriter are tools which are felt as extensions of their users' bodies, thus material resistance of these objects to motion is the same as that of the body itself). Virtual reality technologies modify the bodily proprioceptive sense; at the same time extending and reinforcing it.

IMAGES OF TRANSLATION

Gregor Goethals
Rhode Island School of Design,
Providence, USA

1. Introduction

Technologies for creating and reproducing images have opened up unprecedented opportunities for the discussion of translation. Mass-produced images, now as readily available as printed or electronic words, present translators with a new challenge: to rethink the relationship between word and image. Today, easily accessible visual representations may be combined with words in countless way. Moreover, the widespread use of multimedia - simultaneously combining sound, text, static and moving images - is constantly modifying not only the forms of meaning construction, but audience responses as well.

Translators can no longer assume that they are addressing an audience rooted in a static print culture. In responding to both technological and social changes, the American Bible Society initiated a series of experimental multimedia translations for a youth audience. These experiments have enabled us to identify and explore a number of theoretical and practical design issues.

Biblical scholars and artists who first began working on these translations found it useful to reflect on some of the basic distinctions between image and word. One significant difference is that the vocabulary of visual language – the raw materials of images and objects – is essentially non-discursive. Precise verbal meanings, for example, cannot be directly ascribed to lines and colors; nor can we extract explanatory words from abstract textures and patterns formed by the raw materials of visual language. We may have an emotional response to the color red; but we cannot be sure that others will share our reactions.

Artists in different times and places have, of course, composed visual elements in various ways. The organization – of visual syntax – may range from abstract, non-representational forms to highly "realistic" imagery. An artist may arrange lines, colors, and shapes in ways that attempt to "re-present" our sensory experience. A simple stick figure, for example, with sketchy lines for arms and legs, topped by a round shape, may signify a human figure to people of diverse cultural backgrounds. Or a human figure may be represented with much more illusionistic skill, enabling immediate recognition of a human form in space.

Irwin Panofsky refers to such a basic identification as "pre-iconographical", a phase of image analysis which relies primarily upon ordinary experience of the visible world. Panofsky goes on to describe a "secondary level of symbolism" which depends, by contrast, upon our knowledge of cultural myths. Thus, we may use common sense experience to identify a representation of a woman and a child; but for this image to transfer additional meaning, we require an understanding of a society's religious ideas. To develop a deeper iconographical analysis of this image as the Virgin Mary and infant Jesus, we must bring to the image more than common sense experience (Panofsky 1955: 39-41). In the semiotic terms of Peirce, our signifier or sign vehicle (representation of woman and child) can only point to its object (Virgin Mary and infant Jesus) with the help of an interpretant or body of established meaning (Mariology).

While we all share a basic physiological system for receiving visual data, our individual and culturally filtered brains are constantly translating the raw data of color and light in very different ways. Both simple and complex images are "colored" by our vantage points as responsive viewers. Thus, as we bring particular experiences to an image or object, we actually help to construct its "meaning." Historian and critic Norman Bryson has noted that a work of art calls forth a "production," not a "perception" of meaning. "Viewing," he says, "is an activity of transforming the material of the painting into meanings, and that transformation is perpetual: nothing can arrest it." (Bryson 1983: Preface xiii-xiv)

2. Combining Word and Image

When images and words are presented together, the channels through which we transport our interpretations are more narrow and specific. While the evocative power of images remains strong, our constructions of meaning are, at the same time, prompted and guided by an accompanying text. During the 20th century there has been a remarkable growth of genres which combine words and images into a total symbolic unit. One of the most significant integrations of word and image may be seen in advertising art. Moreover, in the advertising genre, the effective transfer of meaning to a target audience is constantly being measured by sales of particular products and by the attention generated by the ads themselves.

Industries associated with the creation of commercials, both print and electronic, have perhaps become the great 20th century masters of "translation." Combining the emotive, evocative power of images with specific texts resulted in the evolution of an art form in which word and image have become inextricably woven into a total gestalt of meaning. Sometimes the overall pattern of word and image, used repeatedly, may eventually become completely identified with a particular product. In the USA, one recent example of the power of such a combination of word and image was the series of "Joe Camel" commercials. Indeed, because of its effectiveness with children, it was eventually banned. But even as a banned commercial, "Joe Camel" retained its power. To put it in Peircean semiotic terms, billboards offered a related signifier or sign vehicle (a camel in a broken outline) that pointed to the same object (cigarette smoking), but with an even more powerful interpretant or set of meanings (smoking is a now a way of thumbing one's nose at government's regulatory interference).

3. Word and Image in Religious Contexts

The interrelationship of word and image was not, however, invented by advertising artists. Centuries before, monks in medieval scriptoria combined word and image in their illuminated manuscript designs. We see examples of this in such masterpieces as the Book of Kells. Moreover, religions which emphasize liturgy evolve complex, multivalent processes of translation. This is especially apparent in religious rituals prior to the invention of printing. Meaning becomes communicated through a total sensory experience. Like contemporary multimedia events, complex patterns of different communication forms – light, sound, music, human motions and gesture – simultaneously create a web of symbols within which participants interact.

4. American Bible Society's Multimedia Translations Programme

Drawing upon traditional religious integrations of word and image, scholars and artists associated with the American Bible Society Multimedia Programme began to develop a series of experimental prototypes. The following summary will provide an overview of the various facets of multimedia production.

4.1 Word track

At the heart of each multimedia translation is the word track. Working with Greek or Hebrew texts, a team of translators is assigned to produce a text in translation that will address the intended youth audience. One consideration that is getting increased attention is the poetic dimension of the biblical passage; and scholars on the team have reminded us of the *hearing*, not the reading of words, in a pre-print world. Since some of the multimedia productions have featured music and performances, there has been an expanded interest in translations whose sound and rhythms lead to functional equivalents in the form of a target text's words, songs, and dance.

4.2 Preproduction

As the translation proceeds, basic preproduction work begins. A core team works with a producer/director to develop possible treatments for a video translation. For *The Visit* (the story of the meeting of Mary and Elizabeth recorded in Gospel of Luke 1.39-56), the team decided on a musical performance for the major translation. Subsequently, various groups were interviewed and one was chosen for the production. At the same time, directors and producers were chosen for two other video versions of the text. One was a Korean Mask Dance; the other featured a Spanish language musical translation, with a visual narrative for the text.

The ultimate multimedia product was to be a CD-ROM. This CD-ROM would contain the three above-mentioned videos, study materials for a teenage audience, and some lengthier articles on the life and customs, social conditions, and religious background in which the Gospels were written. In light of the diversity of material which would be presented on the CD-ROM, several design issues came to the foreground. The major one was the unification of such diverse material in one programme. Even though the CD-ROM is an interactive medium which encourages viewers to explore the material in a non-linear way, there emerged the need for a visual unity that could serve as an armature or over-arching symbolic look and feel for different levels and genres of material. We began to refer to this symbolic visual motif as the "mega-metaphor." The idea simply is to develop a visual symbol whose features can be highly abstracted, fragmented, enlarged, or combined as recurring marks and colors. The function of the "mega-metaphor" is to contain and unify the disparate parts. Again in Peircean semiotic terms, the "mega-metaphor" provides a signifier or sign vehicle (a nautilus shape in the case of *The Visit*) that points to an object (the programme as a whole). And thanks to an established interpretant or meaning the sign vehicle and its object denote and connote in various ways that the whole programme has an overarching unity and coherence.

The nautilus symbol was chosen because the story of the *The Visit* featured women at the center of its narrative and discourse. The physical features of the nautilus – the logarithmic spiral – furnished a flowing, organic shape that seems appropriate to the text. Moreover, its identification as a basic principle of growth in all life forms brought an additional richness to this passage concerning women.

4.3 Design issues

Particular design issues in the CD-ROM are related to this technology and the ways in which video is presented within a CD-ROM. Due to limitations of CD-ROM technology it was then not possible to play full screen video from a CD-ROM programme. Without full screen video, there had to be a stage-like panorama which served as a context for small video windows. Abstractions of the nautilus design were combined into montages to serve as a backdrop for these windows. As the viewer moved deeper into the textual helps for the translators, they moved deeper into the abstracted proportions of the nautilus. As technology improves, the video window will become larger and particular design strategies will shift to accommodate the new technology.

Indeed, in recent experiments, features of *The Visit* have been transformed for presentation on the World Wide Web. In preparing for this, we had to select parts of the CD-ROM whose meaning could be successfully transferred to the technology of the Web. While video is available on some computer systems, it is still not readily accessible on most. So it became necessary to choose only those aspects of the translation that most average viewers with computer systems of modest power might access. One great virtue of the Web transformation, however, is its possibility as a constantly developing theatre for translation projects. While the visual/technological qualities of the Web and CD-ROM technologies differ, the visual metaphors provide a bridge to the new technology for translation experiments. We have learned that when the basic symbol structure is in place, changing technologies can open up new dimensions of meaning and experience, as well as new opportunities for transferring that meaning and experience from one medium and platform to another.

5. Conclusion

While future plans include the production of CD-ROMs or DVDs (Digital Versatile Disc), or continued experiments on the Web, the heart of the work at the American Bible Society remains translation. What has happened, however, is that, under the pressure of incredible changes in communication technology and audience expectations there is emerging a more inclusive concept of text and translation. Paradoxically, this broader concept of text and translation echoes older, transitional religious forms of transferring the meaning of religious texts – forms in which words and images combined into integrated wholes. Like ancient rituals and illuminated manuscripts, contemporary multimedia return us to the possibilities of translation as a kind of total knowledge through sight and sound. Through dazzling imagery, motion, voice and music, communication technologies have begun to nudge and push us to rediscover the many complex languages available to translators.

TEXT AND CONTEXT IN MULTIMEDIA TRANSLATION

J. Ritter Werner
Expert in Musical Arts,
American Bible Society,
Dayton, USA

1. Introduction

In 1989 the American Bible Society established the NewMedia Project in its Translations Department to produce experimental multimedia translations of biblical texts. To date, the Project team has completed a series of six video translations that combine words, sounds and images in MTV-like formats. In the near future, all of these videos will be available for distribution at www.americanbible.org, in an online catalogue. Over and above these six multimedia texts, the first three videos were combined with supporting multimedia materials and released on CD-ROMS in the early nineties. Since the mid-nineties, the World Wide Web has been chosen as the context for our video translations. One website is completed and two are under construction.

When this experimental project started, electronic-media translation for biblical texts was non-existant. There were no prototypes. At best, Hollywood blockbusters biblical films were paraphrases of translated texts, twice or thrice removed from the original sacred communication. The same was true for audio-visual biblical materials. There was no concept that when a silent, literary document such as the Bible is translated for a multimedia environment, the translator must not only account for the verbal signs of a text, its linguistic parameter, but also for the text's inferred sonic and visual properties, not to mention its implicit and explicit contextual properties.

The inferred sonic properties, which accompany any text's performance, include voice quality, dynamics, tempo, rhythm, and inflection. The inferred visual properties include all the images that a text calls up in the mind of a reader. Such sonic and visual properties are called ”paralinguistic” in functionalist theories of translation. (deWaard & Nida, 1986: 13) The implicit and explicit contextual properties include, for example, a text’s rhetorical structure, the physical environment and the occasion of its performance, as well as the body language of a performer or performers. In functionalist theories of translation such properties are called ”extralinguistic”, (ibid: 17)

The NewMedia team understood that these three parameters (linguistic, paralinguistic, extralinguistic) were not arbitrary or capricious, but demanded by the new technologies themselves which played “electronic texts” containing these three elements in the form of words, sounds, and images. Our task was to render all the implicit and explicit parameters of a silent source text so that a multimedia translation would faithfully communicate the original, multi-dimensional meaning of a source text. (ibid: 10-11). Well-developed tools and methods from a wide range of scholarly disciplines were employed for analyzing and translating these linguistic, paralinguistic, and extralinguistic parameters. What follows is a description of some of our work to date, how we first translate a sacred text, and then produce a context for the text on the World Wide Web. Since biblical texts share many characteristics with other silent texts, it is hoped that this description will prove useful for other multimedia translators.

2. Multimedia Translation of a Source Text: an Overview

The primary question in multimedia translation has two parts: How do the linguistic, paralinguistic, and extralinguistic parameters of a text appear, function, interrelate, and contribute to the total meaning of a text? How is the meaning of these parameters transferred or translated into a multimedia environment?

To answer the first part of the question, a translator needs to remember two axioms, one from translation theory, and one from music theory and aesthetics: "Meaning exists only because there is contrast." (Nida, 1984: 15) And: "Contrast can only be determined and appreciated from the macro to the micro, from the whole to the parts." (LaRue, 1970: 5) To answer the second part of the primary question, a translator needs to be grounded in some form of translation theory – be it formal equivalence, functional equivalence, or semiotics – and understand how translation theory interacts with multimedia technologies, techniques, and context.

2.1 Source Analysis

Source analysis is the more traditional part of the multimedia process. However, since three parameters need to be taken into account, this work can only be done by specialists who are experts in each parameter. For the linguistic parameter, biblical exegetes are needed to do literary, form, and grammatical criticism. Music theorists and musicologists, with a knowledge of the ancient languages, are needed to examine the implicit paralinguistic parameters of the original text and to collect and analyze explicit settings of the text throughout history, if there are any. Since the formative environment of biblical texts was public recital, the extralinguistic parameter needs to be investigated by socio-rhetorical scholars, who can trace the social, cultural, artistic, literary, and liturgical frames of a text. (Robbins, 1984: 13)

2.2 Target Analysis

Target analysis for the multimedia process, while rooted in traditional scholarship, goes beyond the "science of translating." (Nida 1964). It draws on many non-translational disciplines, including orality-literacy studies, media and audience research, play theory, (Hodgson & Soukup 1997: 37-131; Gronbeck, Farrell, Soukup 1991). Again, the reason for this is rooted in the nature of electronic texts and technology which influences the perception and the interrelationship of all three parameters, and which demands different actions and responses on the part of translators, producers and audiences. An example might be helpful at this point.

Part of the extralinguistic parameter in a silent text is the flow of images implied by the words, or stimulated by a performer and/or the performative environment during a recital. The implied images are in the imagination. The stimulated images, while real, are not necessarily related to the words, and can form their own context. In both cases, the implied and explicit images are secondary to the ideal and/or affective content of the linguistic parameter.

In an electronic text, the written words are usually absorbed into a soundscape, while implied or explicit images come to life on a screen in an imagescape. Since the eye takes physical precedent over the ear – Benjamin Franklin invented bifocals to hear better! – attention shifts from word to image. This reality gives new meaning to the old proverb, "A picture is worth a thousand words." In the multimedia context, this means that the visual takes precedent over the auditory. This reality is verified economically by multimedia manufacturers who invest more money in their visual systems than in their auditory systems. This shift has profound implications. For the translator it means being able to successfully bridge the gap between the sacred biblical narrative world, and the secular, video narrative world, and to do so in a way that the visual component is faithfully connected to the verbal source.

For a producer it means discovering a common aesthetic rhythm to interconnect the flow of narrative images to the flow of verbal and musical sounds, so that the sounds, words, and images of a video, for example, can be experienced as a unified performative event. For audiences it means being sufficiently literate in words, sounds and images that they can read a video and understand the meaning of its multivalent content.

3. Implications for Source-Target Analysis and Translation

From the preceding description of source-target analysis it can be inferred that this process is complex. A traditional, print-oriented model of an individual translator, or even small group of translators, doing this type of work, is obsolete. In a multimedia environment, translation can only be accomplished with the help of many scholars and experts. The NewMedia Translation Project of the American Bible Society's Translation Department, for example, at its inception nine years ago, created an interdisciplinary research team of scholars and media specialists to do the source-target research, analysis, and translation. From this larger group of about two dozen specialists, subcommittees stepped forward to do specialized work, and a core team was formed to work with the project manager to make final decisions and to assist in the production.

Very early on, it was discovered that the only way for the various teams and committees to work individually and corporately was to be interconnected electronically in cyberspace, primarily on the Internet. As one team member commented in a project paper, "If we hope to create electronic translations of the Bible, we will also need to discover how to carry on electronic research [...], establish an electronic scriptorium [...], and develop an electronic decision making process" (Roschke 1994).

Over the years, a virtual "electronic community" of scholars and experts has been created. The multimedia tools that were originally means for production and transmission of multimedia texts have become an important means for doing research and communicating between team members. Producing multimedia translations with multimedia tools has turned out to be one of the most important decisions of the project. For as the research team has grown in technical expertise through daily use of multimedia tools, it has learned how better to integrate the new, contemporary world of multimedia with the ancient world of the Bible.

4. Luke 1.39-56: An Example of Multimedia Translation

To better understand how the multimedia translation works, it might be helpful to outline how the research and core teams of the NewMedia Translation Project produced its third experimental video translation, *The*

Visit, a story that recounts Mary's journey and 3-month stay with her cousin Elizabeth. *The Visit* belongs to the six-part series tracing the life and teachings of Jesus. The first production is *Out of the Tombs* (Mark 5.1-20), a multimedia telling of Jesus' healing of the Gerasene demoniac, complete with narration, contemporary rock music, and an analogous contemporary film look using functionally translated images from the original text. The second production is *A Father and Two Sons*, an MTV-like music video with a blues song and country-and-western images and actions, all functionally translated from the original Greek text of Luke 15.11-32.

The Visit uses a format similar to the other two productions, but with one major difference. No attempt was made to functionally translate the implied images of the second section of the source text with an analogous contemporary film. Instead, the research and core teams, together with the producers, decided to script a performance video of the entire text, with singing, drumming, and dancing. Why did they do this? The answer is rooted in the source-target analysis that was made prior to and during the production.

4.1 Source Analysis Highlights

A linguistic analysis documented that Mary's visit to Elizabeth constituted the third story in the Infancy Narrative of the Gospel of Luke. The first two stories announce the births of John the Baptist and Jesus of Nazareth. Now, in the pericope or story about Mary's visit, the two mothers come together, awaiting the birth of their sons. The linguistic and paralinguistic analyses further revealed that the story fell into two sections, followed by a short coda. The first section runs from Luke 1.39-46 and provides a narrative that recounts Mary's entrance into her cousin's household and Elizabeth's prophetic reaction to Mary's divine maternity. The second section contains Luke 1.47-55 and offers a lyric poem in which Mary joyfully responds to Elizabeth's prophetic words. In the short narrative coda of Luke 1.56 Mary departs just before the birth of John the Baptist.

The research and core teams regarded Luke's oscillation from narrative prose to lyric poetry and back again as the most significant piece of information in the source analysis. It signaled a conscious intensification of meaning and aesthetic appeal in the second section, which in turn created a climax for the pericope. (De Waard & Nida 1986: 80). They also concluded that any multimedia production needed to preserve this rhetorical reality to faithfully transfer the meaning of the Greek text from source to target. However, to translate the genre shifts that occurred when the text went from narrative to poetry, and to translate in a way that preserved the aesthetic climax in the target text, were no easy tasks! To do so successfully, the implied paralinguistic characteristics of the genres needed to be appreciated and dynamic equivalences found for a multimedia performance. Since the poetic section of *The Visit* is almost entirely mute about its performance characteristics, the research and core teams extended their source analysis to include other biblical passages to learn more about lyric poetry and its relationship to narrative.

There are not many lyric sections in the Greek Bible. Four are located in the Gospel of Luke (1.39-56; 1.68-79; 2.14; 2.29-33). In general, the Lucan passages are *centos* of verses found in the Greek Septuagint, an ancient translation of the Hebrew Bible. The only important paralinguistic information in the four Lucan poems is the voice of the narrators, Mary, Zachariah, heavenly hosts, and Simeon. And since Mary was the only female narrator in Luke's four texts, the teams decided to study poetic prototypes in the Hebrew Bible. There they found many examples of women singing poetic texts – texts that Luke would have known. In fact, Luke even used parts of these Septuagint texts to compose his own *centos*.

In one of the Septuagint passages (1 Samuel 2.1-10), Hannah thanks God for the birth and weaning of her son Samuel. In another (Judges 5), Deborah sings of Israel's triumph over General Sisera and his Canaanite army. In a final text (Exodus 16.20-21), Miriam, the sister of Moses and Aaron, gathers the women of Israel to sing and dance after the Israelites had triumphed over Pharaoh's army.

In the Miriam example, paralinguistic characteristics began to accumulate. The poetic text is sung, danced, and accompanied by instruments. This "multimedia" performance prompted the research and core teams to investigate these interrelationships in other biblical poems such as 1 Samuel 18.6-7 and Psalm 149.1-3.

In the examples that the teams studied, there were not only paralinguistic characteristics, but also extralinguistic ones as well, for instance notes about time, place, and emotional orientation. The times turned out to be times of victory and triumph; the places consisted of communal spaces; the emotional orientation was joy. All these extralinguistic features turn up in *The Visit*. Mary sings of victory and triumph; she lodges with her cousin; and her joy permeates the whole scene. Mary and Elizabeth are ecstatic in their bearing, while John the Baptist leaps for joy in Elizabeth's womb.

With these extralinguistic and paralinguistic features in mind, the teams decided to produce a multimedia performance video using singing, dancing, and instruments, even though the paralinguistic analysis of the Greek text was not explicit in these matters. After this pivotal decision, the teams focused on how to translate the source text into a target text for an audience of older American teenagers.

4.2 Target Analysis

An MTV "performance video" for American teenagers used images, music, and dancing; as such it provided a genre that fitted nicely into the contemporary electronic culture that delivers images and music to teenagers. However, since the primary emphasis in the genre of performance video lies on instrumental accompaniment, and not on the singing of a text, a performance video of *The Visit* could only partially resemble its MTV counterpart. The center of the production had to be the biblical narrative and its poem with all their rhetorical contrast. To this end a search was made for female performers who could not only sing and dance, but also could communicate texts with feeling. Eventually, an African-American Gospel group was found. It sang the text well, and moved with style and joy. Initial conversations with the group proved very promising, but due to contractual and scheduling issues the choice fell on another group called "The Women of the Calabash."

The process of finding good performers was not the sole responsibility of the research and core teams. Helping in the process was the film's script writer and director, Merle Worth, who also scripted and directed the above-mentioned video translations for the American Bible Society. Merle was particularly helpful in this production since she was not only a well-respected film maker but also a trained musician. She communicated the highlights of the source analysis to the "Women of the Calabash" who began setting the text in song, instrumental accompaniment, and dance. As the "Women of the Calabash" created their setting, an intense dialogue developed between them, Merle Worth, and J. Ritter Werner, the music consultant. At the same time, Gregor Goethals, art consultant, worked closely with all of the above-mentioned people, as well as with the designers of costumes, sets, and lighting.

The end result of this complex collaboration was a video that consciously translates the parameters of the original text into contemporary functional equivalents, be they word, sound, or image. The rhetorical contrast between narrative and poetry permeates the entire production, which is made up of three interlocking parts. The first is the wordtrack, which follows the concepts and process developed by the American Bible Society for translating versions of the Bible such as Today's English Version and the Contemporary English Version. The second consists of the sound-track, which mirrors the paralinguistic elements in the source text, elements such as changes of sound, harmony, melody, rhythm, and form. The third is the film, which through changes in choreography, costume, and lighting, puts into images the extralinguistic elements of the Lucan source text.

5. Contextualizing a Multimedia Translation

The word "complex" amply describes multimedia translation process up to this point, but it is only the first step. The new, multimedia text needs a context. For *The Visit*, this was an interactive CD-ROM, which surrounded this primary multimedia translation with smaller video translations of the Lucan text and supporting educational materials in traditional and multimedia formats. For the next video production, *The Neighbor,* a multimedia translation of Luke's parable of the Good Samaritan (Lk. 10. 25-37), the context is the World Wide Web. Placing multimedia biblical texts on the Web is not without problems, since this powerful medium is primarily directed toward information and commerce. It could easily inundate any biblical text, traditional or multimedia, for two reasons. First, biblical texts are primarily directed toward sacred instruction. Second, biblical texts are most often ritually performed with music, art, prescribed movements, and other sacred texts within the context of public worship.

This ritual context is every bit as important as the biblical texts themselves, for in these "repetitive ceremonial forms", which is a thumbnail definition of ritual, worshipers do more than acquire information. They experience ancient texts as a living reality that appeals not just to the intellect, but to the whole person, body, mind, soul and volition. The overriding question for multimedia biblical translators then becomes, "Can the Web be adapted to mirror this ritual context?" The short answer is, "Yes". The next section of this paper will attempt to demonstrate this.

5.1 Placing a Multimedia Translation on the Web

Even though ritual space and the Web use many of the same elements, the texts, images, sounds, and movements of the former can not be easily translated into the latter. Ritual space is centered on human performance within the confines of "actual" space and time. While cyberspace, the Web's universe, is centered around "virtual" space and time, meaning, "in essence or effect, but not in fact". What is needed are auditory and visual analogues for the various elements of actual ritual worship that dynamically translate their function and meaning for the virtual, electronic environment. The elements include prescribed movements of participants, spoken or sung prayers, vocal and instrumenal music, plus environmental colors, images and architectural shapes. Like *The Visit*, all of these elements contain paralinguistic and/or extralinguistic codes that can be analyzed and translated to establish a ritual context in cyberspace that mirrors traditional ritual worship. This, in turn can provide an environment suitable for a multimedia biblical presentation.

5.2 A Ritual Context for "The Neighbor"

A written description of a ritual context suitable for cyberspace seems recidivistic. To mitigate this anomaly, I recommend that the reader log in on the Web and view the multimedia component for this discussion. The address is www.researchcenter.org. Once connected, go to a Library/Archive area, search for this article by author or title, and follow the directions to view a 20-minute multimedia presentation, consisting of a ritual context and *The Neighbor* video.

The first icon seen in this presentation is of a large planet in space with spiraling satellites. At the same time the opening verses of the Book of Genesis are sung, first in Hebrew, using traditional tropes, followed by a complementary new melody in English, using a poetic translation of the Hebrew text, as found in the Contemporary English Version of the Bible:

> In the beginning God
> created the heavens
> and the earth.
> The earth was barren,
> with no form of life;
> it was under a roaring ocean
> covered with darkness.
> But the spirit of God
> was moving over the water.

The coordinated use of these words, images, and sounds heralds the appearance of the sacred word on the Web, and at the same time telling us all that the NewMedia Project is extending God's creative spirit into this new, electronic universe.

The next icon approaches the center of the ritual context. It is commonly called the Christus Pantocrator, meaning Christ, All-Creator. Beginning early in the first Christian millennium, larger than life-size versions of this image were placed high on apse walls behind the Bishop's chair in eastern and western cathedrals. By doing this, a clear visual message was sent to anyone who gazed upon the figure, that all subsequent words, sounds, images and gestures were rooted in the person of the resurrected and ascended Christ. The icon-like line drawing of this traditional image serves the same function here. Accompanying this drawing is the Lutheran Chorale, *Liebster Jesu,* which invokes the name of Jesus. Invocation is usually the final preparation for the hearing of scripture in traditional Christian services.

> Blessed Jesus, at thy word
> we are gathered all to hear thee;
> let our hearts and souls be stirred

now to seek and love and fear thee,
by thy teachings sweet and holy,
drawn from earth to love thee solely

Words by Tobias Clausnitzer
Trans. by Catherine Winkworth
Tune by Johann R Ahle

Following this invocation is a multimedia presentation of the Good Samaritan, called *The Neighbor* (Lk. 10. 25-37). Like the other videos in the Life of Christ Series, it translates the Greek text into contemporary words, sounds and images. At first glance the results might have seemed far removed from the Lucan text and context. The spoken words, the sound track, and the dramatic images are so contemporary. All the elements of the video, however, are based on translation principles and procedures discussed in the first section of this paper. This modern, multimedia translation is rooted in all three parameters of the ancient source text:

a) *The Linguistic Parameter*
Luke the Evangelist did more than present Jesus' parable (Lk. 10. 30-35). He framed it with a secondary story, a dialogue between an expert in the law and Jesus (Lk. 10. 25-29; 36-37). To differentiate between these two rhetorical units in the video, the frame story is only narrated with scenes and sounds surrounding a train track, while the narration of the parable is accompanied with a dramatization performed by children. The train motif in the frame story is also not arbitrary. Both the parable and the frame story are part of a still larger rhetorical unit, which extends for nearly ten chapters (Lk. 9.51-19. 27). In this major section Luke has Jesus traveling to Jerusalem. The train motif in the video was chosen to hint of this larger rhetorical context.

b) *The Paralinguistic Parameter*
In the Greek text, an emotional watershed occurs when the word *splagchnizomai* is introduced. This word is used sparingly in the synoptic Gospels to signal the presence of "gut-wrenching compassion" in a particular situation. In *The Neighbor,* it describes the internal reaction of the Samaritan when he sees the victim on the Jericho road. Up to this point the music is primarily percussive and fragmented. After the attack, when passers-by start to come over the hill on their bicycles, piano arpeggios are introduced. When the Samaritan begins to help the victim, the piano sounds a simple melody for the first time. A moment before this plaintive tune, as the Samaritan kneels down by the injured boy, a harmonica is also sounded. These two instruments and melodies effectively signal the emotional change that is implied in the source text. The musical score makes explicit what is only dimly expressed in the

original, and, by continuing the lyric style, effectively divides the parable into two sonic sections, the same way the Samaritan's compassion emotionally divides the text.

c) *The Extralinguistic Parameter*
In ancient times, Jews and Samaritans were fierce religious enemies. For Jesus to make a Samaritan compassionate and helpful was more than shocking to an expert in the law or any of his contemporaries. It represents a major reversal of expectations on the part of Jesus' audience. When the parable was eventually told in the gentile world, this dramatic change was not understood. In the new context, the Samaritan was perceived only as helpful and good, since the new audience harbored no ill will toward such people. The radical nature of the story was lost.

In the video, an attempt is made to establish at least some enmity between the victim and the Samaritan and their companions. This happens in the opening fight scene. After the attack, when the Samaritan finds the victim half-dead on the road, flashbacks from the earlier scene tell the audience that the Samaritan's malevolence is turning into compassion. Then, when the Samaritan brings the victim to the inn, the other children, who also participated in the fight, react with stares of disbelief. Since the establishment and reversal of enmity happens very quickly, the director and producer decided to add a written introduction at the beginning of the video to explain the original social context. Between the added text and the visual manipulations, the extralinguistic context of the source text is incorporated into the flow of the video.

5.3 A Sermon in Cyberspace?

Next, a reflection on its meaning of *The Neighbor* is presented. Traditionally, such a reflection would be sermonic, delivered by a knowledgeable religious professional. In cyberspace, this oral art form, which is rooted in the live appearance of a preacher, does not work well since preaching is visually static. The substitute for this ritual element in this presentation is a hymn by the contemporary English poet, F. Pratt Green, On the Jericho Road. Its four verses, which are coordinated with stills from the video, review important moments of the narrative in a poetic form. The hymn also emphasizes the moral of the parable,

> To be a neighbor,' the master said,
> 'On the Jericho Road,
> Is to show compassion as that man did.'
> For even faith without deeds is dead,
> On the Jericho Road,

On the Jericho Road,
On the Jericho Road. (Green 1982: 183)

While this hymn is a good substitute for a sermon in cyberspace, it is far from complete. In a more developed ritual context all facets of the video would be explored in a fully interactive format, with a hypertext version of the word track, linking the contemporary video to its source text, its context, and its history of interpretation. [Such an experience is yours, but out of sequence, if you log on to the NewMedia Project's Good Samaritan website. Its address is: www. Newmediabible.org. On the splash page you will see "Stories on the Web" on the bottom left of your screen. Click on "The Good Samaritan," and travel, explore, and/or locate topics that might interest you.]

5.4 Rooting the Particular in the Eternal

After this reflection, the next screen returns to the Christus Pantocrator icon, but the musical text accompanying it is slightly different. As stated earlier, the purpose of a sermon is not to give factual information but to impart sacred instruction for spiritual growth and development. Of all the elements in a ritual context, it cannot be transmediate, since it depends on the inner disposition of the person who navigates the ritual matrix. Given this reality, all that can be done is to point to the ultimate origin for any insights gained as a result of the reflection sequence. This is done in the singing of the second verse of Liebster Jesu:

All our knowledge, sense, and sight
Lie in deepest darkness shrouded,
Till thy spirit breaks our night
With the beams of truth unclouded.
Thou alone to God canst win us;
Thou must work all good within us.

Words by Tobias Clausnitzer
Trans. by Catherine Winkworth
Tune by Johann R Ahle

In the Judeo-Christian tradition all knowledge gained through sensory input is opaque at best, eternal light or insight coming through divine revelation. Like Paul of Tarsus, the second verse of Liebster Jesu is saying, “For now we see through a glass, darkly; but then face to face: now I know in part; but then shall I know even as also I am known” (I Cor. 13.12, KJV). Both the video and the hymn, “On the Jericho Road”, try to hasten this process by providing revealed insights into earthly living before the beatific vision. Most squabbles between individuals or groups are like the children who were fighting across railroad tracks in the video. From an eternal perspective, they are tempests in teapots. When ill fortune strikes on the road of life, the least expected person, even an enemy, can be the one who feels compassion and helps. Therefore, "...love your neighbor as yourself" (Lev. 19.17; Mk. 12.31). Be prepared to express that love in action, and hope that others do the same!

The final icon of the ritual context is the same as the first, a large planet with spiraling satellites. Accompanying this icon is a Jewish Benediction, chanted in Hebrew and English, with vocabulary echoing the first two verses of Genesis. "Blessed are you, O Lord, King of the Universe, who inspired the act of creation in the beginning". This final act of remembrance and doxology roots the virtual present in the ancient past, and again acknowledges God as the ultimate source for human creativity. It also beatifies cyberspace as a fitting place to express the most sublime Judeo-Christian beliefs and aspirations: that God is one, that humans are of one family, and that love binds both together (Suler 1996).

6. An Overview of this Presentation

There is no way that the thinking used to produce this ritual context will be easily perceived or appreciated by most viewers. On the surface it is too simple and too short. Also, since it is a prototype, there are few multimedia norms for evaluation. This particular ritual context, which is entered with a simple click, frames the video like its traditional counterpart by invoking, remembering, and praising God with complementary sacred words, sounds, and images. The coordination of these various elements is based upon ritual and aesthetic practices, with the hope that balanced variety will produce an aesthetic experience on the part of any viewer. Aesthetic experiences, however, are not necessarily religious, even though beauty and ritual have long been linked in the Judeo-Christian traditions. The plans for the Tent of Meeting in the Book of Exodus are a good example of such linkage (See Chapters 35 through 40 in the Book of Exodus).

Discussions about aesthetic experiences and the interrelation of beauty to ritual seem premature. More to the point would be discussions about how the expanded use of electronic media compels us to rethink the whole translation process and our categories and concepts of quality and fidelity (Lambert 1997: 51-65). However, since the corpus of multimedia translation is so very small, even these important questions are premature. For the near future, what is really needed is the creation of hundreds of diverse multimedia translation teams all around the world to grapple with all these issues while producing multimedia translations. Then and only then, will guidelines be productive, and norms for quality and fidelity be valid, since they will be rooted in the accumulated practical experience of hundreds, if not thousands, of multimedia professionals, and not in theoretical speculation. As Shakespeare tells us, “Experience is by industry achieved, and perfected by the swift course of time” (The Two Gentleman of Verona, 1.3.22-3).

ABOUT REMAKES, DUBBING & MORPHING: SOME COMMENTS ON VISUAL TRANSFORMATION PROCESSES AND THEIR RELEVANCE FOR TRANSLATION THEORY

Karin Wehn
Media & Communication Studies,
Halle, Germany

The profound changes currently taking place in international communication caused by the recent rise and boom of new digitised technologies and media, i. e. the rise of the Internet will bring about new forms of communication.

It is the term "multimedia" that is most strongly associated with those changes. Multimedia refers to the combination of the - up to now - separate types of information (written text, pictures and data) and communication codes (visual, verbal/auditory and binary) and the possibility to converge them in one device: the PC (Meckel 1996: 300). Other prototypicalities of multimedia texts include three-dimensional hypertextual structure and interactivity. However, it not the simultaneous occurrence of different codes that is the real novelty but the integration in one piece of equipment, as it greatly facilitates the production of multimedia texts for more or less anyone who has got access to a computer. Undoubtedly, multimedia texts will soon play a major role in many areas of society, e.g. teaching, advertising and entertainment.

If translation is assumed to be a communicative process, the question is in what way multimedia is going to affect Translation Studies. The point that is argued here is that the subject 'translation' itself, its theoretical reflection in Translation Studies and its methodologies have to become more multimedia. This is to say that translation theory has to pay more attention to other than the verbal code if it aims to maintain and enhance its position in the field of communication.

For a start, I will present different examples where modifications of other than the linguistic code are current practice. Transformation processes that are primarily but not exclusively visual will be focussed on.[1] After that, I will draw further implications about which terms need to be redefined.

1. Dubbing

Body language and gestures are culture-specific. Studies on dubbing have pointed to the fact that if a movie contains gestures and body-language unknown in the target culture, it can be a possible solution to transfer that information to the auditory channel: Take a look at the following example provided by Candice Whitman-Linsen:

> In Robert Altman's *Perfect Couple*, one male character communicates to a woman in sign language from the street below her window. His gestures relate to her and the rest of the English-speaking audience that he will drive by the next day and honk his horn for her. To the Italian audience the same gestures would have so unmistakably suggested his plans for the following day's sexual activities with her that the dubbing director was obliged to fill in the intended meaning in spoken dialogue, adding voice where there was none in the original. (1992: 35-6)

This is actually not a transformation of the visual but an explanation of the visual through the auditory. This type of code-shifting-process becomes necessary when the scene contains information that is relevant to the course of the action, and therefore needs to be understood by the audience.

2. Different versions of films and television shows

While a film is being re-voiced for a foreign audience, some visual transformation processes may also take place. A number of studies have provided examples that one and the same film or television show appears in quite different versions if shown in different countries (cf. in detail Ganz-Blättler 1994). The following types of changes have been recognised: Films and television shows are shortened by a few minutes in order to fit in the time slot of the foreign television channel. Scenes containing sex, violence and, in the case of Germany, allusions to National Socialism and The Third Reich are often erased during the dubbing process because they touch on taboo topics. In Germany, scenes are also cut when they contain topics that are considered to be uninteresting for the target culture. Due to different cultural standards, films are even shot in different versions from the outset: Accordingly, American movies shown in Europe may be sexually a lot more explicit than the same movie shown in the States. All in all, the visual modifications undertaken here serve the purpose to adapt to different cultural needs and prerequisites.

3. Commercials

Blunders committed in international campaigns of the advertising industry provide us with some of the most valuable insights into the cultural-bound significance of images.

For instance, a soap ad which showed a picture of dirty clothes on the left, a box of soap in the middle and clean clothes on the right did not sell well in the Middle East. Why was that the case? The advertisers forgot that in that part of the world people usually read from right to left.

It is also the advertising industry that has commissioned research across cultures regarding people's associations when being confronted with certain words. Compare, for example, the associations triggered by "traditional":

Figure 1. (Kroeber-Riel 1992: 263ff., taken from Dmoch 1996: 197, translated from German into English by the author)

Germans		**Swiss**		**French**	
costumes	33	costumes	38	family	22
dance	14	church	22	costumes	17
clothing	14	celebration	20	house	14
celebration	12	family	16	rural area	14
church	12	England	11	wedding	12
Christmas	9	Switzerland	11	food	11
family	9	army	9	dance	10
wedding	8	mountains	9	church	10
leather trousers	5	food	9	village	9
grandparents	5	suit	9	clothing	7

Italians		**Finns**	
celebration	16	food	16
Christmas	14	rocking chair	10
clothing	10	country house	10
grandparents	8	yoghourt	10
costume	6	church	10
house	6	house	10
cake	4	grandmother	7
family	4	sauna	7
mother	4	pullover	6
food	2	furniture	6

If these findings are applied to the making of a (fictitious) commercial, it follows that a traditional atmosphere would have to be realised differently for different cultures: A rocking chair, yoghurt and a sauna are most likely to carry the connotational meaning "traditional" for a Finnish audience, but not for any of the other mentioned countries.

Consequently, the advertising industry distinguishes between standardised and non-standardised advertising. Standardised advertising such as *Coca-Cola* and *Benetton* is shown world-wide. It realises the philosophy of selling the same things in the same way everywhere. Non-standardised advertising varies the messages and their linguistic and visual realisations regionally. For instance, in Spain the VW Golf GTI is presented as a premium vehicle for acceleration. In the German commercial, the quality, the comfort and the safety of this car are emphasised and strongly tied to environmental concerns (for instance, the use of environmentally friendly paints).

4. Remakes

In capitalistic societies an economic success of a product fosters the production of copies of it until the consumers' needs have been saturated. It is commonplace in film and television audience research that audiences favour local productions with familiar actors and locations in comparison with foreign imports. With good scripts being rare, historical stories or stories from other cultures are adapted to the present cultural needs.[2] Remakes - the making of a new version of an already existing film - are a striking example for comparing the visual and other transformation processes taking place between the two.

Using the French *Trois hommes et un couffin* and its American remake *Three men and a baby* as an example, I will briefly comment on the transformation processes taking place between the original and the 'remade' version.

Both versions essentially explore the same conflicts: The unexpected arrival of a little baby in the lives of three bachelors who have so far avoided taking on any responsibility forces them to rethink and to change their life-styles. Ultimately, this makes their lives a lot more meaningful. Interwoven with this is another storyline: Without the protagonists Michel, Pierre and Jacques (Mike, Peter and Jack in the American remake) actively contributing to it, their flat temporarily becomes a major scene for drug traffic which threatens the life of the baby. The film plays with and subverts traditional sex stereotypes, i.e. the cliché of the working and selfish father and the loving and caring mother. Although both films follow the same storyline, they differ from each other in significant aspects: The French original puts the main emphasis on the exploration of human conflicts and how to deal with them.[3] In contrast, the American remake devotes only little time to human learning processes,[4] but emphasises suspense by employing elements of crime and gangster films. Therefore, the American version contains a number of action film scenes that are not part of the French original: In a race with time, the three men rush out to the airport with squealing tyres in order to persuade Sylvia, the mother, not to go to London and not to take Mary away.

It is also interesting to see how the handing-over of the drugs and its outcome is realised in both versions: In the French version, the drugs are passed over in a nappy that Michel leaves in a bin in the park - all under the surveillance of an ambitious policeman, who as a result of his stupidity loses his job. In the following scene, Michel and Pierre can be seen almost dying of laughter, clearly sympathising with the gangsters and - typically French - ridiculing the police (underlying message: crime does pay). The American remake realises the same scene as a more than 10 minutes long scene full of suspense at a deserted industrial site. After a action-loaded chase around the site, in an heroic act Michael, Peter and Jack trap the gangsters in a lift and hand them over to the surprised police (underlying message: crime doesn't pay). Not only do both films express different values, they are also clearer and more one-dimensional in the remake: In the French film people are portrayed as multi-facetted, having both good *and* bad characteristics. In the American version people are ultimately either good *or* bad. Even seemingly selfish behaviour like that of Jack's grandmother who refuses to look after the baby, can be interpreted as "good" because it is an attempt to teach Jack responsibility. Contrary to the French version, the American remake emphasises long-term-relationships: Growing affection, a more stable relationship and the prospect of marriage are Rebecca's rewards for Peter after he has coped so well with the baby. Sylvia, the mother, moves into the flat with them. Apart from the very obvious change that the French original takes place in a Parisian environment in a typical old-style French flat and the American takes place in a modern and bright American apartment, more could be said about different modes of employing colours and light: the French version uses a lot of warm colours such as different hues of brown and orange. In the remake, dark colours are usually only employed in threatening and suspenseful scenes. Generally, most scenes appear brighter. Media play an important role only in the American remake: many scenes take place in front of the television. Peter's birthday party, the initial scene, is seen through the eyes of a video camera.

Every attempt to compare a source text and its transformation should be accompanied by an analysis of the production context: Obviously, these films were produced in conditions of very different cinematic and aesthetic traditions. This is also indicated by the fact that Coline Serreau, the director of the French version, only consented to selling the rights to the American studios on the condition that she would also be the director of the American remake.[5] However, when two years later the remake came out, it was Leonard Nimoy who was listed as director in the credits. Due to insuperable conflicts with the American executive producer, Coline Serreau had left the production.

5. Morphing

At the conference on "Audiovisual Communication and Language Transfer" in Strasbourg in 1995, Matt McCarthy from Videolondon Sound Studios presented an interesting new procedure which might have the potential to revolutionise dubbing and to abolish the problem of lip-synchrony for dubbing editors all thanks to digitised technology. Showing a commercial in which Alfred Hitchcock can be seen advertising the Nationwide Building Society, McCarthy demonstrated that it is now technically possible to record the dubbing actor's lips as the new dialogue is recorded and to replace the images of the original actor with those of the dubbing actor's lips, whenever necessary (cf. also Reeve 1995: 418ff). Morphing, as this process has been baptised, is still very costly and therefore not widely used yet. However, this method is a product of the digitised revolution and allows us to catch a glance at the possibilities opening up in the foreseeable future.

With the exception of morphing, all examples demonstrated here have their origins in the "old" media and are not new phenomena at all. They also have in common that a lot of money is involved and therefore no risks can be taken.

So what are the implications of those visual transformation processes for translation studies? From a traditional point of view, hardly any of those transformation processes would even be labelled as translations. However, the classification of these transformation processes as mere adaptations would be an (all too) easy way out of the problem.

In his paper at the International Research Seminar on "Multimedia and translation" (Misano, September 1997), Per Quale provides us with two proposals of where to locate multimedia translation: In maximalistic terms, multimedia translation is a multi-semiotic transfer involving written or spoken language. This definition implies the co-occurrence of different codes all of which could possibly be changed. In minimalistic terms, multimedia translation is the translation of written or spoken language in a multimedia context.

Looking at the current state of translation theory, it could at the most be classified as minimalistic. Only recently, the linguistic transfer of multi-semiotic texts such as films, in particular dubbing and subtitling, have been accepted as a subject of translation theory. However, all in all, current translation theory still treats translation as an entirely language-based process.

Maximalistic issues such as whether translation needs to be extended to the transfer of the other codes, for instance the question whether images can be and need to be translated in multimedia texts, and if so, how that is to be done, have hardly been tackled at all. Nevertheless, it is commonplace that not only the meanings of written words but also those of visual objects vary across cultures. Apart from universal symbols, for instance from the realm of traffic signs, e. g. an aircraft taking off into the air signifying an airport, there are plenty of meanings that are conveyed by different signifiers across cultures.[6] Similar to language, the denotational and connotational meanings of symbols differ from each other across cultures. A cow, for instance, is a working animal in Europe, but a holy beast in India. A bicycle is an ordinary means of transport in most Asian cultures, but an instrument of leisure, sports and free-time in most Western cultures. The meanings of colours vary across cultures: Black is the colour for mourning in Western Europe: In South America it is white.

Some of the main reasons for translation theory's neglect of images, as opposed to verbal language, are probably that the conventions of the visual code are by no means as fixed or as tangible as verbal language. The meanings of images cannot be stored in dictionaries. Furthermore, when images are involved (especially with motion pictures), analysts usually have to cope with vast amounts of data. Also, we are dealing with complex signs in which the interaction of the various codes in numerous different ways carries meaning.

However, with multimedia texts the minimalistic approach might not always be sufficient. If we look at it from the stance of translation as a functional and cultural transfer, we have to define translation along the lines of a more maximalistic approach. With the rapidly growing significance of multimedia text types such as web sites, video conferences and CD-ROMs, all of which are ideally a smooth and reciprocally supportive combination of (motion) pictures, sound and written text in a hypertextual structure, a functionally oriented approach to Translation Studies will have to incorporate the other codes as objects of Translation Studies. Otherwise, Translation Studies will soon take a very marginalised position in the rapidly changing field of communication.

Opting for a more maximalistic approach is by no means to say that in multimedia texts all codes always need to be altered. Which elements of the text need to be modified, explained or altered depends on their function, their interaction with the other elements in the text and on the overall function the text is supposed to have in the target culture. Retreating to a famous example, it is easy to image that a CD-ROM on the Scottish poet Robert Burns for the Japanese market illustrating the poems with images would have to consider that the poem "My love is like a red, red rose" translates as "My love is like a lotus flower" into Japanese.

In order to achieve a more maximalistic approach, translation theory will have to become more interdisciplinary. Apart from the examples mentioned above, further impetus could come from disciplines such as semiotics, concerning the relations between the different codes and media studies. Multimedia production should be incorporated in the training of translators.

However, the issue under discussion is not only an extension of the object of translation to multimedia text types: While a perspective of translation being cultural rather than linguistic transfer should be maintained, at the same time it should be borne in mind that - especially with regard to the Internet - the very term "culture" becomes blurred. There are a number of examples that members of the so-called "virtual community" of the Internet enthusiastically speak of themselves as representatives of the "netizens culture" with their own laws (*netiquette*) irrespective of their personal cultural origins. This implies that in the context of the Internet, the concept of culture will oscillate somewhere between the poles of a unified net culture and traditional 'regional' culture.

Notes

1. The research for this article was conducted in the research project "Das Kriminalsujet im ost-, west- und gesamtdeutschen Fernsehen: Die Programmgeschichte des deutschen Fernsehkrimis" at the Martin-Luther-University of Halle, Germany. The research project is financed by the Deutsche Forschungsgemeinschaft.

2. The States are known to be a particularly closed market to foreign movies and television shows as audiences are known for not liking dubbed or subtitled films.

3. When Sylvia, the mother of the baby, comes back after six months and takes Marie away from them, all three pretend to be very happy and go back to their old life-style. As a consequence of important events they are later to experience, they all learn individually to admit that they miss Marie. For instance, Michel watches a mother trying to get a job hiding her baby in the hallway. Pierre listens to a busker singing a song about a girl in a white dress. Jacques goes to visit Sylvia and Marie. Sylvia is out working while Marie is being quite poorly looked after by a baby-sitter. All three get very bored with their respective girl-friends.

4. Here, only Jack, the father of Mary, has to learn that he made a mistake by letting Sylvia go to London. Mike and Peter know it right away. Jack does not find out himself, it is the others that tell him in a moment when he is down and unhappy.

5. Coline Serreau: "This film is like my baby. And if anybody is raising it, it's gonna be me. Whoever wants to do this film, has to let me be the director of it." (Manderbach 1988 : 40; translated from German into English by the author, K.W.)

6. In the discussion, Teresa Tomaszkiewicz provided the example of Polish restrooms where a circle stands for "Ladies" and a triangle for "Gents". If not known, this is likely to cause irritation in Western travellers (see in this volume).

SHOOTING IN ENGLISH? MYTH OR NECESSITY?

Anne Jäckel
University of the West of England,
Bristol, UK

1. Introduction

On the eve of European unification, the outstanding performance of *Cinema Paradiso*, *Cyrano de Bergerac* and Almodóvar's *Tie Me Up, Tie Me Down* outside their domestic market (and particularly in the American market) led Europeans to affirm that "the importance of language alone as a factor inhibiting the ability of films to cross borders had been overestimated": A 1992 Seminar on 'The Challenge of Language in European Film' pointed the finger at "those European producers who had decided to make a film in English (regardless of the demands of the subject matter) as a sure-fire way to international success ending up with the most abysmal critical and commercial failures ever to inflict themselves on the international market" (BSAC 1992: 7). It also blamed European producers for paying "insufficient attention to the way in which the technical aspects of language, dubbing and subtitling could affect the distribution of films".

Building on the initiatives of MEDIA 92, the MEDIA 95 and MEDIA II programmes implemented measures to improve both language transfer and the distribution of European films. At the same time, the development of multiplex cinema theatres and the proliferation of outlets for films raised Europeans' hopes for both increasing levels of film production and getting a wider choice in the cinemas.

However, ever-rising production and marketing costs - as potential blockbusters now routinely open on 2,000 and 3,000 screens in the United States and on more than 400 screens in the larger European countries - have resulted in independent film producers and 'speciality distributors' being rapidly co-opted and absorbed by the major players. Export revenues have become crucial for survival in the global environment, and the larger European players who have entered into 'strategic alliances' with the global 'Hollywood' Majors now see the pursuit of blockbusters as a necessary part of their product portfolio. Shooting in English is regarded by European film producers as a way of breaking into the English-language market, the largest in the world in terms of purchasing power.

While economic analyses of film production history show that economic factors channel the kind of films that are made, cultural studies suggest that "the hegemony of a dominant group is a complex and ever-changing cultural process which can be challenged and modified under certain conditions by the culture of the subordinate groups" (Gramsci 1985 & Lev 1993: XIV). Drawing on research in cultural studies and film history as well as on recent studies made by economists and market analysts, this paper examines the extent to which recent trends affect the production and distribution of 'foreign-language' films. It also discusses the promises and myths of 'the global marketplace' and explores some of the opportunities for non-English-language productions.

2. A long tradition of European co-productions made in English

The production of English-language film is nothing new in Europe. The early sound period saw the development of a substantial number of English-language films by American and European companies. After the war, the Hollywood Majors used their 'frozen funds' in France and Italy to strike production deals with leading domestic producers. Taking advantage of cheaper labour costs and foreign subsidies, Hollywood's international operations continued in the late 1950s and in the 1960's (Balio 1976 & Hubert-Lacombe 1996). Some of those joint ventures - derogatively called 'Mid-Atlantic pictures' by film critics and known as 'runaway productions' in the American film industry - now belong to the classics of World Cinema whether in the categories of popular entertainment (*The Ten Commandments*, 1956; *Ben Hur*, 1959; *The Longest Day*, 1962; *Once Upon a Time in the West*, 1968), Art Cinema (*Fahrenheit 451*, Truffaut, 1965; *Blow Up*, Antonioni, 1966) or both (*Never on Sunday*, Jules Dassin, 1960; *The Leopard*, Visconti, 1963; *Viva Maria*, Malle, 1965). Not all were made in English. Resnais' *Muriel* was in French; Fellini's *8 1/2* in Italian and Cacoyannis' *Electra* in Greek. Some used more than one language. (Godard's *Contempt* is in French, German, Italian and English). While it is true that foreign-language films attracted a wider audience than today, it was not the names of the New Wave directors that broke box office records in the States, but Brigitte Bardot's 1956 film, *And God Created Woman*! (Balio 1998: 63 & Lev op.cit.: 13). More importantly, there was a feeling in the late 1950's and early 1960's that "European films were ahead of their American counterparts in some way" (Lev ibid.: 16). Today, the American film industry produces a large quantity of films which include both family entertainment and adult movie subjects (*Basic Instinct*).They invite European directors to make blockbusters in Hollywood (Emmerich, Jeunet, Verhoeven), co-produce romantic period melodramas (*The English Patient*, *Sense and*

Sensibility), have their own Auteurist cinema (Allen, Altman, Scorsese, etc.) and invest in low-budget independent films (Sundance).

3. European and American strategies in the 1990's

In Western Europe, the existence of regional and national funds along with television funding guarantee a steady film output in most countries. In the European Union there has been a marked increase in the number of national films produced partly due to the support of European and pan-European funds for co-productions. Between 1992 and 1996, the number of European productions rose from 489 to 531 (550 in 1997) and the number of co-productions from 116 to 168.[1]

English-language projects, now on the slate of every major film company in Europe, are also on the increase. In addition, the production budgets of films shot in English are usually much larger than those of co-productions made in other languages, the $90m reported budget of *The Fifth Element* being the highest yet for a "European" film. The trend is set to continue in the next few years. Following the success of Luc Besson's English-language films (*The Big Blue*, *Leon*, *The Fifth Element*), French company Gaumont is planning to increase its budgets and produce at least half-a-dozen films a year in English. The UK-based production company of the other French giant, Pathé, (and the winner of one of the UK National Lottery film franchises) is financing English-language films (including US films in return for European distribution rights). A British trade magazine reported in February 1998 that French producers had currently more than twenty-five English-language titles slated for production in 1998-99 – this figure did not include minority co-productions with British partners such as *The Lost Son* (The Film Co.) or *Catching Fire* (Impact Pictures) (Meaux Saint-Marc 1998).

In Germany where audiences are accustomed to watch dubbed films, German producers have long made English-language features. Bernd Eichinger (Constantin Film) made his name producing the films of Jean Jacques Annaud, *The Name of the Rose,* and Bille August, *The House of the Spirits*. Dieter Geissler (Cine Vox), the producer of *The NeverEnding Story* (Wolfgang Petersen) and *Knight* (Carl Schenkel) co-produced Schenkel's *Tarzan and Jane* with Village Roadshow Pictures (Kemp 1998). Scandinavian filmmakers have been particularly active in making English-language co-productions, and several of their films have been both critically and commercially successful. (Bille August's *The House of the Spirits*, Lars von Trier's *Breaking the Waves*). Spain's Iberoamericana invested in one of the most expensive co-productions of the early 1990's, Ridley Scott's *1492 Conquest of Paradise*.[2] Today, Italian, Belgian and Portuguese producers are also involved in English-language movies. Even Catalan filmmakers no longer wonder "whether 'Catalan Cinema' means making films based out of Catalonia or/and in the Catalan language" and shoot films in English (*Variety* 1998: 54).

4. Mainly a one-way flow

4.1 Europe and the American Myth

In contrast with the 1960's, there is no longer a feeling that Europe is ahead today. Worse still for Europeans, America has not lost its mythical appeal as the land of opportunity and the country of democracy and modernity. To many Europeans today, the English language continues to be seen as a passport to a mythical America.

However, for all European producers' efforts, their English-language films have not been able to capture a significant share of the American market. Whether under the helm of British or continental directors, large-budget European co-productions starring an array of European talent have rarely grossed over $8m at the US box office. (An average American blockbuster normally takes twice that amount in its opening weekend.) Ridley Scott's British-French-Spanish co-production *1492* only took $7.15m (compared with $18m in France alone) in 1992, a disastrous performance for a film budgeted at $44m. The same year, the Franco-British co-production, *The Lover,* took $4.17m in the US, $19m in France and a mere $2m in its minority partner's country in spite of being shot in English. Annaud and his French producer Claude Berri targeted their film to an international audience but to their surprise, *The Lover* tended to be received as a "French film". This was particularly the case in Japan where Annaud's adaptation of Marguerite Duras' novel took $12.4m. Recent European ill-fated English-language films include *Mesmer,*[3] a multilateral co-production between Austria, Germany, Canada and the UK, Mark Peploe's *Victory* (£8.6m, UK-France-Germany, 1994) and Philippe Rousselot's film debut, *The Serpent's Kiss*. Few have escaped the dreaded label "Europudding".

The marked improvement in the performance of European films in the US since 1995 – from a low 1.16 per cent the market share has risen to 3.03 per cent in 1997 – is due to the outstanding results of three films, all shot in English in the UK and with some American (creative and/or financial) input, *The Fifth Element*, *Bean* and *The Full Monty*. As for European foreign-language pictures, their fate on America's large screens has deteriorated over the years.

4.2 Lack of success of foreign-language films in America

The number of art-theatres declined steadily in the 1980s, and many independent distributors handling foreign films collapsed in the late 1980s and early 1990s leaving a handful of survivors (Balio 1998: 65). Among them, Miramax, the independent distributor of *Tie Me Up! Tie Me Down* and *Cinema Paradiso*, is probably the most aggressive. Famous for its marketing skills, Miramax has won more Academy Awards than most major film companies. However, when in 1993 North American combined box office grosses for foreign-language films reached a record of $48.5m and one per cent share, it was not a European film, but Mexico's *Like Water for Chocolate*, which became "the all-time foreign film box office Champion in the US". (A Miramax acquisition, the film took more than a year to gross in excess of $20m).[4] With one or two hits each year doing most of the business, foreign-language pictures have played a small role in the business of the other two main distributors of foreign films in the US, Samuel Goldwyn Co and Fine Line. After heavy losses, the two companies were put up for sale in 1995 and 1996 respectively (Balio ibid.: 72). *Il Postino* is always cited as evidence that foreign-language pictures can succeed in the US, but it took three years for Michael Radford's film (distributed by Miramax) to take $31m. Moreover, in 1995, the relative success of both *Il Postino* and *Belle de Jour* was attributed to the two films providing "counterprogramming to the summer US blockbusters".

International awards have done little to change the trend although they are an incentive for an American distributor to pick up a foreign-language film. Only 23 per cent of the films that win awards at the major festivals around the world are subsequently distributed in the US. The Oscar for best foreign-language picture may confer prestige on the winner and translate into longer runs (and better box office grosses), but it offers no guarantee of success. In 1991, Xavier Koller's *Journey of Hope* (Switzerland) took under $260,000. The last few years have seen a slight improvement in the performance of foreign-language films (particularly French films with a little help from Unifrance). In 1996, nine films took more than $1m in the US, six of them French. Yet, France's attempts to dub its more popular fare (*Les Visiteurs*, *Un indien dans la ville / Little Indian, Big City*) into American-English have not been successful. (The latter took just over $720,000 in 1996.) On the whole, European non-English-language films continue to perform badly in the US, and there has even been a drop in the number of European films securing theatrical distribution.

5. Distribution and performance of European films in Europe

In the late eighties, Europeans feared that the impact of multiplexes would lead to "a greater Americanisation" of their screens. Film critics even talked of "the end of cinema". Yet today, moviegoing is booming and the upswing in European cinema attendances is not simply due to a few successful American blockbusters. The number of European films distributed is increasing and several local films have performed extremely well in their respective domestic markets. Recent 'local' box office hits include France's *La vérité si je mens, Pédale Douce*, Germany's *Männerpension* and Italy's *Il Ciclone* and *A spasso nel tempo*. Scandinavian films regularly appear in their Top Ten chart. In 1996, Sweden had three entries, and, in Iceland, Fridrik Thor Fridriksson's *Devil's Island* – one of the only two Icelandic films distributed that year – was the most popular film of the year, making 80,000 admissions in a country with a population of 270,000 (Sverrisson 1998: 190-91).

On a less optimistic note, many of the domestic films which meet with considerable success at home are comedies, and, British films excepted, European comedies do not travel well. Moreover, the 1997 figures given by the European Audiovisual Observatory (Table 1) show that only European English-language productions with a UK input managed to enter the Top Ten in several European countries and to achieve a considerable degree of success with North American audiences.

Table 1. *European films making 1m admissions and over in Europe in 1997 (Source: Statistical Yearbook 1998, European Audiovisual Observatory. Strasbourg)*

Rank	Film	Country
1	Bean	UK
2	The Full Monty	UK
3	The Fifth Element	France
4	The English Patient	USA/UK
5	Tomorrow Never Dies	UK/USA
6	Evita	UK/USA
7	Fuochi d'Artificio	Italy
8	La vérité si je mens	France
9	Le pari	France
10	Rockin' on Heaven's Door	Germany
11	Rossini - Oder die Morderische Frage Wer Mit Wem	Germany
12	Kleines Arschloch	Germany
13	Didier	France
14	Fierce Creatures	USA/UK
15	Ballermann 5	Germany
16	La vita è Bella	Italy
17	Airbag	Spa/Port/Germ.
18	Miss Smilla's Feeling for Snow	Ger/Den/Swe.
19	On connait la chanson	Fr/UK/Ita/Swi.
20	Le Bossu	Fr/Ita/Germ.
21	Lucie Aubrac	France
22	Carne Tremula	Spa/France
23	Ovosodo	Italy
24	Apothekerin	Germany
25	The Borrowers	UK/France
26	Les randonneurs	France
27	Nirvana	Ita/France
28	Marius et Jeannette	France
29	A Life Less Than Ordinary	UK
30	A spasso nel tempo: L'avventura continua	Italy
31	Western	France

32	Amor perjudica seriamente la salud	Spain
33	Shooting Fish	UK
34	Kolya	Cze/Fra/UK

"British films" accounted for 47 per cent of the admissions generated by the top 60 films produced in the European Union. The five top films had UK links, involving either British producers or British facilities. From slapstick comedies (*Bean*) and period adaptations of novels and plays (*Sense and Sensibility*) to James Bond movies and contemporary dramas (*Trainspotting*, *The Full Monty*), Britain is the only country in Europe to offer a wide variety of successful films both at home and abroad. Outside the British output, hopes for more diversity on European screens have largely remained a myth. Despite the promises of multiplex operators, the range of films available to mainstream audiences has to date not been enhanced by the development of multiplexes. With a few exceptions in the large urban centres (Les Halles Ciné-Cité in Paris, for example), multiplexes tend to show the same picture on several screens rather than risk a lesser known / non-English-language film on one of their screens.

6. On the rise of the blockbuster as a model

Gaumont regarded *The Fifth Element* as a test of whether it could challenge the Majors in the global film market. On the strength of the worldwide performance of Besson's film (ranking at number eight with an estimated 50m admissions and reported box office grosses of $235m - over a third of which in the US), Gaumont can now claim that Europeans have finally challenged the American hold on the blockbuster - a form invented in Hollywood and exploited to perfection in the multiplexes. With European production of 'high-concept English-language films' starring American and British talent on the increase, production costs are rocketing and European producers are forced to seek revenues outside their domestic markets. Even a minute percentage of the huge American market is not insignificant to European producers (and local talent) who have to contend with much smaller domestic markets. To many filmmakers today, a distribution deal in the US signals international recognition and confers a certain status (Karlin 1998: 40). From being only one of the European producers' risk-reduction strategies, the English language is turning into a status symbol. Other strategies include screen previews and the development of products related to film. Even in France, the country where directors still enjoy an "Auteur" status, producers are now using "sneak previews" and launching a whole range of gadgets and products on a film's release, in the hope of increasing the market potential of their domestic productions (*La crise*, *La vérité si je mens*, *Le Bossu*). To a large extent, the present rise in national audiences for domestic films with popular entertainment value owes much to Europeans adopting Hollywood's strategies.

7. No future?

7.1. European film policy

Film policy is also changing in Europe. Where rules to access local film funds have not already been altered to accommodate international co-productions made in English - Soficas in France has been able to invest in non-French-language films since 1993 - national governments are considering legislation to make it easier for producers to make international English-language films. The 1992 report on *The Challenge of Language in European Film* ended by saying that "the Seminar reaffirmed that language [could] never be treated simply as an inconvenient post-script to the primary business of film-making. The challenge of language must be taken into account through the development, production and post-production of the entire film" (BSAC op.cit: 54). Six years later, non-English-language films are increasingly treated as an inconvenient post-script to the business of film-making by the large European media players operating on a global scale, with the tacit approval of local governments. Rather than the challenge of language, it is the international potential appeal of a film and its marketing strategies which are taken into account throughout the development, production and post-production of films.

7.2 American concerns and strategies

All this is happening at a time when box office results are not keeping up with the increase in production and marketing costs and the Majors are expressing concerns about the blockbuster strategy in terms of profitability and the imbrication of film with a system of global capitalism. James Cameron's *Titanic* may have broken all records, but in America it has done little to relieve Hollywood's anxieties. Since a major part of their revenues comes from abroad, and several foreign-language films have become huge hits in their domestic markets, the Majors have announced they are now considering multi-picture deals which include a small number of non-English language films (Columbia TriStar, Miramax in Germany). In the UK, Warner has pledged to set aside between six and ten screens, within several of its planned multiplexes, exclusively for foreign-language and locally produced films. At home, the Majors are paying particular attention to the development of specialised niches targeting, among others, hispanic communities. It is ironic that, at a time when the unpredictability of the business is undermining the confidence of Americans in their traditional strategies and forcing them to adopt new ones, Europeans are so eager to embrace a traditional Hollywood formulaic approach.

7.3 European efforts: too little too late?

Distribution has been the stumbling block of film policy, and Europeans have taken measures to address the problem.[5] There is little doubt that, with the derisory sums at their disposal (compared with most EU budgets), the various MEDIA initiatives have helped create networks and a "new consciousness among linguistic territorial minorities that they are not alone" (Thomas 1993). Nevertheless, they have not substantially improved the crossborder appeal of non-English-language films. Europa Cinemas[6] does not consider "language" criteria in the definition of "national" or "European" films, and the Felix (European Film Academy Award) has not really raised the profile of films nominated for this top European award. While the controversial Television Without Frontiers Directive (TWFD) has been temporarily extended, European regulators continue to dodge the language issue. Although the European video market now already accounts for more than twice the revenues of theatrical exhibition, only small amounts of support are available from MEDIA II. As far as broadcasters are concerned, there is hardly any large European broadcaster involved in film production – whether public or private – which does not invest today in English-language films.

7.4 Role of sales agents and cultural differences

In 1996 Patrick Frater (1996) suggested that the language problem might have "less to do with audience resistance and more to do with movie buyers, as films that are made in English appeal more to distributors and exhibitors wary of foreign-language films and their traditional low grosses". Whether films are shot in English or not is probably far less important to audiences than sales agents and other middle-men assume it to be. Yet, decades of relegating foreign-language films to art-house theatres have taken their toll. A few examples may suffice here. In 1982, Fassbinder shot his adaptation of Genet's play *Querelle* in English but it was in its German version that the film was released in the US, "its distributors having probably found *Querelle* too bizarre for anything but art-house release" (Lev op.cit.: 60). A decade later in Japan, *The Lover* was released in both versions, English and French, but it was the (dubbed) French-language version that drew the bigger audience. In 1996 the dubbed version of Josiane Balasko's *Gazon maudit* (*French Twist*) took less than its subtitled version on the art-circuit in the UK.

There are variations between territories even in Anglophone countries. For instance, the subtitled version of Mathieu Kassovitz' *La Haine / Hate* was, in relative terms, much more successful in Britain than in the United States. Even though the film did not have "the normal appeal" of French films to the middle-class audiences of art-theatres, it received both critical acclaim and substantial media coverage in Britain. *La Haine* did not find the youth audience targeted by its distributors in America: Its lack of appeal to American youth (who found the film and its characters "quaint") had less to do with subtitling than with cultural differences (see Jäckel in this volume: Part III). Quality dubbing proved a success for *Les Visiteurs* in Spain and to a lesser extent in Germany, but not in the UK and in the US. While some foreign-language films can be enhanced by an art-house release (the films of Godard and Rohmer for example), others can be damaged by it (comedies such as *Les Visiteurs* in the UK).

8. An international business

8.1 On budgets, profitability and the myth of "the global market"

Yet, an international audience for the so-called "art-films" continues to exist. For such an audience, language has never been an issue, and there are signs that a new audience for those more demanding films is emerging. (In the UK for instance, the 35-plus age-group has doubled since 1991 and they make up 57 per cent of the art-house audience today.) When so few films recoup their cost on the theatrical circuit, the current obsession with film budgets and box office ratings seems misplaced. Whether in America, Britain or France, statistical surveys clearly demonstrate that the films with the highest profitability ratio are low-budget films such as *The Full Monty* (£2.2m), *Brassed Off* (£2.5m) or *When the Cat is Away / Chacun cherche son chat* (FRF 6m). Contrary to what is commonly assumed, small-budget European films can perform extremely well in their domestic markets and, with a little help from the European and pan-European programmes, in other European countries too (two 1997 hits were the French films *Marius et Jeannette* and *Western* with reported budgets of FRF32m and FRF23m respectively) and non-English-language films are not the losers the media claim them to be. Even in Britain, a study of the domestic performance of all UK films released in 1997 – ranked by box-office takings per print (rather than the ratio between box office earnings and budget) – shows that *Ma Vie en Rose*, a French-language UK-France co-production, came in fifth place with £37,190 per print after taking £409,095 with just 11 prints. The 1997 Oscar-winner *Kolya*, a British-Czech-French co-production, was in eigth position with £30,989 per print after grossing £494,870 on 16 prints. Those two foreign-language films beat much bigger "UK-produced films" released with over 200 prints.[7]

Screen availability and "a reasonable run" are essential to a film's success. One of the reasons why French – and indeed other European – films perform better in Paris than anywhere else in Europe is that distributors there are prepared to show and keep films for longer runs. Films released with a small or non-existent promotion budget rely on word-of-mouth. Nurturing an audience takes time. In today's environment, films which do not perform well in their opening weekend are too often taken away to make room for "the bigger pictures". Yet, in terms of recoupment and profitability, blockbusters score no better than low-budget films and all films today rely on ancillary markets to cover their costs and make a profit.[8]

8.2 New (and old) outlets for films

There is much speculation but little agreement on what the new technologies have already brought and are about to bring as far as feature films are concerned. At present, the response to video cassettes, digital video discs, Pay-Per-View television services is very different in the American and in the various European markets.

On the one hand, there are those who argue that the major studios are not likely to do anything that will adversely affect overall revenues from the various revenue sources. American film and the "integrated structure" of the Majors may have changed but, in an industry known for its conservatism, innovations tend to be constrained and risks minimized. On the other, there are those who insist that in an environment undergoing such transformations as film and audiovisual production and distribution, all the riches of cinema, including those of non-English language cinema will find an audience. As for *cyberfans*, they are already celebrating the arrival of virtual reality, where digital images and sound - including language - can be altered according to the wishes of viewers/readers.

Curiously, such wide range of opinions is also reflected in the assessments of the present situation of foreign films in North America: Examining the performance of foreign-language films in the new outlets, the American trade journal *Variety* noted in 1996:

"The one element that's remained virtually consistent is that foreign-language movies remain almost entirely a theatrical phenomenon. Revenues from cassette and cable exploitation have increased, but they still generally lag 75 per cent to 80 per cent behind comparably grossing English-lingo pics".[9]

Writing a couple of years later, Geoffrey Nowell-Smith (1998: 15) gives a totally different picture of the American video market situation: According to the British scholar, "the market for European (and Asian) films has now moved to video. There may not be many new European films on theatrical release, but huge numbers of recent and classic European films are available on cassette or laserdisc."

Such contrasting views – and the lack of reliable data – on the exploitation of a film that occurs via video assettes or cable television may not be incidental. If television and video have been "the commercial salvation of cinema in recent years" (Falcon 1998) theatrical releases continue to serve as a marketing platform for the more remunerative new outlets for films. In a domain which represents the second US export revenue and the largest potential growth forecast, predictions may be no more than wishful thinking.

In any case, films have not the same impact nor the same status in the various countries of Europe and in America. While in US the major film studios have a powerful influence on the broadcasting industry, within Europe, "the broadcasting-based giants" are more powerful.[10] Local broadcasters may have started to invest in English-language films, but their investments in local productions have also continued to rise.

All experts agree on three points: (1) the market structures presently in place for the distribution of films will change in the next ten to fifteen years; (2) the economic impact of the new technologies will cut drastically the cost of distribution[11]- and affect the role of the middle-men; and, niche markets may soon become more important than theatrical distribution. The role and (3) importance of distributors and sales agents are also set to change dramatically. Examining the theoretical concept of "role as a resource", Baker & Faulkner (1991) assert that:

> In stable environments, "traditional positions" are produced and reinforced (White 1981), resulting in the reproduction of old and conventional roles [...] But in environments undergoing deep transformations, such as culture production, the likelihood that new roles can be created is much greater. In changing contexts, new roles can help create and sustain the transformation as social actors claim and use them to fight for their interests.

They cite the rise of what they call "the artistic hyphenate" in the New Hollywood. Even though Baker & Faulkner's study is mainly concerned with the impact of the blockbuster on roles and positions in Hollywood filmmaking, some of their findings may be used to further the interests of foreign-language productions and the role of social actors in the latter. For instance, the role which stars can play in enhancing European films is worth exploring.

9. Hopes and Opportunities for European films

9.1 Role of Stars

There is little doubt that the cross-border appeal of Gérard Depardieu, Sophie Marceau or Jean Reno has improved following their English-language/Hollywood roles. It needs not be a one-way traffic. Indeed, British stars (Helena Bonham-Carter, Kristin Scott-Thomas) have already appeared in French-language films. Arguably, the relative success of the French-language *Portraits Chinois* on the art-circuit in the UK was partly due to the curiosity effect of Bonham-Carter in a non-English-language part. Emma Thompson speaks French, Arnold Schwarzenegger German, Jean-Claude van Damme Dutch, and one can easily imagine them speaking another language than English in European productions. After all, disaster movies – for which multiplex audiences seem to have a limitless – appetite have hardly any dialogue. American and British audiences probably never understood all of Marlon Brando's mumblings in *Apocalypse Now* or John Rambo's big speech in *First Blood* (Taylor 1993) and despite the purported dislike of American mainstream audiences for subtitling, subtitles are commonly used to communicate messages of fast-breeding *Aliens*.

9.2 Multilingualism

Global advertising is becoming more multilingual, not less: the use of foreign words and catch-phrases to promote foreign – and domestic – products has proliferated in recent years and is on the increase. Advertisers are eager to enrol new foreign players – not just in the world of football. One of the effects of the growth in co-productions with several European partners is that television programmes and films with characters speaking more than one language are also on the increase. In the latest film of Radu Mihaileanu, for instance, the Romanian Jews embarking on the *Train de vie* speak French, German, Yiddish and Romanian. While the French input – to comply with co-production treaty regulations – appears contrived, other languages do not.[12] A sign of the times, several European comedies are exploiting problems of communication between people who do not speak the same language (Ian Sellar's *Prague*, Tony Gatlif's *Gatjo Dilo*, etc.). Is multilingualism soon to become universally accceptable in our multi-ethnic and multicultural societies?

9.3 Use of local songs

Given the links between the music and the video industry on the one hand, and the growing importance of the soundtrack in films on the other, another strategy is to further exploit the use of local songs in European films (*Le huitième jour*, *On connait la chanson*). At a time when the distinction between high and popular culture is blurred, making use of a lively cultural form such as "local chansons" can only serve to celebrate the cultural (and ethnic) diversity of Europe.

Anthropologists may be questioning the notion of language both as a model for culture (Bloch 1991) and as the vehicle or medium of culture (Street 1993) but it is language that immediately provides meaning and identity to a particular group or community. Yet, languages are insufficiently supported by the MEDIA programmes, and European regulators continue to dodge the language issue. What languages need, along with films, is not so much protection as exhibition. The new incentives for the distribution of non-national films in Europe are to be welcome, but more can be done.

It has been suggested that investment in nationwide and/or Europe-wide "circuits of art-house multiplexes" could constitute an alternative to the commercial sector (Anderson 1997: 26-27). This might even contribute to the emergence of a new cinephilia. One could also think of remakes being shown alongside the foreign-language originals in the same multiplex. Another suggestion is to "include rival distributors offering hyper-links between their Internet websites to help increase the overall audience for films" (Anderson ibid.).[13]

Markets are not stable entities. Old markets can be revived (as illustrated by recent theatrical re-releases of old movies) and new niches can be created. Two examples may suffice here, one from Britain and the other from "the continent": In the last decade, Britain has been at the forefront in home programming, with 68 per cent of households having a video-recorder already in 1989. One of the reasons for this rapid development of the UK video market is the appetite of Asian communities for Hindi-language films from "Bollywood". (Falcon op.cit.) The other example is that of the Franco-German channel ARTE. Despite a derisory small budget, its film production arm La Sept Cinéma has been involved in over 120 films since its inception in 1992. They include many co-productions in languages other than French, German or English, among them, Ademir Kenocvic's *Perfect Circle* (in Bosnian), Lucian Pintilie's *The Oak* (in Romanian), Theo Angelopoulos' *L'Eternité et un jour* (in Greek), Vitali Kanevski's *An Independent Life* (in Russian) and Rithy Panh's *Les Gens de la Rizière* (in Cambodian). Many films which received support from La Sept-Cinéma speak more than one language (Theodopoulos' *Ulysses' Gaze* is in English, Greek and other languages from the Balkans; Tran Ahn Hung's *Cyclo* is in French and Vietnamese, Yolande Zauberman's *Toi Ivan Moi Abraham* in Yiddish, Russian, Polish and Tzigane). Many have been selected for festival screenings and received universal critical acclaim. Along with ARTE, the pan-European fund, Eurimages, has also played an important part in encouraging the co-production of films made in the various languages of the member states of the Council of Europe.

Despite the fact that it is increasingly difficult to assess a film's nationality, nationality criteria continue to be used to access subsidies as co-production treaties stipulate the number of nationals involved in any agreed film. However outdated international co-production agreements may be today, the reciprocity clause written in many of them is worth preserving. Reciprocity requires that partners treat each other on equal terms. Peter Lev who pointed out that "the hegemony of a dominant group [...] can be challenged and modified under certain conditions by the culture of the subordinate groups", also insisted that internationalism should not be conceptualized as "a neutral arrangement among equal partners".

9.4 The British paradigm

In the struggle between large conglomerates with global ambitions and independent film companies trying to survive, the new British cinema, popular with audiences worldwide, represents an interesting paradigm. One of its biggest hits, *The Full Monty,* provides a fitting example of a film "which succeeds in its own terms in constructing specific imagined worlds" where its (British) filmmakers managed to achieve a successful compromise between the demands of their American financiers (Fox wanted "known actors") and their own desire for the film to retain its cultural identity (including the Yorkshire accents).[14]

Another, *Trainspotting,* was, in some quarters, originally deemed to failure because of its "incomprehensible Glaswegian accents". Today, encouraged by the international acclaim of films such as *Trainspotting*, Scottish cinema is asserting its own cultural (linguistic) identity, and an increasing number of British script-writers are refusing to submit to "commercial pressures": Rather than coveting American inflections, they prefer to use the home-grown equivalent (Shone 1998). Veteran filmmaker Ken Loach, whose early films were released with subtitles in the US, is no longer an exception. In 1999, a British film, *The Slab Boys*, may tour the US - in a subtitled version - as part of a festival of critically acclaimed foreign-language films because its producers refuse to have the film dubbed, in order to preserve the film's integrity.[15]

The Scottish examples along with the video market for Hindi-language films in the UK clearly illustrate the rise of identity politics placing a subculture's rights over those of the mainstream. It is because they value their local culture that some minorities in Europe have been able to successfully challenge the mainstream culture. In the new political and technological environments, conditions are such that "special-interest groups" can modify the hegemony of a dominant group. The economic and cultural domination of the market by one group cannot be taken for granted and needs to be constantly re-assessed. Public rhetoric is no longer about containment but about seeking to enforce a recognition that there is an enormous diversity, and people need to value it. Over the last decade, the European Community has provided a new forum for Europe's many linguistic minorities to articulate their demands and defend their right to exist (Coulmas 1991: 14).[16] Today the new technologies present Europeans with unique opportunities to challenge and modify the current cultural process which contributes to the dominance of the English language in European film and audiovisual cultures. The current financial upheavals show that capitalist economies cannot always rely on pure market forces if economic stability and political consent are to be preserved. Governments must accept responsibility for maintaining stability and managing both macroeconomic demands and cultural plurality. The 1998 Strasbourg Forum on Cinema concluded its session on globalisation and international legislation by emphasizing the importance of promoting a European model of society founded on the promotion of the old continent's riches in cultural and linguistic diversity (Scotto 1998).

Yet, American dominance of the film markets in the Western world is achieved through attractive popular elements, not just through economic advantages. It is part of a wider cultural process in which for almost a century, the American way of life has dominated people's imagination. The supremacy of English is also part of this process.

Ultimately, the extent to which European values differ from the present current of individualism and free-marketeer mentality (where everything is valued in terms of economic performance) will no doubt contribute to determine whether Europeans prefer their dream factory to speak in their mother tongue or to operate in English in the future. One thing is certain as more national/local films embrace the trend towards English-language internationalism: interest groups, local communities, national governments (and European policy-makers) will find it increasingly difficult to argue for cultural exception.

Notes

1. Source: European Audiovisual Observatory, Strasbourg 1998.

2. Arguably, *Belle Epoque*, a Spanish-language feature – and the winner of the Oscar for best foreign language picture – did more to consolidate Iberoamericana's international position in the early 1990s than *1492*.

3. The UK sales company Mayfair Entertainment International refused to take delivery of the film claiming the completed product differed fundamentally from the project they had first agreed to back. (Source: *Screen Finance,* 7 (19), 19 October 1994)

4. Source: *Variety*, 29-4/5-5-1996.

5. Among the projects supported by MEDIA I, the most important contributions to the circulation of European films and audiovisual programmes within Europe came from: SCALE for helping joint initiatives between countries with a limited geographical and linguistic area; BABEL for promoting multilingualism in television programmes through financial support for dubbing and/or subtitling; Media Salles and Europa Cinema for the theatrical exhibition of European films, and EFDO and EVE for distribution.

6. Europa Cinemas, the MEDIA II distribution programme to reduce the financial risks of distributors of foreign-language films, offers distribution loans up to 50 per cent of the total cost of releasing a film.

7. Source: *Screen Finance*, 9 July 1998.

8. The argument: "in the multimedia age, a theatrical release has lost much of its significance for a film's career" is strongly denied by ever-increasing promotion budgets and the subsequent media attention generated when films are released.

9. *Variety* (29-04/05-05 1996) gave the examples of *Il Postino* which had by then taken, $19m at the US box office, but "was unlikely to ship as many cassette units as *Priest* - an English-language film that had a domestic box office of $4m". They quoted a specialist distributor saying: "This part of the industry isn't obviously about big bucks".

10. 82 % of French films were pre-sold to Canal Plus in 1997, and the French conglomerate is now investing in Italy, Poland and Spain. German films are financed by local broadcasters and CLT-UFA is today backing French theatrical distribution operation with a chance to exploit rights to movies it controls. The renaissance of British cinema in the 1980's was largely due to Channel 4. Today, the BBC is also producing films for theatrical distribution and BSkyB has a special deal with British Screen. The latter administers the government-supported European

Co-production Fund (ECF) responsible for backing, among other UK co-productions, foreign-language pictures such as *Ma vie en rose*, *Portraits Chinois* and *Before the Rain*.

11. According to a recent study conducted by Denton Hall Consultants, "it is not unrealistic to anticipate that an expensive French film (with a production budget of $8m) could cover [all] its costs ($15m) during the video-on-demand window in Europe only, leaving the whole rest of the world and all other media for profit". Today, the same film needs to earn around $80m at the box office to recoup the net cost to recover from distribution (Flint, 1996: 31-32).

12. The latter example also illustrates that "national languages are not necessarily more democratic than any of the *linguae francae* that we tend to criticise" (Lambert, 1998: 29).

13. Anderson (1997: 26) questions the inability of independents on this side of the Atlantic to come up with joint initiatives to give the sector "power through numbers". He gives the example of the US independents "responding to the likelihood that a greater public appreciation for niche products would increase commercial prospects for everyone by coming up with *Independents*, a free quarterly publication distributed in both art houses and multiplexes in which all leading independents get full-page ads and editorial".

14. The producers were reported to have made a 15-minute cut for the version released in the United States.

15. *The Slab Boys* tells the story of three factory workers in Paisley, a suburb of Glasgow, in the 1950's. American distributors were reported to be "balking at buying the film because of its Glaswegian accents".

16. For a discussion of the role of intellectuals in minority language cultures, see Mike Cormack (1998).

THE POSITION OF FOREIGN LANGUAGES IN THE FLEMISH MEDIA

Reine Meylaerts
Katholieke Universiteit Leuven,
Leuven, Belgium

1. A hidden phenomenon

In March 1994, the Flemish Council, the Parliament of the Dutch-speaking community of Belgium, invited other Dutch- and Afrikaans-speaking communities[1] to an international colloquium.[2] The goal of this colloquium was to stimulate a common media policy in order to preserve or even to improve the position of Dutch- and Afrikaans-speaking media all over the world. Therefore, as a kind of preliminary phase, it was considered necessary to describe the linguistic structure of the media in each participating community or country and to analyse the influence of this structure on the position of the language involved. In fact, the knowledge gained from this description would offer the only possible way to develop a common linguistic policy or – in terms of the colloquium's report – a "culturally responsible media policy". In this respect, the colloquium was an answer to the 1993 conclusions of the Uruguay-round of the GATT-negotiations for which the EU refused to incorporate the film and audio-visual sector into the liberalisation agreements.

In the context of protecting one's own media and language and of stimulating future collaboration, each participating community was invited to make an analysis of its own media landscape, i.e. the printed, audio-visual and electronic media. Language would be at the core of the study. Moreover, as there is a clear link between the position of language in the media on the one hand, and the socio-economic and political factors determining the media structure on the other, an analysis of language in the media had to be carried out in relation to these socio-economic and political elements.

As follows, some of the report's main conclusions on the media in Flanders[3] will be briefly commented. It will be pointed out in what respect these conclusions cannot count at all for what was presumed to be their goal: the analysis of the position of (a) language in the media. This is due to a general unawareness of the language component and more especially to a lack of distinction between the crucial categories of "imported/not imported", "translated/not translated" and the various links of these categories with the language issue. Or to quote the report (my translation): "Lack of time and space have forced us to leave aside relatively important aspects of the issue as for instance the translation policy" (1994: 224).

In other words, if delocalisation of ownership and economic structures is becoming increasingly important in any kind of research into the media, the possible consequences in terms of delocalisation of production and of the related translational activities especially remain a hidden phenomenon. This is part of the reason why the Flanders report can – erroneously – confirm that:

> There are actually very few tendencies that confirm that internationalisation of capital structure refrains the "domestic" national character of a medium. (my translation)

How to explain that the Dutch language is prominently present in the Flemish, whereas in most cases the ownership of the media is foreign?

For the audio-visual and printed media, i.e. for the new and old media, some of the main conclusions of the Flanders report will first be highlighted. It will be pointed out in what respect they are in straight contradiction with the real market situation just because of ignorance of import and of translational phenomena.

2. Distribution of films and TV programmes

The report confirms that the production and the distribution of films in Flanders are dominated by American productions and American distributors. They control about 70% of the market. Consequently, in this sector, the American dominance is undeniable. This dominance also extends to language. Film in Flanders is an anglophone medium because of the fact that films are always subtitled and not dubbed. When it comes to films, the market structure seems to overlap with the ownership and the linguistic features of the product.[4]

The average Flemish family has got cable television, which means that they can watch between 25 and 30 different channels, broadcasting in almost as many languages. Among them, there are five Flemish channels. Apart from public-service television broadcasting on two channels (TV1 and TV2) there are two commercial television stations. One of them also operates with two channels (VTM & Ka2)[5] and is partly Dutch owned; another commercial station[6] (VT4), is broadcasting on one channel and is owned by Scandinavian Broadcasting Systems.[7]

The report estimates that Flemish television in Flanders is doing well, as 60% of the Flemish public watch one of the Flemish stations. During prime time, this percentage even reaches 75%. This leads to the optimistic conclusion that Flemish television enjoys a very sound position and that the Flemish public is strongly attached to their own television productions. The report does mention a high presence of American fiction, but predicts an increase of domestic Flemish fiction productions.

This kind of conclusion ignores the major issue of the origin of the programmes (domestic production vs. import) and of the related issue of translating[8] or not translating programmes. All foreign programmes are subtitled; dubbing is virtually non-existent on Flemish television.

3. Origins of programming: buying and subtitling programmes

A limited investigation comparing the origin of the programmes during the first week of each new television season in 1994, 1995 and 1996, reveals the importance of the above mentioned delocalisation of production activities and the parallel importance of translation activities.

First of all, in those three years, there is, looking at all channels together, a gradual increase of foreign, anglophone (mostly American[9]) programmes (table 1). Whereas in October 1994, 57% of all programmes were local productions, in February 1996, these only reached 45%. Moreover, in October 1996, probably for the first time in Flemish television history, American programmes occupy the absolute majority of the total Flemish television supply! On the commercial channels Ka2 and VT4, American productions constitute respectively 88% and 70% of the supply. But also TV1 and VTM dedicate more than one third of their time on air to American programmes. In absolute numbers, the import of American productions has almost tripled: from 3555 minutes a week in February 1994 to 9525 minutes a week in October 1996.

As for fiction programmes (table 2), in two and a half years time, the supply of American fiction (series and films) on the Flemish channels has increased with 175%, from some 2000 minutes a week in 1994 to some 6000 in 1996. In comparison, local productions only reached 690 minutes (9,5%) in 1996.

Table 3 shows the evolution of the origin of fiction programmes in percentages. For all channels together, American fiction reaches 80% of all fiction in October 1996. On the commercial channel Ka2, fiction programmes are 98,5% American, whereas the lowest share is found on TV1, with no less than 69%!

These percentages become even more significant considering that the majority of programmes broadcast are fiction programmes (table 4). Especially for the commercial stations Ka2 and VT4 some 75% of the total programme supply.

In this respect, the report's conclusions – and predictions – about the sound position of Flemish television and its language combined with the public's attachment to a television "made in Flanders", are at the least relatively contradictory. These conclusions reveal the ignorance of the real origins of the Flemish TV supply. Of course, one can either like or dislike this situation and its evolution, but it is not of our concern here.[10] However, these phenomena do matter, whatever the language policy in the media may be. There even seems to be an internal contradiction as to subtitling. Whereas the report concludes that in film the use of subtitles leads to the dominance of the American language and that film in Flanders is an anglophone medium, the omnipresence of subtitles on television is not dealt with in the report. Still, with regard to the ever-growing presence of American – subtitled – programmes on Flemish channels, television – in terms of the report's reasoning – necessarily becomes more and more an anglophone medium.

4. Foreign formats

4.1Television channels

If one considers translation in the media from a broader point of view, it might embrace borrowing and importing foreign – in this case American and Dutch – models. It then appears that the phenomenon of import and of translation on TV is even more overwhelming. During the first week of February 1996, 12% of the above identified (low) supply of Flemish programmes on all channels were based on American or Dutch[11] formats. In October 96, some 20% of the "domestic" Flemish programmes were based on foreign formats: a concept can be borrowed from a foreign format[12] and elaborated for the domestic public, or a totally preconceived pattern can be copied so that even the colours of the decor are dictated by the foreign licence holder.[13]

4.2 Book market

The report does not only overlook delocalisation of production activities, import and translation in the audio-visual media but also in the printed media. Once again, unawareness of these phenomena can only compromise investigations on a language policy for the media.

With regard to the book market the report again concludes that the Flemish book is in a comfortable position. As a proof, table 5 shows how during the last decade, the number of Dutch books published in Flanders increases. The percentage of books published in foreign languages in Flanders is on the contrary almost zero. Table 5 also reveals that more than 50% of these Dutch titles are imported from Holland. For fiction, the percentage of import from Holland represents about 60% of the market.

In this respect the report does stress the important structural dependence of the Flemish market on Dutch publishers: the latter realise 54% of the total turnover of books in Flanders. This means a great deal of the production and distribution of Flemish books is in Dutch hands because of direct import from Dutch publishing houses and their majority participations in Flemish publishing houses. Moreover, the few editors with Flemish capital are dependent on Dutch partners for the distribution of their products. Still, according to the report, this is of no importance for the publications themselves as they are published in Dutch. Import from Holland only contributes to the sound position of Dutch literature and language.

Once again the report does not take into account the origins of the titles available on the book market. Translation as such is completely ignored and the phenomenon of delocalisation of the translation activity on the Flemish book market gets no attention. Let us take the situation for printed fiction between 1980 and 1985 as an example. Figures will be taken from an analysis of Belgium's national bibliography.[14]

Between 1980 and 1985, about 60% or more of the titles of fiction mentioned in the national bibliography are translations (table 6). More than 80% of these translations are made and edited in Holland only to be imported to Flanders (table 7). The major publishing houses like Bruna, Elsevier, Het Spectrum are Dutch publishing houses. They monopolise the translation of popular anglophone fiction edited in cheap, successful pocket series and make substantial turnovers with these publications. Popular authors like Stephen King, Danielle Steel and Joan Collins are systematically translated and edited in Holland and read by the Dutch and Flemish public. Table 8 shows how these English translations occupy an important percentage of the title export into Flanders (of the respective editors).

5. Conclusion

In a world of globalisation and internationalisation, the categories traditionally used for description of and research into the linguistic structures and functioning of the (printed and audio-visual) media, have revealed themselves as surprisingly unadapted. Unlike discussions of the internationalisation of economic structures implying the well-known idea of import and export of goods, of capital etc., research dealing with cultural products, their linguistic component, and especially with language policies in these international(ised) media, are still dependent on a local, national(istic) frame of reference, which ignores the most crucial aspects of this global problem.

Origin of television programmes on Flemish channels.

(Fl: Flemish; A: American, Canadian, Australian; O: other)

Table 1. Origin of Programmation throughout the year (%)

Year		Total	VTM	Ka2	TV1	TV2	VT4
94	Fl	57	53		59	63	
	A	33.5	39.5		32	21.5	
	O	9.5	7.5		9	15.5	
95	Fl	47	45.5	32.5	63	70	21.5
	A	43	48.5	55.5	24.5	22.5	66
	O	10	6	12	12.5	7.5	12.5
Feb. 96	Fl	45	59	30.5	60.5	61	19.5
	A	41.5	37	58	20.5	22	64
	O	13.5	4	11.5	19.5	17	16.5
Oct. 96	Fl	40	66	12	59	40	21.5
	A	52.5	31.5	88	36	32	70.5
	O	7.5	2.5	0	5	28	8

Table 2. Origin of the Fiction programmes throughout the year (in minutes/week)

Year		Total	VTM	Ka2	TV1	TV2	VT4
94	Fl	550	405		145	0	
	A	2115	1360		645	110	
	O	435	135		300	0	
95	Fl	530	330	0	175	25	0
	A	4895	1900	1170	560	495	770
	O	1269	204	285	450	150	180
Feb. 96	Fl	860	390	180	240	50	0
	A	5140	875	1325	445	485	2010
	O	1613	150	360	448	145	180
Oct. 96	Fl	690	380	0	235	45	30
	A	5850	1005	1540	630	495	2180
	O	765	120	0	165	275	205

Table 3. Origin of fiction programmes throughout the year (%)

Year		Total	VTM	Ka2	TV1	TV2	VT4
94	Fl	18	21.5		13.5	0	
	A	68	71.5		59	100	
	O	14	7		27.5	0	
95	Fl	8	13.5	0	15	4	0
	A	73	78	80.5	47	74	81
	O	19	8.5	19.5	38	22	19
Feb. 96	Fl	11.5	27.5	9.5	21	7.5	0
	A	67.5	62	71	39.5	71.5	80
	O	21	10.5	19.5	39.5	21	20
Oct. 96	Fl	9.5	25	0	23	5.5	1
	A	80	67	100	61	60.5	90.5
	O	10.5	8	0	16	34	8.5

Table 4. Variation in Programme Offer throughout the year (%)
(N: non fiction; Sp: sport; S: fiction series; F: films)

Year		Total	VTM	Ka2	TV1	TV2	VT4
94	**N**	49.5	44		50.5	62.5	
	Sp	3	2		3	4.5	
	S	29	40		25.5	7	
	F	18.5	14		21	26	
95	**N**	44	38	34	57	52.5	39
	Sp	4.5	2.5	0	3	19	1
	S	39	51	53	30	24.5	32
	F	12.5	8.5	13	10	4	28
Feb. 96	**N**	39	46	24.5	50.5	53.5	22.5
	Sp	3.5	3.5	0	2	12.5	1
	S	44	37	60	31.5	25.5	63
	F	13.5	13.5	15.5	16	8.5	13.5
Oct. 96	**N**	36	50.5	12.5	52.5	45	22.5
	Sp	3.5	6	0	2	8	1
	S	40.5	35.5	42.5	28.5	32.5	58.5
	F	20	8	45	17	14.5	18

Table 5. Dutch bookproduction in Flanders and import from Holland

Year	Flemish Titles	Import Holland	Total
1980	2200	3756	5956
1981	2472	4600	7072
1982	2394	3961	6355
1983	2654	3867	6521
1984	2889	4278	7167
1985	2714	4536	7250
1986	2625	4376	7001
1987	2858	4057	6915
1988	3052	3797	6849
1989	3141	3956	7097
1990	3027	4401	7428
1991	3528	4264	7792

Table 6. Fiction: Number of titles according to the national bibliography

Year	Original	%	%	Translation
1980	288	38	62	470
1981	233	32	68	484
1982	239	41.5	58.5	337
1983	303	44	56	387
1984	201	35	65	365
1985	184	38	62	304

Table 7. Fiction: Edition of translations according to the national bibliography

Year	Edited in Flanders	%	%	Edited in Holland
1980	72	15.5	84	392
1981	81	16.7	83	402
1982	49	14.5	85.5	288
1983	56	14.4	85.5	330
1984	63	17.2	82.8	302
1985	62	20	80	242

Table 8. Fiction: Relation between original titles and English translations of the major Dutch publishing houses present on the Flemish market

	BRUNA		ELSEVIER		SPECTRUM	
Year	Original	Engl. Trl.	Original	Engl. Trl.	Original	Engl. Trl.
1980	21	90	47	107	18	73
1981	29	80	35	121	7	71
1982	4	25	2	41	10	44
1983	0	4	14	64	13	71
1984	3	26	11	65	10	83
1985	13	43	6	41	21	104

Notes

1. Among the participants were Flanders, Holland, Namibia, South Africa, Suriname and the Dutch Antilles.

2. The colloquium's proceedings were published in an extensive volume: Van Zutphen, Nan & Johan Nootens (eds.). *Nederlandstalige en Afrikaanstalige media [...]. Tweede internationale colloquium Nederlands in de wereld, Brussel 1994.* Brussel VUBPress. 1994.

3. Siebelink, S., D. Biltereyst & J. Burgelman. "Vlaanderen", Van Zutphen et al. (eds), *op. cit.* 1994: 221-277.

4. In this respect, the report appreciates the recent evolution towards co-productions in a European context.

5. Ka2 was created after the report was published.

6. When the report was published, this channel did not exist.

7. SBS is owned by the American company ABC which again is owned by the Disney group.

8. As will be illustrated below, the word "translated" does not only refer to subtitling versus dubbing, but also means "based on a foreign format".

9. For the sake of the argument, we will use the term "American" in the following, considering that the Australian and Canadian television productions are mainly following American models, certainly with regard to fiction programmes (soap series and TV-films).

10. For a more elaborate analysis of the dependence on and the impact of American television in Europe, see for instance: Biltereyst, Daniël. 1995. *Hollywood in het Avondland. Over de afhankelijkheid en de impact van Amerikaanse televisie in Europa.* Brussel: VUBPress.

11. In this respect it is worth mentioning that the commercial channels VTM and Ka2 have a 44,4% Dutch ownership.

12. As for instance, the concept of *Ushuaïa*, an adventure-travel programme based on a French format.

13. The most famous example is that of *Rad van Fortuin* (*Wheel of Fortune*) a very popular quiz, broadcast every day.

14. *Nationale Bibliografie - Bibliographie Nationale*, 1980-1985. The numbers in the tables are based on the national bibliography. It means that they do not represent the market situation in absolute numbers but they have proved to represent accurately the tendencies on the market.

DISENTANGLING AUDIOVISUAL TRANSLATION INTO CATALAN FROM THE SPANISH MEDIA MESH

Patrick Zabalbeascoa & Natàlia Izard,
Universitat Pompeu Fabra, Barcelona
Laura Santamaria,
Universitat Autònoma de Barcelona
Spain

1. Introduction

In this paper we aim to outline a complex situation of intertwining relationships between media, languages, language transfer mechanisms and strategies, politics, technological advances, and even sociological and educational factors. All of these factors seem to combine in such a way that makes research in the field both fascinating and challenging. As new factors seem to be popping up all the time, new research tools will be needed as well as a continuous updating of information and explanations. To begin with, this report on the state of affairs in Spain, laying particular emphasis on Catalonia, needs to be compared with that of other countries, near and far.

2. The Spanish mesh

In Spain, the major television networks mirror the geopolitical and language borders quite closely, which is noteworthy given the number and complexity of the divisions. Thus, just as there is a Central Government there are nationwide television networks; just as there are parts of Spain which also have a considerable degree of autonomy and a Regional Government and Parliament, so too there are regional broadcasting companies. In a very brief account of this situation we can say that on a nationwide level there are two public channels,

TVE1 and TVE2, both part of the RTVE corporation that used to hold the monopoly of television broadcasting in Spain. RTVE has now added satellite broadcasting to their offer (Hispasat). The private sector offers two "open" channels (Antena 3 and Tele 5) and one "subscription" channel (Canal +). Apart from these terrestrial channels there are two subscription satellite broadcasters (Canal Satélite Digital and Vía Digital). All of these channels cover the whole of Spain, but there are other channels that can only be seen in certain parts of Spain, the regional or peripheral networks. They are to date all publicly owned and funded by the Autonomous Administrations. Some are Spanish-speaking only: Telemadrid in Madrid and Canal Sur in Andalucía. Others are mostly or partly non-Spanish-speaking: TVC (TV3 and Canal 33) in Catalonia, Canal 9 in Valencia, Euskal Telebista in the Basque country, TVG in Galicia. Cable television is no more than a local pilot project in Spain.

2.1 Further complicating factors

There are a number of factors that make it very difficult to establish a clear-cut statistical account of aspects that in other countries might seem much more straightforward, such as number and distribution of languages, which channels are public and which private, percentage of foreign-language imports, and the question of whether Spain is a dubbing or a subtitling country. To start with, there is a media war going on at the moment. Even the Government has been accused of interfering and taking sides. Secondly, RTVE has shares in the privately-owned digital satellite broadcasting company Vía Digital, and TVC has a stake in both digital platforms. There are also various network alliances for exclusive rights of sporting events and films. Access to RTVE archives is another matter of controversy. Satellite broadcasting includes a lot of repeats of past and present terrestrial product. Thirdly, the regional networks form an alliance called Forta, which enables them to purchase programmes and sign contracts as a single consortium. Among other things, this means that a single television series may be dubbed into as many as four different languages and sometimes separately for the Valencian variety of Catalan (there is serious political controversy over whether Valencian is a dialect of Catalan or a language in its own right). In consequence, after fourteen years of programming in Catalan, two minor standard varieties have consolidated: one is the variety spoken in Barcelona and its surrounding area, to be shown all over Catalonia - also seen from the Balearic Islands, the other is the variety spoken near Valencia, 350 km. south of Barcelona, the capital of another "autonomous community", the Valencian Country. Thus, TVC can be seen in parts of Valencia, (and on most of the Balearic Islands) but not vice versa.

2.2 Quotas

There are quotas regarding the ratio of Spanish feature films and foreign films shown in cinemas (1 to 4 approximately). In the case of peripheral non-Spanish-speaking channels the aim is to avoid using Spanish as much as possible and promote Galician, Basque or Catalan, through home production and dubbing. For example, the Catalan Government is pressing all networks broadcasting in Catalonia to provide a certain percentage of their programming in Catalan. In fact, the first TV broadcasts in Catalan appeared before the existence of TVC and were done by TVE in Catalonia; TVE2 still offers a considerable amount of time in Catalan. Tele 5 occasionally offers Catalan through the bilingual stereo system. Antena 3 offers a few programmes in Catalan, most noticeably football. Canal + shows films in Catalan on "special occasions".

3. Problems in counting the percentage of imported programmes

Below is a schematic account of relevant factors, genre not included:

- The distinction between fee-paying (where imported programmes are far more numerous) and free ("open") television is more relevant than private vs public. Particularly important is the distinction between thematic channels and those that offer a wide range of programmes.

- Monolingual broadcasting systems (Antena 3) vs bilingual-stereo (TVC-English/Catalan); Tele 5 Catalan/Spanish. Monolingual channels (Catalan: TVC; Spanish: Tele 5, Canal Sur) vs bilingual (TVE in Catalonia, Canal 9 in Valencia, EB in the Basque Country).

- Spain is generally regarded as a dubbing country although subtitling is steadily but slowly gaining ground. In the foreseeable future the two major forms of audiovisual translation will probably coexist and complement each other. It is important to note other strategies (dub and sub versions of the same film shown at different times on the same channel; bilingual stereo broadcasting and multilingual digital broadcasting offer the viewer a choice of language for a given programme; remaking a film, as an alternative to either dubbing or subtitling it (dub or sub), is unheard of in Spain, with the exception of commercials which can be dubbed, adapted, remade, or made completely different for each market.

- Peripheral languages not broadcast outside their respective areas. The exception to this are satellite broadcasts.

- The relative importance of the actual number of programmes must be weighed against other factors: duration, time slots, and ratings.

- Not all imports are foreign-language imports (South American films in Spanish-speaking channels). Are we to consider Spanish programmes as foreign-language "imports" in basically non-Spanish monolingual peripheral networks? This political mine-field is usually avoided by arguing in favor of complementarity with Spanish-speaking networks. There are occasional "exports" from minority-language producers dubbed for the whole of Spain, e.g. the Catalan soap *Poble Nou* dubbed by Antena 3 as *Los Mejores Años*.

- With the advent of so many new channels, newspapers are becoming much more selective and telegraphic in the information they provide regarding TV programmes. Most papers tend to highlight friendly networks and give them much more space, a more central position on the page, and more favourable criticisms, while doing exactly the opposite for enemy networks, sometimes ignoring them completely. Much the same could be said for radio programmes that deal with television.

- Foreign imports include a wide range of different programmes, mostly feature films, soap operas and serials, situation comedies, documentaries, and cartoons; but never or hardly ever (except via satellite): sports broadcasting, news and weather reports, quiz shows, variety shows, chat shows, gossip programmes, reality shows, political satire. In the case of quizzes and contests, what is imported is the idea and format (e.g. *Wheel of Fortune*). Due to the variety of genres, various forms of screen translation can be found at any time of the day, although traditional (non-teletext) subtitles are mostly limited to off-peak hours, especially the small hours. There is a tendency to introduce new genres through dubbing and then gradually produce them locally. It is difficult to tell to what extent some Pan-European satellite broadcasts can be regarded as imports.

4. Technological factors which bypass the traditional "dub or sub" dilemma:

- Simultaneous radio broadcasting of the original soundtrack and language (late 70's to mid 80's) was the first alternative to "dub or sub". Today, some people prefer to watch football on television with the sound off and listen to the radio commentary. This may involve a change of language.

- Bilingual stereo makes it possible to listen to the original sound or a dubbed version for the same picture, pioneered in Spain by TVC in the late 80's (for viewers who do not have the right set only the dubbed version can be heard). Recent digital technology allows for more than one foreign version for both dub and sub. It does not reach many people yet so the actual offer is much smaller than the technology's capability.

- Dub and (teletext) sub versions conceived for people with special needs tend to include narration and description as well as dialogue.

- TV subtitling as the only option is still infrequent. Documentaries mostly resort to sub in the case of political figures, although it used to be done only for "special voices" (e.g. Hitler, Martin Luther King).

- Dub-sub hybrids: limited almost entirely to the subtitling of songs or *foreign* speech (e.g. a third language or a special dialect) within dubbed versions. The rule is: a dub may include sub in some part of the text, but a sub version may never resort to dub as a solution. Dubbing, subtitling, interpreting, voice-over narrative or dialogue, and non-translation are all resorted to for documentaries and news programmes, or parts of them, in the case of hybrid versions.

- Digital manipulation of the picture could make screen translating much less constrained; normally the translation of the oral elements of the audiovisual text is constrained by the need for it to be synchronized and coherent with the nonverbal and visual constituents. There are already several commercials that manipulate the picture to make small babies and animals move their mouths and lips in perfect synch with song lyrics.

5. The Process of Dubbing in Spain

Dubbing clearly prevails over subtitling in Spain. In commercial cinema there is a big difference between large cities and small towns. In a big city like Barcelona about 65% of the films shown in cinemas are in dub format and the remaining 35% are subtitled (this situation, though, is quite recent: until 1995 subtitled films were rare, only shown at "art cinemas" and public cinemathèques). In smaller towns, subtitled films are rare, with a few exceptions in the non-commercial circuit (e.g. *cine-clubs*). The percentage of subtitled films is even smaller when it comes to television. In 1996, the overall average was one film per month, increasing, in 1997, to one per week. It is important to note that the offer in subtitled versions is steadily growing, however slowly, both for the cinema-goer and television viewer. It has a lot to do with greater audience appreciation.

English is the source language for practically 90% of all television imports. The other 10% is mostly French, German and Japanese (especially cartoons). In the beginning of the television era (the early 60's in Spain) some US productions were dubbed in the USA by Spanish-speaking American actors. This was Hollywood's last effort to control every aspect of their exports as they had done in the past. Some of these versions are still repeated once in a while, producing a nostalgic effect on the older generations. Today, the dubbing process is carried out in Madrid and Barcelona for Spanish; and the peripheral languages, Basque, Catalan, and Galician, are each produced in their respective geographical areas.

5.1 Dubbing for TVC

The technical facilities to make the process of dubbing into Catalan possible were consolidated in Barcelona from the very beginning since all programmes shown by the various Spanish channels used to be dubbed in Barcelona, and many of the actors were native speakers of Catalan. So, it was quite easy to put the whole machinery to work for a new language. Every year TVC puts out to tender the total amount of films and programmes to be dubbed among the dubbing studios. When the year is over, the quality of each studio's work is evaluated. Each dubbed version is marked according to linguistic, aesthetic and technical criteria, including the quality of the translation, synchronization, sound mixing, and the actors' performances. The aim is to have a continous assessment of quality and compliance with the conditions.

Usually the dialogues are translated and dubbed while all other sound effects remain untouched. The original tapes sometimes have two separate soundtracks, one for the dialogues, and one for the music and effects. In this case, it is possible to mix the original background sound with the dubbed dialogues, at the end of the process. When there are no separate tracks, sound effects either disappear from the dubbed version or are recovered by reproducing and recording them in a studio. Technicians make sounds of slamming doors, ringing phones, footsteps, etc. The noises can also be recorded live from schoolyards, traffic jams, crowded bars, etc. The latter option is much more expensive and rarely done, since dubbing for television is done on a tighter budget than commercial cinema.

5.2 The impersonating voices

Dubbing actors are classified according to a limited number of voice-types or profiles that neatly cut up the whole spectrum of film characters, generally resulting in a few broad categories: villain, hero, heroine, clown, vamp, child, and so on. Dubbing actors do not tend to be creative but rather imitate the dominant speech and intonation patterns, which makes each category even more paradigmatic. Children are dubbed by women.

Voices are selected on the basis of the film character, not the original actor playing the part; typically then, male characters should be dubbed with low voices, unless the character is a to be laughed at or is effeminate. This produces mismatches between the actor's original voice and the dubbed version. Clear examples can be found in actors like Tom Selleck who looks 'macho' and usually plays the 'good guy', and is given a deep mellow voice in dubbing although his own voice is quite high-pitched and creaky. In contrast to this, Dustin Hoffman is dubbed with a high-pitch voice to fit his anti-hero image, despite the fact that he really has a rich deep baritone voice. Interestingly, this norm coexists with an effort to dub famous film stars with the same voice as much as possible, regardless of the character they might happen to be playing, in an attempt to create an illusion that each star has his or her own voice in Spanish or in Catalan, thus enabling actors to be recognised in Spain by their dubbed voices since they can't be by their own. The so-called radio-play effect is produced (all too often) when the same dubbing actor is recognised by the audience as having lent his voice to many actors already, i.e. Geena Davis might have the "same voice" as Mia Farrow. Disney likes to use famous local (non-dubbing) actors to dub their cartoons (e.g. Robin Williams as the genie in *Aladdin* is dubbed by an actor who, like Williams, is well-known to Spanish audiences for his face as much as for his voice and had never before worked in dubbing). It should be noted that Disney is almost the only company which tries to control the target versions of their productions. This kind of control is otherwise only applied occasionally, as when Stanley Kubrick commissioned the Spanish cinema version of *The Shining* to the Spanish film director Carlos Saura.

5.3 The translators (the case of TVC)

In Spain, translators are selected by the dubbing studio, which is responsible, after the approval of their client, for the whole process, from the translation to the final revision and recording. However, the selection of translators for TVC dubbings is slightly different because of the particular situation of the language. Catalan was banned from public use for many centuries, particularly under the Franco dictatorship (1939-1975), and is now being restored to widespread use as a "normal" language. TVC selects but does not train its translators. The dubbing studios receive a list of authorised translators for Catalan, updated every year by TVC. TVC also selects copy-editors to revise the translators' work. TVC has the right to make the final revision of the whole process, and to demand certain changes (called *retakes*). This is done when the dubbed version deviates from the standard language norm. Training and experience varies considerably from one translator to the next; a few have received formal academic training, but most are self-taught. They usually have experience in translating written texts before starting to work with audiovisual texts. Some are specialised in screen translating, others work in a variety of areas. The translator initiates the process by writing a translation of the script. Then, all the other participants in the process (the copy-editor, the synchronizer, the dubbing director, and the dubbing actors) use the translated text as a rough copy and reshape the text to their convenience. The names of the translators are never shown to the viewers on the screen, so they never become household names. In Spain, translators are paid, not according to the number of words they translate but according to the footage of the film. All of this suggests that the audiovisual translator's social and professional standing is rather low.

On a positive note, we must say that recent years have shown a growing awareness of audiovisual translation in Spain (Ávila 1997, Izard 1992, Lopez Escobar 1993). TVC started a periodical intended as a constant update of their style-sheet, and in 1997 it bore the fruit of a full style-book written mostly for screen translators (Televisió de Catalunya 1997). Spanish universities now offer more and more audiovisual translator training both in translation degree courses and in film studies. Some translation textbooks have special sections devoted to audiovisual translation. Research in this field is growing, both in popularity and in the volume of its publications.

Basically, the problems translators for the media face are caused by the fact that technical professionals, dubbing actors, and adapters of dialogues, are all very much concerned about the constraints imposed by the length of the sentences and the movement of the actors' lips, and thus the process of translation is considered a minor step. Therefore, while the rest of the professionals work as a team, the translators are left alone, once more, usually working at home, and are accused for any problem in the dubbed text.

6. Foreignization vs Domestication in TV dubbing into Catalan

In the last two decades, the discipline of translation studies has taken a new turn, changing its focus to look at the reasons for producing a given translation - i.e. the origins of the distance between the original text (OT) and its translation (TT). Accordingly, the objective of this part of the article is to extend the analysis of the translation process from OT to TT beyond the consideration of the actual words used.

We have analysed, among others, the translation of various TV series in English (British, American and Australian) for TVC since its very beginning fourteen years ago. Among the series, there are well known productions such as *Dallas, Neighbours* and *Eastenders*, sit-coms of varying quality (*WKRP in Cincinnati, The Nanny, Roseanne* or *Mad About You*), and what we might call historical cartoons, such as *The Flintstones*. So, although for this analysis, we will have to take into account the actual words spoken by actors in the TT, we are interested in approaching the translation from different angles, so that we can have a wide perspective of the non-linguistic factors that eventually affect and modify the TT. We have arranged these factors into three categories: (i) plot; (ii) users' preferences; (iii) images (not so much how the TT has been adapted to fit the lip movements as how viewers elicit information from scenes).

6.1 Plot

It is quite clear that, generally speaking, the reason for making a film is to tell a story. Therefore, in most cases translators must consider translating messages related to the plot as a priority. Probably, if we refer to certain genres, for instance sit-coms, where humour plays a more central role within the programme, the priority for the translator, in consequence, must be to make the TT audience laugh. If we were capable of separating language from pictures in a script, the assumption could be that we would encounter the same translation problems that any work of fiction may pose to translation.

In a recent publication by TVC (Televisió de Catalunya 1997), it was made quite clear that they are differentiating between the two subtexts within scripts. On the one hand, dialogues carry information on the plot, and on the other they are adapted to their environment and settings. In this style-book, it is made clear that translators should try to produce a dubbed text which does not sound like a translation. As one of the established norms for the translation of literature into Catalan is that readers should have the feeling that they are reading a novel written originally in Catalan, it is clear, then, that literary norms apply also to television.

6.2 Users' preferences

Usually dubbing in TV is associated with countries with widely spoken languages whereas films with subtitles are shown in countries with a relatively small number of speakers. In the case of Catalan, the decision to show all foreign films and TV series dubbed into Catalan was taken in order to fulfil the audience expectations. Until 1967, during the dictatorship in Spain, it was explicitly forbidden to show any film in the original version. The reasons are quite clear: dialogues can be manipulated more easily in the dubbing process than through the subtitles (although this gave rise to all kind of funny situations: lovers turned into siblings as in *Mogambo*, someone nodding "yes" while saying "no" whenever the answer did not fulfil the censors' expectations).

Although dubbing was closely linked with the censorship of this period, the Spanish audience got used to it and nowadays the tendency is to believe that subtitles require an extra effort since they have to be read. This situation is beginning to change, but very slowly. Younger viewers, especially if they have a good knowledge of English, prefer to watch films in their original versions with subtitles. In addition, everybody who wants to prove his/her knowledge of the film industry never watches a dubbed film. Another factor to be taken into account is that TVC has as one of its aims to improve the population's knowledge of Catalan. Thus, translators must follow the rules of the Catalan prescriptive grammar and this constrains the translators' translation.

Summing up, in the first place, the choice to dub foreign language programmes made by the audiovisual media in Catalan has been conditioned by the previous political regime which was perceived in a negative manner by the potential viewers themselves, but which, nevertheless, has modified the viewers' preferences. Secondly, most foreign television programming translated into Catalan is dubbed twice into its two main dialects. Since Catalan is a minority language, political reasons recommend the unnecessary public investment of dubbing for a potential audience of seven million people in Catalonia and the Balearic Islands plus three million people in Valencia. Thus, we are witnesses to the division of a lesser-used language, a split made possible thanks to and through the mass media and due to a politically motivated decision with the excuse of satisfying viewers' preferences. Thirdly, TVC has been selected as one of the main means to raise the number of people able to understand Catalan and to improve the overall level of Catalan in the viewing public. To meet this aim, media translators must always follow the prescriptive rules of the language. Therefore, in some instances utterances spoken by actors have little to do with the characteristics of the oral spontaneous variety spoken in similar real situations.

6.3 Images

In this section, we will relate the manipulation of the OT to the process of domestication, and how viewers elicit information about characters in a film through their words. It would not be too daring to guess that the language used in TV films and series also carry information about the different characters and that translators should try to recreate the language to give the same impression.

But contrary to theatre, and specially in TV series, TV characters tend to look unreal. They are stereotypes, archetypes, that would not work if they were not placed in the appropriate context and settings.

In a recent publication addressed to script-writers, a Catalan soap-opera actor complained about the tendency that in TV series things happen because the characters say so, but not because they are a part of the character's interior dialogue. He was missing the subtext underlying the words spoken in the dialogues.

Since we have said that literary translation norms affect the segments of language that carry information about the plot (thus rendering any distance between the OT and the TT unacceptable) and since, in the case of TVC, language must follow the prescriptive rules of grammar, the question is how can dubbing show the different speech habits of each actor?

In American series such as *The Nanny* and *WKRP in Cincinnati*, it is the actual tone of voice and affectation of the dubbing actor which compensates for the loss of social dialect characteristics in the OT that gave evidence of a character's social status.

A much more far-fetched solution that TVC adopted was for the dubbing of a well-known cartoon series: *The Flintstones*. The possibility of watching *The Flintstones* in Catalan was highly welcomed by the audience, specially by the middle-age section of the population, and for a very clear reason. This series was one of the first programmes to be broadcast at the beginning of television in Spain. So, it meant being able to go back in time with the added bonus of now watching the series in Catalan.

Nevertheless, this was a quite an old-fashioned series, technically and ideologically. In order to find a way to make the series work, and thereby capture a new audience, some changes had to be introduced, and they could not be linguistic – otherwise it would have been "unfaithful". The solution was to dub some characters with artificial-sounding voices. The dialogues were kept intact, but the effect they achieved was completely different. In this way, Fred was no longer a parody of an American middle-class husband from the fifties, politically incorrect with women, but an unreal character, quite a rough male-chauvinist, and therefore someone to laugh at because he usually made a fool of himself.

This is not the only example of how by manipulating the tone of voice, you can manipulate the effect on an audience.

Solutions like these have been widely adopted. For instance Magnum had a clear macho voice when he was dubbed into Catalan and there was some fruitiness in Roseanne's voice.

6.4 Concluding remarks on domestication strategies

Some years ago, when there was no home production in Catalonia, the tendency was to avoid all sorts of cultural references that would have helped the viewers to properly locate the series. Therefore, although the names of persons and cities were not changed, in *Eastenders*, for instance, "Albert Square" became "the Square" in to order to make it sound more neutral.

Nowadays, the tendency has been reversed. The reasons have not yet been studied, but probably it will shed new light on how the actual process of translation is conveyed by the dubbing professionals.

Cultural elements are still manipulated. Cultural conventions (saying "thank you", expressing apologies, etc.) are not modified, but names of brands, whenever the audience cannot associate them with any concrete product, are substituted with other brands with English-sounding names, so that the audience can identify them at two levels.

In fact, our belief is that this subtle transformation of the text is hidden within the foreignization of cultural elements.

On the other hand, we have to go beyond the word-level to define how a text has been translated, but, as we have seen, in dubbing, paralinguistic strategies produce parallel texts.

INTERPRETER-MEDIATED TV LIVE INTERVIEWS

Bistra Alexieva
St. Kliment Ohridski University of Sofia, Bulgaria

1. The Media and Interpreted-Mediated TV Live Interviews

The niche of interviews is expanding at a very rapid pace in all the media, but its vigour in terms of scope and variety seems to be enjoying the greatest boom in the electronic media space. What are the major reasons for it? Firstly, an interview provides audiences "with the feeling that they are sharing in the ever-evolving nature of current affairs" (Mulholland 1991: 98). And this is valid to the highest possible extent for TV live interviews, particularly for the Interpreter-Mediated (IM) events, because in them the dialogue takes place before the very eyes of the TV viewers, which creates a sense of spontaneity and credibility, much greater than in the case of previously translated programmes. Secondly, the greater credibility the IM TV live interview enjoys amongst viewers in Bulgaria today, is also due to the high social status of the interviewees, who are all eminent personalities from abroad, and from whose answers Bulgarian viewers can glean information about the way the world sees them. Therefore, this type of TV live interview can be assigned a more informative rather than an entertaining function (cf. Mulholland 1991: 105), a hypothesis which finds support in the answers elicited from viewers. The difficulties interpreters encounter in mediating TV live interviews suggest that it is necessary to study the specificity of this type of interlingual communication, with a view to identifying the more dangerous areas, and elaborating strategies for the optimisation of the process. The present attempt to attain this goal (based on 15 samples of interviews with English-speaking interviewees and one in German, and two enquiries amongst TV viewers) will focus on:

(1) The participants' status and role;
(2) The nature of the text, however with the focus not on the "What about", but on the "How", i.e. on the text building strategies, determined by the participants' goals;
(3) The setting and the mode of interpreting, and
(4) The interpreter's output.

2. Participants in Interpreter-Mediated TV Live Interviews

2.1 Two Sets of Primary Participants

One of the most important characteristic features of TV interpreting in general (Alexieva 1997a: 171-174) is that the interpreter is a mediator in two communicative channels, that is, between two sets of primary participants:
(1) The on-screen cast consisting of the primary interlocutors – interviewer and interviewee in our case, who alternatively perform the roles of speaker and addressee, and
(2) The off-screen cast, which consists of: firstly, the initiator – the TV channel via its programme managers, who are in fact responsible for the invitation of the interviewee, and secondly, the TV viewers, who are the final addressees of the performance of all the other participants.

2.2 Status and Role of the Participants

Another important feature of the type of IM TV live interview most frequently employed in Bulgaria now is related to the status and role of the participants in it. The people interviewed in these TV live programmes, as has been already mentioned, usually belong to the world elite, and the difference in social status and rank (relevant to the particular communicative situation at least) between interviewee and interviewer places certain requirements before the latter to strictly observe a number of verbal and non-verbal norms of behavior. Another reason for the need of strict observation of the politeness principle here (Grice 1975: 41-58) derives from the additional roles the primary participants acquire, namely: the interviewee, apart from playing the role of interviewed, is also a guest of the TV channel, especially invited to come to the studio, while the interviewer, apart from the task to do the questioning part, is also expected to play the role of host, because s/he is usually one of the leading journalists of the TV channel.

2.3 Participation of TV Viewers as Additional Interviewers

Direct participation of viewers in TV interviews is rather rare, much rarer than in radio interviews, the main reasons probably being of a technical nature. However, there might be other reasons as well, since it is the practice in the Sunday "Hotline" programme of Channel Two, in which the interviewees – mostly Bulgarian politicians – often become the target of a merciless crossfire from different quarters. And one of these reasons, in my view, is the guest-host relationship between interviewee and interviewer discussed above, which seems to prevent the host from exposing the guest to a volley of awkward questions.

3. Textual Parameters. Cohesion. Pre-Planning. Communicative Goals

As has been already pointed out, the "What about" of the text will not be discussed here for lack of reliable data, due to the great diversity of topics and the difficulties in handling the "shared knowledge" parameter, particularly in designing questionnaires for eliciting information about a person's knowledge. Therefore, the focus will be only on the "How", that is, on the way a text is made up, in terms of:
(1) The cohesion of the interview as a whole;
(2) The role of pre-planning and the semantic density and implicitness associated with it, and
(3) The goals of the primary participants, their involvement in the communicative act and the strategies they employ for its realization.

3.1 Cohesion

An interview is an asymmetrical dialogue (or an asymmetrical exchange, Macaulay 1996: 498-507), which can be described as a macro-text with a specific internal structure, because (a) it consists of micro-texts produced by two people; (b) the micro-texts are different in length, the questions usually being shorter, than the answer, and (c) the cohesion within each of its question-and-answer sequences is often different from the linking between the sequences themselves.

The fact that the macro-text is produced by two different people is responsible for the specific zig-zag linking between the sequences, which, in about 20 per cent of the samples, is employed by the interviewer as a topic-changing strategy. This is especially the case when the answer of the interviewee contains a word or a phrase (a mere slip of the tongue or part of some peripheral detail), which the interviewer can link with an issue s/he is desperate to ask about, but has not had the chance to do in a casual and non-aggressive way. In other words, if the interviewee mentions "X", the interviewer may snatch the opportunity and digress in a slightly different direction by asking about "X1", or "X2", or about any member of the "X-family" that can serve the purpose. Thus the cohesion between the micro-texts can be described mainly as lexical, with the near-synonym type (Halliday & Hasan 1976: 288) having the highest frequency. This lays additional traps for the interpreter, if the latter chooses a near synonym that may lead the discussion in an undesired direction (see 6.3).

3.2 Preliminary Planning

One of the most important features of a TV live interview derives from the fact that it is usually preceded by a pre-planning stage and the sketching of a scenario about most of the questions the interviewee will be expected to answer. Even if the primary participants do not have the chance to do any pre-planning together, the nature of their professions makes it plausible for us to presume that they probably rehearse their parts beforehand, working out alternative versions, trying to anticipate the moves of the other. The person who is in the most disadvantageous position is the interpreter, who has much less chance, if any, to know the real scenario in advance. The suggestion about the pre-planned nature of the interview finds supporting evidence in the recorded samples, which can be described as semi-improvised dialogues, with segments of a higher semantic density, a higher degree of implicitness, more formal lexis, a well measured degree of involvement often bordering on a surface neutrality, and a parsimonious use of non-verbal codes, features which are in full harmony with the goals of the primary participants.

3.3 Shared or Conflicting Goals

An interview can be defined as "a cross between a conversation and a legal cross-examination", says Mulholland (1991: 98). In the type of interviews we are discussing here, however, the "legal cross-examination" part of this definition appears in a highly mitigated form, due to the guest-host relationship between the two primary participants, which entails respect for the guest on part of the TV channel and its interviewer, observation of the principle of politeness, tolerance to otherness and avoidance of overt expression of hostility (cf. Baker 1997: 113-131). Another reason that may account for the tendency towards mitigation derives from a similarity in the intentions that the initiator and the on-screen primary participants seem to have with regard to the fourth participant – the TV viewers. The data suggest

that the two most important shared goals the former have with regard to the latter are:
(1) To build a good image of themselves, that is, to make a good impression on the audience by coping with their respective jobs in a tolerant and cooperative manner, with due respect for social status and role and without threatening the other's face, and
(2) To handle an exchange of different views in a constructive, yet unyielding way, avoiding overt expression of antagonism, and mitigating conflicts.

Beneath the surface however, the two interlocutors will always have conflicting goals, even if these derive only from the desire of the interviewer to receive an explicit answer which the interviewee does not want to give: conflict is the gist of the genre. What is important in our case, however, is that the avoidance strategies employed to disguise a conflict create additional difficulties for the interpreter.

4. Text-Building Strategies

Concerning the strategies and counter-strategies of interviewer and interviewee (see Mulholland 1991: 107-9), the data suggest that it will be more rewarding to study them in a polysemiotic perspective and identify the way the primary participants use language and non-language for the attainment of their pragmatic goals, namely:

(1) To conceal their involvement;
(2) To avoid overt expression of modality;
(3) To change the topic in a covert way;
(4) To undertake face-saving moves, and
(5) To employ the kinesthetic code in a parsimonious way.

4.1 Means to Conceal Participants' Involvement

As is well known, involvement is one of the parameters on the basis of which a text can be assigned a position on the orality-literacy scale (Shlesinger 1989: 10-25), and the greater the involvement of its author, the more spontaneous it sounds, and the closer it is to the orality end of the scale. Spontaneity, however, seems to be only a surface structure feature of an IM live interview, because, as has been pointed out, the latter is a fairly well planned exchange, which implies that the participants have ready-made moves for concealing their involvement if necessary. The most frequent strategems employed for the purpose are:

(1) Avoidance of 1st person singular when asking or answering a question, and use of 3rd person instead, with a subject of a more general nature, often referring to an indefinite group of people, e.g. "some (of)/one", "some/most people", etc.;
(2) Use of impersonal constructions, e.g. "There are those who might object to.../It's very unlikely that...", and
(3) Use of the passive in order to avoid explicit mention of agent, e.g. "It's been suggested that...".

4.2 Avoidance of Overt Expression of Modality

With regard to the degree of commitment to the truth of what the two participants say, the most frequent means of making a claim less categoric, thus leaving some space for manoeuvring, is the use of (1) verbs of the "seem" family; (2) adverbs and adverbial phrases such as "probably, (un)likely, by all appearances", etc, and (3) non-witness phrases of the model "X is said to have done Y/ X is quoted as saying", etc.

If these three major stratagems for covert epistemic modality are employed by both interlocutors, the implicit imperative type is more frequently resorted to by the interviewer because s/he is the one who asks the questions and insists on receiving an answer, while the interviewee's major purpose is to say only what s/he wants to say. The most frequent means the interviewer employs for softening the cross-examination nature of the interview can be summed up as follows:
(1) Mitigation of the questioning: the asking of a question is in itself a demand for an answer, therefore it is often mitigated by the "asking to ask" strategy (Macauley 1996: 491-509), e.g. "Would you please let me ask you about...". The asking can be still further mitigated by using an interrogative clause instead of a direct question, e.g. "After what you've just said I was wondering whether you would encourage investments in..."; and
(2) Avoidance of explicit imperatives: this tendency is even stronger and the samples abound with the following three major means of mitigating a demand:

(a) The "Let + me + bare infinitive" construction;
(b) Conditionals used as implicit imperatives (Alexieva 1986: 225; 233-4), e.g "It will be extremely interesting for our audiences if you could tell us more about...", and
(c) The use of questions, and tag-questions in particular, because the latter imply a kind invitation to the interviewee to supply the desired answer.

4.3 Change of Topic

It is much easier for interviewee to change topic without warning (Mulholland 1991: 108) by means of the well known pattern, "Yes, but may I first say something about...", a stratagem which does not create difficulties for the interpreter. The interviewer, however, is in a more delicate position, because the guest – host relationship does not allow her/him to overtly digress from the scenario, and the only way out is the use of subterfuges. The avoidance of overt change of topic, however, lays many and various traps for the interpreter. And this is particularly the case when resort is made to lexical repetition by means of near-synonyms ensuring the specific zig-zag cohesion of the macro-text discussed above, and allowing the interviewer to finally get the word on which to build her/his long-awaited question. One of these chains, for example, starts with the interviewee's mention of the more or less neutral phrase "a certain attitude to foreigners", a chance snatched immediately by interviewer who, with each new turn, increases its markedness in a negative direction (via the negatively marked "prejudice/lack of tolerance/ intolerance", etc.), and finally works her way to the heavily negative "xenophobia" and "racism".

4.4 Face-Saving Strategies

It may seem strange, but both participants engage in moves to save the face of the other, certainly in addition to what they do for saving their own. The explanation one may venture to suggest is that a face-redress operation to help your interlocutor is a show of good will that, in fact, may add to your own prestige. For example, the interviewee's failure to give a satisfactory answer is followed by a face-redress operation on the part of the interviewer (the Host), who uses apologetic phrases such as "Perhaps, I was too pressing with my questions / I shouldn't have insisted on so much detail... ", etc.

In this way the interviewer so to speak takes the blame upon her/himself, however in such an ostensibly "noble" way that the move, instead of redressing the face of interviewee for an unsatisfactory answer, adds a positive touch to the image of the interviewer.

The interviewee, too, may undertake such moves, knowing that saving the face of the other participant can be crucial to the success of the whole show. The need of remedial moves on the part of interviewee, for example, arises as a reaction to interviewer's compliment-fishing questions, such as "Do you like Bulgaria / Do you enjoy your stay here", which compel interviewee to give a positive answer. And if the latter does not feel like doing so, s/he may look for other ways of saving the face of interviewer for being tactless. For example, as a first reaction to the question "Do you know the names of any Bulgarian actors?", Lundgren (the actor) blurted out a "No", and then immediately added, as if by way of apology, "I don't know the names of any Swedish actors, either".

4.5 Parsimonious Use of the Kinesthetic Code

The tendency towards covert verbal strategies, discussed above, refers to the non-verbal component as well, and even to a greater extent. The non-language codes here play a lesser role as markers of implicit meanings because as a rule, the primary participants are people with great experience and perhaps even training for public appearances. Therefore one can hardly expect them to allow their body language to betray what they want to conceal. (Unlike on-the spot interviews, where interviewees can be caught off their guard, as for example, the way the smile disappeared from the face of Ann McGurk, the representative of the International Monetary Fund, when asked at her arrival, about the Fund's plans for restrictions on pay increase). That is why an interpreter in a TV live interview cannot rely on kinesthetics as a means of deciphering the speaker's intentions. Apart from that, the proxemic arrangement in the studio does not give the interpreter the chance to make use of two of the most important functions of eye-contact, namely the "Information-Seeking" and the "Channel Opened/Closed Signalling" functions.

Eye-contact is also relevant to the other two communicative channels, namely, between:

(1) interviewer and interviewee and
(2) the on-screen cast and the audience. The data suggest that body language and eye contact, together with the other visual codes (appearance, way of sharing the immediate space, etc.), determine, to a very great extent, the Trust/Distrust parameter, i.e. the degree to which the viewers may trust or distrust what is said.

5. The TV Live Interview Setting. Mode of Interpreting

5.1 The Setting

One of the major problems for the interpreter of this type of TV interview derives from the total lack of privacy, because s/he is in the studio, sitting at a desk on the right-hand side of interviewee, which means frequent appearance on the screen. This places tight restrictions on body language (facial expression, eye and hand movements in particular) and diminishes the possibility of using eye contact as an information-seeking device. The only non-language code the interpreter has the chance to use is interviewee's lip movements.

5.2 The Mode

Thus the setting and the dialogue form of the interview suggest that the best option in this case is conference interpreting (CI), which lends a more natural rhythm to the interaction. However, the shortage of time TV programmers always complain of, recommends simultaneous interpreting (SI) as less time consuming. But there are other factors which work against the choice of SI, and these are:

(1) The effect the mode of interpreting has on the Trust/Distrust parameter, and

(2) The time the two primary interlocutors have for making decisions about their next move, for which CI creates more favourable conditions.

Concerning the Trust/Distrust parameter, the data shows that the Bulgarian TV viewers want to hear the original wording, because this precludes manipulation via the interpretation. Therefore, the optimum choice for the direction "Foreign language → Bulgarian" is CI or voice-over, because they give the viewers the chance to follow both the original and the translation. However, enquiries point to CI as the more favoured mode, while SI proper (via which the viewers receive only the translation) is not well accepted. In the direction "Bulgarian → Foreign language", chouchotage seems to be the best option, because firstly, with regards to chances for public control, one can judge about the adequacy of the translation of the question from what follows (i.e. from the answer) and secondly, it saves time.

6. Inferences Concerning the Interpreter's Performance

The programmers' choice to include the interpreter in the visual component of the TV interview, and not only in the audial one as a disembodied voice, is highly appreciated by the TV viewers, as the enquiry shows. Being in the limelight, however, means greater stress, which often leads to a number of shifts (Shlesinger 1995: 193-214), diminishing the degree of approximation to the original. The samples suggest that there are areas where certain shifts – quite innocent at first glance – may easily turn into inadequacies hampering the felicitous realisation of the communicative act, inadequacies that give us the right to place the interpreter's output in such cases closer to the right-hand side of the "Shift-Inadequacy" scale.

6.1 Shifts in Prosody

It is interesting to observe that in almost all the samples the interpreters do not take notes. The strategy they resort to when they get afraid of forgetting the content of the segment is to slip into the simultaneous voice-over mode. This is particularly the case when the segments the interviewee offers vary much in length, which upsets the interpreter and diminishes her/his capacity to correctly predict the end of the turn. The resultant uncertainty affects the prosody of the final product, as if the expectation that "this can't be the end and there is certainly more to come" makes the interpreter finish every turn with a rising intonation, even such well marked statements as "I can't say anything about it" pronounced with a fall in English and a rise in the Bulgarian version. The "Rise → Fall" can be assessed as an innocent shift only if it is sporadic, as is the case in the larger part of the data. But in two of the samples the shift has such a high frequency (an average of 57%) that it turns into a noise in the channel, a jamming that places the interpreter's output on a position closer to the Inadequacy end of the scale.

6.2 Shifts in Lexis and Syntax

An interview is a spoken genre, but as has been already mentioned, it may contain portions that are pre-planned, or even rehearsed. The result is an interesting mixture of more formal syntax and lexis (in conformity with the public nature of the event), and of more everyday expressions employed to create the effect of spontaneity. In the conditions of great stress, however, the interpreter is not always in the position to preserve the exact ratio between the two, and the solution s/he most often resorts to is a shift towards more formal and emotively more neutral lexis and syntax. For example, a reference to Clinton's affair by means of the words "tryst" and "romance" in the English text is rendered in Bulgarian by more general and neutral terms; and direct speech is often transformed into indirect, a syntactic shift which lends a more formal flavour to the text. The data, however, show that unlike the other cases, shifts of this type do not create "noise" in either of the two communicative channels.

6.3 Shifts in Intertextual Cohesion

Too great a liberty, however, on the part of the interpreter in choosing amongst synonyms may lead to a communicative disruption, because, as is well known, differences between near-synonyms can be negligible in one context, and vitally important in another. For example, the interpreter's choice of a Bulgarian word with a slightly stronger negative load (e.g. "intolerance" instead of "lack of tolerance"), gave the interviewer the chance to use a word with a heavier negative load, which had an adverse effect on interviewee, who seemed unwilling to have the discussion propelled in such a direction. In another sample the translation of "the more or less fixed general image of what the Balkan nations are" in Bulgarian by what can be glossed back in English as "the stereotypical image of the Balkan nations", provoked a question on the part of the interviewer, containing the word "stereotype", and the English version of the latter produced a slight frown on the face of the interviewee, who was obviously reluctant to introduce the more marked word in the discussion. Therefore shifts of this type can be more precisely described as inadequacies which may substantially affect the pragmatic component and lead to break-ups in the channel.

6.4 Shifts in Implicitness

Another type of danger for the interpreter that may turn a shift into a blunder is associated with the primary participants' effort to avoid explicit expression of their involvement and commitment when necessary, particularly in the case of conflicting goals, and to resort to subtle face-saving strategies and a variety of mitigators for the different types of modality. For example, segments with a higher degree of implicitness in the rendering of disapproval signaled by words such as "unfortunately; to regret, express deep concern, doubt; to be disappointed, to be puzzled", etc., acquire an entirely different pragmatic meaning in the cases in which they are translated by means of explicit negative statements. Therefore here the rendering of implicit meanings in an explicit way is not a mere shift: it is an inadequacy that can have a disruptive effect on the interaction and may, in some cases, even induce a note of hostility.

6.5 Kinesthetic and Proxemic Shifts

If we consider the interviewee's performance and its rendering by the interpreter as polysemiotic texts (PSTs), we can expect them to differ in their non-verbal component, too, as well as in the way the latter complements the verbal one, because they are produced by two different people. In other words, we can expect certain shifts in the kinesthetics and proxemics of the original and in the interpreter's output affecting the intersemiotic cohesion and coherence of the PST (Alexieva 1997b). The study of the data shows that if the shift is in the direction of a more reserved sharing of the immediate space and a lesser kinesthetic markedness, the interpreter's output is a PST with a greater harmony between the verbal and the nonverbal components, that is, a PST with an acceptable intersemiotic cohesion and coherence, which can ensure an adequate response on the part of the audiences. And vice versa, a shift towards overuse of body language (facial expression, movements of the eyes/head/shoulders/hands, etc.) that is in striking contrast with a more moderate kinesthetic behavior on the part of interviewee, may lead to an intersemiotic dissonance, as a result of which the interpreter's PST cannot be assessed as an adequate reproduction of the original.

CONFERENCE INTERPRETERS ON THE AIR: LIVE SIMULTANEOUS INTERPRETING ON ITALIAN TELEVISION

Gabriele Mack
Università di Bologna, Italy

1. International communication and language transfer - some concepts of analysis useful for media interpreting

The nineties have been characterized by globalization on the one hand and diversification on the other in all areas of social activity – in economy as well as in communications. In the field of television, satellites and the decline of public broadcasting monopolies have led to a high differentiation of programmes and to a marked growth both in the national demand for and in the international exchange of TV productions. Yet, three main characteristics of mass communication, identified thirty years ago by Umberto Eco in *La struttura assente* (1968), still hold true: mass communication is a typical feature of industrial societies, it uses channels which can reach non-predefined groups of recipients with different social backgrounds, and it consists of messages made by producer groups using industrial production facilities.

Exchanges of TV programmes across linguistic borders require some kind of localisation in order to convey foreign language messages to local audiences; this can be carried out in different modes (for tentative systematisations see Hindmarsh & Luyken 1986 and Gambier 1994) by people with different professional profiles. The growing use of new terms such as *language transfer* instead of *translation* underlines the fact that linguistic, pragmatic and semiotic aspects of interlingual communication cannot (or at least should not) be looked at in isolation.

According to a functional approach, translations are the result of a series of decisions taken on various levels in a given situational framework. They are influenced by the norms recognised by a certain group at a particular time in a given place. Each translator/interpreter contributes to the perpetuation or change of existing norms with her/his work (Toury 1980 and 1995). Descriptive translation studies aim at studying both prescriptive norms and rules and those created by facts and practice, in order to better understand translation as a social phenomenon.

The categories mentioned above (undefined recipient groups; industrial production by teamwork and the concept of norms) can be used in order to establish a framework of analysis apt to cope with the specificity of interpreting for the media compared with traditional conference interpreting. In the following study, rules and requirements stated in literature for simultaneous TV interpreting are compared to the practical experience of some interpreters working for Italian television, with the aim of describing the current situation and anticipating future trends and research needs.

2. Interpreting on television: operational framework and requirements according to literature

Interpreting (sometimes called *live voice-over*) is increasingly used as a language transfer mode in Italian TV. According to Luyken & al. (1991) it is a so-called "revoicing" method, together with lip-sync dubbing, narration, free commentary and classical voice-over (i.e. a previously translated text, read by a professional speaker while the original sound is inaudible or reduced to a low level). These authors judge voice-over as a rather simple and fast transfer mode compared to dubbing - especially live voice-over, which can do without pre-recording or post-editing. Yet non-live broadcasting of programmes leaves scope for different realisation modes of simultaneous interpretation. The programme types eligible for interpreting are mainly concerned with information such as internationally broadcast summits, meetings and conferences, political statements, press conferences and parliamentary debates, but increasingly also with national TV productions in infotainment and confrontainment such as interviews, panel discussions, talk shows etc. A special programme category is that of media events (Dayan & Katz 1992), i.e. the live broadcasting of exceptional facts allowing people all over the world to take part in facts arousing particular public interest such as the first Apollo space missions, official visits (heads of state, the Pope etc.), funerals (Lady Diana), judicial proceedings (O. J. Simpson, B. Clinton) or big award ceremonies (the Oscars). Interpreting on TV is generally performed by conference interpreters using their traditional techniques - consecutive, simultaneous and chuchotage (or whispering) interpreting; yet, most authors underline the special difficulties arising from the particular working conditions in television (already mentioned by Pinhas 1972; see also Strolz 1997) which force the interpreter to adapt or even change her/his usual approach and strategies in order to cope with the specificity of this particular field of communication (Laplace 1997). This leads to the creation of completely new job profiles which also require an updating of traditional training practices (Kurz 1990, Dries 1994, Kaufmann 1995, Alcandre 1995).

One substantial difference between TV interpreting and conference interpreting is that the first is fitted into a much more complex and articulate setting than the second. The unity of time, space and action of a traditional conference situation is not given in television, where there is an off-screen cast (e.g. the TV audience and the initiator of the event or programme), and an on-screen cast involving a host of participants with different roles, functions and mutual relationships. The interactions within and between these two levels are quite complex and vary according to programme typology, but generally speaking, for the former there is only a very limited possibility to use a backchannel. Some members of the on-screen cast have the task of making the representation of reality captured by the camera accessible and comprehensible for the viewers while attracting their attention and keeping it alive. In the international media events on which this analysis is focussed, what is shown on-screen is usually mediated for the domestic TV audience by a commentator / presenter on the spot or in the studio and, if enunciations are made in a foreign language, sometimes by an interpreter (Balestrieri 1984). In other cases language transfer is also needed between the on-screen participants, not only for the secondary participants watching TV. All this is possible only with the help of sophisticated technical equipment and a high degree of labour division, involving many other people behind the scenes.

The presence of interpreters on TV can be dealt with by commentators / presenters in different ways. One extreme choice is to virtually ignore them: no mention at all is even made of their existence, neither by commentators nor in the running titles, efforts are made to make their work as unobtrusive as possible. The other extreme is to specifically mention and highlight their presence, putting, for example, the interpreter on the stage and exploiting his/her presence as a factor which contributes to the authenticity and even spectacularity of the TV event (Straniero 1999; see also Nishiyama 1988).

The peculiar difficulties of media interpreting identified in the literature, mainly by professionals, can be grouped into three main categories:

a) logistic problems (e.g. unusual working hours, short notice for assignments, deficiencies of technical equipment);
b) medium-related circumstances and requirements which can also have a psychological impact on the interpreter (such as lack of contact with speakers and of audience feedback, strict requirements on voice quality and speech presentation, the awareness that one's work is accessible to a huge public and that most listeners are unaware of the constraints of

simultaneous language transfer (a fact already underlined by an AIIC status report, Reddmann 1984) and thus not prepared for active, cooperative listening as conference audiences generally are);

c) stemming from all this, the potential need for supplementary processing strategies to meet special requirements (reduced décalage, i.e. time lag between the original speaker and the interpreter, request to let the audience hear the initial part of the original, increased attention on clear and simple wording, voice and presentation).

As far as prescriptive norms are concerned, the literature mostly offers descriptions of specific events, programmes or initiatives given by practising interpreters (e.g. the projects Apollo and Eurikon, single events in Germany, France and Austria; see among others Daly 1985, Bros-Brann 1993 & Kurz 1993). Authors mostly state what they consider important for TV interpreting according to their experience: maximum ease and intelligibility of the translation, a voice quality comparable to that of professional TV announcers, a very short décalage and close synchrony of text segments in source and target text (see Mizuno 1997 for a general overview). Other authors also mention the ability to manage the intersemiotic redundancy of the audiovisual message and coordinating words with the images (Alexieva 1997c), to autonomously prepare texts and to give supplementary information if needed so as to avoid ambiguity, as well as the capacity to deal with sophisticated technology and the readiness to cooperate with technicians and other TV operators (Kurz & Bros-Brann 1996).

Rather surprisingly, the requirements of TV producers and initiators of interpreting services and the perception of the audience as users of the interpreters product have been studied very rarely. Kurz (Kurz & Pöchhacker 1995 and Kurz 1996) carried out a series of studies designed to investigate the opinion of media interpreters and TV people in Germany and Austria about the quality requirements for interpreting in this field, using criteria which had already been used in earlier investigations into user perception in international conferences. Her main findings were that TV professionals tend to pay more attention to a pleasant voice and a fluent delivery rather than to completeness of content. Yet they rated sense consistency with the original message and logical cohesion as foremost objectives - exactly as conference participants and professional interpreters did in earlier studies. Most interesting was the fact that the judgement of media interpreters as to the ranking of the criteria proposed was practically identical with that of TV people. A couple of articles illustrate the pragmatic criteria applied to the selection of simultaneous interpreting by a bilingual TV station like ARTE (Moreau 1995).

These are, in broad overview, the state of the prescriptive norms for interpreting on TV covered in the relevant literature and some research findings. This picture was compared with the experience of some Italian media interpreters in order to identify hypotheses for future investigations in this field.

3. Live simultaneous interpreting on Italian TV: an exploratory inquiry

A small group of simultaneous interpreters who regularly work for public as well as private Italian TV stations were interviewed in order to analyse the extent to which the picture given above matches their personal experience. The following observations are focussed mainly on their interpreting for Oscar awards ceremonies and cannot be generalised, but the interviewees agreed that these observations do apply to the current practice of TV interpreting in Italy.

As to logistics, the notice for TV assignments tends to be very short even for events scheduled long before. If there is any preparatory documentation, the interpreters receive it with considerable delay and it is often incomplete. Very often interpreters have only a very rough idea of how the programme is going to proceed. Working hours frequently are unusual (early morning, late night), with long waiting periods before actual work. In most cases the interpreter goes on the air only for a few minutes, but there are also cases with virtually non-stop interpreting for hours (e.g. during the Gulf war or for the Oscar ceremonies). Generally there aren't any stand-by interpreters for emergencies, not even in the case of very important events. Studio equipment is often not comparable with standard conference equipment, owing both to different technical means and to the fact that interpreters are still looked upon as occasional actors in routine TV work. Only very few TV studios in Italy are equipped with interpreting booths, and even adequate headphones cannot always be taken for granted. Very often the sound input the interpreters receive is of extremely bad quality, hampered by breakdowns of satellite transmissions, disturbed by interference from other channels or even by the feedback of the interpreter's own voice.

While it is rather obvious that contacts with speakers thousands of miles away from the TV studios where the interpreter works are virtually impossible, surprisingly enough contacts, let alone cooperation, with the TV people on the spot seem to be extremely rare and difficult, mainly for reasons related to time planning and work schedules.

Sometimes recruiters of interpreters make their quality requirements quite explicit, but more often than not, substantial diversions both from these wishes and from traditional interpreting quality standards are imposed by prohibitive working conditions. Voice-matching is not a general rule, though it can be requested on special occasions even if it causes a heavy imbalance of workload within the team. The very first priority for television producers seems to be a natural sounding, continuous speech flow, produced by the interpreter under any given circumstances, not leaving any room for hesitations, let alone interruptions or self-corrections. Completeness and even sense consistency with the original seem to be considered as fairly secondary aspects, as long as the interpreter's output sounds coherent and plausible. Voice quality as such is not generally regarded as a selection criterion. Debriefings, appreciations of audience feedback or other kinds of quality control are apparently considered superfluous as long as the required smoothness and continuity have been reached.

As to interpreting itself, the peculiar working conditions described impose processing strategies that differ from those of conference interpreting. Little or no preparation for specific subjects tend to deter interpreters who are not prepared to rely heavily on improvisation; the awareness that there is no chance to have a second go must be dealt with successfully; absence of coordination and eye contact with other on-line speakers (journalists, moderators, sometimes even other colleges) can make turntaking very difficult and confusing; the often rapid pace of utterings requires as short a décalage as possible both at the beginning and at the end of an interpreted discourse; short interventions often leave the interpreter no time to warm up and become accustomed to a person's voice, accent and way of speaking, making anticipation more risky; inadequate monitor images further reduce predictability and bad sound quality can even make it impossible to hear parts of the discourse to be interpreted, imposing emergency strategies to fill in the gaps.

All these imponderables make the job of Italian TV interpreters extremely risky and stressful. According to all interviewees, the main characteristics required are strong nerves and an extreme flexibility as well as plenty of inventiveness in coping with the problems mentioned in a satisfactory way. Also teamwork between interpreters is less practicable than in a conference setting; everybody struggles to survive on his/her own, coping with situational constraints in order to make the best of it for him/herself, the producer and the audience. Apparently an often encountered dilemma is the impossibility under these conditions to respect the principle of the "honest spokesperson", mentioned by Harris (1990) as one of the universal norms in conference interpreting. Paradoxically, the interpreters' output tends to be judged not in relation to the original speaker's discourse, but to the presentation of other TV speakers who often read prepared texts. The interpreters interviewed thus admit that working for TV is often frustrating because of the impossibility to meet their interiorised quality standards, mainly related to sense consistency and completeness. For most of them, the sum of these aspects make TV interpreting an experience completely different from traditional conference interpreting, abiding to its own rules which each of them has had to learn on the job at her/his own risk.

4. Conclusions and suggestions for future research

A comparison of the two situations depicted above has led to the formulation of a series of reflections and hypotheses which, if substantiated by other surveys, could be pursued in future research in this field.

(1) The market for TV interpreting in Italy is growing and diversifying while there seems to be virtually no research into the requirements of initiators and recruiters and their selection criteria for interpreters. The same can be said about the Italian audience perception of interpreting on television. Such studies would be a prerequisite for developing specific training modules designed to qualify traditional conference interpreters for working with the media instead of leaving the selection process to sheer trial-and-error.

(2) In Italian TV at least, interpreting as a mode of language transfer seems to be considered as a secondary aspect not requiring any specific expertise except general language knowledge and sometimes experience acquired in the field; interpreters (at best) play a marginal role in programme planning and production, and they are generally also excluded from teamwork with TV people, a tendency encouraged by their status as free-lancers working mostly for intermediary agencies. Making TV producers and staff more knowledgeable about constraints and potential benefits of interpreting could have a positive effect both on working conditions and on the quality of overall results. This should possibly lead to a closer involvement of interpreters at an earlier stage of programme preparation (see in this respect the positive experiences described in Kurz 1986 and 1991).

(3) The interpreters' profession in Italy is presently confronted with radical changes affecting traditional job profiles. The trend towards greater subordination and improvisation might be opposed by claiming and defending a more autonomous and responsible professional role. This would also imply making a distinction between the loyalty to all communication partners, a loyalty which is traditionally guaranteed by qualified interpreters (the already mentioned "honest-spokesperson" principle), and the request for externally determined, potentially manipulative text production.

(4) This raises the question of decision-making at different levels and of the responsibility of individuals, professionals, companies and institutions involved in TV communication, the consumers of which are also citizens of the modern information society. Judging from the practice applied for TV interpreting in Italy, it seems that the specific problems of language transfer in TV communication are often ignored by the actual decision-makers who lack awareness in dealing with linguistic and cultural differences in TV discourse. More detailed analyses of and comparisons with interpreting practice abroad, e.g. within ARTE (Rozat 1995) or in Switzerland (Mona 1995), could perhaps contribute to awareness raising. Such a process is needed especially in public

service TV companies which cannot ignore the cultural dimension of their activity.
(5) This exploratory case study substantiates the hypothesis that Italian programme makers employing interpreters on the one hand, and those media interpreters, themselves on the other, refer to different norms when stating what interpreting is or should be in this context. Especially under extremely adverse working conditions, there seems to be a clash between the idea of the interpreter as a responsible mediator in intercultural communication, still sustained by most professionals, and the idea of the interpreter as an external contractor for subordinate language substitution – the latter being apparently predominant among Italian TV makers. In this respect a study of the historical evolution of norms for interpreting on TV could shed some light on ongoing and future trends.

TRANSLATION QUALITY
AN ORGANIZATIONAL VIEWPOINT

Eivor Gummerus & Catrine Paro
YLE Finnish Broadcasting Company Swedish Department,
TV Translations & Versioning
Helsinki, Finland

In this paper, we aim to discuss the impact of organizational design on screen translation quality. Our experience is that to ensure good quality, you need to focus on at least the following variables: criteria for the recruitment of translators (qualification, selection, testing), methods for and time-span of on-the-job training, continuing training, and revising and editing translations. Other factors affecting the translation quality are naturally the general working conditions (fees, tools, schedules, professional status etc.). In addition to these fairly evident variables, we want to stress the impact of organizational factors and management: How is the translation production organized? Is translation seen as an integral part of programme production? What is the position of the translators in the organization?

The structure of the paper is as follows: First we give a brief description of our organization and the work we do, followed by an outline of the development our translation department has undergone in the past ten years. Then we move on to a discussion on our views on translation quality and quality assurance, and an account of our methods of quality assurance, summarized as six steps of action.

1. Broadcasting for a language minority

We share a ten-year experience of working for the Swedish section (Finlands Svenska Television, FST) of the Finnish Broadcasting Company (YLE), both as in-house translators and editors, and as educators responsible for the recruitment and training of free-lance translators. Catrine Paro also has a four-year experience of managing the translation department. YLE currently has two national networks, TV 1 and TV 2, broadcasting about 7,000 hours annually. FST produces programming in Swedish for the Swedish-speaking audience in Finland (about 6 % of the population), and has an airing time of about 900 hours per year, divided on both national channels.

FST's organizational structure consists of five programme-producing departments (news & current affairs, sports, children's programmes, fiction and documentaries) and a department for acquisitions and co-productions. Since the beginning of 1998, the translation department has been an independent unit with the same organizational status as the programme-producing departments.

Out of the 900 hours of Swedish broadcasting, about two thirds are FST's own productions, and one third consists of imported programmes. Since one of FST's aims is to make its programming accessible not only to the Swedish-speaking population, but also to the Finnish-speaking language majority in the country, there is a general principle that as far as possible, Swedish programming should be translated into Finnish. In practice, this means that our department handles the translation of about 2/3 of FST's total programming, and we manage the translation both into Swedish and Finnish (roughly fifty-fifty). We do mainly subtitling, but also narration, and dubbing of animated children's programmes.

The FST translation department consists of one head of department, three co-ordinators with administrative duties (commissioning the translations, billing, technical checking of the material etc.) and seven in-house translators / editors. There are about 40 free-lance translators working on a regular basis for our department, plus a number of free-lancing actors and narrators.

2. Developing the translation department

2.1 Growth and rapid change

Over the last ten or twelve years, the FST translation department has faced a number of major changes. Translation volumes have trebled, production schedules have tightened, new technologies have transformed our everyday work, and both translators and viewers have become increasingly quality-conscious. In a sense, the situation at FST seems to reflect, on a micro level, what is happening in the field as a whole: As the TV industry grows more and more international, issues of language transfer can no longer be overlooked as secondary to programme production, or they will turn into major problems. Our hope is that a case study of FST, because of its bilingual sphere of action, can serve to illustrate the relationship between translation management and translation quality.

Broadcasting its Swedish language programming in fixed slots on the national YLE channels, FST has a long history of subtitling its programmes into Finnish for reasons of goodwill. Until about ten years ago, it was a question of only two or three programmes a week, but when translation was computerized, it became possible to subtitle an increasing part of the FST productions. Costs, however, still kept the output at a fairly modest level.

In 1993, however, the picture changed. There was a channel reform in Finland, which coincided with the appearance of dozens of cable and satellite channels, at a time when the economic recession was at its worst. Such was the political climate, that competition for viewers grew very fierce, and even national public-service broadcasters had to start looking to their laurels. "How can we defend publicly funded television, if nobody is watching it?" went the argument.

In FST's case, it meant Finnish subtitling wherever possible, and beyond. As the subtitling of FST's own production increased, so did the distress signals that the translation department received from the translators: "The schedules are so tight that we can't do our job properly"; "They keep putting captions at the bottom of the screen, interfering with the subtitles"; "I got an earful of abuse when I asked the reporter how his interviewees spell their names" etc.

Until then, most of our programme producers and journalists had been used to addressing mainly a monolingual audience. Only a few of them had ever had to allow for translation in their schedules, or reflect on where to put their captions. At the translation department, we had mainly been dealing with foreign programming, completed somewhere else, in plenty of time, and it had hardly ever occurred to us to try to get a word in edgeways at the production stage. We had no history of taking part in programme planning, or offering our advice on relevant issues.

Suddenly, we had to lift ourselves by our bootstraps; first, to realize that translation can actually be taken into account in the planning of a TV production; secondly, to realize that when it comes to crossing language barriers on television, we were the experts; and thirdly, to make our programme producers realize the same.

2.2 Enforced co-operation

Like in so many other aspects of life, the problem bore the seed of its own solution. Only because there were problems co-operating with the programme producers did we in earnest start to reflect on how to establish co-operation with them. They, of course, would stand no nonsense from translators telling them how to do their job. In order to carry weight with them, we had to start by educating ourselves, defining and developing our knowledge, and learning to explain what we do and why. Furthermore, if we demanded more favourable working conditions for our translators, we had to ensure our ability to offer translation quality in return.

Only a few years before the channel reform, we had set up a reviewing system at the translation department. Before that, translators were usually left to their own devices after their introduction to the job, consisting of feedback sessions on their first two or three translations. Not surprisingly, the reviewing system revealed that standards varied greatly amongst our translators, and that a certain amount of further training was needed. Also, as we lacked sufficient resources for an all-embracing reviewing system, we had to pay special attention to the recruiting and training of new free-lancers, making sure of quality from the beginning.

Recruiting can be quite a challenge, because there are very few formally trained translators, especially among the Swedish speakers in our country. If you want to study translation on an academic level in Finland, you have to do it in Finnish, which might not be the first thing that springs to mind if you want to work in Swedish.

This does not mean that we do not have very competent and professional translators, but most of them have studied something else, and learnt their trade on the job. They lack the formal knowledge that would help them analyse, assess and discuss their work, and they lack the support of academic research in their own field.

For want of trained translators, ready to pick, we have found ourselves looking for people with vast experience as translators, or as writers; testing their knowledge and skills thoroughly, and training them ourselves.

For further training, we place a lot of trust in the "greenhouse effect" provided by an in-house translation department. We encourage discussion and co-operation between free-lancers and in-house translators, emphasizing the importance of the reviewing system as a means of education, rather than mere quality control. About once a year, we arrange a screening or seminar focussing on some aspect of screen translation, like subtitling rhythm or text linguistics.

Although our recruiting and training have improved considerably, our co-ordinators, assigning a job, still face a colourful array of translators with very different backgrounds, skills and levels of knowledge. This, of course, is a great advantage, as topics on television tend to vary considerably. But it also means that somebody who is brilliant at a certain type of programme might make a complete mess of things if given the wrong kind of job.

Our co-ordinators also have to monitor overall employment among the free-lancers. Many of our free-lancers work only part-time as translators, whereas others rely entirely on working for FST, and everybody should be kept suitably busy. Also, translators of languages less frequently needed should be given opportunity to keep up their skill, translating from another language, usually English. In this sense, we are constantly walking a tightrope between not having enough people to get the jobs done on the one hand, and on the other, losing people we have trained to other employers.

To keep track of all this diversity, the co-ordinators should really have the training and experience of senior translators themselves, to evaluate the difficulty of each assignment and the competence of each translator. In practice, though, we have found that we cannot have translators tied down to a full-time job of co-ordination. A translator needs to translate to keep his pencil sharp, and a rotating system, for instance, would not work, because continuity is so important, especially in creating good relations with the programme-producing departments.

The answer, so far, seems to be constant co-operation between the co-ordinators and the in-house translators, where the translators help to assess the tasks, and, as reviewers, report back to the co-ordinators about the individual skills, strengths and weaknesses of the free-lancers.

2.3 Making translation visible

When it comes to "educating" our programme-producing colleagues, we have adopted a policy of generally making the translation department more visible within FST. For a few years now, we have distributed our monthly newsletter, primarily aimed at our free-lancers, to all FST employees; we make a point of nominating translated programmes for FST's annual "best programme" award, and so on. However, the lion's share of the job is done by individual translators and co-ordinators, co-operating with individual producers and journalists on a daily basis.

It has not always been easy, because in many cases, producers and journalists must have felt the translators to be trespassing on their creative freedom with their demands or suggestions, or just being a general nuisance. But on the whole, they seem nowadays to appreciate our contributions to their programmes, and most of them really try to ensure smooth co-operation with the translators, offering background information and assistance with proof-reading, for instance, and taking a general interest in the translation of their programmes.

The management, too, seems to have gained greater understanding for the role of translation in overall programme quality. Here, we have certainly been helped by the fact that we work in a language minority setting. Language, of course, is of special importance to FST, as are issues of quality, because of limited airing time; we cannot afford to broadcast rubbish.

In 1997, the improved profile of the FST translators was formally acknowledged when the translation department was given the same organizational status as the programme-producing departments. Before that, we were subordinate to Programme Acquisitions. This rise might prove important, because earlier, we have had something of an uphill struggle, trying to make our voice heard in the organization. Already, we can see the benefits of having a more direct line to the management. Getting things done and decisions made has become easier.

Of course, our department is still far from perfect. Developing it is very much an ongoing process, and at times a very painful one, with enormous pressures on the individuals involved. Still, it is also rewarding, and as a team, we have reached a new level of professionalism – soon to be challenged, however, by the advent of digital broadcasting and all the new technology and increase in volume that *that* entails.

Let us now try to summarize the main lessons in translation quality control that we have learned through the development described above. But before we move on to the concrete steps of action to be taken, let us linger for a while on a few matters of principle and the basic conditions for good translation quality.

3. Defining translation quality

3.1 Focus on the viewer

First of all, an important question to be considered when dealing with translation quality is: What do we mean by quality? Quality from whose point of view? Who defines quality? The viewer, the translator(s), the reviewer, the translation department, the broadcasting company, the researchers or teachers in the field (the list could be made longer) – or is it the film producer's or director's intent and interest that should be the decisive factor in judging screen translation quality?

When our team talks about translation quality, we tend to take the view that quality refers to the total viewer experience and the translation's role in or contribution to it. Consequently, when we assess translation quality, we very often express it in terms of whether or not the translation functions or "works" in its audiovisual context. What we are looking for could also be expressed in terms of *functional adequacy*, and we sometimes use terms such as *optimal and minimal quality*, to stress the fact that we are dealing with a relative, not an absolute concept.

3.2 Quality is the result of a joint effort

Secondly, when our team talks about quality control/assurance, we tend to refer to organizational matters as well as e.g. merely the revising of translations. We take the view that every step in the translation production process is important from a quality point of view. To ensure good quality, we need to make sure that everybody involved in the production process are aware of their role in it, and that they have the skills and the means to do a "quality job". Although the individual translator bears the responsibility for the quality of his own work, we want to stress the fact that ultimately the responsibility for good translation (and programme!) quality lies with the company commissioning the translation (broadcasting the programme). Translation quality is thus not only a matter of the competence of the individual translator, but a result of good co-operation between all the people involved in the production process: on the one hand, the programme producers and the journalists, and on the other, the co-ordinators, the reviewers and the translators. In other words, translation quality is seen as the result of a joint effort and the keyword is co-operation.

3.3 Quality based on a solid infrastructure

Thirdly, there are a great deal of factors affecting translation quality that reach beyond the control of the translation department, or even the broadcasting company as a whole. We are referring to the general working conditions of professional translators.

In Finland, we are fortunate in having a very active translators' association (Suomen kääntäjien ja tulkkien liitto, SKTL), which has worked vigorously for the rights of the screen translators almost since the first TV translations appeared on the screen. Consequently, the terms of contract for free-lance screen translators in Finland are among the best in Europe. SKTL's section for TV-, film- and video translators, established in 1970, has also ensured that there is a long tradition of common translation conventions and norms among the professional screen translators. SKTL takes an active interest in the further education of screen translators, co-operating among other things with the adult education departments of the universities. Translation as a discipline has been taught in Finland since 1966, and on an academic level since 1981.

The "greenhouse effect" among the screen translators as a professional group is, in our experience, at least as important as the greenhouse effect within FST's translation department. On the whole, it is our view that the translators' professional awareness has a lot to do with the quality they produce in their work.

The Finnish translators' association is, however, facing quite a challenge at present through the emergence of new commercial subtitling companies on the market. These companies tend to offer lower fees than YLE, for instance, and they might very well turn out to threaten the unity of professional conventions and standards in the field, unless the newcomers are made aware of the importance of this tradition. The risks are all the greater, since the translators' association functions on a basis of voluntary work, and it is a continuing struggle to find people willing to put in the time and the effort to further the common interests.

Yet, on the whole, one can justifiably say that there is a functioning infrastructure in the field of translation in Finland, and this constitutes a solid foundation for companies, as well as for individual translators to build on. In FST's case, there is a lot to be gained through this infrastructure. It is also true, however, that the minority language position is reflected in this, as in so many other social contexts in Finland. There are, for instance, very few translation courses offered in Swedish, the translators' association offers most of its services only in Finnish, there is no university training for translators in Swedish, etc. Therefore, our department has been forced to – or rather, we have had the advantage of having to – focus on matters of quality assurance to a much greater extent than our Finnish colleagues, even within the same company.

Let us now move on to a more detailed description of how our department at present tackles the issue of translation quality assurance.

4. Lessons learnt on Translation Quality Assurance

4.1 Step one: Start an in-house translation unit

First of all, the basis for good translation quality at FST has been laid through the decision to have an in-house translation department, with a responsibility to guarantee and monitor translation quality. Every once in a while, the question has been raised within YLE whether or not the translation services should be outsourced. At the moment, this is not an option for FST, since there are almost no other employers in the field of screen translation into Swedish in Finland.

4.2 Step two: Pay special attention to requirements of competence when recruiting translators

Since there are no self-evident, formal qualifications that we can demand of our applicants (e.g. a university degree in translation studies), we have – mostly through trial and error – developed an aptitude test package to test the following skills:

(1) productive competence in the mother tongue: written test, summary of a newspaper article,
(2) translation skills: two written tests, both requiring some adaptation for the intended audience and purpose of the translation,
(3) "listening comprehension" skills in the foreign languages: literal translation from audio tape,
(4) motivation: short subtitling task from videotape with the aid of written instructions.

We also require a long experience in the field of translation, and we have found that a higher university degree in languages, or any other field for that matter, is important as an indicator of the applicant's maturity. Furthermore, familiarity with various computer systems is an absolute must.

4.3 Step three: Provide thorough training on the job

In our experience, it takes between six and twelve months for a beginner – even for an experienced translator – to gain the necessary routine and confidence in screen translation, mainly due to all the technology and the spotting techniques involved, but also because of the great diversity of the translation tasks.

We usually start off with a one- or two-day crash course. The first exercise often consists of intralingual subtitling, i.e. subtitling from Swedish into Swedish or Finnish into Finnish, which we have found to be an effective way of demonstrating the timing (spotting) and compressing techniques. After that, the beginner is assigned a personal tutor for the next six months or more, depending on the candidate's progress.

4.4 Step four: Pay special attention to the commissioning stage

In our experience, it is crucial that the translator, accepting a task, is fully aware of what the task consists of and what is expected of him or her. This applies not only to the contents of the translation, but also to the overall broadcasting policy and aims of FST and YLE as a whole (minority culture and language interests, public broadcasting responsibility etc.). It is also extremely important that the translators are aware of their individual strengths and weaknesses, so that they can refuse unsuitable tasks.

In this context, we want to emphasize the role of the co-ordinator: The person commissioning a translation should be aware of the special demands of the task (special terminology, songs, poems, wordplay, jokes, high-speed dialogue, or any other features that have an impact on the level of difficulty). The co-ordinator should also be familiar with the individual translators' competence and special talents, so that the right job can be assigned to the right person.

4.5 Step five: Make sure that the "production line" works smoothly

Oiling the machinery is a very important part of quality assurance. In our case, this has meant going over every step in the production process, improving co-operation with the programme-producing departments, maintaining good contacts with the foreign television companies and distributors, looking over the working routines of our co-ordinators and arranging additional training for them, improving communication with the free-lancers (newsletter etc.), co-operating with the YLE computer engineers in developing new subtitling software, and in every possible way improving the communication between all parties involved.

4.6 Step six: Establish a reviewing system

We have had a reviewing system operating for 7-8 years now, where the in-house translators take turns, one week at a time, revising translations, and helping the free-lance translators with advice and assistance in practical and technical matters as well. We always review a translation in its completed form, i.e. the spotted version in its audiovisual context. We regard reviewing to be one of our most important means of not only educating the translators further, but also of monitoring the general level of competence among our translators and spotting needs for courses and screenings.

Unfortunately, our department lacks the resources to review all the translations, and since all our in-house translators are Swedish-speaking, the reviewing of the Finnish translations has also lagged behind. We are now starting an experiment where Finnish-speaking free-lance translators are paid to do reviewing one day a week.

5. Water the plants in your greenhouse

All the above steps of action will, in an ideal world, create a “greenhouse effect”, i.e. an atmosphere of co-operation and understanding, where all parties involved, through their individual efforts, work for a qualitative end result. The belief, often repeated, that translation is solitary work for lone wolves who sit in their chambers, buried under dusty dictionaries and piles of paper, is no longer valid in the age of modern technology. Increasingly, translation is based on team work, and the translator’s role in the production of a film or a TV programme is becoming increasingly versatile, changing from a mere post-editing function to consulting work in the planning stage of a production. And this is as it should be, when (multi-) media products are designed to be distributed over linguistic and cultural boundaries, and multilingualism is becoming not an exception, but the rule, in the dawning of the digital era.

QUALITY DOWN UNDER

Felicity Mueller
SBS Corporation,
Sydney, Australia

1. SBS Subtitling and Language Services

I am a German subtitler and editor of subtitles with Subtitling and Language Services at the SBS Corporation in Sydney, Australia, where we subtitle for television and work primarily into English.

Our subtitles are yellow and are easily visible against any background. Because they are for television, they are relatively large. Australians from a variety of backgrounds are very fond of *Derrick*, our 3rd most popular programme for many years. It does not present too many challenges to the subtitler, as Derrick and Harry and all the actors speak slowly and clearly with frequent repetitions. For this reason, *Derrick* has been useful for testing and training new subtitlers.

The principal function of the SBS Corporation is to provide multilingual and multicultural radio and television services that inform, educate and entertain all Australians and in doing so, reflect Australia's multicultural society. SBS Radio was established in 1975 and SBS Television in 1980. The broadcasting of subtitled films from around the world has always been an integral part of SBS Television.

Since its inception in 1980, SBS Subtitling and Language Services has developed its skills to a high level. It employs 26 subtitlers (13 full-time, 13 part-time) and 10 editors (5 full-time, 5 part-time) as well as contract staff to work on films from over 60 countries in well over 100 languages and dialects. We subtitle and produce renarrated scripts primarily into English, although Language Services does a great deal of voiceover work into other languages, primarily Asian languages. In such an environment, quality standards are essential. How do we go about producing quality subtitles and what standards are in place?

A subtitle can only be as good as the person who prepares it, so the first part of this paper will deal with the standards developed by SBS Subtitling and Language Services for the selection, training and monitoring of subtitlers and editors of subtitles. The second part will attempt to answer the vexed question of what is quality in a subtitle and how it (or, more likely, the lack of it) is recognised.

2. Standard Procedures

2.1 Selection criteria for subtitlers

The selection criteria for subtitlers include native-speaker level aural comprehension of all registers of the source language, a high degree of written facility with English, a wide vocabulary in both languages, sound general knowledge and bicultural skills. Tertiary qualifications, preferably gained in the source language, and experience in subtitling or related work, such as translation and interpreting, teaching or writing, are desirable but not essential.

100% comprehension is absolutely essential. It includes all varieties of slang, cultural references, half-finished sentences, body language, irony, puns, etc.

With the German film *The Boys,* subtitled by SBS for the Berlin Film Festival, even though our native German subtitlers had lived in Australia for many years, they realised that they needed help from two sources: people who grew up in Australia and young city-dwelling Germans (preferably just off the plane) familiar with drug terminology, etc. The ability to recognise one's limitations is, to my mind, absolutely essential in any translator, but particularly in a subtitler.

Lack of knowledge of the cultural context can also cause problems. In an Australian film set in lush rural Victoria, one character comments on the beauty of the scenery, saying "This looks just like a Bunny". The subtitler, after having a good look and failing to see any rabbits hopping about on screen, decided it must be a reference to Bugs Bunny and subtitled it accordingly. What the subtitler did not realise was that Rupert Bunny is an early 20th century Australian landscape painter. This is yet another example of the need for input from native speakers of the source language and persons familiar with its culture.

Excellent idiomatic English expression, both oral and written, is almost as important as comprehension of the source language. In order to condense well, subtitlers must have a large range of vocabulary to choose from and must be able to differentiate between subtle nuances suggested by the editor.

The personal qualities required are maturity, clear and logical thinking, reliability, initiative, perseverance, thoroughness, cooperativeness and flexibility. A subtitler needs to be able to work under pressure, to a schedule, with the minimum of supervision and both alone and as a member of a team.

2.2 Recruiting

Up to about 1996, new subtitlers were recruited for ongoing work by testing a large number of candidates (sometimes up to 150) in an audio translation test, and then giving the top candidates a 5-hour subtitling aptitude test. Successful candidates were then interviewed and those found suitable were included on our panel. This was complex, expensive and, as it was the public service, extremely slow. Many excellent candidates had disappeared into thin air by the time they were found suitable for training.

All new subtitlers are now on contract. They are selected according to the needs of the schedule from those who send us an appropriate CV and, if need be, from a directory of accredited translators and interpreters. Compared with the previous method, we have found the quality of the candidates to be similar and the process to be much cheaper and more efficient, as the initial time-consuming culling of unsuitable candidates has been eliminated.

2.3 Training

We have two senior subtitlers who recruit, train and monitor new subtitlers. An experienced subtitler sits with the trainees, first subtitling with them for about two hours and then checking every subtitle at regular intervals. Their linguistic performance and subtitling progress is evaluated constantly. This continues for a minimum of three months.

Then a progress report (Appendix 1) is prepared, rating criteria such as expertise in the source language, facility with English, technical skills, general knowledge and editability from excellent to unsatisfactory. It is then possible to pinpoint further training needs. The points covered in the progress report can, I believe, be taken as quality standards to assess a subtitler.

Obviously, those who meet the exacting standards will continue to be asked to work; others will not. We believe that someone who satisfies the selection criteria mentioned above and then gains an excellent result in the progress report has the potential to become a proficient subtitler. It takes much longer to develop real skill in the art of subtitling.

2.4 The subtitler does not work in a vacuum.

As well as an excellent library of monolingual and bilingual dictionaries and reference books and access to the Internet, we have a Subtitling Manual and a Style Guide which provide essential information for subtitlers and editors (see brief excerpts in Appendices 2 and 3).

In addition, in the major languages, we have a mixture of native speakers of the source language and native English speakers fluent in that language who can and do consult one another constantly. We believe that this interaction can lead to complete understanding of the original utterance and the meaning underlying it (thus avoiding the Rupert Bunny problem I just mentioned) and also to finding the best possible equivalent in the target language.

2.5 The editor's role

The editor is a native English speaker who does not generally know the source language. Selection is on the basis of a practical test in editing subtitles. The main selection criteria are demonstrated professional ability in either editing subtitles or editing books or periodicals; excellent command and understanding of English in formal and colloquial registers and the ability to write in a wide range of styles and command of idiom and spelling.

The editor is given a subtitled script, and looks at the programme from the viewer's perspective, checking the sense, grammatical, lexical and semantic correctness, flow and general readability of the subtitles. This may include changing time codes, additional condensing or even pointing out nuances of meaning (from visual cues) which the subtitler may have missed.

In the unedited subtitles for the Taiwanese film *Rebels of the Neon God*, lack of quality is evident in poor timing, poor legibility, poor blocking, lack of flow, inappropriate slang, overcondensing, failure to comprehend the original or to recognize a reference, failure to convey humour or irony and lack of response to visual cues. These may distract discerning viewers from enjoying the programme, which is, after all, their main purpose. Therefore, anything that makes viewers do a double-take should be avoided.

One example is the subtitle "Can you pass water?", said, not by a urologist talking to a patient after an operation, but by an ordinary person asking for a glass of water. Linguistically it is not incorrect, but it is inappropriate to the context. It was clearly written by someone whose command of English was limited and was almost certainly not edited.

We believe that this editing process and the subsequent "conference" between subtitler and editor constitute one of the main factors contributing to the quality of SBS subtitles. Depending on the complexity of the programme, the "conf" can range from 2 minutes to many hours.

In multilingual films and in an increasing number of documentaries, the editor's role is significant. Individual subtitlers do their sections, and the editor is called upon to put them all together in a unified stylistic form.

3. What is quality in a subtitle?

These procedures all work well, as far as they go. However, there is far more to quality in subtitles than external standards. The quality of subtitles is not like that of microchips or stages in the management of an engineering project, which can be totally standardised. It is at its best when the subtitles are not even noticed. Good subtitles are unobtrusive - we would really prefer it if nothing came between the viewer and the film:

> Ultimately, the aim is to fashion subtitles which are attuned so thoroughly to their audiovisual environment that they appear to "melt" into the total fabric of the programme. By making the linguistic sign as unobtrusive as possible, the very best subtitling seeks to foster the illusion of unmediated comprehension on the part of the viewer. When an audience stops being aware of reading the subtitles, the subtitler has achieved a major goal. In effect, the material substance of the subtitles shrinks and vanishes before our very eyes, leaving only the message. (McCormick 1997: 5)

By its very nature, unobtrusiveness is difficult, if not impossible to measure and is thus hardly suitable as a quality standard. Quality in subtitles is not easy to define - its absence is far more noticeable than its presence, as I have illustrated above

4. Conclusion

Quality in subtitling as seen by SBS comes from a combination of measurable standards for the judicious selection, training and monitoring of the best possible candidates and more subtle standards which are virtually impossible to measure but the absence of which is obvious.

Appendix 1

PROGRESS REPORT (Trainees)

1) Expertise in original language

Aural ability to comprehend original language
• unsatisfactory • adequate • good • excellent

2) Facility with English

Ability to write idiomatic English
• unsatisfactory • adequate • good
• excellent

Ability to translate into idiomatic English
• unsatisfactory • adequate • good
• excellent

Ability to choose the appropriate register
• unsatisfactory • adequate • good
• excellent

Ability to condense while maintaining the narrative flow
• unsatisfactory • adequate • good
• excellent

Range of vocabulary
• unsatisfactory • adequate • good
• excellent

Spelling
• unsatisfactory • adequate • good
• excellent

3) Technical skills

Timing
• unsatisfactory • adequate • good
• excellent

Blocking
• unsatisfactory • adequate • good
• excellent

Line breaks
• unsatisfactory • adequate • good
• excellent

Punctuation
• unsatisfactory • adequate • good
• excellent

Attention to detail
• unsatisfactory • adequate • good
• excellent

4) Processing skills

Data entry expertise
• unsatisfactory • adequate • good • excellent

Ability to provide PPU with the appropriate information
• unsatisfactory • adequate • good • excellent

Ability to provide Censorship with the appropriate information
• unsatisfactory • adequate • good • excellent

Ability to provide appropriate details on the information sheet
• unsatisfactory • adequate • good • excellent

5) Background

General knowledge
• unsatisfactory • adequate • good
• excellent

Ability to research
• unsatisfactory • adequate • good
• excellent

6) Editability

Ability to explain idioms occurring in the original language
• unsatisfactory • adequate • good • excellent

Ability to discriminate between various suggested translations
• unsatisfactory • adequate • good • excellent

Ability to distinguish between nuances of meaning in English
• unsatisfactory • adequate • good • excellent

7) Ability to work as a team member

Willingness to work with other colleagues
• unsatisfactory • adequate • good
• excellent

Willingness to cooperate with others in problem-solving
• unsatisfactory • adequate • good
• excellent

Willingness to accept direction
• unsatisfactory • adequate • good
• excellent

Ability to train new members of staff
• unsatisfactory • adequate • good
• excellent

8) Reliability

Conscientiousness
• unsatisfactory • adequate • good
• excellent

Productivity
• unsatisfactory • adequate • good
• excellent

Punctuality
Ability to work to the schedule
• unsatisfactory • adequate • good
• excellent

Ability to work unsupervised
• unsatisfactory • adequate • good
• excellent

Ability to work unsupervised
• unsatisfactory • adequate • good
• excellent

Appendix 2

From *SBS Style Guide:* "Slang"

Do not use Australian, American or other slang in contexts where it would jar *or* make sure it suits the style and period of the programme

Appendix 3

From *SBS Subtitling Manual:*

COMMAS

1. In general, punctuate lightly, consistent with keeping the sense clear. Commas can often be dropped at the ends of blocks.
2. Use the vocative comma; its omission can cause confusion or unintended vulgarity: "What's up Fred?" Use it also when the vocative comma begins the block: "Fred, what's up?"

QUALITY CONTROL OF SUBTITLES: REVIEW OR PREVIEW?

Heulwen James
Subtitle Editor, Testun,
Cardiff, Wales, UK

> A person who reads a book in translation or sees a dubbed film must go to the original text to check what they suspect is a faulty translation… The subtitler is in a much more vulnerable position [than the translator] since the original is available for all to see and hear.
>
> Jan Ivarsson, 1992.

1. Quality control to meet clients' expectations

Anyone who has ever subtitled a television programme or a film will know that trying to create a file of perfect subtitles is a neverending challenge. Besides, perfection may be interpreted differently from one client to another. The product is the subtitle, but there is no one particular client. The subtitling industry is anything but a straightforward business. Different clients have different expectations.

The author or scriptwriter, whose original script has been converted into subtitles, would expect his or her intentions to be reflected accurately and authentically. Whether the intention is to entertain, inform or do both, the author or the scriptwriter of a soap opera or a detective series would expect the subtitles to present a credible portrayal of the action and the characters; the scriptwriter of a documentary or a news bulletin would expect the subtitles to present the facts as plainly as possible. But the script is only a part of the picture.

The manner in which a programme or film has been produced has an impact on the subtitles. Long camera shots and few changes of speaker, will result in longer length subtitles. Here, the subtitler is able to create his or her own rhythm of appearance and disappearance of subtitles. Short camera shots, a fast-moving dialogue and frequent speaker changes will result in shorter subtitles of a shorter duration and the subtitles will be constrained by timecoding conventions relating to shot cuts. A producer will expect subtitles which are not only accurate and authentic but which are in keeping with the rhythm of the dialogue.

The broadcaster of the subtitles will have its own technical requirements for the transmission of subtitles. For instance, in Teletext subtitling, it is expected that the subtitles file carries the appropriate holding captions, cue dots and subtitles credit caption.

Of all the clients, viewers and their expectations are the most important. A viewer must be able to follow the subtitles with ease and be able to have faith in their contents. Subtitles should be correct, clear, credible and give the impression of being part of the action on the screen. Above all, the viewer should enjoy following a subtitled programme or film in such a way that the subtitles form a natural part of the action. In order to help achieve these aims, subtitling conventions are intended to provide guidelines to ensure consistent high quality. These conventions (relating to timecoding, duration of subtitles, shot cuts and formatting) must be respected in the same way as the principles of subtitling - reduction of original dialogue, simplification of language, character portrayal, cultural adaptation, and so on, must be respected.

In addition, the product must seek to satisfy the expectations of the other clients. This is not always an easy task. Clients' differing expectations may oblige the subtitler to make choices or to compromise between one subtitling principle or convention and another. A scriptwriter may consider character portrayal more important than correct grammar. A producer may consider correct grammar more important than character portrayal. The subtitler may have had to choose between, say, character portrayal and correct grammar, reduction and effective cultural adaptation or descriptive detail and adequate duration on screen.

The purpose of such a thorough type of quality control is therefore not only to eliminate routine errors, to ensure that the "product" (the subtitle) meets the requirements of specific criteria (subtitling conventions) and to reduce the potential for perceived errors. A thorough quality control also seeks to ascertain whether or not the subtitles satisfy the different expectations of the clients.

2. Quality control: review or preview?

Quality control arrangements vary from one country to another and from one broadcaster to another. From the perspective of the subtitle editor, quality control can range from a spellcheck to a preliminary reading or preliminary viewing of the subtitles to implementing the amendments directly onto the screen.

A spellcheck could be termed as the most elementary form of quality control. A spellchecker is an useful tool but it cannot detect all types of spelling errors. Words which are spelt correctly but which appear in an incorrect context remain undetected, e.g. *your* and *you're*, *sum* and *some.* Neither will it detect proper nouns, titles, foreign language words etc. Additional manual checking of the spelling of proper nouns and unusual words is a necessity. A quality control exercise based solely upon a spellcheck is totally inadequate.

2.1 Preview

A preliminary reading of the subtitled texts only, without a viewing of the video tape, has its limitations. Although a useful exercise, instances of inaccurate interpretation remain undetected, character portrayal cannot be appreciated adequately, timing difficulties cannot be recognised, and so on. The full picture, in the literal sense, can only be envisaged. A preliminary reading of the subtitled texts alone cannot possibly give the subtitle editor the full opportunity he or she needs to carry out a thorough quality control.

A preliminary viewing of the subtitled programme or film, without a preliminary reading of the subtitled texts, also has its limitations. While the subtitle editor is familiarising himself or herself for the first time with the contents of the programme as well as the subtitles, oversights which may result in obstructing the natural flow of the subtitles often go unnoticed. Although a preliminary viewing of the subtitled programme probably yields better results than a preliminary reading of the subtitled texts alone, it is likely that the subtitle editor's task remains incomplete. A previous reading of the subtitles, without the distraction of the video tape, gives the editor an opportunity to focus more intently on the contents of the subtitles. As a result, he or she is subsequently in a better position to detect instances of ambiguity, incoherence, discrepancy, and so on.

Neither a preliminary reading of subtitled texts nor a preliminary viewing of a subtitled programme alone could be considered as an effective form of quality control. The two forms of quality control could be termed as variations of a "preview", which according to the Concise Oxford Dictionary is, "the act of showing in advance"; the task remains incomplete.

2.2 Review

A form of quality control which comprises a spellcheck, a preliminary reading of the subtitled texts followed by a full viewing of the subtitled programme is likely to produce a more satisfactory quality control outcome; the subtitle editor will have viewed the subtitles twice and from two different standpoints. A preliminary reading of the subtitled texts provides the subtitle editor with an opportunity to concentrate solely on the linguistic contents of subtitles without being influenced by the soundtrack and the screen. The editor is more likely, at this stage, to notice instances of lack of clarity, ambiguity of meaning, inconsistency of terms, missing links between subtitles, and so on. He or she is far more likely to notice anything that prevents subtitles from running smoothly. The subtitle editor is also in a better position, at this stage, to make a house-style consistency check. The next stage, a full viewing of the subtitled programme, gives the subtitle editor the opportunity to concentrate on the overall impression created by the subtitles in relation to the programme, thereby appreciating the subtitled work in full before proceeding to carry out any amendments. This form of quality control could be termed as a "review". According to the Concise Oxford Dictionary, a "review" is "a general survey or assessment" or "a revision or re-consideration".

3. Practical experience of quality control in television subtitling in Wales

Responsibility for quality assurance of S4C (Channel Four Wales) subtitles lies with Testun. Testun is an independent company contracted by S4C to carry out, on their premises, a package of services comprising quality control, preparation and transmission of S4C subtitles – either as closed captions via Teletext or as burnt-in open subtitles.

Since its creation of its subtitling service in 1987, S4C has been conscious of the need to achieve high standards in order to develop a successful subtitling service and attract as many non-Welsh-speaking viewers as possible. Wales is a bilingual country which has a high percentage of bilingual households. Many viewers of subtitles are learners of Welsh. Welsh-language programmes with English subtitles are regularly viewed by both Welsh-speakers and non-Welsh speakers at the same time. Consequently, any errors in subtitling are apparent to many viewers. They register their complaints with S4C quite quickly if they are not happy with the contents of a subtitle or any other aspect of the subtitling service. As a result, there is very little one can get away with. The subtitling service must simply strive to meet the high standards expected by the viewers.

Subtitle editors in Wales carry out a quality control based upon a three-stage review of subtitles. It is a model that has been practised by editors working for S4C over the past twelve years. In S4C's view, this is considered to be the most effective form of quality control.

3.1 Time pressure

Turnover in television subtitling is much higher than the film industry. Subtitling for television without a script is a normal occurrence in Wales. For many programmes, filming will be completed only a day or two in advance of transmission. This clearly puts pressure on subtitlers to complete their work very quickly. There is potential for error when subtitling directly from the soundtrack onto the screen without a script, while working to a deadline. In this situation, it is essential to have high quality subtitlers backed by rigorous quality checking of the finished product.

3.2 Quality checking

An editor usually takes up to two and a half times the length of a programme to carry out the three-stage review and to carry out amendments as necessary. The amendments are implemented directly on the screen. If the programme is particularly difficult, more time is necessary. If the subtitles need more editing than usual and time permits, the subtitles file is returned to the subtitling company. If time does not permit the return of the file, Testun will carry out the additional editing as necessary and reserve the right to withdraw the subtitle credit caption. In such instances, S4C also reserves the right to withhold payment to the subtitling company. The additional cost to the subtitling company and the loss of professional credibility is a keen incentive not to submit inferior products.

There is a clear analogy between the process of television subtitling and any production line where different stages of production add value to the raw material: it is better to intercept errors early in the production process. In terms of the subtitled programmes, the raw material could be considered to be the script, or in some situations, a novel or a play which has been adapted for television. The different stages in the production process in this case are:

(1) the original script or novel as written by the scriptwriter or author;
(2) the translation into another language;
(3) the adaptation into a screenplay;
(4) the interpretation by the producer, director and actors;
(5) the conversion by the subtitler of the screenplay dialogue back into written texts.

Cases have arisen where authors have been critical of the subtitles convinced that difficulties had originated during stage (5) above. In one case, the difficulties which had arisen at stage (2) had gone undetected and were therefore continued inadvertently in the other stages. In this particular instance, the final product was adequately amended for transmission following discussions with the author. A case such as this only goes to show that the ideal situation in the subtitling process is that which takes place on a production line – quality control at each stage of the production process. The subtitle editor cannot influence stages (1) to (4) but can help subtitlers improve the quality of their work by providing feedback on editing at quality control stage. This is discussed later on in the paper.

3.3 A three-stage review as carried out by subtitle editors in Wales

Subtitle editors in Wales carry out a three-stage review of all English language subtitles transmitted on Welsh-language programmes on S4C. There are exceptions, namely, live subtitled programmes and programmes where subtitles are cued live during transmission.

The three-stage review comprises a spellcheck, a preliminary reading of the subtitled texts followed by a full viewing of the subtitled programme. Any amendments are carried out by the subtitle editor directly onto the screen during the viewing stage. Occasionally, the subtitle editor will contact the subtitler about a particular point. The subtitle editor is responsible for the final version of the subtitles file before transmission.

4. Some examples of subtitle editing

4.1 Clarity of meaning

Literal translation constitutes an occupational hazard for subtitlers, especially under time pressure. Unless the subtitler allows adequate time for editing, instances of literal translation may result in lack of clarity, ambiguity, incoherence, and so on. Unscripted speech requires particular attention in this respect. The unedited examples show how literal translation of unscripted speech can disrupt the viewer's reading rhythm and cause him or her to stop and wonder about the intended meaning.

unedited version	**edited version**
How are you connected to this mill, Hugh?	What's your connection with this mill, Hugh?

unedited version	**edited version**
A day soon goes by with the jobs that need doing.	I've enough to keep me busy all day.

unedited version	**edited version**
Do you have big muscles?	Do you have big muscles?
No, I'm hopeless.	Not at all!

4.2 *Accurate interpretation*

Telyn is a Welsh common noun meaning *harp; delyn* being a soft mutation of *telyn*. But *Delyn* also happens to be a proper noun which is the name of an area in north east Wales and where a local choir carries the same name.

unedited version	**edited version**
We were accompanied by the harp choir.	We were accompanied by Côr y Delyn.

4.3 *Cultural adaptation*

While the subtitler strives to compress the original dialogue, clarity of meaning can sometimes be sacrificed. In this example, *Cardis* is an acceptable shortened Welsh name for the people who live in Cardiganshire but the term may not be easily recognisable to non-Welsh speaking viewers. In the edited version, the length of the subtitle was increased in order to take into account the necessary cultural adaptation.

unedited version	**edited version**
You know what they say about Cardis, don't you?	You know what they say about Cardiganshire people, don't you?

4.4 Character portrayal

In this example, it is character portrayal that has been sacrificed for reduction of original dialogue. However, given that the unedited version gives a different impression to the one intended, it was necessary to amend the contents not only to adapt to the character who is speaking but also to fit the character who is being spoken about.

unedited version	**edited version**
He got a job at the BBC.	He was appointed to a post at the BBC.

4.5 Selective reduction of original dialogue

Small omissions of inconsequential words are common in subtitling but omissions of whole units of meaning are less common. In this example, the subtitle editor re-instated the sentence which had been dropped, "It's made me want to see him." instead of, "It's made me quite emotional!" so as to provide the viewer with as much information as possible about the development of the story in the unedited version.

unedited version	**edited version**
It's made me quite emotional!	*It's made me want to see him*

4.6 Correct grammar

On occasions when the line can be very thin between credible character portrayal and correct grammar. This is an obvious example. While the unedited version may appear more credible in the context of certain type of character, it is felt that subtitles which adhere to basic rules of grammar make it easier for the viewer to read them.

unedited version	**edited version**
There's the keys.	There are the keys.

4.7 Perceived errors

Potential for perceived errors is an area of concern for the subtitler as well as for the subtitle editor. In this example, there is a possibility that the unedited version would result in an incorrect interpretation in that the viewer might assume that the subtitle contains a mistake and that it should read "You finished off the car quickly" as opposed to the meaning the car has been repaired quickly.

unedited version	**edited version**
You finished the car quickly.	You fixed the car quickly

Part of the original dialogue may be ambiguous, whether it was the original intention or not. Given that a subtitler's task is to interpret what is said in the original dialogue, it follows that an ambiguous statement should remain ambiguous in the subtitle. But the line between an intentional ambiguity and an unintentional one is not always clear. The subtitler or an editor may feel the need to clarify the ambiguity on the basis that clarification will make it easier for the viewer to follow.

4.8 A capital letter makes all the difference

In this example, the correct edited version is a reference to the threat of a global war and not a war between the less developed (Third World) countries.

unedited version	**edited version**
..the Third World war...	..the Third World War...

5. Poor quality original script

Occasionally, subtitlers may spend time wondering about the meaning of piece of the original dialogue, particularly unscripted speech. Spoken language can be ambiguous, repetitive, incoherent, contradictory, and so on. If a meaning is unclear in scripted speech, does it mean it was the scriptwriter's intention? Or is the lack of clarity it due to the unstructed nature of spoken language?

The question arises – to what extent should a subtitler or subtitle editor edit spoken words for the sake of clarity of meaning for the viewer? If the unscripted speech of a person is limited in vocabulary, whether it be the language of a learner, a child or someone who's just searching for the right word, how far should the subtitler and subtitle editor attempt to clarify the meaning? A dilemma to the subtitler is whether or not to impose clarity on ambiguous statements.

6. Feedback to subtitling companies

S4C considers it essential to provide quality editing feedback to their own clients, the subtitling companies. One way in which this is done is by means of reports which are compiled by the subtitle editors on the editing carried out. S4C's Head of Subtitling, selects programmes for reports on a regular basis. The reports and the subtitle editor's accompanying explanatory notes are then forwarded to the relevant subtitling companies for information and ideally, response.

S4C's Subtitling and Teletext Department holds fortnightly review discussion sessions with Testun subtitle editors. Individual review discussion sessions also take place between Testun subtitle editors and subtitlers.

The all-Wales Screen Translation Forum, under the auspices of University of Wales, Lampeter, brings together organisations and companies involved in the subtitling industry in Wales (S4C, Testun, subtitling companies, independent television companies, media production companies, authors, scriptwriters, university teachers and students) to debate issues of common concern.

7. A sense of balance

From our experience, a three-stage review of subtitles, as outlined in this paper, is the form of quality control that contributes the most to achieving high standards of subtitling. Not only does this method enable the subtitle editor to correct routine errors, check subtitling conventions and ensure house-style consistency, it also enables him or her to detect more subtle hindrances to the flow of the subtitles. At quality control stage, what the subtitle editor is looking for is whether or not the subtitler has made the most effective choices between the different factors at play. Compromise is part and parcel of subtitling. The right compromise helps to achieve a certain sense of balance which is central to successful subtitling.

SUBTITLING FOR CHANNEL 4 TELEVISION

Hazel R.Morgan
GGSM Subtitling, Channel 4 Television
UK

I have been looking after Channel 4's subtitling since the week after the Channel went on air in November 1982. Like so much of the media we are in the throes of technological change, but at the moment we put the subtitles on screen as follows:

When Channel 4 buys the rights to a film which needs subtitling, we ask the distributors to send a *complete* English translation (whether we get it is another matter). Similarly with a commissioned programme; we ask the producers to provide a complete translation with the unsubtitled master tape. When the tape arrives we make a VHS copy with two timecodes – one in vision, that is Burnt-In Time Code, BITC – and one not, which is VITC, Vertical Interval Time Code, so called because it goes in the interval between frames. This timecode – concurrent with the one in vision – drives our subtitling equipment, which at present is the PU2020 system linked to an Insight character generator. The timecoded VHS is then sent, with whatever paper-work has come with the film, to one of the freelance subtitlers who are on our books.

One of these is John Minchinton, who has been subtitling films for around 30 years for both cinema and television. I quote him unashamedly:

> It is our job to do justice to the authors of the work. We are not the authors, but we are their intermediaries. Dialogue in film and videotape is measured and the measurements are noted on the original language dialogue list. This, internationally, is 'spotting'. Thus the texts are broken into sections, initially depending on the speed at which dialogue is delivered. If a few words are spoken rapidly, followed immediately by a few words spoken by another character, and so on, the subtitles are, perforce, of short duration – sometimes only one second. If the speech is long, the spottings follow the speech rhythms, using pauses and aspirations as stop and

> start points, but almost never spotting one title longer than six seconds. Cuts (shot changes) are carefully respected, because they punctuate the action and they can be used to punctuate the flow of subtitles; the general rule is never to carry a subtitle over a cut unless there is no alternative... The subtitles translating the dialogue are then written to the spottings, which indicate how much time is available for each translation. This is the classic method, developed over the last half century in many lands for film and television purposes. (Minchinton 1993)

The spotting is done using the timecode on the unsubtitled VHS (which I mentioned at the start). The subtitler plays the cassette, pausing at *every point* where speech starts or stops: finger on the Pause button or Search knob, and allow about 4 frames for "finger time" i.e. how long it takes for the finger to hit the button after the ear/eye notes the speech point. Subtitlers soon get used to this and develop their own ways of working, and they write in the appropriate place on the script the timecode of each start or stop point. As well as speech, the subtitler will note cuts, also any text on screen which should be translated such as notices, newspaper headlines etc.

When the subtitler has worked through the whole film they have a script broken up by pairs of timecodes, In (where the speech starts) and Out (where the speech stops). They write the subtitles by condensing the translated text to fit these spots, to be readable in the time, and limited to one or two lines. They then write their work to a 3.5" computer disc and return it all to me, with a printout from the disc. I read the disc on my equipment, check it through – mainly for spelling but also with a look at the timecodes – and I write these changes to the disc. I then make a *rehearsal cassette* by playing the unsubtitled VHS linked in series with the subtitle disc on the PU2020 and a second cassette recorder, resulting in a VHS with both the picture and the subtitles on it. It is not broadcast quality, and there is a timecode running at the top of the picture, but it does give an idea of how the programme will look on screen. Anyone can see this who cares to: the subtitler to check their own work, the production company in the case of commissioned programmes, a viewer for content/ classification/commercial references – and any further changes that these people want are made *on the disc***.** When it is as good as we can get it, a final printout is made for Archives and the disc is taken to the technicians, who make a subtitled dub by running the master tape in series with the disc (on the PU2020) and a blank tape, the timecodes on the disc locking into the synch pulses on the master tape. That, give or take breaks or any further editing, is what you see on screen.

It's a great advantage to be able to proofread, as it were, without disturbing the film itself – it waits in the library until the disc is ready. The use of computers has made subtitling much more flexible than it used to be, and changes can be made quite easily. But computers cannot do all the work; for a start, not all of them are compatible – the PU2020 has a unique program which our subtitlers are able to use only because a cybernetist copied it for them (and it took him eighteen months to decode). The PU2020 now has a Windows-compatible program, which is fine if you are committed to that system. Technical matters aside, there still has to be the knowledge of the individual film and of language – that is, *the language of the subtitles*. If you see a subtitled film and find the translation odd, it is probably been done in the film's country of origin by a non-native speaker, who could be perfectly fluent in the language but not conversant with *idiom*.

When writing subtitles to fit the spots, the good old English A Level art of precis comes into its own; also, having seen the film almost frame by frame, the subtitler should have a better idea than most of what dialogue is essential – much better than some programme-makers, who have come back to me complaining that "you've left half of it out". They know their film *too* well; it is very hard for them to place themselves in the position of the first-, perhaps only-time, viewer. My ultimate weapon in these cases is "If the viewers see too much text on screen, they'll switch off."

Another constraint is the number of characters per line available in the *font* used for subtitling. In programmes subtitled for the deaf we still use a font specially created for TV subtitling, called CGM; it allows 42 characters per line, and has a small square serif which helps legibility – essential for Deaf subtitling. We used to use this font for all our subtitling because it was built into the system and we did not need a separate character generator. When choice became available, senior Commissioning Editors – not, please note, the people who actually process the subtitles – chose the fonts they wished their programmes to have. For documentaries we now use a slightly taller font, Arial Narrow 30, which also allows 42 characters per line. Even with the ghost box, that is the translucent box around the letters, it does obscure a considerable amount of the picture because of its height, but if we had used the next size down the letters would have been too small to read, especially having no serif. The font we use for arts programmes and films, Gill Sans 28, allows only 38 characters per line; it was chosen by someone who wanted the effect to "look like the cinema". With a very talky film this can be a serious restriction, a test of the subtitler's craft.

Reading speed is another consideration – and another complaint too: "We can't read the subtitles, they're not on screen long enough". Take 2 seconds per line as an average time; if a spot is less than 2 seconds, certainly less than one, is that subtitle really necessary? Help-help murder-murder is usually fairly obvious, no matter what the language. But subtitlers are paid *per subtitle,* and the temptation to put in as many as possible is not always resisted.

So what makes a good subtitle? One which, within the time available, conveys the author's intent. To start with, basic is best. A quote from a well-known British journalist of the 1950s, Nancy Spain: "Begin by putting in all you want, end by cutting out all you can." She was talking about newspaper articles but could well have been talking about subtitles. The viewer is here for the view, first. The best subtitles are the ones you hardly notice because they make you feel you are understanding the original as you hear it. They do *not* draw attention to themselves – great big fancy fonts are not on, neither are very strong colours. A producer's recent request for a blue box (instead of the usual grey) was reversed when she saw what it looked like.

How long does all this work take? The people who ask me that are usually producers of commissioned programmes who want to deliver as close as possible to transmission. I never give a time, because it depends on the programme; some are surprisingly easy to subtitle, others surprisingly difficult. Length is not what matters; editing – in other words cuts – is far more important. What does speed the process up is good paperwork: a full translation, with every um and er, plus a full original-language transcript if possible. I discourage producers from shrinking their own text; some of them really think this is helpful – "I've written the subtitles, all your subtitler's got to do is put them on". (One wonders how much they know about the subtitling process.) The subtitler would much rather have the full text, then they know where they are – especially if they do not speak the original language.

If none of this paperwork is supplied, the subtitler may be reduced to making a transcription from the soundtrack; and transcription is nothing like as easy as it sounds.

But the better the film, the easier it is to subtitle it well. Good subtitles cannot save a bad film, but bad subtitles can spoil a good one. Bad: badly spotted = poor timing, text on screen when there's no speech, or speech left unsubtitled which ought to be. Too much text on screen for the reading time. Over-punctuation, including massive use of exclamation marks; too many of these – in English at any rate – devalue their impact, and using more than one at once makes the screen look like a skittle alley!!!!. Channel 4 does not use a full stop where a subtitle ends at the end of a sentence – we believe that it is obvious, and it takes up another character. Where a sentence is split over two or more subtitles, three dots are used to indicate the breaks; the first subtitle ends with three dots... ...and the next subtitle starts with three dots. Dots should be used only where essential; too many and the programme looks like a case of the measles. And self-conscious or unsuitable use of language – would a mayor's chauffeur in provincial France really ask his employer "You're being hassled, sir?"

Good subtitles are accurately timed, and convey concisely the author's intentions in a style as close as possible to the original; they should give the impression of coming from the film rather than being imposed upon it. And although humour is the first thing to go in translation, occasionally a phrase lends itself to the situation and should be seized upon. In the Czech film *The Ear,* which has a political background, the subtitler (Mr Minchinton again) took the opportunity to call a ministerial residence "Czechers".

The people likely to be best at this work are those who are fluent in the *subtitling language* – in our case English. If you speak the film's original language, whether as mother tongue or acquired, you hear so much detail and so many nuances that it can be very difficult to do the necessary reduction – you can't make up your mind as to what to leave out.

Rates of pay are per reel – that is 10 minutes of programme, based on the 10-minute reels of film which make up cinema prints; plus so much per subtitle. (Current rates are about £60/reel and 85p-£1/subtitle.) Any extras can be charged for: transcription and/or translation, if these have not been supplied; work with a third party such as a language specialist or the production company; and perhaps an extra percentage if the work has to be done in a hurry.

When work really *has* to be done in a hurry – topical news stories, for example – this is perfectly possible provided every aspect of the job is well organised and all the people involved are working to one purpose. In September I was involved in the subtitling of *Algeria Daily*, a series of 3-minute programmes filmed and edited in Algeria by a French company and line-fed to us at 10.30 every morning for transmission at 19.55 the same day. Scripts in French and English were faxed through; our VT technicians received the line-feed and made timecoded VHS's, and while the subtitler, an Algerian translator and myself did the subtitling in my office the programme was captioned in the edit suite. A VHS of the captioned version was delivered to me, I recut the subtitles to fit it and made a rehearsal cassette for the commissioning editor; as soon as any changes he wanted were made, I took the subtitle disc to the technicians who then proceeded with the dub which went out as that evening's programme. Everybody, not all in the same country, worked together as a team; it was hard work but very rewarding, and succeeded because people (rather than technology) were in contact and knew what was required.

Sadly, neither Channel 4 nor BBC2 are showing the number of subtitled programmes they used to, because they are not deemed to boost the ratings or bring in advertising revenue. We do not have a subtitling unit as such at Channel 4 – I am a checker, a proofreader, not a subtitler as such. Our subtitlers are all freelance, working from home, and at the moment (late 1998) we do not have enough work to keep them busy and they have to do other work. It sounds rather depressing. But more depressing, perhaps, is the standard of literacy; what is the use of having text on screen if viewers will not read it fluently? But if our current government really means business in its education policies, then literacy standards might rise again and eventually people could enjoy reading intelligent, concise subtitles while hearing the language of a culture other than their own.

LIVE INTERLINGUAL SUBTITLING

Corien den Boer
NOB Subtitling & Translation,
Hilversum, The Netherlands

1. Introduction

The subject of this paper is live interlingual subtitling. By this I mean subtitling a television programme while it is on the air, from one language into another.

It must be every film producer's dream: You make a terrific film, a fascinating documentary or any type of television programme and you can show it to everybody all around the world, because as if by magic, it will have subtitles in the correct language as soon as it goes on the air. That is what live subtitling can do: furnishing a programme with the desired type of subtitles broadcast. When I say "as if by magic", I am of course being cynical. It is a lot of hard work.

2. A short history of live subtitling in the Netherlands

The only live subtitling found in the Netherlands is done by Teletekst, a department of NOS. NOS is the national news and sports broadcaster, among other things. Teletekst runs the information pages behind all three public TV channels in the Netherlands. They supply the Dutch - Dutch intralingual subtitles for the deaf and hard of hearing. And they provide live subtitles for the news, for current affairs programmes, and for practically every programme that cannot be prepared in advance. About 50% of those are sports programmes. At the moment, live subtitling cannot be done without a velotypist, someone who types in syllables rather than letters on a special keyboard and can produce up to 1000 letters a minute. In that way, velotypists are almost up to normal talking speed. But Teletekst subtitles are often a condensed version of what is actually being said, if only because every "er" and "well" is left out. Velotypists cannot do the subtitling on their own, for two reasons: first, because usually they are not linguists but typists; and second, because the thought process would be too complex for any normal human being. They need to be fed, line by line, the exact text that is supposed to appear on screen. So they pair up with an editor who streamlines the spoken text into easily readable chunks: subtitles. In the case of a news bulletin, there usually is a script of the newsreader's text, even though the news is aired live. Teletekst has the script and can prepare a fair amount of subtitles in advance. News items are usually more problematic, and if an extra news item is suddenly put in at the last minute, subtitlers have to improvise. When that happens, we can speak of a truly live subtitling situation, albeit in one language only. So far, occasions where live interlingual subtitling was involved were of an incidental nature in the Netherlands. There was an experiment in 1992, two more in the course of '93 and '94, and in 1997 a pilot project was set up. The way things are at the moment, live interlanguage subtitling involves the very close and concentrated cooperation of two subtitler-interpreters, one velotypist and, in complicated cases, an editor.

3. The pilot project

The Teletekst people and our translation department linked up for a live subtitling project for translated subtitles. There appeared to be a market for them, and innovation is always a good thing.

Two things happened that warranted such a pilot project. It all started with Bill Clinton's inaugural speech in 1993; typically an occasion that would be broadcast live by NOS. The White House was not kind enough to supply copies of Clinton's speech in advance to any news broadcasters, so NOS had the usual set of choices:

(1) Broadcast the speech live with a live interpreter (expensive and not very elegant)

(2) Broadcast the speech live with a running commentary by a journalist (even less elegant)

(3) Tape the speech, run it through the translation department at terrific speed and broadcast it an hour later with Dutch subtitles (and let CNN or BBC run away with your viewers)

(4) Broadcast the speech live with live translated subtitles. Expensive, but new and exciting and so never mind the elegance.

Two freelance interpreters, one of whom also had considerable experience as a subtitler with NOB, were given two training sessions of two hours each before Inauguration Day. They would interpret and condense the source text simultaneously. Whatever came out of their mouths would be put on the screen by the velotypist. They would have to combine the jobs of interpreter and subtitle editor. And they did so remarkably well with a modest lapse of time between source text and subtitles. The client was very pleased. We do not know what the viewers at home thought. Besides, they may have listened to the oral interpreter that was also put on the job for safety's sake. The teletext-page with the subtitles was optional.

Even before the pilot project was started, Diana, Princess of Wales, sadly lost her life in a car crash. Her funeral service was broadcast on Dutch television with "normal" NOB subtitles, because we were given a script beforehand. One part of the service was kept secret and did not appear in the script: the thundering speech that Diana's brother Charles delivered. Dutch viewers could watch it with live translated subtitles provided by a team of NOS/NOB people.

Another client appeared interested and another live subtitling session was organised to cover an awards ceremony. Two things went horribly wrong. Firstly, the presenter peppered her audience with quips and jokes, moving from one guest table to another. The live subtitles were inevitably so far behind that she was two tables ahead of the subtitled conversation, and the whole thing became incomprehensible. Secondly, the client insisted that the programme should have open subtitles. This meant that they would appear on every TV set that was tuned in to this programme, and not just on the ones that called up the appropriate teletext page. It also meant that we couldn't use different colours for different speakers, a technique that *Teletekst* uses frequently. Accordingly, everyone who watched the show also watched the live subtitling disaster. A black day in the history of subtitling. But again, the client was happy.

After this, NOS and NOB set up a pilot project. NOS supplied the trainers, velotypists and facilities. NOB supplied the trainees and the course material (video tapes). The aim of the project was to create a group of permanently available live subtitle-translators, or interpreter-subtitlers if you like, in order to meet any short-term requests by clients for this particular service. The pilot project started in November 1997. Five volunteers, experienced subtitle translators who also had some experience in interpreting, were trained for two hours a week for a period of four months. I was one of them. We used mainly video tapes of monologues or speeches and sometimes of people being interviewed. Several velotypists were involved; every practice session we worked with other people and discovered more about the process. To be honest, I bowed out after two months. The practice sessions never failed to give me a raging headache and it usually took me three hours to get over an hour's worth of practice. My colleagues really enjoyed doing it and I just didn't. I felt I had practiced enough to be able to do it if called upon in an emergency. The rest of the team will practise with some regularity to keep in shape. Practice makes perfect, and quality will improve with experience. By the end of the project, we were able to conclude that we made a lot of progress and were ready to deliver whenever live interlingual subtitles were required.

4. The Clinton tapes

No sooner had we drawn that conclusion than a political drama exploded in The White House, involving sex, lies and video tapes. The latter were of extreme interest to us live subtitlers. They turned out to provide me with a perfect example of the pros and cons of live subtitling. The Clinton interrogation was broadcast worldwide on September 21st, 1998. SBS, a commercial TV channel in the Netherlands, asked NOB to subtitle it live. Initially, we warned them that the quality would not be great. Apart from anything else, we were unable to use the NOS teletext equipment. This meant that the subtitles would be open and not on a teletext page. It also meant that we had no access to velotype keyboards or their operators. SBS said they would take full technical responsibility; if the whole thing fell apart after two minutes, they wouldn't hold it against us. The tapes were to start somewhere around three o'clock that afternoon. At two o'clock, NOB said yes. We scrambled together the appropriate equipment: a Screen subtitling software unit and a normal Qwerty keyboard, among other things. The live subtitling team was briefed. At three thirty, the tapes went on air. Five interpreters and numerous typists and technicians got stuck in for four hours without stopping. We subtitled the complete set of tapes from beginning to end. The client was deliriously happy. Many TV viewers rang up to say how impressed they were. We were pretty sure that no other country pulled this off. This was a historical day for the subtitling industry. Commercially, it was a success. Technically, considering what we had to work with, it was a success. But what about linguistically? A twelve-second delay was built in between the incoming satellite material and the outgoing broadcast onto the SBS network. This gave the subtitlers just enough time to do their work. Some of the subtitles flickered on and off. This is because Screen software works with a buffer and occasionally, the buffer would overflow. The Screen system would present the latest subtitle in a flickering fashion and throw all the previous ones away, even though they hadn't been broadcast. That caused quite a serious interruption of continuity. (Afterwards we were told that this was a fairly simple technical matter that could have been solved quite easily). On top of that, the sound quality of the satellite feed was bad. The interrogators in particular were very hard to understand. They never once appeared on screen, so lip-reading was out of the question. This made life difficult for the interpreters. There were a lot of typing errors as there was no time to correct your mistakes. The presentation time of some subtitles was ridiculously long, but again, that couldn't be helped. In short: If you compare these subtitles to no subtitles at all, they're great. If you compare them to normal Dutch subtitles of the quality we aspire to and are used to, they're awful. All this from a linguistic point of view. In the real world, SBS and NOB had a field day.

5. The product - pros and cons

There is obviously a market for live interlingual subtitling. In this day and age, speed is all, and potential clients are very attracted to the concept of live subtitling, even if it costs a bit more. It is important for a company like NOB to offer as wide a product range as possible, and also to be on the cutting edge of innovative translation procedures. The fact that NOB can offer this new product is great. It is really worth investigating; it is really worth the investment. The one thing that has my particular attention is the quality of the product. Subtitling in itself is still in many ways a debatable product. Can we really afford to leave so much of a source text untranslated? Do we really want to comply with all these technical restrictions such as reading speed, presentation time, no more than two lines on screen etcetera? Are we sure dubbing is not the better option? Live subtitling is therefore even more debatable. It involves combining two very complicated mental processes: translating one language into another and one type of text into the rigourous strait-jacket of another. All this within seconds. The only alternative which is just as quick is a live oral interpreter. The content of the source text will come across loud and clear, but a number of other qualities will be lost in the translation. To clients, a live broadcast is a very prestigious thing. They do not want to be delayed by anything. An artificial delay such as was used for the Clinton tapes is acceptable. But where is one to draw the line? If twelve seconds is OK, what about twenty? A technical restriction hovers into view at this point: if your delay is too long, but the subtitlers still work as if the programme is aired live, the subtitles might appear before the speaker has even spoken the words. You would have to have an extra person who decides when the subtitle is to appear. So why not wait half an hour and have normal quality subtitles? Time is money, it is said. We live in an era that reduces many things to how much they cost. In my opinion, time spent on making something of some quality should be more valuable than money. I can say this because I am a linguist and not a manager or a producer. And as a linguist, I want to defend the quality aspect. It worries me that most people were aware of how bad the Clinton subtitles were, but nobody seemed seriously worried about it. So let us talk about quality. Of course there is the *loss of information* that occurs in most subtitles for all the usual reasons, aggravated in live situations because of the time pressure. Some *delay* is inevitable in live subtitling. This can be very disturbing to two groups of viewers:

(1) Those who are used to 'normal' subtitles of some quality will expect them to synchronize with the spoken text and to consist of no more than two lines for

legibility's sake.
(2) Viewers who have no experience with subtitles, but understand enough of the source text to be able to follow it, will be disturbed by the lack of synchronisation. At best, it looks funny. At worst, it is confusing to the point of making the programme unintelligible.
Viewers who have no experience with subtitles may find it difficult to read them at the best of times. Live subtitling would be even harder to follow. One may end up having *read* the programme without actually having *watched* it. Of course, watching Clinton's head for three hours would make anyone glad to see something else appear on screen. But this was a rare event. The Clinton subtitles also showed a number of *spelling errors*. Again, this demonstrates that the quality of live subtitles is not great. Obviously, a highly experienced subtitler delivers a better product than a beginner. Experienced velotypists hardly make any spelling errors at all. But as long as live interlingual subtitles remain in relatively low demand, people who can do the job will have relatively little opportunities to gain experience. To me, quality is the operative word. If you are going to offer a service like this one, you have to be able to guarantee a quality product. Our experiences in the pilot project have taught us that some programmes are just not suitable for live interlingual subtitling. I think that only speeches, monologues and non-heated one-on-one discussions can have live subtitles. During the church service for Queen Elizabeth and Prince Philip's wedding anniversary, Archbishop Carey quoted a number of lines from a Shakespeare play. Our live subtitle-translator was stunned. There was nothing he could do except explain the subject of the quote in very general terms. So poetry and songs are out of the question. Feature films will prove impossible. Jokes are a nightmare. The ideal person for the job would be someone who is a qualified interpreter and a professional subtitler. These are two different fields of expertise. People who combine these qualities are extremely thin on the ground. The chances of being able to deliver a quality product are therefore quite small. There's a difference of opinion, I think, between language experts and clients when it comes to the importance of the quality of live subtitles. Clients are aware of the quality issue, but do they agree that it is an important issue? More commercially-oriented people would say: "What if the clients don't care? What if we simply can't do any better? Delivering a product that our client is happy with, that's quality too, isn't it?" That is what worries me. It would be like CNN in their early days saying: "OK, the quality isn't great, you can't see what's happening, you can't hear properly, but hey, we're here live, isn't that terrific?" My fear is that linguists will have little or no influence on the client's decisions. Linguists should have a serious input when it comes to developing this new product and define its possibilities and limitations very clearly. Pilot projects like ours are a good start. Once we are familiar with the ins and outs of live subtitling, we can start on the do's and dont's.

PUNCTUATING SUBTITLES: TYPOGRAPHICAL CONVENTIONS AND THEIR EVOLUTION

Clara Cerón
Freelance translator
Paris, France

1. Introduction

Although viewers usually do not pay much attention to it, punctuation plays a very important part in the readability of subtitles. At a very early stage, subtitling has tailored the usage of punctuation signs to suit its specific needs. But today, new technologies, among other reasons, have caused an evolution in punctuation conventions. This has resulted in the coexistence of contradictory norms, which impedes readability and hence comprehension of the subtitles. Obviously time for standardization has come, but here again who should decide which standards to apply?

Whenever movie and TV viewers are watching a subtitled film, they are deciphering a whole set of codes. They may be unaware of it, but they will react immediately to a departure from the norm. *Desperanto (Let Sleeping Girls Lie)*, Canadian director Patricia Rozema's contribution to the film *Montréal vu par... (Montreal Sextet)* provides a perfect example of this.

The main character, an Ontario housewife, is visiting Montreal, which she views as the height of sophistication. She crashes into a preview at an art gallery, feels out of place within the French-speaking in crowd, starts drinking and gets herself into an embarrassing situation. Throughout the film, subtitling is cleverly used: it even takes part in the action. The character "crosses the subtitle line" (thus hiding them to the viewers) in order to read them and understand the conversations going on in French. She then plays with them as with objects. At the end of *Desperanto*, the subtitles become the flying carpet on which she escapes reality.

In this movie the comic effect derives from the defeat of audience expectations. The audience is expecting subtitles to behave in a certain way and they don't. Subtitles are not supposed to move across the screen, to land into the cleavage of an actress or to disappear melting away into a glass of red wine. The audience unconsciously expects them to follow certain rules concerning their visual aspect on the screen and dealing with layout, typography and punctuation. We do expect subtitles to appear at the bottom of the screen, to be one or two lines long, to be centered or justified to the left, to be written in a not too ornate font, to be yellow or white or white in a black box, and so on. But these rules are not set once and for all; they depend on the country we live in or the language we speak, or even on the subtitling lab, and, as we will see later, they are undergoing an evolution.

General punctuation is a set of conventions which varies according to each language. The same applies to subtitle punctuation. That is, what is allowed in one country may be an absolute no-no in another, e.g. hyphenation at the end of the first line. This is why I will base my observations on what is happening in France and Spain, but from what I have heard similar situations are found in other countries.

2. The idiosyncrasies of subtitle punctuation

Obviously, punctuation in subtitling is based on the rules existing for other written texts in a given language. It tends to follow the established typographical rules, but not always. At a very early stage, subtitling has created new uses for some punctuation signs in order to cater for its specific needs.

We must keep in mind that subtitles are not just like any other written text. Time and space constraints account for their idiosyncrasies. Unlike books, it is impossible to go back and reread what was not understood at first glance. Each subtitle is a clean slate, as it erases totally what came before. As our brain has limited storage capacities, we can only keep in mind a fleeting memory of the previous subtitle as we read on the next one. Each subtitle is a world of its own, an island isolated by huge gaps. So, when a sentence starts in a subtitle and goes over onto the next one, it has been felt necessary to throw a bridge in between. A suspension bridge if I dare say: in most countries the punctuation sign used to inform the viewer to read on is the suspension dots, both at the end of the first subtitle and at the beginning of the following one. In some countries, this usage is now disappearing.

Another innovation is the way subtitling uses italics for other purposes than the standard ones, for instance for transcribing voice-over (narrators, unseen speakers on the phone, the radio, the TV). Italics are also used for foreign languages other the main language used in the film, and for songs.

But, of course, the area in which subtitling has shown the biggest creativity and taken most liberties with conventional layout, typography and punctuation is captioning for the deaf and hard of hearing. For instance, different colours will be used for each character. Or for different kinds of speech (yellow for voice-over, red for songs, etc). Text will be placed according to the position of the speaking character on the screen. And so on.

3. The recent evolution in punctuation conventions

Lately, punctuation conventions in subtitling have undergone an evolution. In itself, this is not necessarily a bad thing. But the problem is that this evolution has led to the present situation where different norms – sometimes contradictory – coexist.

There are several reasons for this evolution and for the resulting chaos. New technologies have improved some aspects of subtitling. For instance, the machines which carried out chemical subtitling had a slow reaction speed and made it compulsory to leave a space of a foot, or at least half a foot, between each subtitle. The introduction of laser engraving and computerized subtitling systems has enabled more precision. We could jump directly from one subtitle to the next one if we wanted. Of course, we do not do it, because otherwise the viewers would not realize there is a new subtitle starting. Usually, we now leave a gap of only 2, 4 or 6 frames depending on the habits of the subtitling lab involved.

Since the time between each subtitle is now shorter than it used to be, it has been somehow felt that the suspension dots warning the sentence is not over are no longer necessary since the next subtitle will arrive soon enough. They have now disappeared altogether from French subtitles. In Spain, where this new norm arrived along with the French laser machines, some film translators still stick to the older convention.

In France, as this space-consuming habit was suppressed, another one was reintroduced: it was decided to follow standard French typographical usage and put spaces before question marks, exclamation marks and some other signs, which had not been done before in subtitling, to save a few characters. But instead of the half-space that should be used, we usually find a full space since most subtitling software does not allow the use of the half-space.

Ironically, though you would expect the use of computerized systems to open new possibilities, their introduction have impoverished punctuation. We often find full spaces instead of half-spaces, hyphens instead of dashes, and so on, because subtitling software developers have not thought of automating this, whereas the typesetters of old who prepared the plates used in chemical subtitling had more respect for this kind of punctuation subtleties. Then, we are also victims to this very common plague of computer science: the incompatibility of codes when it comes to diacritic marks and the so-called extended characters. Very often, when subtitling into Spanish, we have to do without accented capital letters, because many subtitling software applications cannot deal with them.

Another paradox is the bad influence a cultural TV channel has had on subtitling punctuation in France. The channel ARTE has chosen the teletext format for technical reasons. But the version of teletext used so far is very poor as far as typography and punctuation are concerned. It does not permit the use of italics, nor accented capital letters, nor even the capital c cedilla, which is so common in French sentences.

One of the reasons for coexisting conventions is the relative globalization of the field. For instance, a Belgian documentary shown on French TV will follow the Belgian usage regarding subtitle layout (i.e. justification to the left), whereas in France centred subtitles are favoured.

And let us not forget the recent trend in commercials which overuses typography and subtitles, and introduces new norms never seen before, thus adding to the confusion.

All these coexisting conventions make reading subtitles a bit tiring for the viewer at best, since he has to adapt each time to a new one, and, at worst, they can even prevent his good understanding of the show he is watching.

It is when it comes to punctuating subtitles which enclose two-person dialogues that the situation is most chaotic. Dashes come and go, turn into hyphens, etc. Since it would take too long to list all of the different cases we might find (there are at least a dozen of them), I will give a final, and simpler, example that sums up the confusion existing today. In the same country one might come across at least three different ways of punctuating a sentence which carries on to the next subtitle:
(1) Old punctuation style, with suspension dots at the end of the first subtitle and at the beginning of the second one.
a. Full stops are suppressed when they coincide with the end of a subtitle.
b. Full stops are maintained.
(2) New punctuation style, with no suspension dots at all, but with full stops when necessary.
(3) Mixed style (no suspension dots and no final periods).
Here, the absence of the full stop at the end of the subtitle creates the most confusing and even irritating situation of all, as it may mean two contradictory things: either that the sentence stops there or that it goes on. Needless to say, this makes subtitles following this style very difficult to read.

This style comes from the older punctuation style which assimilates subtitles to newspaper captions (cf. the Portuguese name for subtitling *legendágem* and the American synonym for it *captioning*), where the last sentence will have no full stop, maybe because subtitles are seen as text at the bottom of a picture. However, in my opinion, this choice of punctuation is not the best one, for a subtitle is no more a newspaper caption than it is a book page; it can only work while the suspension dots are maintained. As soon as they are dropped, it becomes very hard to make any sense of the subtitles.

4. Conclusion

This last example is enough to prove the blatant need for standardization. But who should decide which norm to use? As things go now, each subtitling lab, each TV channel, has different rules. And this is not only true of punctuation; it also applies to other subtitling aspects such as reading speed and the number of characters available for each subtitle. In France, the reading speed may vary: 12, 15, 17 or even more characters per second. Such technical aspects of subtitling would also benefit from standardization. But, is it likely everyone will agree on the same rules, even within a single country? And the pending globalization brought by satellite channels and DVD are bound to add to the already existing confusion.

And how to decide upon which norm to use? Obviously, it is a good thing punctuation conventions in subtitling are based on standard typographical usage in a given language, so the audience does not have to learn a whole set of conventions each time. But to apply strictly typographical rules that were created for other kinds of written text can be a mistake in some cases. It is OK to do so only as far as it does not create situations of ambiguity within the specific context of subtitles.

However, I am convinced there is still room for more creativity. Maybe we should consider creating new uses for existing punctuation signs and – why not? – maybe new signs, as long as it is done for the sake of readability. Reading subtitles requires an effort. We should always make it easier for the reader. And we should take advantage to the full of the possibilities offered by computerization, instead of letting it dictate which letters and punctuation signs we can use. Some subtitling labs cleverly use these possibilities (using a wide array of fonts to render those used in the original credit titles, for example), while others are slaves to insufficiently developed subtitling software and the impoverished typography imposed by teletext.

So maybe it is time to carry out a comparative study on which convention is easier to read. This may be the only way to get everyone agreeing on a standard norm for punctuation and other technical aspects of subtitling.

SURTITLING OPERAS
WITH EXAMPLES OF TRANSLATIONS FROM GERMAN INTO FRENCH AND DUTCH

Linda Dewolf
Brussels, Belgium

Technological progress is revolutionising the translator's profession. After word processing and computerised translation assistance tools, surtitling is now getting into the act. All this progress is compelling us to rethink our profession.

This contribution addresses the problems involved in the evaluation of surtitling according to four parameters: the original (film, theatre, opera), the method: surtitling or subtitling, the translation system (slide projection, software system) and the quality of the translation, based on a case study containing examples of Wagner's opera *Parsifal*.

Everyone knows what subtitles are. Surtitling in opera houses and theatres is a technique which produces similar results for stage productions. It is a new rapidly expanding field which enables plays and operas to be understood by larger audiences, since advance in technology have made new software available and affordable to meet an increased demand of translation. With regard to the state of the art, the topic is relatively unexplored as translation studies seldom deal with the problems related to the quality of the end-translation. The question of the visibility of the titles, the colour, the size and the type of characters, which determine the legibility of the surtitles has hardly been analysed so far. Existing research about audience perception is also limited, except maybe in countries like Austria and the United States, where studies of opera translation seem to flourish.

The question is usually phrased as a simple dichotomy: with or without titles? Opera translation is surrounded by controversy over its feasibility. Since the question here is not whether to translate or not, I would like to put an end to the myth and break away from preconceived judgements that concentrate on the "disadvantages" of different forms of translation. Rather,

I would suggest to look at the rhythm of live performances and the textual aspects which affect the comprehension of the titles.

So what are the advantages of titles? What has the titles phenomenon brought to live stage performances? What does it take away? Projected titles are considered one of the most important developments in recent years. They have changed the experience of opera profoundly, and there is no doubt about what is being done and how it is being done. During most of opera history, two principles ruled: either an opera was sung in the language of the audience, or it was sung in the language of the singers. In a greater number of cases, the two principles were not even in conflict; singers and audiences shared a common language, and many singers who performed in other than their native language restricted themselves to a single one they had learned fluently. Recent years however have brought a distinct improvement. That titles are an innovation and not merely a convenience, is demonstrable - titles are a technical device to make opera more user-friendly.

There are basically two methods of projecting titles on a screen over the proscenium. The first, and historically the oldest, involves the use of slides, each of which has texts that are flashed onto the screen through the means of a slide carousel. Two people must work in coordination: a stagehand with the text backstage and an operator in the projection booth, in constant touch with the person backstage. About 400 to 500 slides are necessary for most repertory operas. The advantages of using slides are that the initial costs are lower and that the graphic definition is sharper and clearer.

The other method uses a computer-generated text, which is then projected onto the screen in the same manner as the slide method. It is a word processor with a graphics editor which creates a sort of slide on the computer screen containing texts and/or graphics. Text display and removal, and the insertion of the next text can be adapted to perfectly match timing variations in lyrical performances. This electronic slide is directly transmitted to the video projector through a specifically designed video interface (Saario & Oksanen 1996: 194). La Monnaie in Brussels has developed its own surtitling system called Libretto and VLOS in Antwerp is using Focon, a Danish software product also used in Berlin at the Hebbel Theatre. Not to mention that in Paris, at the Théâtre du Châtelet, the titles are projected on the back of opera seats.

The point is that operas are not abstract musical structures; they are dramas, in which words and music interact to create a theatrical effect. Without reasonably full comprehension of the words on the part of the audience, opera inevitably becomes pantomime accompanied by music, not integrated musical drama. Titles are one element in a whole event that conveys what singers are actually saying in the context of the staging and the dramaturgy:

> Vor allem für die Übertitelung ergeben sich aufgrund der Struktur des Operntextes eine Reihe von Problemen, die nur in enger Beziehung zur szenischen Darstellung gelöst werden können. (Kaindl 1998: 10).

With this approach, projected titles are not simply a utilitarian adjunct to understanding but an integral part of the performance and of the creation. Titles give the audience the illusion they are receiving verbal meanings directly.

The basic principle of surtitling is to avoid distracting the attention from what is happening on the stage. Let me explain how this is done in a little more detail. There are five major elements that need to be considered.

(1) First, repetitions and secondary details are not translated, unless this would give the public the feeling that they are missing something. The basic decision is thus which lines to include and which to eliminate.
(2) Although the surtitles are based on the libretto and follow as closely as possible the original text and style, they have to be easily understandable as regards syntax, vocabulary and content (one glance at the title should be sufficient to understand the text, so that for one brief moment alone the attention is distracted from the stage).
(3) Surtitles should form a logical unity (minimum sense blocks).
(4) Surtitles should never appear before the entry of the singer/chorus.
(5) Lastly, but perhaps most importantly, surtitles may never give the impression of nervousness.

Under-translating is preferable to trying to get every word into titles. The overall rhythm, duration and timing are crucial, because titles should not be exposed there after the singer has stopped singing, yet long enough for the audience to be able to read them. Therefore, the closer the conductor and the director are in conceptualising the use of titles in the design, the better.

Another key issue is the quality of the translations. As titles are made by several surtitlers, the quality is often said to be uneven. Even in the biggest opera companies, there is seldom anybody who sits down to review the title scripts, analysing which one is right for the production. One reason is that they are not really equipped to make a literary or aesthetic judgement. Those who denounce the literary quality of translations have little conception of the defects in the original. Another point is that it means that they have got to look at the text while listening to the opera, because it is the only way you can judge it. You cannot read it as a text, because it is an integral part of the total opera. Music and dramaturgy are 75 to 80 percent of the opera experience and the lines sung account for some 20 per cent. Titles reverse the ratio, the 20 percent experience becomes the 80 percent experience, with the music receding into the background.

During the stage-orchestra rehearsals, the content as well as the pure technical aspects of the surtitles (layout) can and will be tested and adjusted to the staging and the interpretation of the music. With the Libretto surtitling system it is always possible to make changes in layout. Even though the type and size of the characters, as well as their brightness and colour (red/green/yellow) have been selected on the basis of previous experiences, the system has the capacity to alter any of those parameters rather quickly.

One major drawback of many current titling systems lies in the clarity of the text on the display, especially for brightly lit sets. Working on getting greater contrast in the system could perhaps alleviate this. What I would like to argue is that the advantages of projected titles outweigh the shortcomings. Opposition to this method is, I suspect, based on mere conservatism, habit, misplaced aesthetic canons or resistance to a small but beneficial, pleasure-enhancing innovation. However, while the performer expresses one thing at one time, the screen is saying a related thing at a not-too-distant time: disparity is inescapable. Adding to this is the loss inevitable in verbal translation, such as rhymes abandoned, wordplay obscured by more concise phraseology.

What are the implications for the translation of an opera, besides the purely linguistic factors?

It is a truism, though an important one, that the words to which composers set their music are of crucial importance, especially in opera, where the words are an intrinsic element not only in the expression of the meaning of what is sung, but of the dramatic action, and not only the words, but syllables, inflections, accents, rise and fall, emphasis. Consequently there arises a problem: should accessibility of the meaning of the words be sacrificed in favour of fidelity to the composer's intended fusion of words and sound? Or, on the contrary, should the fidelity on which purists insist yield to intelligibility? Is there an inescapable incompatibility between the two approaches?

This case study will exemplify the way the mechanics of opera and the mechanics of titles interact. The examples taken from *Parsifal* must be followed word by word, if its impact is to be fully responded to - and the effort is worth it – even more to the majority of Wagner's operas, where the words play a significant role.

Parsifal is notoriously difficult to translate, let alone phrase in surtitles. The libretto is a strange mixture of elements from three sources: the Christian liturgy (Percival or the Grail legend of Chrétien de Troyes), and Wolfram von Eichenbach's poem Parzifal a manuscript dating back to the 14th century called Mabinogion. Adding to this, he was inspired by Schopenhauer's philosophy. Although we must concede that the score is one of the most beautiful edifices ever raised to the glory of music, we appreciate the fact that translation in the titles is concise: just enough to render the text, but not the repeated phrases.

Before we get further into our discussion, let us take a few minutes to look at some examples. Just after the opening, the titles give a bold interpretation and reading of the score of the German lines whilst they ideally should gain in refinement and bring out more transparency for the opera audience who cast their eyes above the proscenium.

(1) Libretto[1]
Gurnemanz : *Hi! Ho! Waldhüter ihr, Schlafhüter mitsammen,*
so wacht doch mindest am Morgen!

Dutch literary translation[2]
He! Ho! Gij woudhouders, -
slaaphoeders bovendien,
wordt ten minste toch 's morgens wakker.

French literary translation[3]
Hé! Ho! gardiens de la forêt.
Gardiens tout endormis vous-mêmes.
Eveillez-vous au moins le matin!

De Munt - Dutch titles[4]
Hé! Woudwakers! Word tenminste's morgens wakker!

La Monnaie - French titles[5]
Hé! Gardes du bois!
Veillez au moins à l'aurore!

VLOS - Dutch titles[6]
bewakers van het woud, hoeders van de slaap
word toch wakker

French subtitles[7]
Hé! Ho! Gardiens de la forêt
Qui ne pensez qu'à dormir
ouvrez l'oeil au moins
quand c'est le jour.

Dutch subtitles
Hee daar! Woudwachters
die alleen aan slapen denken

Hou tenminste de wacht –
als het dag is.

Notice that in the former example surtitles have no standard convention as this can be seen in the different use of typography (capitals, fonts…), punctuation and layout.

(2) Libretto
Jetzt auf, ihr Knaben!
Seht nach dem Bad!

Dutch literary translation
en nu op, gij knapen! Zorgt voor het bad.

French literary translation
Debout, jeunes gens … Préparez tout pour le bain.

De Munt - Dutch titles
Sta nu op! Zorg voor het bad

La Monnaie - French titles
Debout!
Veillez au bain!

VLOS - Dutch titles
sta op, knapen
en zorg voor het bad

French subtitles
Allons, debout, enfants!
C'est l'heure du bain.

Dutch subtitles
Vooruit nu, jongens!
Tijd om te baden.

(3) Libretto
Heil euch! Wie geht's Amfortas heut?
Wohl früh verlangt er nach dem Bade:

Dutch literary translation
Heil u! - Hoe gaat het heden Amfortas?

Hij wenst zijn bad wel vroeg:

French literary translation
Salut à vous... Comment se porte Amfortas aujourd'hui?
Il a demandé bien tôt qu'on le baigne

De Munt - Dutch titles
Hoe gaat het vandaag met Amfortas?
Hij verlangt vroeg naar zijn bad.

La Monnaie - French titles
Comment se porte Amfortas ?
Il a demandé son bain de bonne heure

VLOS - Dutch titles
hoe gaat het met Amfortas?
hij wenst zijn bad wel vroeg

French subtitles
Comment est Amfortas ce matin?
Il veut son bain bientôt il me semble.

Dutch subtitles
Gegroet!
Hoe maakt Amfortas het vandaag?
Hij wil zijn bad vroeg
Dunkt me.

In surtitling, projected titles are kept at a minimum of the entire text, even of ensembles when the various characters may all be saying something quite different. To me, the key points of the analysis and of the courageous experiment of surtitling *Parsifal* seem to support the assumption that operagoers – above all those who underrate the beauty and depth of operas because they cannot follow the words, can be made enthusiastic by becoming able to understand the meaning musically and emotionally of what is going on. Articulation, as diction, in opera – whether original or translated – are rarely intelligible. Since nobody expects to understand, nobody complains about the real cause, which is not the inadequacy of translated opera but the absence of it. The comprehension factor is dependent on such factors as the style and the range of the vocal writing, the complexity and subtlety of the orchestral texture. Many of those involved in the birth of projected titles assumed that they would work much like the subtitles in foreign films, but things did not turn that way. Moreover, translating drama with the assistance of titles is less evident, because of the speech tempo, the dramaturgy and not the least, because of improvisation. The example of *Arturo Ui,* Brecht's play[8] subtitled for ARTE and surtitled for deSingel, illustrates two differences: from the audience's point of view, subtitles are right there on the screen in the same field of vision as the actors, which is not true in the theatre. There is an obvious difference between a television screen, which can be taken in a simple glance and the stage, where projected titles do require a brief upward look:

> Durch die Übertitelung entsteht für den Zuschauer ein neues Seherlebnis. Die Blickrichtung bewegt sich zwischendem über der Bühnen geschehen selbst durch multidirektionale, je nach Situation fokussierende oder aufganzkeitliches Erfassen ausgerichtete Sehbewegungen. (Kandl 1998: 13).

A great deal depends on precise synchronisation, the angle of vision, the size of the letters, the type of illumination, punctuation, the exact position above the proscenium and, this is unavoidable, selection and compensation of the text. In movies, subtitles do not require the plasticity that goes with live performances.

Another main difference between drama and lyrics is that in an opera, we have music and a concise dramatic plot, whereas within a play, the narrative structure plays a key role. In Brecht's plays, the technique based on the so-called "*Verfremdungseffekt*" (alienation effect) is increased by the titles creating two levels of viewing. *Arturo Ui* offers an example of combination of prose and verse which is not reflected in the titles since their purpose is to clarify the dramatic situation.

(4) *Sein oder nicht sein, das ist hier die Frage*:

Dutch surtitles
Zijn of niet, dat is de vraag

French surtitles[9]
Etre ou ne pas être, c'est la question

(5) *Ob's edler im Gemüt, die Pfeil und Schleudern*
Des Wütenden Geschichts erdulden, oder…

Dutch surtitles
is het edeler voor de geest de pijlen
van het lot te dulden…

French surtitles
Est-il d'âme plus noble de subir les traits du sort...

(6) *Sterben - schlafen-*
Nichts weiter! - und zu wissen, daß ein Schlaf
Das Herzweh und die tausend Stöße endet,

Dutch surtitles
Sterven, slapen, niets meer.
En weten dat de slaap het einde is
van zieleleed en ingeboren angsten...

French surtitles
Mourir. Dormir. Pas plus.
Et savoir que dormir est la fin de l'angoisse du coeur et des affres...

A little more comparative research makes it clear that captions in a video opera recording function like those in a foreign film and are open to the objections raised against projected titles in theatre, i.e. that they impede communication. Video titles require minimal optical diversion from the picture itself, and if applied after the actual performance, can be fine-tuned for timing and content.

Recognising the role of new technologies in the dissemination and enjoyment of stage productions, titles have done more than anything else to increase the size of the audience. The viewer of an unfamiliar opera can understand the plot at first glance, without having previously read the libretto. As surveys attest, an overwhelming portion of the public enjoys titles. Their well being is crucial. This is part of a cultural problem in which everything is consumer-oriented and has to be fully accessible immediately. But whatever the problems – and a few must still be addressed – surtitling, one kind or another, is here to stay.

Notes

1. Libretto by Richardt Wagner based on a text by Wolfram von Eichenbach.
2. Dutch translation of the libretto by Georgette Gorus-De Rijcke.
3. French translation of the libretto by Georges Pucher.
4. Surtitles in Dutch for De Munt by Koen Van Kackenberghe.
5. Surtitles in French for La Monnaie by Brigitte Brisdan.

6. Surtitles in Dutch for VLOS by Jacques Peters & Simen Van Machelen.

7. Subtitling in French by Bernard Fraylich - movie by H. J. Syberberg.

8. Heiner Müller, Berliner Ensemble, 15-16/11/1996 deSingel, Antwerp.

9. French surtitles by Monique Nagelkopf for deSingel.

THE CHOICE TO SUBTITLE CHILDREN'S TV PROGRAMMES IN GREECE: CONFORMING TO SUPERIOR NORMS

Fotios Karamitroglou
University of Athens, Greece

1. Introduction

Greece has been traditionally described as a predominantly subtitling country. A research conducted for the years 1994-1996 indicated that 91.4% of the total volume of foreign programmes was broadcast subtitled, 5.7% dubbed, 1.9% in free commentary and 1% in voice-over + subtitling (Karamitroglou 1998: 157). As a matter of fact, all non-children's TV programmes were broadcast subtitled except for some documentaries and news/information programmes which were broadcast in voice-over + subtitling, as well as some sports programmes which were broadcast in free commentary.[1]

But what about the specific case of children's TV programmes? In most of the other predominantly subtitling countries across Europe, it is purported that when it comes to children's TV programmes in particular the subtitling norm tends to be modified since "cartoons are invariably revoiced even in subtitling countries [...] because of the age-range of their expected audience and because of the need to preserve their visual integrity" (Luyken et al. 1991: 134).[2] In Greece, however, it has been discovered that in the same years under study (1994-1996) only 55% of the total children's TV programmes were released dubbed, whereas 45% were released subtitled (Karamitroglou 1998: 117). So, what are the reasons behind such a choice? What are the motivations that drive the commissioners into deciding to subtitle children's TV programmes too? In order to investigate this normative phenomenon I will follow a systematic approach and try to account for all the factors which participate in the formulation and perpetuation of normative situations in audiovisual translation. I classify these factors under

a) the products themselves (children's TV programmes),
b) the audiovisual mode in question (TV),
c) the targeted audience/recipients (children), and
d) the human agents / commissioners involved (in children's TV programmes).

2. An analysis of the factors

2.1 The products

A first step that one should take before analysing the startling 45% that subtitled children's TV programmes get in Greece, is to examine the distribution of the various programme types amongst this final overall amount. Astonishingly enough, all (100%) of the children's *movies* are released subtitled. In other words, it is only *series* that get dubbed. This shows a first clear indication that the programme type of the specific children's programmes plays a crucial role in the decision to broadcast it subtitled. The answer to the question "why this special treatment for children's TV movies?" comes easy if we accept that the language transfer choice for this particular programme type cannot but be inevitably influenced by the language transfer method that dominates the cinema medium, i.e. the major representative of movies in the audiovisual media. During the same years (1994-1996) in Greece 94.3% of the total volume of foreign cinema products was released subtitled. All non-children's movies were invariably subtitled. As for children's cinema movies, the norm was to release them subtitled (68.4%), unless their theme and humour were clearly targeted at younger children, in which case they were released dubbed or in a double version (subtitled and dubbed). Apparently, no such distinction is made for TV programmes; and since the cost of a double broadcast / release is immensely high, commissioners of children's TV programmes quite logically opt for the cheap - and at any rate dominant - method of subtitling.

Even within the same programme type of series, however, it is the percentage that *cartoon* productions manage to collect which increases the share of dubbing. 70% of all TV cartoon series were broadcast dubbed. When it came to live action or cartoon + live action series, however, the share of the dubbed products dropped to 23.6%. It is actually the excessive number of cartoon series occupying the airtimes of what is characterised as children's TV programmes which manages to sustain the overall percentage of dubbing after all. But why is there a differentiation in the treatment of live action series? The answer lies in the conceptualisation of what a children's programme is and the visualisation of its target audience. Cartoon productions strike automatically as children-oriented; the notion of cartoons, of unreal drawings moving on the screen, is associated with something targeted at children, bearing a children's theme or even perhaps humour. Live action productions, however, although probably made to appeal to children, do not automatically carry the above features; on the contrary, in terms of their filmic perception and psychology of viewing they resemble very much the rest of the live action productions made for adults. Since the rest of the live action productions made for adults are broadcast subtitled on Greek TV, why not these ones too? At any rate, children do watch adult programmes as well, so we can presume that they get accustomed to the use of subtitling at quite an early age.

But what kind of products comprise the 30% of the subtitled cartoon productions? We notice at a glance that most of these products fall into one or more of the following categories:

a) they have a theme/humour that appeals more to older children (44%),
b) they are re-releases or new episodes of older productions which had already been released subtitled in the past (8%), or
c) they are productions with established high status (in the eyes of the target community) most often coming from one of the large and respectful studios like Walt Disney or Warner Brothers (25%).

For those products with adult theme/humour, the argument behind the choice to subtitle them is based on the presupposition that older children (who are expected to constitute the core of the target audience) are already accustomed to the norm of subtitling through their watching other "adult" material. For the new episodes or the re-release of older subtitled productions, commissioners seem to be reluctant to invest more money into having a production dubbed since this would employ the risk of de-customising their audience from a firmly established norm. And finally, as far as the highly esteemed productions are concerned, the choice to respect the status of the original entails the decision to leave the soundtrack intact and opt for subtitling. For the remaining 23% of the subtitled cartoon series one should consider to the possible late arrival of the episodes, and – most of all – the cost factor, in combination with the expected low viewing rates for the specific programmes.

In closing, the language of the original was found to play some role in the choice to release some children's cartoon series subtitled, since only 17% of the productions which did not have English as the original language on screen were released subtitled; the small amount of such productions, however, could not really affect the overall picture.

2.2 The audiovisual mode

The ultimate argument that is put forward in favour of subtitling children's TV programmes is that since TV is such a popular mass medium it can promote reading skills better than any other kind of activities (Aaltonen 1995: 387; O'Connell 1998: 65; ITC ed. 1996: 12). At the same time, children have been found to be more vulnerable to linguistic phenomena around them than adults are (Davies Messenger 1989: 11). From an educational point of view, therefore, subtitling could prove better than dubbing not only because it can promote children's reading abilities but also because it accommodates fewer idiomatic expressions and anglicisms that could influence their language use especially when their carrier is the mode of TV (Herbst 1995: 259; Ross 1995: 48; Whitman-Linsen 1992: 108). Since, however, children watch TV mostly for fun and less for information/education purposes (Palmer 1988: 143) and dubbing can allow an audience with limited reading abilities to access a product with less cognitive effort (Volmar 1950: 540; Gottlieb 1994a: 102; O'Connell 1998: 65; Karamitroglou 1996: 35) it is natural for children to favour dubbed material precisely because it involves less cognitive effort. This, however, does not mean that commissioners have to follow this suggestion; especially when recent studies have indicated that the act of reading subtitles does not require any conscious cognitive effort on the part of an audience already accustomed to this specific language transfer method (Delabastita 1990: 98; Chalier & Mueller 1998: 100). It becomes an automatic process (d'Ydewalle et al. 1991: 650; cf. Gunter 1982: 8). Thus, if children, especially of older age groups, watch a great number of adult products too, where the norm of subtitling is overwhelming, we can assume that their reading behaviour gets accustomed to processing the cognitive load of subtitles much faster than children from other countries at quite an early age. It is quite reasonable to suggest, therefore, that Greek children, especially of older age groups, do not find the use of subtitles particularly disturbing. This can explain to a large extent the decision to subtitle children's TV programmes with a more adult theme or humour, namely products that are expected to appeal more to older children, especially since children have been found to be better lip-readers than adults (Fodor 1976: 53), so they are more liable to spot bad lip-sync and be disappointed by a hastily dubbed production.

However, it should be noted that the much acclaimed use of subtitling for the educational purpose of promoting *second language* learning by the presence of a foreign spoken language on screen has been proven false, since it is actually reverse subtitling (spoken native language with second language subtitles) that has this beneficial effect (Blane 1996: 123).

In Greece, the issue of the eyes focusing on flashes on the screen when reading subtitles and its effects on children's vision still creates controversy with some doctors claiming that it "wears eyes out" (Papageorgiou 1981: 7) and some others pointing out that "the weariness of the eyes as reported by many viewers after prolonged TV watching is due to the weariness produced as a result of their usual labour, simply emphasised by television" (Kanavakis 1977: 24) [my translation].

Other constraints of a more technical nature related to the mode of TV and the need for subtitled multiple-language broadcasts available via teletext, as e.g. in the case of the European satellite Children's channel some years ago (Kilborn 1993: 656) did not prove applicable to the Greek situation.

2.3 The recipients

The company that measures viewing rates in Greece (AGB) describes as "children audience" the group of viewers which range between the age of 6 and 14 (AGB Hellas ed. 1996: 100). Overall, it is believed that the lack of reading proficiency amongst children in general makes them favour dubbing (Luyken et al.1991: 136). Detailed studies have indicated that the lower the children's social background, the more they are likely to stay at home, watch TV, regard it as a means of entertainment and, therefore, the more they favour dubbing (Koronaiou 1992: 128; Palmer 1988: 151). On the other hand, the higher the children's social and educational background, the less they watch TV, the more they regard it as a source of information and not just entertainment and, therefore, the less they favour dubbing (ibid). Apart from these studies, however, it is also reported that it is children under 6 who mainly watch children's programmes, whereas children between the age of 10 and 12 mainly watch adult material (Gunter & Svennevig 1987: 10; Stipp 1993: 301). And although my research did not attempt to investigate the viewing habits of children according to their social background and therefore did not produce any results that could relate such parameters/factors with the choice to broadcast any of the children's TV programmes subtitled rather than dubbed, it did manage to highlight differences between the viewing habits of younger and older children. In general, it was proven that children between the age of 10 and 12 watch three times as much adult TV material than children between the age of 6 and 10 (AGB Hellas ed. 1996: 101).

As children grow older and watch more adult TV material, they are consequently expected to be more conditioned by it; and since the predominant language transfer method for adult TV material in Greece is subtitling, Greek children of an older age are expected to be conditioned by subtitling and prefer or even sometimes request it. On the other hand, and more importantly in our case, children's programmes themselves are not viewed by children alone; a large sector of the adult audience watch them too. In Greece, most children in the household (78%) watch TV with other members of the family (AGB Hellas ed. 1995: 33). This seems reasonable considering the fact that only 1% of all TV sets are placed in children's bedrooms; 79% are placed in the living rooms and another 16% in adults' bedrooms (AGB Hellas ed. 1996: 32). As a result, private TV watching by children is rarely feasible. As for who decides what to be watched, 31% say that this is a decision they take together, and only 4.5% say that it is children who take the final decision (AGB Hellas ed. 1995: 33). As a matter of fact, the average market share[3] for children's TV programmes occupied by the "children audience" in 1994-1996 is only 27.3%. Interestingly enough, it is 20.1% for young men and women aged 15-24, and 16.4% for men and women aged 25-44, i.e. potential parents (Karamitroglou 1998: 129). In this respect, we cannot claim that children's TV programme commissioners can clearly idealise a potential homogeneous "children audience"; they rather have to cater for the needs of adult viewers too. If, then, the viewing rates[4] – and not only the market shares – for adults as far as children's programmes are concerned proved also relatively high, whereas the viewing rates for children proved relatively low, it would be reasonable to assume that the language transfer commissioners would not risk a potential investment in dubbing in order to satisfy the children audience since dubbing, even in Greece, is approximately 10-15 times more expensive than subtitling.

For children's movies, which, as we saw, were released invariably subtitled, the average viewing rate for children was 1.8% whereas the overall viewing rate (including adults) was 1.2% (Karamitroglou 1998: 138). We see, therefore, that the choice to broadcast these specific products subtitled rather than dubbed is justified by the relatively low percentage reached for children viewers and the relatively high overall percentage. When it comes to cartoon series on TV, however, the average viewing rate for children is 1.9% for the subtitled productions and 3.1% for the dubbed productions. The overall viewing rate for cartoon TV series is 0.6% for the subtitled productions and 0.7% for the dubbed productions (ibid). We notice, therefore, that children do finally prefer dubbed cartoon productions. This is an incentive for the commissioners to release such products dubbed and justifies the overall trend that TV cartoon series tend to be dubbed. On the other hand, though, the relatively low overall percentages cannot justify the high investment risk of dubbing. And in addition, the balanced overall viewing rates prove that the actual targeted audience are not children alone; and if adult viewers are to be satisfied too, why should commissioners of TV cartoons overrule the choice to release some of these products subtitled rather than dubbed? This hypothesis is reinforced by the fact that a general move towards more dubbed children's TV programmes – as experienced in 1996 – was not found to be accompanied by higher viewing rates.

What is most extraordinary, though, and proves the intricacies and complexities of the issue is the case of live action series. The reason is that out of all children's TV programmes, the one with the highest viewing rates is a dubbed live action series (*Power Rangers)* which in March 1995 and March 1996 reaches the astonishing 10.7% and 13.8% amongst children (2.5% and 2.7% overall) (ibid: 142); and this considering the fact that only 23.6% of the live action or cartoon + live action series were broadcast dubbed. The result is even more surprising once we realise that this was the only dubbed children's live action series in March 1995. The massive success of the series was obviously the motive for the TV station which broadcast it dubbed (ANT1) to dub another live action series in March 1996 (*VR Troopers)* which also reached astonishing viewing rates (10.8% amongst children and 2.1% overall) (ibid). The rest of the (subtitled) live action series, by contrast, record very low viewing rates, somewhere between 1.7% amongst children and 0.7% overall on all other channels (ibid). These contradictory facts and figures suggest that there may be something other than the language transfer method alone involved in the success of the two ANT1 broadcasts, and the choice to release the rest of the live action series subtitled is perfectly justified. The answer lies in the boost given to the programmes by the toy industry that produces *Power Rangers* and *VR Troopers* merchandise. This toy industry supports and commissions the programmes, markets them in the best way possible and caters for the best quality dubbing available. Which brings us to the role and contribution of the human agents involved in the choice to dub or to subtitle children TV programmes.

2.4 The human agents

The structure of the audiovisual translation industry is different in every country, rather complicated, often quite cliquey, and even more often based on connections and networking. Greece is not an exception to this rule. In most cases, it is the TV station's administrative board (plus staff from the marketing department) who will decide on the language transfer for all programmes, including children's programmes, unless there is an in-house translation department which is sometimes also consulted. The role of film distribution agencies also seems to be important, since quite often they tend to intervene directly in the audiovisual translation process (cf. Delabastita 1989: 202) – less so in television, more in cinema – guiding or supervising choices at every step of the process. In the case where the commissioning of a children's programmes is supported financially by an international TV programme distributor, dubbing is more likely to be used.

Due to the oligopoly-based structure of the audiovisual translation market, commissioners throughout Europe tend to pay whatever price they are quoted for the audiovisual transfer of their programmes (Luyken et al. 1991: 89). Audiovisual translators' unions strengthen the professionals' position in the industry and provide them with some voice of resistance (Hempen 1998: 53; Dries 1995: 11). In Greece, however, there are no such unions at all. As a result, commissioners will still pay the price they are asked, but they will not negotiate with the audiovisual translation studios or with the free-lance translators any choices to do with the language transfer method to be followed. They will rather impose these choices directly and with no further discussion. At the same time, however, they will not interfere too much with linguistic choices below the text level (cf. Gambier 1994: 280). All this, of course, provided that the TV stations do not have an in-house audiovisual translation department (cf. Vitkus 1995: 319).

Greece seems to be wrongly classified as a country where TV stations tend to have their own in-house translation departments (Luyken et al. 1991: 93). The truth is that out of the whole range of TV stations operating on Greek territory, only one state-owned channel (ET1) and a relatively new cable corporation (Filmnet) have such departments. Clearly, then, when dealing with national norms and practices concerning the choice of language transfer method, it is not helpful to examine the role of the translation agencies; it is the norms and values of the film distributors and the receiving TV network people that will have to be primarily investigated. The particular structure of the committee that decides which language transfer method will be implemented is important for the following set of reasons:

a) the fewer the people involved in the decision, the more flexible the committee, the easier it is to change already established norms and habits and as a result, the more likely it is that the committee will vote for the more radical solution of dubbing;
b) the more involvement on the part of departments of marketing, trading and purchase, the more likely it is for financial considerations to be raised and the less probable that a financially risky solution like dubbing will be finally implemented; and
c) the more involvement from people from the audiovisual translation department, the more awareness of the special nature of the targeted children audience and as a result, the more likely it is to decide on dubbing, the theoretically preferable method for children's TV programmes.

Quite surprisingly, a questionnaire that was distributed to and filled in by Greek TV programme commissioners revealed a unanimous preference for dubbing as the optimum language transfer method for what was described in generic terms as "children's TV programmes". If this is the case, however, why do they finally choose to broadcast many of such programmes subtitled? The answer came with a question related to their perception, visualisation and classification of "children's TV programmes". Almost all of them indicated that they differentiate between programmes targeted at older (10-14 years old) or younger children (6-10 years old), and for the former they explicitly recommend subtitling.

In general, Greek children's TV programmes commissioners claim that they base their choice of the language transfer method on:

a) the potential recipients of the programme; this means that for a potential young children audience they would most likely vote for dubbing;
b) the time this programme will be broadcast; this means that a programme shown at non-peak hours is less likely to be dubbed, but it also means that a

programme broadcast at times when viewers are mostly adults is likely to be subtitled;

c) the specific programme type and genre; this means that they prefer to dub series and cartoon genres; and

d) the language of the original, meaning that if it is not in English, the programme has more chances of being dubbed.

Out of these four acclaimed parameters we saw that three were finally implemented. What was found not to play any role in the choice language transfer method was – surprisingly enough – the time that the products were shown. One would expect the commissioners to be more reluctant to dub a production that would be broadcast very early in the morning, i.e. at a time when the number of viewers is by definition considerably restricted. Such concern, however, did not seem to play any role in the commissioners' final decision.

They all claim emphasis on the feedback they get from viewing rates, meaning that if a dubbed programme does not eventually prove successful it might switch from dubbing to subtitling. At the same time, most of them seem to be very cautious and reluctant towards dubbing because of what they perceive as "inherent difficulties" that hamper the prospects of good quality work, pointing at the need for an ideal match of target voices with characters on the screen and paying particular attention to the quality of the oral verbal material used (i.e. easily comprehensible, not offending children). In terms of broader subtitling norms that influence the commissioners' decisions, however, it is only the people from one station (Filmnet) who explicitly explained occasional preference for subtitling some of their children's TV programmes with the strong subtitling tradition in the country. This is the most straightforward acknowledgement of the existence of powerful norms in Greek audiovisual reality.

3. Conclusions

All the above indicate that in Greece, human agents i.e. audiovisual language transfer commissioners, seem to be tightly bound and strongly conditioned by established norms which they are reluctant to break. Children's TV programmes are victims of the overall tendency that the whole country seems to follow and accept towards subtitling. The fear of an audience familiar with subtitling already at quite an early age distinguishes Greece from other traditionally subtitling countries around Europe which seem to be less dependent on the predominant superior subtitling norm and allow for dubbing to be implemented. The astonishing viewing rates achieved by one particular dubbed live action series, however, prove that there is nothing in the programme genre (cartoon or other) which is inherently related to the appreciation of either language transfer method. The higher response of the audience towards some dubbed productions seems to be more the result of the promotion and individual quality of the specific programmes than an outcome of the choice of language transfer method. In this respect no one can claim, exclude or predict any future developments in the country. As a matter of fact, the tendencies for children's TV programmes seem to be highly in favour of dubbing. It is only that the deep roots and the omnipotence of the subtitling tradition will make it hard for any attempt to alter the setting and reverse the current situation overnight. Time – and money – is required. However, I believe it won't be long before Greece will join the practices of other predominantly subtitling countries around Europe and will start making a clear distinction in favour of dubbing children's TV programmes in general.

Notes

1. It is true that in the last couple of years some soap operas have started to be broadcast dubbed but unfortunately these cases fell outside the time span covered by this study.

2. A similar deviation from the overall subtitling norm is claimed to apply not only to cartoon programmes but also to live-action or puppet children's TV movies or series in general.

3. The "Average Market Share" is defined as the percentage of viewers of a specific programme in relation to the number of people watching TV at a specific time-point (AGB Hellas ed. 1995: 107).

4. "Viewing Rates" (or "TV Rating") is defined as the percentage of viewers of a specific programme in relation to the total potential viewership, i.e. the number of people who own a TV set (AGB Hellas ed. 1995: 106).

STRIVING FOR QUALITY IN SUBTITLING: THE ROLE OF A GOOD DIALOGUE LIST

Jorge Díaz Cintas
University of Surrey, Roehampton
London, UK

1. Introduction

There are certainly several factors that impinge on the quality of subtitles that appear on screen. For the purposes of this paper, I will divide them in three loose categories. Some of the problems we encounter are of a physical nature, and therefore easily noticeable and closely linked with the constraints imposed by the medium itself: lack of synchronisation, excessive reduction, insufficient time to read the subtitle, etc. Most of these problems can be overcome easily nowadays thanks to the help of computers and specific software for the subtitling profession.

In addition to this set of time-and-space constraints, there are some metatextual factors that are at least as important in determining the quality and nature of the end product. These are concerned with the working conditions under which the subtitler is forced to work, of which, as Fawcett (1983: 189) points out, "The most important are: poor wages [...]; absurd deadlines [...]; poor originals [...]; and finally, poor training of translators". We could also add two other factors to this list. Firstly, the excessive atomization of the profession with the unfruitful and unnecessary split between translators, spotters, subtitlers, adaptors, etc. – though it has to be mentioned that not all studios apply this distinction. At Titelbild (Berlin), for instance, the person who does the spotting also formulates the subtitles (Smith 1998: 144). And secondly, the excessively endogamic nature of this job circuit that renders entrance to the profession rather difficult in many countries.

There is still a third category, derived from the actual linguistic transfer. And it is here that I would like to focus my attention. The basic aim of any translation is to reformulate a source language message in a given target language, avoiding at all costs any misunderstandings in the process. In other translation practices mistakes can easily pass unnoticed, but this is rarely the case in a mode of translation as uniquely vulnerable as subtitling, always challenged by its concurrent *tertium comparationis*. In this sense, a determinant factor that facilitates the task of the subtitler and helps to reduce potential comprehension mistakes to a minimum, is a good dialogue list.

2. Different types of dialogue list

There are several types of list, as I shall mention in this paper, but in essence, a dialogue list (not to be mistaken with the script) is the compilation of the dialogue exchanges that materialise in the film, and that, according to Minchinton (1986: 8), is "the essential text" for the subtitler, although unfortunately its use is rather rare in the professional world. This regrettable reality may be one of the reasons why in many subtitling training courses students work directly from the screen, without the help of any dialogue list, in preparation to enter a working environment that tends to work without this valuable document. James et al. (1996: 182) state that "Students do not work from a script and the course requires that they gain experience of creating subtitles directly on screen on the basis of the sound-track alone, as is normal for professional subtitlers in Wales". And according to Gottlieb (1994b: 267) the same attitude is adopted in courses run in Denmark: "on our courses we rarely use manuscripts. The students, like simultaneous interpreters, must rely on their eyes and ears in order to receive the message correctly".

Such a list is usually supplied by the film distributor or producer and in its ideal format it offers, besides all the dialogue, metatextual information on the implicit socio-cultural connotations, explains punning, word play and possible double entendre, explains the meaning of colloquialisms and dialectalisms, elucidates the origin and the usage in context of certain terms that may be obscure at first sight, gives the correct spelling of all proper names, advises on the convenience of using a particular font type for some words in the subtitled version, clarifies implicit as well as explicit allusions to geographical realities, etc.

The inclusion of this avalanche of details may lead some to believe that it is purely spoon-feeding the subtitler. After all, most translators in other fields must work only with the original text and some reference books such as dictionaries and the like. However, it cannot be stressed enough that here we are dealing with a totally different working context, where deadlines are nearly impossible to keep, and therefore time for the research of a particular problem can be very limited or nonexistent. Besides, linguistic hurdles that can be easily distorted or even deleted in other translation practices, without the target reader noticing at all, are problematical in the case of subtitling due to the aforementioned concomitance of both languages. This is why the provision of a good dialogue list makes the difference between a high quality product and an inferior one.

In terms of layout, the dialogue may come unprocessed and it is the task of the translator to do the spotting of the linguistic exchanges. It may also be that the dialogue has already been broken up by spottings, a *spotting dialogue list,*[1] and in this case it is assumed that the subtitler will have some latitude to decide what to transfer to the target language. In other cases, we encounter what is known as a *standard list* that contains the dialogue already compressed into subtitle lengths in the original language, *master subtitles*. In many instances, the latter document may come without the full dialogue list.

There are general guidelines aimed at homogenising the production of these lists and at setting minimum standards, although the heterogeneity of layouts seems to be the norm these days.[2] In the United Kingdom, for instance, there is a *British Standard Specification* called *Recommendations for the Preparation of Motion Picture Export Scripts* (Minchinton 1986: 13). On a wider level the *European Broadcasting Union* (EBU), based in Switzerland, resulting from the *Conference on dubbing and subtitling* that took place in Stockholm in 1987, launched a proposal with the guidelines that should hopefully be followed in the submission of material that accompanies audiovisual products that need to be translated. These recommendations can be found in the *EBU Review, Programmes, Administration, Law* 38(6): 31, november 1987,[3] but since they are not compulsory, they are not always followed. In the case of contemporary films this choice of including a dialogue list is optional, and the common practice is that the films come with a rather incomplete one. With old movies it is usual that the subtitler does not have a list and that the original linguistic material must be transcribed directly from the screen, a practice that can lead to misunderstandings of the original message and, therefore, to subtitles that are at odds with the original message. However, even in the lucky event that one of these lists is provided by the distribution or production company, Minchinton (1986: 13) is nevertheless sceptical regarding its absolute validity and advises us to: "Be prepared to find omissions in dialogue lists where texts are not dialogue: newspapers, letters, captions, recordings of speeches, songs, radio voices and so on. This is because dialogue list compilers usually forget that there are other texts in a picture besides the actors' dialogue". To which we could also add the caveat to double-check the spelling and meaning of loan words that come from a language different to the two in play; another potential minefield for the translator.

As mentioned earlier, lists reaching the subtitler can be very rudimentary, a mere transcription of the film dialogue (see dialogue list 1, Almodóvar), or be extremely complete and include a large number of clarifying notes both linguistic and extralinguistic (see dialogue list 2, Allen).[4] On occasion these annotations may seem rather insubstantial. However, the asides as well as the explanatory notes may fulfil a function closely linked with the commercial dimension of the film industry, a factor sometimes neglected by scholars when commenting on the quality of the product. With all this information included in the dialogue list, the translator should not need to watch the film, and the distribution company can prevent the circulation of the film before the commercial launching, an element that is particularly important in the case of films that are preceded by big publicity campaigns that whet the appetite of future spectators.[5] Needless to say, the detrimental effect that this practice can have on the final product is obvious.

3. An example of a complete list

In the case of *Manhattan Murder Mystery / Misterioso asesinato en Manhattan*, directed by Woody Allen in 1993, I can confirm with total certainty that the dialogue list[6] provided is scrupulous and accurate and would be hard to match, with its large quantity of detail and explanation. Its 329 pages comprehensively register information considered to be relevant to the translator, including an introductory note on behalf of Woody Allen, addressed to all translators and thanking them for their ingenuity. We are certainly presented here with a very complete standard list (see dialogue list 2, Allen)[7] On the left hand side of the page we find the combined continuity and dialogue; that is, the detailed and faithful reproduction of what the actors say on screen, including repetitions, exclamations, redundancies, linguistic fillers, etc. together with the asides that help contextualise the performance of the characters. This side of the list is meant for dubbing translators who, according to Zarmati, "need the full text with every utterance" (e-mail exchange). On the right hand side of the page, in English, we find the master subtitles, that is, the dialogue pruned into which is meant to be the material that the translator has to transfer into the target language and that, once more according to Zarmati, is meant for subtitle translators. What is debatable here is whether it is possible, or even advisable, to make such a clear cut division. Since it is on the right/subtitler side that we find lots of explanatory notes whose aim is to facilitate the translator's task, it seems rather probable that the dubbing translator will resort to this side of the page to profit from it as much as possible. On the other hand, resorting to the material compiled in the left/dubbing translator side of the list can pay dividends to the subtitler, as I hope to demonstrate with my examples below. It is, therefore, my contention that to cross-reference in both directions is beneficial for both the subtitler and the dubbing translator, so there is no need to establish a rather artificial divide in the document.

4. A valuable co-operation

Returning to the actual list, what is relevant in the case of the compressed dialogue on the right hand side of the page is its generalised rationalization and naturalization when compared with the 'gross' dialogue on the left. Hesitations, repetitions, false starts, etc. have all been neutralized in a much more compact and logical, yet at the same time more clinical and less colourful discourse, as we can appreciate in the following examples from pages 2-(15), 11-(9) and 12-(3)[8]:

2-(15) TED (overlapping) You said she liked- She liked eating high cholesterol desserts. Is that what you said?	TED (to group) You said she liked eating high cholesterol desserts.
11-(9) CAROL Well, yeah, it's, excuse me, hey don't worry, yeah, okay	CAROL (to Larry) Yeah, don't worry, okay?
12-(3) LARRY (into telephone) Yes, yes. Yeah, no, no, no, no, I-I-I-I understand. I, uh yes, no	LARRY (into telephone to Paul) Yes, no. I understand

Somehow the translator's task has been lightened (the overlapping of dialogue, for instance, has been dealt with), but it could be argued that this lightening is at the expense of the translator's freedom, since there is always the possibility that the subtitler would have opted for a different way to fracture and reconstruct the original dialogue. In House's terminology (1986), the translator's framework of negotiability is, *a priori*, of a castrative nature, with severe limitations as far as the selection of original material is concerned. And the same opinion is shared by Smith (1998: 144-145) when he states that "a ready-made spotting list would tend to encourage translators to divide their subtitles to fit it, even where better solutions could be found". Although Allen's detailed standard list imposes some restrictions, there always exists room for manoeuvre for the translator, in direct connection with the above mentioned advice from Minchinton (1986) not to blindly follow the dialogue list. And this is precisely the attitude adopted by the Spanish subtitler[9] when, contrary to what has been 'recommended' to him in the right column, he has preferred to recuperate information from the 'gross' dialogue that had been originally ignored, as we can see on page 1-(6):

1-(6) CAROL (overlapping) I know. Can you believe this guy in Indiana? Killed twelve victims, <u>dismembered</u> them and ate them	CAROL (to Larry) I know CAROL (to Larry) Can you believe this guy in Indiana? Killed 12 victims and ate them.

Here, the Spanish subtitler has preferred to sacrifice the substantive "victims" and place the emphasis on the gruesome aspects of the killing:

[7] Ya lo sé. Es increíble /// lo de ese tipo de Indiana.
[8] Mató a doce, los /// <u>descuartizó</u> y se los comió.

In other instances, this policy pursues a clear objective as in the following example from page 7-(3):

7-(3) LARRY You want to lie down for a while? We'll put a cold compress on your head, or a hot compress on your back, or--	LARRY (to Carol) You want to lie down? We'll put a cold compress on your head.

Here, the subtitler has preferred to transfer to Spanish a version more complete than the one proposed in the right column, with the aim of reinforcing the ironic value of the English statement. At the same time the translator has opted to resort to a synecdoche and substituted the whole *head* in English for the part *frente* [forehead] in Spanish:

[898] Túmbate, te pondré /// compresas frías en la frente,...
[899] ...o calientes en la espalda. O...

In this particular example, had the subtitler blindly followed the instructions in the right hand column, the humour of the original would have been irrevocably lost, since there is nothing strange in putting a cold compress on the forehead of someone ill or dizzy.

One of the paralinguistic singularities that predominate in the film is the nervous and agitated characterization of the protagonists, especially the one played by Woody Allen. The personality of the various characters that appear in the film is determined by a very particular sort of behaviour in the way in which they exteriorise their feelings. And this is the reason why their linguistic performances are characterized by false starts, syntactic readjustments, repetitions, exaggerated intonations, semantic and syntactic hesitations, unfinished sentences, etc. The subtitler has quite rightly realised the importance of these stylistic strategies and, once again refuses to follow what has been prescribed, deciding instead to retrieve information from the on-screen dialogue in order to recreate the same impact in the target language, through the written medium:

3-(3) LARRY (overlapping) She worked on those for-- [327] Lleva preparándolo desde...	{remark not meant to be translated}

3-(11) LARRY (off) Maybe he didn't want to spend eternity next to the beloved. So he-he told us that, uh-- You know, what's the difference?	LARRY (to Carol) Maybe he didn't want to spend eternity next to the beloved. So he told us that. What's the difference?

[370] Puede que no quiera pasar /// la eternidad junto al ser querido,...
[371] ...y nos dijera eso, ¿comprendes? /// ¿Qué más da?

Returning to the meticulousness of the dialogue list, some of the clarifications offered are of limited value, since they add information that cannot be transposed into the target message. This is the case of the conversation between Ted and the would-be actress, Helen, who, when boasting about her artistic achievements, tells him:

> 11-(24) and I was even, uh, Miss, uh, Teenage Passaic.
> (note that Passaic is a working class town in New Jersey)
> [1790] ...y llegué a ser "Miss Quinceañera /// de Passaic".

In this particular instance we can ask ourselves if the loss of the connotative dimension, pregnated with irony, is not a price that most of Woody Allen's films have to pay. The director's umbilical relationship with the urban environment in which his characters move, leads to the inclusion of references of use only to those fully familiar with the city of New York and its surroundings. On this level, the geographical connotation can be as alien to a Californian or Briton as to a Spaniard or German. In direct relation to this, and related with the semantic dimension of the dialogue exchanges, Desroches (1984: 7) gives us his opinion when he states that "they approach the limits of adaptability, partly due to their frequent word play, partly because of their many allusions to the precise context of New York (allusions that, one should note, are sometimes even incomprehensible to English-speakers that do not live in this metropolis of the United States)".[10]

In the search for perfection, minute details are taken care of, such as the inclusion of intratextual references pointing back to previous dialogue exchanges, with the objective that the subtitler can achieve the greatest degree of internal cohesion and coherence. Here is an example from page 2-(13):

> 2-(13) LARRY (to Carol)
> I get the urge to conquer Poland.
> (Humorously referring to the fact that Wagner's work was a favorite of Hitler and the Nazis, who invaded Poland in 1939)
> (See Title #1-3)

The result is a product that not only the spectator but also the critic would perceive as being of high quality. It has to be acknowledged that there are several factors that contribute to this final perception besides a mere adjustment of synchronization between oral and written material. One of them is what I would call *overtranslation strategy*, that allows the subtitler to reclaim elements from the "gross" dialogue, not only to convey to the spectator the psychological comfort that no information is being kept away from him/her, but also to reinforce the comic impact of the original as well as to recreate, in written form, the hesitant, broken nature of the characters' speech.

An extratextual factor that cannot be overlooked is the one concerning the director's persona. If at a literary level any work by say Shakespeare enjoys the halo of a canonized product that requires a greater respect on the part of the translator, it seems fair to say that in the linguistic transfer that takes place in the film world, the figure of Woody Allen is the closest to this canonization phenomenon.[11]

The communication channel is another factor to be taken into account since it can be argued that the attitude adopted by the subtitler, or the person responsible above him/her, when confronted with a product meant to be televised and aimed at a passive customer is not the same as that adopted when having to translate the same product for a video version, as is the case here, aimed at an active client that has bothered to go out and buy it.

But probably most important of all factors is Woody Allen's own attitude towards translation. There is no doubt that he is aware of the great importance that the linguistic transfer (be it subtitling or dubbing), and therefore the translator, has in the appreciation of his movies in non-English speaking countries. This is the reason why the dialogue list can be seen as a sort of *clin d'oeil* to the linguistic mediator. It is an act of co-operation and understanding that is patently obvious not only in the mentioned "Thank you for your ingenuity!" that ends the introductory note, but also in all the multiple additional explanations that are scattered in this valuable working document and that, as in the example from page 2-(15), are presented more as a confirmation of the director's well-known hypochondriac nature than as elements *sine qua non* to satisfactorily bring about the linguistic transfer:

2-(15) TED (to group) You said she liked eating high cholesterol desserts. (cholesterol: note that deposits of cholesterol form in certain pathological conditions, as gallstones or arteriosclerotic plaques and high strum. Cholesterol is linked to heart attacks)

The artistic zeal of Woody Allen is evident in several European countries. In France, for instance, a married couple of dialogue translators for dubbing, Anne and Georges Dutter, has the monopoly over all the films directed by Woody Allen (Seren-Rosso 1989: 33). This factor guarantees a high degree of homogeneity amongst all the works by the same film director that have been dubbed into French, promoting at the same time a closer and more productive interaction between the director (or the person that acts on his behalf) and the professional responsible for the linguistic mediation. As far as Allen's filmography in German is concerned, Johnson (1992) mentions that the American director keeps a close eye on the dubbing of his films, and he is very aware of what is going on, to the extent that he has even said that "Wolfgang Draeger's German voice in Manhattan suited him better than his own" (ibid.: 62). He has also followed very closely the dubbing of his movies in Spain and has shown his human dimension when after the death of Miguel Angel Valdivieso, the professional responsible for dubbing Woody Allen himself for several decades, the director sent a telegram to the deceased's wife, "in which, among other things, he acknowledged the great job that her husband had done with his films" (Avila 1997: 105).[12] In direct relation to this artistic zeal, Whitman-Linsen (1992: 151) mentions that "since 1987, Woody Allen has employed a supervisor for the dubbing of his films in Europe", a measure that the American scholar considers very successful since "there are therefore fewer blunders and misrepresentations of his work".

5. A high quality target product

As I mentioned at the beginning of this paper, there are certainly many factors that contribute to the final linguistic quality of the subtitles for this Woody Allen video. The discursive cohesion and coherence, the numerous attempts at attaining the same impact as the original, the recreation of the different linguistic registers, the implementation of the compensation strategy, the absence of deficiencies or errors, etc. are all key elements in this positive perception of the whole. But we should not forget that these achievements are closely linked with the dialogue list, hence its prime importance. A detailed dialogue list is imperative if we are to create a high quality target product, and it is the director's duty, possibly through some supervisor as in the case of Woody Allen, to guarantee that the subtitler receives one of these lists as well as to control the end-product quality. In one of his works, Ivarsson (1992: 11) deplored that "Unfortunately, film directors and TV producers seldom show any interest in what happens to their works once they are exported to other countries", and the same idea is shared by Krogstad (1998: 62) when, after recognizing that contemporary films are increasingly being produced for the international market, he goes on to deplore that "Still, it doesn't seem to be an integral part of the planning of a film that its reception abroad depends on the quality of the verbal transmission". It is high time this situation changes. In an increasingly globalized market, with the great potential for boosting box office receipts abroad, translation is a fundamental part to the international success of a movie, and many directors still have to wake up to the reality that the translation process is an artistic factor on which more control needs to be exerted and in which it is worthwhile to invest the necessary amount of money – which generally is very little compared with the overall budget. Subtitling, as dubbing, has to be understood as an integral part in the process of the artistic creation of a film and not as a mere appendix subject to market forces.

It is somehow understandable that, due to time pressure, dialogue lists are not available for the subtitling of news programmes, but it is lamentable that detailed lists are not provided for the subtitling of films, which cost millions and are long term projects. At the very least, it would be an act of goodwill and acknowledgment towards the linguistic mediator. However, when dialogue lists are inadequate or simply nonexistent, translators ought to be able to retaliate by inflating the price of their services. Although not resorting to it as a weapon, Dries (1995: 13 & 25) is aware of the negative effect caused by the absence of a dialogue list and mentions this factor as one to be taken into consideration when setting the price for a programme. In countries such as Finland, rates are increased by 30% or 40% when the list is incomplete or nonexistent, respectively, and according to Ivarsson (personal communication), Swedish television pays 60% more to subtitlers that have to work without a dialogue list.

From my analysis of the linguistic data, there is plenty of evidence in the Spanish version of *Manhattan Murder Mystery* that the subtitler has not fully respected the way the dialogue was spotted for him/her, creating, nevertheless, a high quality product for a particular audience. This discovery seems to point out the fact that the ideal situation should be one where spotter and translator are the same person, thus contradicting Luyken's debatable view (1992: 167) that the verification/spotting task ought to be carried out by someone other than the translator, in order to improve standards and increase profits.

Finally, a good dialogue list should be compiled by a professional with a flair for the sort of problems involved in linguistic transfer and should contain as many details as possible, even if, as in the Passaic example mentioned earlier, the metatextual information proves too elusive to convey. Some translators may, and in fact do, find these explanations an irritant and often too basic, but it cannot be forgotten that the ultimate aim of the list is to be useful to as many translators as possible, working in different countries and coming from very different cultural backgrounds. So, when translating an American or French film, what may seem straightforward for a European audiovisual translator may not be so for a translator from an African or Asian country.

By now, I hope to have made clear the prime importance of a dialogue list. But translators, beware, because it is not a sacrosanct document and should be used with a critical eye and a pinch of salt.

Notes

1. In the use of the terminology I follow Minchinton (1986).

2. Torregrosa (1996: 74-75) offers the reader four of the most common models of dialogue lists.

3. Some of the proposals directly affect the translator's ethics, such as number four that stipulates that "new slang expressions or local jokes should be explained in the script" (Ivarsson 1992: 184).

4. These asides offer metatextual information of a varied nature: camera movements ("Camera pans L. and tilts down to Carol and Ted seated in Ted's car") or character moves ("Helen opens the rear passenger door and starts to get in the taxi"), intonation of the statement ("chuckles", "moans"...), character's attitude ("indistinct to"), etc...

5. This situation arises in some cases, despite the fact that this practice contravenes the 1976 UNESCO recommendation that translators have the right to use original documents when transferring from one language into another (Chalier & Mueller 1998: 100).

6. I would like to show here my gratitude to Elio Zarmati, President of Gelula & Co., for his comments on the terminology they use to refer to this document. According to him, this list should be referred to as a CCSL (*Combined Continuity and Subtitle/Spotting List*). The use of terminology in this field is certainly in need of some harmonization. Without the intention of debating this issue on these pages, I prefer to use the term *dialogue list* which, in my opinion, is of a more global nature.

7. The Spanish subtitles quoted in this article come from the subtitled version of the film that was released in video format by *Columbia Tristar Home Video* in 1995.

8. In the pagination of the dialogue list the first digit refers to the film reel in which the dialogue exchange can be found (from a total of 12), whilst the number in brackets corresponds to the page in the working document. Thus, 10-(23) indicates that the dialogue exchange can be found on page 23 in the section that compiles all the information for film reel number 10. On the other hand, the number in square brackets that precedes the subtitles in Spanish makes reference to the numerical order of the subtitle within the film, out of a total of 1944.

9. This attitude seems to contradict the somehow over-confident statement by Torregrosa (1996: 78), who assumes that with a spotting dialogue list (like the present one) the problem of having to select and purge the linguistic material that has to be transferred to the target language "queda resuelto" ["is solved"]. What is clear is that following the advice by Minchinton, the subtitler has to be constantly on the alert and should not accept blindly what is imposed to him/her in the compressed dialogue.

10. My own translation of the French original "frôlent la limite de l'adaptabilité, tant en raison de leurs nombreux jeux de mots que de leurs allusions fréquentes à un contexte précis, celui de New York (allusions qui, soit dit en passant, sont parfois même incompréhensibles à des anglophones qui n'habitent pas la métropole des États-Unis)".

11. With the scarcity of material dedicated to the linguistic transfer that takes place in the audiovisual world, it is noticeable that the only name that comes up with some regularity and authority is that of the New Yorker Woody Allen: Desroches (1984), Seren-Rosso (1989), Johnson (1992), Whitman-Linsen (1992), Pisek (1994), Avila (1997), Díaz-Cintas (1997). This is undoubtedly a clear indication that the figure of this film director is well on the way to (semi)canonization in this field.

12. My own translation of the Spanish original: "en el que, entre otras cosas, reconocía la estupenda labor que había realizado su marido con sus películas".

Dialogue List 1: *The Flower of My Secret,* Pedro Almodóvar (1995)

LEO:	Eres mi marido. ¿Tengo que explicarte cuáles son tus obligaciones conmigo?
PACO:	Me prometiste que agarcaríamos nuestros problemas hasta que terminara el conflicto.
LEO:	¡Lo lamento mucho, pero no estoy hecha de metal! No se me puede aparcar como a los coches...
PACO:	¿Por qué no intentas entender la situación?
LEO:	No hay nada que entender. Entre yo y tu trabajo, tu trabajo es lo primero...
PACO:	¡Estoy intentando salvarle la vida a mucha gente!
LEO:	¿Por qué no salvas la mía?
PACO:	Leo, estoy hablando de gente inocente, gente que no tiene para comer, gente a la que matan mientras hacen la cola del pan, que no tiene luz, ni medicinas... ni esperanza!
LEO:	¡Estás hablando de mí!
PACO:	¡Eres el colmo del egoismo! ¿No puedes dejar de pensar en tí aunque sólo sea un momento?
LEO:	¡No! ¡Y eres un hijo de puta por poner a los pobres desgraciados de Bosnia como pretexto!... Solicitaste voluntariamente la Misión de Paz para huir de la guerra que tenías aquí... y de esa guerra la única víctima soy yo... Desde el momento en que decidiste pertenecer a las Fuerzas Internacionales de la OTAN ya te estabas separando de mí... Podrías haberte quedado en tu despacho del Ministerio de Defensa, si hubieras querido... al menos hasta ver cómo solucionábamos nuestros problemas. Pero tú sólo querías huir de mí... ¿Por qué no tienes el valor de reconocerlo, eh?...! Respóndeme!
OFF LEO:	"¡Le odio! ¡Ojalá pudiera seguir odiándole como ahora! Este odio me ayudaría a arrancarle de mi vida. Dios mío, no creo en tí, pero ayúdame."
LEO:	¿Te vas ya?
PACO:	Sí.
LEO:	Paco, por favor, te estoy hablando…
PACO:	¿Qué?

<u>Dialogue List 2:</u> ***Manhattan Murder Mystery*, Woody Allen (1993)**

Manhattan
Murder Mystery
Title & reel R/7 P/34 Spotting list footages & titles

Combined continuity & dialogue	**title no.**	**start**	**end**	**total**	**title**
SCENE 9 - (continued)					
LARRY (overlapping) That meant absolutely nothing. She hated me. Julie despised me.	7-192	979.12	985.14	6.2	LARRY (to Carol) That meant absolutely nothing. Julie hated me, despised me.
CAROL (overlapping) What?					
LARRY You know that. She-She thought I was lowlife, and a wimp, and a vermin, and a roach.	7-193	986.2	991.2	5.0	LARRY (to Carol) She thought I was a lowlife, a wimp, a vermin and a roach. (lowlife: colloquial for 'low-class, vile, comtemptible person')(wimp: colloquial for, 'cowardly, timid,effeminate, contemptible person') (vermin: colloquial for, 'despicable person') (roach : colloquial for, 'disgusting, despicable person')
CAROL (overlapping) (sighs)					
LARRY Just-Just jump in any time you want to defend me, you know.					
CAROL (overlapping) Hey, I mean, I'm waiting for you to say something I don't agree with, okay?	7-194	991.6	994.12	3.6	LARRY (to Carol) Jump in any time to defend me. (i.e., 'against these charges of Julie's') (Jump in: i.e., 'Interrupt me')
LARRY (chuckles) Ho-Ho!					
	7-195	995.0	1000.0	5.0	CAROL (to Larry) I'm waiting for you to say something I don't agree with.
CAROL (overlapping) (chuckles)					
LARRY Hey, you're nailing me. Jesus.	7-196	1001.0	1005.0	4.0	LARRY (to Carol) Hey, you're nailing me. (nailing me: colloquial expression used to acknowledge a telling remark or rejoinder on the order of 'touche')

FEATURES OF ORAL AND WRITTEN COMMUNICATION IN SUBTITLING

Alexandra Assis Rosa
Universidad de Lisboa, Portugal

1. Subtitling and dubbing in Portugal

Media translation of foreign-language programmes in Portugal is almost synonymous to subtitling, for it is the most common choice of translation in Portuguese television,[1] films and video. In television, dubbing is confined to advertisements, children's films or cartoons, as well as to South-American soap-operas dubbed in Brazilian-Portuguese. This habit has built a preference of the Portuguese audience for subtitling which has recently coaxed cable television channels to start substituting dubbing, which was adopted in earlier stages, by subtitling. Nevertheless, dubbing continues to be a subject for discussion as a possible alternative with the purpose of also reaching a still considerable illiterate audience.

2. Subtitling of dialogue as both interlingual and intesemiotic translation

As "interpretation of verbal signs by means of some other language" (Jakobson 1959: 233) subtitling is interlingual translation. As such it is here considered mainly in its attempt to draw a correspondence between the group of linguistic varieties (dialects and accents) of the Source Text Language (STL) and the system of the Target Text Language (TTL), i.e., finding a parallel between historical, regional, socio-cultural and situational varieties of ST and TT Languages.

Subtitling is also intersemiotic translation because it transfers to written verbal language a source text which in most cases corresponds to face-to-face communication, and therefore is multi-channel and multi-code:

made up not only of verbal signs but also of non-verbal signs – such as visible and audible gestures.[2] Therefore, subtitling involves:

(1) a change of medium: from speech and gestures (both visual and audible) to writing;
(2) a change of channel: from mainly vocal-auditive to visual;
(3) a change of the form of signals: mainly from phonic substance to graphic substance and, as a result,
(4) change of code: from spoken verbal language (and non-verbal language) to written verbal language.

This considered, subtitling faces several different problems, among which I would like to point out the following. Firstly, finding a correspondence between historical, regional, socio-cultural and situational varieties (dialects and accents) of the ST Language and the TT Language is no easy task. This is the case not only because in some instances the parallel does not exist but also because the linguistic variation of a language has not always been thoroughly described by scholarly work, and the translators are left with little more besides their intuitions about the languages concerned. This is even more so due to the characteristics of the source text that consists mainly of speech and is therefore likely to include evidence of linguistic variation, irrespective of its being real-life or fictional discursive interaction. Secondly, considering the multimedia nature of the ST, some problems may also arise from the effort to transfer that part of meaning also conveyed by the non-verbal component of oral communication, namely comprising features such as visible, audible gestures and prosody, among others. When left untranslated these elements may in some cases assume the same meaning in ST and TT cultures. However, in other cases they can not only be impossible to interpret but also assume different or even opposite meanings thus confusing the audience. This is particularly important when the non-verbal signs convey information which is necessary to interpret the verbal component of communication, when they are in counterpoint to the verbal component, and especially when they are in contradiction to the information conveyed verbally, as often happens in the case of irony (see Teresa Tomaszkiewicz, in this volume). Thirdly, as for registers determined by the medium, the translator is faced with the choice of textual features ranging from those of a TT oral register similar to the ST – since subtitles are the representation of spoken verbal communication – to those of a written register in the TT – in accordance with the norms of the medium of the subtitles: writing.

Focusing on the third item mentioned above – the change from mainly oral verbal language to written verbal language – the intersemiotic transfer creates the problem of a possible hesitation between situational varieties that range from the oral register of the source text to the written register of the target text. These two registers differ in terms of functional and structural features, and the point here is to raise some questions about the choice of structural features of oral and / or written register in subtitling of films shown on Portuguese television.

3. Choice between structural features of oral and written register

The choice of structural features of oral and written registers in subtitles naturally involves the decision about the TT's adequacy and/or acceptability (Toury 1995) in terms of register. However, as I see it, this choice also poses a few problems rising from the way native speakers value the characteristics of these two media –speech and writing – and those of their respective registers. The attitudes of native speakers organise the different varieties of their mother tongue in a centre of prestige mostly occupied by standard, formal *written* language. Compared to this centre every deviation, whether standard or non-standard informal *speech,* is promptly pushed towards the edges and regarded as something beyond the border of what they consider correct. This value system may be a conscious or unconscious motivation behind the choice of what I have called strategies of centralization or decentralization (Rosa, 1999). As Lambert and Delabastita remark: "le type exact de traduction, que nous préférons rattacher à une *stratégie* (largement inconsciente) ne manque pas d'être aussi influencé par des rapports de prestige ou de pouvoir, bref par des rapports entre des cultures et des institutions (systèmes de valeur)." (Lambert & Delabastita 1996: 48).

To the consideration of this evaluation of speech and writing in terms of prestige and its relation to translators' choices, one must add the circumstances of the particular case of media translation. One of the consequences of this evaluation of speech and writing is also present in the criticism that audio-visual media are subject to. As Robin Lakoff points out: "much of the current unrelenting attack on non-literate media – earlier, comic books; currently, TV and movies – can be traced to the terror that we are about to regress as a civilisation into a new Stone Age, bereft of logical linear thought, that literacy alone allows for sensitivity, intelligence and complexity of thought." (Lakoff 1982: 239).

3.1 Predominance of written register features in subtitling

Most subtitles in Portuguese either do not present features of the oral register or reduce them to a hardly perceptible minimum. This is even more obvious in subtitles of spontaneous oral communication, such as extracts of interviews in the news. Most examples surveyed of non-spontaneous oral communication, such as films, convey the impression that the characters speak like a printed page. To name but a few features, this means that the subtitles:

a) mainly consider *referential function*, ignoring expressive and phatic functions
(question tags; emphatic markers);
b) emphasise *content* and not interpersonal involvement;
c) focus on *communicative* and less on informative signals;
d) concentrate on *linguistic signals* and overlook the importance of prosody and paralinguistic signals in the expression of meaning, usually not conveying nuances of loudness, rhythm, tempo and pitch (prosody);
e) omit overlaps, repetitions, hesitations, reformulation, and expletives, ellipsis, emphasis markers, interjections, incomplete sentences, forms of address, reference to mental processes, etc.;
f) concentrate on the *meaning in the text* vs. meaning in the context, e.g. omitting expressive illocutionary acts and reducing them to merely assertive ones;
g) use a TTL *standard variety* (usually equated with writing) to correspond to a STL non-standard variety. This means that the phonetic, morphological and syntactic features of sub-standard varieties are a) omitted, or b) sometimes lexicalised. As for informal and colloquial registers, slang and taboo words (often occurring in speech), they are usually levelled to less informal standard discourse. As remarked by Jose Lambert: "le sous-titre standard opte délibérement pour une représentation standardisée du discours (fictionnel) en recourant à un style zéro, au langage non-dialectal (l'exception confirme la règle) et grammatical." (Lambert, 1990: 235).

Despite the general fact that in Portugal, television subtitling complies with the norms of the TT written register and the standard variety, there is, nevertheless, a slight difference to be noticed between private and public channels. Although still exceptional, the presence of features of oral register in subtitles is more evident in films aired by private channels than in those aired by public channels. This reveals a possible difference of strategies in subtitling produced by private subtitling companies who work for private Portuguese TV channels, and in those produced by the department of translation of the public channels.

3.2 One example of the exceptional attempt to portray structural features of oral register

The corpus analysed includes evidence of the inclusion of features of oral discourse in the subtitles. The ST chosen corresponds to two film adaptations of *Pygmalion* by George Bernard Shaw. The usage of sub-standard and standard varieties of British English is central for the plot, (which, as known, may be summarised as teaching a speaker of sub-standard British English the standard variety). It is therefore essential that the target text portray this distinction, otherwise the audience who does not understand the spoken English version will be excluded from access to this central issue of the plot.[3]

The two examples surveyed were, firstly, the film *Pygmalion* by Anthony Asquith and Leslie Howard, produced for cinema in 1938 and aired in February 1994 by RTP, Canal 1 (public channel) and, secondly, an adaptation for TV by Alan Cook, produced by Twentieth Century Fox in 1983, and aired by SIC (private channel) in March 1995.

Faced with the impossibility of illustrating translation choices with real examples, I chose to briefly summarise the main types of phenomena observed.

In the first case – subtitles produced and aired by one public TV channel – there is a choice of Standard Portuguese for the representation of phonetic, morphological and syntactical characteristics of non-standard Cockney but some substandard lexical features of the ST are maintained by the choice of vocabulary in the TT. Most ST features of oral discourse are omitted, e.g.: ellipsis, markers of emphasis, interjections, incomplete sentences, hesitations, forms of address, etc.

In the second case – subtitles aired by a private TV channel – the effort to portray features of oral and sub-standard discourse is conspicuous. Several examples of alteration of spelling (though not coherent) portray not only a different accent (mainly different vowel quality) but also ellipsis or contractions characteristic of speech. The choice of vocabulary is used to portray substandard lexical features and there is also an effort to maintain the force of expressive illocutionary acts – characteristic of speech – instead of levelling them to merely assertive ones. The altered spelling, on the one hand, enabled the Portuguese audience to recognise the characteristics of the speech of Alentejo as the southern Portuguese dialect chosen as counterpart for Cockney. On the other hand, it also marked the non-standard status of the discourse portrayed. Interestingly enough, some oral discourse features included in the subtitles seem to have been used to mark the discourse as non-standard.

4. If representation of certain features of oral communication is possible, why is it an exception?

In view of the above, representing certain features of oral communication in subtitling is indeed a feasible option. However, the choice not to omit or not to reduce features of oral communication in subtitling remains exceptional, and this may be due to several motives.

Reductions may result from the *change of medium, channel* and *code*. Translators may feel a need to coherently comply with the rules of the TT register: writing. Reductions may be due to the *selective criteria characteristic of subtitling*, such as the need for text compression due to the use of 2 lines of 30 characters each, exposed for an average of 4-6 seconds. Another reason for the choice to reduce features of spoken verbal language may be associated with the *particular circumstances of the work done by translators*, who work mainly with scripts and thus with a written ST, who are insufficiently paid and subject to sometimes very serious time constraints. Under these circumstances, it is impossible to afford the time needed to create written representations of features of oral discursive interaction; and it is also easy to be influenced by the written features of the script used as ST. Another motive was mentioned by a representative of the subtitling department of the public channels: given that the main purpose of the subtitles is understood to be to help understand images as quickly as possible, reductions may be due to *avoid readability problems*. Therefore, the reductions or omissions may also be a consequence of the secondary or marginal function of the subtitles, which should not concentrate the attention of the audiences in themselves and are expected to exclude non-intentional informative elements of the discourse of the characters.

However, as I have already pointed out, these reductions may also be interpreted as the result of socially and politically significant choices influenced by value systems. If we consider the way native speakers value written language and regard features of oral discourse as incorrectness, the pervasive choice of a consistent written register to portray oral discourse acquires a different significance. As remarked by Gambier: "The anthropology of writing has shown how much power is based on writing and how much power the written word possesses" (Gambier 1994: 373).

Moreover, the choice to include oral register features in the TT involves risks because it is likely to be regarded as wrong translation by the average native speaker, as remarked by Lefevere: "*flavored* translations that deviate significantly from dominant linguistic norms may be dismissed as *incorrect*" (Lefevere 1992: 70). And, of course, translators who produce "incorrect" translations run the serious risk of being out of work.

5. How can we interpret the choice of a written register and standard variety in subtitles?

The apparently pervasive strategy of subtitlers to reduce or ignore non-verbal signs and reduce or exclude the translation of features of spoken verbal language may be due to several motives. Among the ones already mentioned, I would like to stress that this choice may result from an effort towards greater acceptability and coherence in terms of target text register. It may also be understood as an effort by public TV channels to uphold standard written Portuguese.

However, it may also be explained as an attempt to transfer the prestige of written language and standard variety to the work of translation and to the medium of television, already considered "sub-standard culture", mass culture or, even worse, an attack on *the* culture – which, of course, is a written one. This choice may, therefore, be considered a result of what I have called a strategy of centralisation, a choice of characteristics of the prestigious centre occupied by writing and by the standard. The greater predominance of written register norms in subtitles may be due to the fact that these norms are still considered by most average native speakers as the example of correctness. Translators are therefore, explicitly or implicitly, consciously or unconsciously, led to produce "correct", coherent written register TT versions of the ST.

6. How can we interpret the choice of features of oral register and non-standard varieties in subtitles?

Against a background of almost generalised use of a written register in subtitling, it is interesting to notice some still exceptional choices of features of oral register and non-standard varieties, resulting from what I have called a strategy of decentralisation.

This may be interpreted as an effort of bestowing adequacy on the oral register of the ST, even if this implies less acceptability in terms of TT register. Since this tendency has been noticed in subtitling aired by private TV channels, it is possible to conclude that private companies may feel less responsible for upholding the standard, hence allowing for a certain degree of "artistic freedom". Moreover, since the STs surveyed are considered works of art, informative as well as communicative signals are deemed relevant. This strategy may also be interpreted as a result of the ideological atmosphere. It may be considered a "politically correct" attempt to produce an accurate, adequate translation of the source text. Therefore, the inclusion of features of oral discourse in subtitles may be interpreted as a proof of the present and future rising prestige of speech and of the gradual change of the value system concerning writing and speech.

Prestige seems to be moving "down market", so that writing may portray non-standard and orality features. Thus, these exceptional examples may be interpreted as evidence of the beginning of an evolution experienced in Portugal. As Bolinger and Sears remark: "Universal literacy has partially closed the gap between the language of the models and the language of the learners; the more they have been able to write, the more up-to-date the writings have become" (Bolinger & Sears, 1981: 282). In Portugal, literacy is still not universal. Nevertheless, features of speech and non-standard varieties are acquiring a prestige that becomes evident in some attempts to include them in subtitles, following an evolution already started some years ago, for instance, by some prestigious Portuguese weekly newspapers.

Here the value system seems to be changing not only due to the influence of "political correctness" in the evaluation of standard and substandard, writing and speech, but also due to a positive evaluation of innovation and to an association of the notion of modernity to speech. The following remark by Jose Lambert has a bearing on this issue: "Le passage d'un medium à l'autre rend particulièrement significatives les décisions et priorités suivies en la matière [les tiraillements entre l'écrit et l'oral]. Préférer l'écrit à l'oral, ou l'inverse, n'est-ce pas se prononcer en même temps sur les hiérarchies de valeurs *du passé et du présent*?" (Lambert, 1990: 234) (my emphasis). Therefore, the exceptional presence of features of the oral register in subtitles may be indicative of the trend towards a choice for value hierarchies of the present.

7. Final remarks

A lot remains to be said and studied about the far from simple relationship between attitudes towards standardisation, writing and orality, on the one hand, and translation and media translation, on the other.

The present remarks were based on the analysis of a fairly limited corpus of subtitles and are to be regarded as part of a study in progress, the first results of which were published in Rosa 1999. They are also to be seen mainly as a series of questions formulated during preliminary research on the way in which the system of value associating prestige and correctness with writing may influence the translational choices made in subtitling. Some of these questions point the way for future research I would like to carry out to contribute to the description of the "how and why" of subtitling in Portugal.

Notes

1. The Portuguese audience can choose between to two public television channels (RTP Canal 1 and RTP Canal 2), two private ones (SIC since 1992 and TVI since 1993) and at present over 400 000 households have access to more than 40 cable television channels.

2. The terminology used here is that of Bolinger & Sears 1981

3. This also raises the question of excluding or including the reader/audience which, as mentioned by Peter Fawcett "has always been a driving force in translation" (Fawcett, 1995: 187) and is therefore related to consciously or unconsciously exercising power against the reader/audience. However, whether the translator/subtitler is actor or victim of this power play is in itself a topic for another paper.

PYGMALION BY G.B SHAW AND ITS TRANSLATIONS INTO PORTUGUESE

Shaw, G.B. (1856-1950)
1916 (1973) *Pygmalion*, Harmondsworth: Penguin.

1961 *Pigmalião: análise de peça de Bernard Shaw, precedida da respectiva tradução portuguesa*. trad. Port. Marina B. L. Prieto (dissertação de licenciatura apresentada à Faculdade de Letras da Universidade de Coimbra).
1972 *Pigmalião*, trad. Prot: Fernando Mello Moser, Lisboa: Verbo.
1987 *Pigmalião* (edição bilingue) trad. Port. Mário César Abreu, Mem Martins: Publicações Europa-América.

SUBTITLED VERSIONS OF *PYGMALION*

1938 *Pygmalion,* directed by Anthony Asquith and Leslie Howard, version subtitled by Ruth Saraiva, aired by RTP, Canal 1, 9.2.1994.
1983 *Pygmalion*, directed by Alan Cook, version subtitled by Eulália Ramos/Sintagma, aired by SIC, 28.3.1994.

THE SUBTITLING OF *LA HAINE*: A CASE STUDY

Anne Jäckel
University of the West of England, UK

1. A controversial film

This contribution applies an interdisciplinary approach which draws on globalization and postglobalization communication theories (Anderson 1983; Ferguson 1992; Cunnigham & Jacka 1996), theories of register and genre (Lefkowitz 1991; Hunston 1993), and audience-based reception studies (Ang 1996; Liebes 1990; Morley & Robins 1989; Hall 1992). It examines assumptions made about specific targeted audiences by film-makers and subtitlers and their implications in political, cultural, and economic terms. It also explores to what extent these assumptions play a role not only in multimedia translation but also in the reception of one film in various countries.

1.1 A mixture of influences

The film in question, and the object of our study is *La Haine* (Hate) a 1995 film directed by 28-year old French filmmaker and actor, Mathieu Kassovitz. *La Haine* presents a low-budget feature film, shot in black and white, using a mixture of "authentic material", fiction, and cinematic references. It blends a powerful soundtrack with sophisticated visual effects and cinéma vérité techniques. Hailed as an inflammatory political pamphlet, *La Haine* raised several burning issues: youth unemployment, youth culture, integration of ethnic minorities, urban violence. Costing 17 million French francs, the film was accused of sparking riots in Noisy-le-Grand, outside Paris, in June, 1995, just a month after its screening at the Cannes Film Festival.

The film clearly reveals France as a multicultural and divided society. Its three young heroes, unemployed and surviving on petty crime and drug-dealing, include Hubert, who is black, thoughtful, and a would-be boxer;

Vinz, who is Jewish, impulsive, and full of rage; and Said, who is hyperactive and a *beur* (a young French citizen of North African origins).

La Haine's youth speak a language that some critics call "prose-combat". It combines the particularities of the spontaneous languages spoken today in several French *cités.*

A mixture of many influences, it offers an almost perfect example of every possible deviation from standard French: sloppy language, bad grammar, misuse of words, use of local colloquialisms, slang, *verlan* (back-slang), Americanisms, Arabic, and all this intermingled with funk rhythm.

Critics describe *La Haine* as France's answer to Spike Lee's film *Do the Right Thing*. Two points are worth making about this alleged response to Lee. First, although one can speculate on the exact degree to which Lee's films appeal to French *cités* youth, it is clear that his films belong to their favourites. *Cités* youth language abounds in Americanisms, and *Malcom X* T-shirts belong to their dress code. Second, while most American blockbusters are released in France in both their dubbed and subtitled versions, the films of Spike Lee only run with subtitles.

Given this response, it comes as no surprise that *La Haine* seemed to have strong potential appeal to American youth. As a result, *La Haine* was subtitled for the Anglophone market, and distributors circulated this subtitled version in the English-speaking world. American actress Jodie Foster helped promote the film in the US, saying that it had much to bring to American audiences.

The variety of the film's speech forms created difficult problems for the subtitlers. For one thing, there are more instances of unusually fast speech rate and dense visual and non-verbal phonic information than is the case in an average film. To what extent did the subtitlers find suitable equivalents in the target language? What factors determined their choices? How problematic were those choices? To what extent did the subtitling determine the reception of the film in the English-speaking markets?

Before examining these questions, one should briefly refer to the extraordinary attention the film received in its country of origin and to the particular language in the film.

1.2 A popular film in France

In the 1995 Cannes competition, *La Haine* won the Best Director Prize for Mathieu Kassovitz. In Berlin, the film won Europe's Felix Award for the Best Young Director. Additionally it garnered three (French) Césars in 1996 for best film, best producer, and best editing. In June, 1995, the French prime minister, Alain Juppé took the unprecedented step of arranging a special screening of *La Haine* for his cabinet.

In France, the film played to both critical and public acclaim. With almost 2 million admissions in 1995, it reached thirteenth place in the French box office rating. It was particularly popular in urban areas (Paris region/province ratio: 3.25), becoming one of the most discussed events of the year. In the summer of 1995, reports circulated about young, upwardly-mobile viewers (*BCBG branchés*) sitting next to young, less sophisticated ones (*jeunes de cités)* in Parisian film theaters.

The French government's interest in *La Haine* may have triggered interest from unexpected quarters: older middle-class audiences, eager perhaps to gain some cultural insights into new sociocultural forms to which they had no direct access. When the film ran at Cannes in its subtitled version (ostensibly for Anglophone members of the audience), a substantial number of French people said they were glad for the subtitles. The subtitles helped them understand the language spoken by the characters in the film!

Reviewers praised the film for raising contemporary issues and focusing on the difficulty of communicating in today's France. The cinéphile magazine, *Cahiers du Cinéma,* hailed the film as both a deserving rival for, and a remarkable tribute to American film in so far as the dialogue only existed through the actors, delivery and gesture. *Jeune Cinéma,* on the other hand, criticized Kassovitz because he "had filmed the defeat of language". For this magazine, the verbosity of the characters only served to highlight "the impossibility of communication in a country losing its culture" (June, 1995).

In media interviews, the *cités* youth were divided over the portrayal of French youth in Kassovitz's film. While some believed the characters to be true to life, others expressed anger and thought the film potentially damaging because it could reinforce people's misconceptions about life in an environment consisting of bleak estates on the edge of a city. The film even evoked violent reactions when it played, for example, at the Grand Rex venue in Marseilles.

Being a young filmmaker and making a film about youth and the underprivileged did not necessarily mean that Kassovitz had produced a film that was accessible to young audiences. Even in France, many viewers felt confused and asked Kassovitz to explain his choice of language and the meaning of some scenes. Some youth criticized the film sharply. For example, in an interview published in *L'Événement du Jeudi*, one youngster named Rachid, said he did not like Vinz, whom he described as "a Frenchman who pretends to be an Arab: he does not know who he is, he speaks *verlan,* he adopts the culture of the *cité*, but it does not ring true. It is not a problem of race but of culture". (May 18-24, 1995: 77). In a country proud of its culture and keen to defend and promote the French language, *La Haine* provoked heated debates about language.

1.3 The Language of "La Haine"

In the last decades, Anglicisms and Americanisms have proliferated in France. On the other hand, the popular word game called *verlan* has only recently arrived on the youth scene. The game consists of inverting the syllables of a word, for example, *femmes* (women) becomes *meufs,* while *flics* (cops) turns into *keufs, mec* (guy) is pronounced as *keum*, and *juif* (Jew) is *feuj.* Other examples include *Arabe* (Arab) and *noir* (black), which become *reubeu* and *renoi,* respectively.

Franglais and *verlan* are not the only deviations from standard French. Bad grammar, misuse of words, local colloquialisms, and slang all appear in the film. Such verbal usage reflects different value systems.

Like *verlan*, the spontaneous languages spoken in the French *cités* have developed in reaction against the standard modern French language used by a largely middle-class French society. Initially, their primary function is one of differentiation. (Hunston 1993). For their users, such languages provide a way of asserting their right to be different and to challenge authority. While some see such developments as an enrichment, others regard them as the result of exclusion. Feeling excluded from mainstream society, people develop their own mechanisms of exclusion, in this instance, a verbally aggressive language mainly comprehensible to peers. Today, however, *verlan* has transcended social barriers and penetrated standard French language and mainstream French society. As a result, other varieties have emerged. *Beurs,* for example, like other groups, have developed language varieties in opposition to both the penetration of *verlan* into standard French and the appropriation of *verlan* by a particular group. For both *verlan*-users and speakers of other language varieties, code-mixing is considered a source of pride. With different groups in different locations developing their own language varieties and value systems, the situation is extremely complex. Worse still, it is constantly changing. Experts explain that such forms of speech vary from one region to another and even from one housing estate to another! It should also be noted that

> Such varieties usually have strong individual connotations: they depend on the speakers' feelings toward each other, what topic they are discussing, and where their conversation is taking place. (Lefkowitz 1991: 45).

Faced not only with an untranslatable *verlan* but also colloquialisms meant to be incomprehensible to the majority of viewers, how did the subtitlers cope?

2. Subtitling "*La Haine*"

Two Paris-based writers, Alexander Whitelaw and Stephen O'Shea, provided the subtitling, and they did so with great care. Whitelaw, a former film producer, has written the English subtitles for more than 500 French films over the last 20 years. O'Shea, a film critic for the magazine *Variety* has collaborated frequently with Whitelaw. In an interview given to *The New York Times,* the subtitlers said that Mathieu Kassovitz made only one request:

> His first movie, *Métisse,* which was released as *Café au Lait* in the United States, used subtitles whose language came straight out of the American inner city. This time, he said, he did not want ghetto slang to be used, because he felt that it had alienated the audience. (Riding 1996)

As a result, Whitelaw and O'Shea opted for what they called a mixture of styles. Certain political and cultural references to French society disappeared while other references were transposed and replaced by American equivalents. The comic book character Astérix became Snoopy, while *Les Schtroumpfs* (the Smurfs) became Donald Duck. The retail store *Darty* became WalMart, and Malik Oussekine's quote was replaced by one from Rodney King, an African-American beaten up by Los Angeles police officers. Dialogues such as *ta mère, elle boit de la Kro* (for Kronenbourg beer) in the French version became "your mother drinks Bud", (for Budweiser beer) in the American/English version.

Verlan, described by a British journalist as "the subtitler's nightmare" (*Independent*, 1995), posed a particular challenge. Whitelaw and O'Shea thought they could not hope to be understood if they borrowed or invented American back-slang. (Riding 1996). So they opted instead for simplicity: *keufs* became "pigs", *meufs* turned into "babes", and *keums* equaled "homeys".

Despite the endeavours of Kassovitz, Whitelaw, and O'Shea, most reviewers concurred that the subtitling was "frankly geared towards the American market". (Barry 1995-1996). In Britain, *The Independent* complained that the subtitles were too American. Ryan Gilbey, writing for *Premiere,* thought that "in English, the authenticity of the dialogue [was] almost entirely lost" and found himself "more stung by the picture when its characters' roaring and bragging was unintelligible (Gilbey 1995). David Styan wrote in *Vertigo*: "Sadly, Kassovitz's multiple meanings, his nuanced visual and verbal puns, are likely to be lost on a non-French audience. The subtitles, which are a sloppy pastiche of black American slang in which Vinz and Hubert talk as if they were *homeboys* in the *hood*, hinder rather than help an understanding of this dimension of the film." (Styan 1995).

By way of footnote, we can add that in 1996-1997 the author conducted a survey in the West of England among largely middle-class and educated audiences (teachers and their students) in an art house film theatre. Though these respondents may be fairly representative of British art house audiences, they do not typify the majority of multiplex cinema-goers in Britain. Still, this survey showed that British audiences did notice the American-style subtitling. Many found it inappropriate, noting, for example, that dollar signs and other US references felt wrong in a French-deprived environment. Others found certain references confusing.

At the same time, the subtitlers' choice of American amply justified itself. After all, American culture undeniably influences Europeans, and similarities exist between urban unemployed youth lifestyles the world over. In the French *banlieues* video stores stock an abundance of Stallone, Murphy and Schwarzenegger posters. With young *beurs* and blacks wearing *Malcolm X* T-shirts, baseball caps, and trainers, the male-dominated suburban environment of many French suburbs does not seem to differ much from the African-American ghettos of America's large cities. In 1996, visiting the set of Merzak Allouache's *Salut Cousin!* in Clichy (a northern district of Paris) and meeting the "homeboys" of the community centre, Hadani Ditmars noted that "American street lingo had now seeped into *banlieue* consciousness". (Ditmars 1996)

3. Problematic Choice of American Slang: Consequences for the Film Text

Although the choice of American slang can be justified on the grounds that no other form is universally recognizable in the English-speaking world, such a choice presents serious cultural implications. In the first place, it has consequences for understanding the film text, as illustrated by the following examples.

The subtitled version differentiates less between the three heroes' speech than does the French original version. Saïd's volubility, for example, leads him to often repeat three or four times the same utterance. But the subtitles rarely express this feature. In *La Haine* verbosity does not require a perfect knowledge of a language. In the film, the most talkative characters (those who take a whole scene to tell stories or lengthy jokes) show up either as foreigners like the old Eastern European gentleman, or as Arab or *Beur* (Said and Sam, the young boy on the estate). This point of characterization gets partly lost in language transfer.

Some have argued that the main usage of slang and *verlan* is related to their ludic function. Burling (1992: 34) refers to language games as a deliberate manipulation of language which shows more individual variety and innovation than the normal usage. Here, subtitling does the opposite. As a result, such energy and creativity on the part of the *Beur* characters for example, can be lost in the subtitled version. On the other hand, there is the suggestion that *verlan* resembles subtitling in so far as it emphasizes the essence of the characteristic it is describing. A more powerful form than standard French, it often functions as caricature. In addition, rude words, less used in their written forms, have more impact when shown as subtitles (One four-letter word appears 83 times in some 1,500 subtitles). Subtitled, rude words may appear more negative, aggressive, and hateful than their French equivalent.

To what extent does this approach affect people's reception of the film? Are non-Francophone audiences less sympathetic to some of the characters?

Audiences reading the subtitles often commented on the characters' poor mastery of the language (with the exception of Hubert who is the only one capable of code switching). Non-Francophone audiences seemed to notice less the greater verbosity of the Arab and *Beur* characters. This observation, suggesting that their gestural communication does not compensate for the verbal loss, leads to the question: To what extent does a necessarily simplified language rendering reinforce cliches about peer culture, youths, blacks, and immigrant minorities?

4. Socio-political Implications

There are citations of American films in *La Haine*, for example when Vinz in a comic scene looks at himself in a mirror and utters in French Robert de Niro's immortal line from *Taxi Driver* "Are you looking at me?" Given such references to American film and youth culture, the subtitles and the translation choices within the subtitles have cultural as well as political implications. For example, the subtitles reinforce a notion of American hegemony and a purported vision of America as a trend setter, whether in mainstream or minority culture. They do this because they resort to an American model (although a variant model of a non-mainstream kind): African-American ghetto/youth popular culture. Arguably, the written word reinforces a given discourse, elevating minority speech forms to authoritative discourse and helping a given discourse achieve and reproduce dominance, in this case, American dominance.

Given the anti-American stance of French cultural policy, best illustrated during the 1993 GATT negotiations, or in the grand project of Francophony (the defense and promotion of French language as a central cultural policy), the decision to award *La Haine* the French César for best film sent an ambiguous message. Kassovitz claims that his film is a pamphlet against police brutality, but the film's use and misuse of the French language challenges the whole French establishment. At a time when intellectual debates are dominated by cultural specificity and integrity, the role of the French language is seen as particularly important. For example, in 1996, the French Minister of Culture, quoted Francois I, Condorcet, and Richelieu before making his own eulogy of the French language. In that eulogy he said,

> To the weaker, the less educated, and no doubt, to the more recent French citizens, the French language represents their first capital, the sign of their dignity, ... a share of the common [national] heritage, a part of the French dream. (*Le Monde,* August 1996).

Clearly, the speech forms of those who do not speak or write French properly, like the young people in *La Haine,* pose a threat to French language policy, both in its national and international aims. Still, the film was sold to many countries with the support of *Unifrance,* the French film export agency. As a result, *La Haine* turned into a French "ambassador" to the rest of the world, an irony not lost on the subtitlers.

5. Impact of Subtitling on Other Signifiers

Subtitling seems to play down the unifying role of the soundtrack. It is no coincidence that in the film a popular chanson of post-war times (*Non, rien de rien, non, je ne regrette rien...),* intermingles with more contemporary music sounds (*Nique la Police!*) in one dream-like sequence. A British reviewer, cited on the film's *Tartan* video release, inferred that Kassovitz wanted

> to translate his characters' dreams and spirits, not just their anger, into visual language, hence the astral-planing, and the soundtrack's incongruous fusion of Edith Piaf with some relentless break beats.

A sociocultural approach would give a different reading and indicate that such fusion, far from being incongruous represents an attempt to reconcile the old and the new in a definite populist vein. It could be argued that, combined together, the tunes express (and encourage?) a sense of community at a time of disillusionment and economic hardship. Yet, here in the film, where one normally expects subtitles, there is only blank screen space, creating an impression of a void that may well reinforce the demoralization and emptiness of life in the *cité.*

6. Economic Implications

Translation choices also have serious implications in economic terms and, in the case of film, in terms of box office results. Although linguists agree that subtitling strategies should be adapted to the structure of the targeted audience(s), such agreement does not make subtitling easier. The term "audience" has an abstract and debatable character. Mass communication researchers have shown that communities are both real and imagined (Anderson 1983) and that, strictly speaking, one cannot know an audience (Ang 1996; McQuail 1997: 83). An audience is fragmented, for example in terms of its gender, age, class, and religion. And, like the language of the suburbs, an audience is not fixed but constantly changing.

The dominant position of American films on world screens may be well established, but use of Americanisms may not be universally acceptable to all English-speaking/reading cinema audiences. Given that *La Haine* was subtitled into American English, one could expect the US market to respond more positively to the film than the British market. In fact, just the reverse occurred: in the Anglophone world it was not in the US but in the UK and in Australia that the subtitled version of the film found greater success. Audiences in the UK (a fifth of the American market) turned out in numbers twice as large as audiences in the US. One possible explanation is that in the UK art-cinema audiences are more familiar with the French language. Another is that, like in France, curiosity and pedagogy played an important part in the relative British success of the film. The above-mentioned Bristol survey showed how eagerly teachers and their students saw/learned about French youths, French *cités*, French slang, and youth culture. By offering such insights to teachers and students it proved to be a pedagogical tool that gave access to French youth culture – a fact that no doubt made the director and his young cast shudder with horror. (In France, faced with an uncontrollable mediatization of some of the issues raised in his film, Kassovitz complained the film no longer belonged to him!)

7. Reception

7.1 In the U.K.

La Haine opened in Britain in November, 1995, shortly after its London Film Festival screening. Film reviewers took a largely positive view, and the French director's presence in London at the launch of the film helped give it substantial media coverage. In Britain, as in France a few months earlier, nobody realised the film's immediate relevance. By an ironic twist of fate, three weeks after the film's UK release, in December, 1995, a riot erupted in Brixton. The coincidence struck a British reviewer who subsequently wrote: "In the morning after the riot, amidst the shattered shop windows and charred, pulverised cars, there was the same eerie calm and paralysing tension which hangs over Mathieu Kassovitz's devastating film." (Gilbey 1995). Outside London, art-houses, not multiplexes on the edge of British towns, screened the film.

7.2 In the US

In the US, *Variety* magazine described *La Haine* as a film "bowing at the decidedly downtown Sony Village VII in the East Village". In order "to make the film matter to the crucial teen audience – a market not known for its acceptance of subtitled films", the trade journal suggested that Gramercy, its American distributor, had to "take it to trendy neighborhoods as the film platforms". It quoted Gramercy, saying they had "to be very careful where [they] placed the picture". The film was "not a film that should be in the midtown Sony Paris theater", since the latter was "often the home to the arty, genteel and historical epics more characteristic of American taste in French cinema". Gramercy gave the film exclusive runs in New York and Los Angeles and prepared to send out 200 prints "if the film scored with the right mix of young ticket buyers and the more conventional foreign film buffs". (Evans 1996). Talk even circulated about releasing a dubbed version.

La Haine opened to good reviews in New York on February 9, 1996. The *Jody Foster Presents* tag, reflecting the actor's admiration for the film, proved beneficial. Reports gave out the first weekend's results as "very correct", the film having earned $20,128 in three days. *La Haine* played in 11 theatres throughout the state of New York, the venues being one theatre in Buffalo, one in Albany, and seven in and around the New York City metropolitan area. Most of these engagements lasted one week, though one theatre in New York City played a six-week engagement. By the end of June, 1996 total box office receipts amounted to $280,547.

In New York City and elsewhere it was clear after one week that the targeted market was no longer the inner cities but the usual audiences for foreign-language films. Gramercy revised its original marketing strategy. Like most foreign films exported to the US, *La Haine* continued to play in art houses and on college campuses across the country. The French press, keeping a close look on the film's performance in the US, reported that in the line of cinema-goers queuing at the Multiplex Cinema Village of Manhattan on February 10, 1996,

> One heard French spoken (a little), English (a little more), Spanish and the language of the Blacks from the ghettos (a lot).... After the

film, some spectators said they found it surprising that French youth imitated so much American youth (same taste in clothes, music, same attitude) but they noticed a difference in time, the French were lagging behind. One young hip-hopper said, "Break-dancing, that was ten years ago." (*Le Monde,* February 1996).

8. Cultural Differences

The subtitlers of *La Haine* knew about the time lag between French and American cultures. They recognized that the enormous influence of American popular culture on French youth created what they described as another language-related problem.

In *La Haine,* for example, there is mention of the *McGyver* television series that was initially broadcast in the US in the late 1980's. It is very popular with unemployed French youth who watch it in the afternoons. But for Americans the series was outdated, so the subtitlers just used the word "television". (Riding 1996). In January, 1996, Shane Barry of *Film Ireland,* remarking on the divergence between French and American underclasses, predicted that audiences in east Los Angeles "might find this type of subtitled European dramas almost quaint". She wrote,

> One of the main threads of *La Haine's* story line concerns a gun lost by riot police during the previous night's disturbances. The media hysteria about a stray revolver in a housing project might appear touching to a society in which prepubescents tote Uzis but not to American youth for whom the young men's inability to drive would be "quaint".

She also found Vinz's replaying the scene from *Taxi Driver* "fairly old-hat". (Barry 1995-1996). Ultimately, the film's lack of appeal to targeted US audiences had less to do with subtitling (in comparison with Britain, the subtitles were hardly noticed in the US), more with perceptible cultural differences.

Critics usually attribute the French failure to penetrate the American market to the resistance of American audiences to subtitling (and dubbing) and/or to the poor quality of language transfer. This case study points towards another cause: deep cultural differences. *La Haine* did not have the normal appeal of French films to middle-class US audiences. What's more, as a youth cult film it did not align with American culture, and the choice of American slang did little to help. By contrast, British art house and cinema audiences flocked to see the film out of curiosity.

Martine Danan has convincingly argued that American films recently released in France in their original version with subtitles have acquired a cultural added value for an upwardly mobile educated French audience. (Danan 1995). The same audience which went to Spike Lee's subtitled films may have rushed to screenings of *La Haine* in France, but there is little evidence that the release of Kassovitz's subtitled film in the US had the same effect on either American art house audiences or young cinema-goers.

The subtitlers' choice certainly squares with Jose Lambert's and Dirk Delabastita's assertion that the

> culture of the media continues to be perceived as a product, in economic terms, and according to configurations often very universalist, and which tend therefore to be American. (Lambert & Delabastita 1996: 57).

The subtitlers of *La Haine* acted as cultural experts, but their efforts to bridge the cultural gap between France and America did not go far enough. Using their knowledge of the original and target cultures, they might have greatly and profitably extended their role as translators-mediators. For example, had they been consulted on the best way to crack the American market, they might have suggested a complete remake, and not necessarily one featuring stars and colour. They might have even suggested doing away with the episode in which the three young men attempt to steal a car; or they might have opted for a story line focusing on an event other than a lost gun.

True enough, such major repairs may still belong to the domain of translation. But it is unlikely that France (a country which calls cinema the "seventh art" and where film directors continue to enjoy auteur status) will turn to such adaptations in the immediate future.

9. Conclusion

Taking into account the film director's own assumptions about young French audiences and their familiarity with popular American youth culture, one can easily justify the subtitlers' choice of American slang. And while it is true that language transfer is partly responsible for the loss in the characters' differentiation, it is unlikely that additional work on the verbal exchanges would have resulted in a greater acceptance by American audiences. The divide between original and target cultures stood too wide.

Ultimately, this case study provides specific examples of, and raises questions about, the role of cultural discount. (Hoskins et al. 1989). It also sheds light on the varied allegiances and interpretations multimedia practitioners and audiences bring to a film text and how these allegiances and interpretations affect a film's reception. The relative success of the film among British critics and audiences and its failure in the American market also bring into question some long-cherished beliefs about what genres are characteristic of French film and what genres of French films are suitable for subtitling and thus for export.

This study also suggests what might have happened if the translators/subtitlers had taken a more decisive role in adapting Kassovitz's film-event to the target culture. In such a case, the film might have more easily overcome differences between original and target cultures and posted not only a solid artistic performance but an economic one as well.

TRANSFERT DES RÉFÉRENCES CULTURELLES DANS LES SOUS-TITRES FILMIQUES

Teresa Tomaszkiewicz
Université A. Mickiewicz
Poznań, Pologne

1. Références culturelles

Tout texte est indissociable de son contexte. Ainsi un texte de départ apparait dans un milieu socio-culturel comportant toute une série de codes: moeurs, modes, rapports sociaux, conceptions esthétiques, normes linguistiques, normes d'écriture, normes littéraires etc. Le milieu d'arrivée n'est pas le même, surtout si la distance géographique ou temporelle est importante, que celui de départ: les codes, caractéristiques de chacune des deux cultures en question, peuvent donc varier dans une plus ou moins grande mesure. Ces différences culturelles ainsi que certaines différences entre les systèmes linguistiques en contact posent évidemment des problèmes de traduction.

Selon Wojtasiewicz (1992: 30), les difficultés de traduction peuvent se ramener, grosso modo, à deux types de phénomènes:

(1) la langue d'arrivée ne dispose pas de moyens structuraux comparables aux moyens de la langue de départ;

(2) la langue d'arrivée n'a pas de correspondants pour dire certaines notions de la langue de départ.

Avec le premier type, on peut penser aux langues qui n'ont pas développé certaines catégories grammaticales, telles que par exemple le genre, ou qui ne disposent pas d'articles ou de système flexionnel, etc. Dans le processus de traduction, il existe toujours néanmoins une possibilité de compensation d'un moyen linguistique par un autre qui permet d'obtenir le même effet signifiant.

Par contre, avec les manifestations de la spécificité culturelle d'une société, comme ses moeurs, ses plats, son argent, ses fonctions administratives, son système juridique, ses institutions, son patrimoine historique et culturel, ses lieux géographiques, etc, on constate qu'une langue, faute de refléter dans son lexique les faits ou les notions d'un univers donné, peut être dans l'impossibilité de les faire passer dans son propre univers.

Le problème en traduction ne concerne pas tellement le manque, dans la langue d'arrivée, de termes ou d'expressions équivalentes, mais la non-existence, dans la culture cible, de fragments de la réalité comparables à ceux de la culture de départ ou encore la méconnaissance d'une certaine réalité évoquée par l'original. "Il appartient alors au traducteur de donner au lecteur étranger des connaissances supplémentaires, minimum mais suffisantes pour entr'ouvrir la porte qui mène à la connaissance de l'autre. (...) Le traducteur aide [le lecteur de la traduction] en explicitant certains des implicites du texte original et en employant des moyens linguistiques suffisants pour désigner les référents pour lesquels il n'existe pas de correspondance directe dans sa langue." (Lederer 1994: 123).

Les stratégies des traducteurs, face à ces problèmes de transfert culturel, peuvent être au moins de trois sortes:

- trouver un substitut dans la culture d'arrivée;
- sauvegarder les éléments de la culture étrangère, en y ajoutant explications ou explicitations supplémentaires;
- neutraliser l'information culturelle spécifique, en se bornant aux phénomènes de nature universelle et générale.

Evidemment la stratégie adoptée va dépendre de la finalité de la traduction, de la forme et du sens général du texte d'origine, ainsi que des caractéristiques du public visé par la traduction. Les procédés qui permettent de réaliser l'une ou l'autre de ces stratégies peuvent être des opérations paraphrastiques, explicatives, définitionnelles, descriptives, des calques ou emprunts, ou tout simplement l'omission de certains éléments dans le texte d'arrivée.

2. Spécificité de la traduction au cinéma

Le cinéma intègre plusieurs éléments signifiants à la fois, à savoir l'image, les bruits, la musique, le verbal. Le sens dans un film est exprimé par les diverses relations qui s'établissent entre tous les éléments signifiants. Avec la traduction un seul élément de tout le message filmique original est soumis au transfert linguistique, c'est le texte parlé par les protagonistes.

La traduction au cinéma est réalisée le plus souvent par deux techniques différentes: le doublage et le sous-titrage. Dans ce qui suit, nous allons nous concentrer sur ce dernier.

La présence, dans les messages audiovisuels, de divers éléments signifiants (bruit, musique, image) peut faciliter la saisie du sens, même si la présence verbale se voit réduite. N'empêche, ces autres systèmes sémiotiques, ne sont pas nécessairement compréhensibles de la même manière par le récepteur d'origine et le récepteur étranger (par exemple certains gestes, certaines normes de présentation de l'image, etc.). Ces difficultés de compréhension sont dues à la fois aux différentes conventions qui unissent les signes non-linguistiques et leur signification et aux différences entre le savoir cognitif du récepteur d'origine et celui du récepteur des sous-titres. Cette deuxième difficulté n'est pas propre à la traduction au cinéma, mais elle est peut-être plus sensible parce qu'il n'y a pas de retour en arrière possible et qu'on ne dispose pas de moyens d'explication comme les notes en bas de page ou les astérisques.

Tous les films sont plus ou moins ancrés dans un contexte socio-culturel spécifique. L'importance de ce paramètre culturel est certes variable, dans les images, parce que l'action se passe dans un contexte géographique, culturel, social donné, dans le comportement des protagonistes – membres de la société en question, mais aussi dans le discours des personnages où certains éléments linguistiques renvoient directement à des références culturelles connues du spectateur d'origine. Comment rendre ces références culturelles?

3. Procédés pour les références culturelles

3.1 Omission des termes

La solution la plus simple ou la plus radicale, consiste à supprimer le terme qui pose un problème de traduction. C'est possible dans le cas où le contexte et le cotexte sont suffisamment sélectifs pour comprendre la totalité de l'énoncé:

- *Słuchaj, podobno wystawiacie ten music-hall w* ***Syrenie***. (Ecoute, il paraît que vous montez ce music-hall à **Syrena**.)	- Il paraît que vous montez un music-hall.

Comme cet énoncé est émis dans les coulisses d'un théâtre et que dans le cotexte on parle d'un *music-hall*, la précision de l'endroit n'est pas fondamentale pour la compréhension. Pour le public de Varsovie, où se passe l'action de ce film, mais aussi pour les habitants d'autres villes en Pologne, le nom du théâtre (*Syrena*) renvoie à un lieu concret, bien connu. Ce théâtre n'a cependant aucun sens symbolique, dans le récit en question. L'omission de son nom, donc de cette réalité culturelle, n'entrave pas la compréhension de l'énoncé contextualisé. On peut déduire les mêmes conclusions de l'exemple suivant:

- *Kawiarnia "Maskota",* ***ulica Chimery****. Co to jest ?* (Café "Maskota", **rue Chimera**. Qu'est-ce que c'est ?)	- Café "Mascotte"...qu'est-ce que c'est ?

- To jest napewno adres pracy jego matki. (C'est sûrement l'adresse de travail de sa mère).	- L'adresse de travail de sa mère.

Dans la traduction, on a traduit le nom du café, et supprimé le nom de la rue. Mais, ce qui importe, c'est de savoir que les enfants à l'école se moquent de l'endroit où travaille la mère de Rafał: un café, plus que son adresse précise. La suppression n'empêche donc pas de comprendre les réparties et les connotations qui en découlent.

Nous pouvons donc avancer que l'omission de certaines informations relevant du culturel est parfois possible, sinon nécessaire. Cette tactique est d'ailleurs pratiquée également par les traducteurs d'autres types de textes. Par exemple, dans la traduction des textes de Szczypiorski (1990), nous avons trouvé:

*Cieszyły mnie wyprawy do kina **"Mucha"** przy ulicy Długiej.* (Szczypiorski, 1990: 153)	Je me réjouissais des expéditions au cinéma de la rue Długa. (trad. 1995: 191)

L'omission du nom propre du cinéma n'était pas dictée cette fois-ci par la contrainte de concision, comme pour le sous-titrage; mais simplement cette information a paru au traducteur inutile, inappropriée pour le récepteur du texte cible.

3.2 Transfert direct

Comme nous l'avons dit, certains éléments de la réalité d'origine possèdent leurs noms propres sans équivalents nécessairement dans la culture d'arrivée. Pour sauvegarder la couleur locale de l'original, on se permet dans certains cas de conserver ces termes, en leur forme originale, dans le texte cible. C'est le procédé de l'emprunt.

Dans chaque langue il y a une quantité d'emprunts qui au bout d'un certain temps sont intégrés dans le vocabulaire. C'est par exemple, le sort de plats comme *pizza, schaschlyk, hamburger* etc., c'est le sort aussi des termes désignant l'organisation administrative d'un pays: *Land* allemand, etc.

Dans le transfert linguistique au cinéma, introduire des emprunts peu ou non assimilés dans les dialogues d'arrivée, sans explication, peut bloquer la compréhension. Parfois ces éléments sont certes bien contextualisés, ce qui permet au spectateur de saisir leur sens. Par exemple, au début du film de Rohmer *L'ami de mon amie*, il y a le nom d'une banlieue parisienne: *Cergy.*

- "Tu habites où ?"
- "A Cergy Village."

Du dialogue, on peut conclure que *Cergy* est le nom d'une petite ville ou d'un village, même si dans la traduction on a sauvegardé ce nom dans sa forme originale: *Cergy Village.* Cette projection du sens est due au verbe *habiter.* Le nom apparaît par la suite plusieurs fois, mais une fois contextualisé, il commence à fonctionner comme un emprunt, dans le cadre du film en question.

Parfois, le référent d'un nom propre est déjà explicité dans l'original, ce qui permet de le transférer par une *traduction littérale*, par exemple: *The August Strindberg Award* → *Le prix Strindberg,* mais évidemment, pour celui ou celle qui ne connaît pas ce fragment de la réalité, il est difficile de saisir quelle est la nature du prix qu'on évoque.

La même remarque concerne l'exemple suivant. Dans un film polonais de F.Falk, *Le héros de l'année*, on énumère les différents théâtres de Varsovie, en envisageant la possibilité d'y monter un spectacle. Les noms de ces théâtres renvoient à des institutions concrètes, dont la renommée et les dimensions de la salle sont importantes: plus la salle est connue, plus on valorise le spectacle envisagé. En plus, chacune de ces salles a sa propre histoire à forte charge connotative.

Ainsi *Kongresowa*: ce fut à un moment la plus grande salle de Varsovie où on organisait des rencontres importantes, des congrès internationnaux, mais aussi les congrès du parti communiste. Rendre donc ce nom par *Salle des Congrès* ôte au référent toute cette charge connotative. *Teatr Wielki* est l'*Opéra de Varsovie*, unique et perçu comme la scène nationale. Le traduire par *Le Grand Théâtre* ne souligne pas le caractère exceptionnel de cette institution. Et finalement, quand on constate que pour le spectacle en question *La "Halle"* ne convient pas, il faut savoir qu'il s'agit d'une salle de spectacles sportifs ou de variétés, inadéquate donc pour un spectacle de gala.

La contrainte de concision peut avoir parfois des influences néfastes sur le sous-titrage, si elle est poussée à l'extrême, même pour des noms autrement connus. Cornu (1983) cite ainsi des exemples de traduction littérale abrégée:
- "Voir Shakespeare dans le *Park*" (pour *Central Park* à New York)
- "Il va exposer au *Moderne*" (pour en fait *The Museum of Modern Art* à New York).

Parfois on emprunte les noms et les prénoms de l'original et en même temps on conserve la structure de la langue de départ. C'est le calque. Dans un des films analysés (*Kochankowie mojej mamy – Les amants de ma mère*) on a conservé parfois les termes d'adresse dans leur forme originale :
Pan Witek (*Monsieur Witek*); *Pani Lena (Madame Lena.)*
De fait, il y a des divergences dans l'emploi contextuel de ces termes d'adresse. Les formes en français (*Monsieur Witek, Madame Lena*) ne correspondraient pas au contexte d'énonciation du film et au type de relation sociale qui s'établit entre les protagonistes.

3.3 Périphrase définitionnelle

Les exemples précédents ont montré les limites du transfert direct d'un terme relevant du culturel dans une autre réalité. Souvent une explication supplémentaire est nécessaire; par exemple:
- *Random House* → ***aux éditions*** *Random House*
Ce procédé est aussi exploité dans la traduction des textes littéraires:

Po drodze, jeśli zdarzyło mi się mieć pieniądze, jadłem w barze na ***Powiślu****.* (Szczypiorski, 1990: 66)	Quand par hasard j'avais de l'argent, je prenais un petit déjeuner dans un bar ***du quartier de Powiśle****.* (trad.1995: 86)

Avec les sous-titres, il est difficile d'introduire toute explication supplémentaire, à cause de la contrainte de temps et d'espace. En comparant différentes traductions d'un même film, on peut constater que les décisions concernant la valeur sémantique à sauvegarder peuvent varier. Par exemple:

- You look like you stepped right out of Life magazine.	- On te dirait sortie d'un Life **1960.**	- *Jakbyś zeszła z* ***okładki*** *Lief'u.* (On te dirait sortie de la couverture d'un Life.
- That's my own theory based on a mexican food called burrito.	- Ma propre hypothèse, née de l'**omelette mexicaine,** burrito.	- *Jest to teoria wzorowana na* ***meksykańskim burrito.*** (C'est la théorie qui repose sur le burrito mexicain.)

Dans le premier de ces exemples, il s'agit du magazine américain: *Life.* Ce référent n'est pas évident pour tout le public français ou polonais. Dans le contexte, il s'agit d'un compliment concernant l'habit d'une des protagonistes du film de F.Coppola: *Peggy Sue got married.* On peut donc en déduire que *Life* est un magazine de mode. Mais l'important ici, c'est de savoir que c'était un magazine des années 60. Le traducteur français l'a donc précisé, préférant évoquer la date, puisque Peggy Sue, pendant le bal de sa classe, vingt ans après le baccalauréat, a voulu imiter la façon de s'habiller de l'époque. La solution du traducteur polonais (*la couverture d'un Life*) ne rend pas le même service que la version française.

Quant au deuxième exemple, le traducteur français, tout en gardant l'appellation originale, a essayé de la définir: *l'omelette mexicaine,* pour donner au spectateur français une idée de ce que c'est qu' *un burrito*. Pour le spectateur polonais, cette notion n'a aucun sens; il peut comprendre seulement qu'il s'agit de nourriture, grâce au cotexte qui suit (*Je l'ai mangé à Disneyland*), sans pouvoir imaginer d'aucune manière la nature de l'aliment.

En développant un nom ou un terme de manière définitionnelle, on peut parfois se passer de ce terme dans la traduction:

- *Mój trzeci mąż był sanitariuszem w* ***Tworkach.*** (Mon troisième mari était infirmier à Tworki.)	- Mon troisième mari était infirmier **chez les fous.**

Tworki est le nom d'une ville, près de Varsovie, où est situé un hôpital psychiatrique. Quand on dit: *tu iras à Tworki*, d'habitude on ne pense pas à la ville même, mais à cet hôpital. Dans ce contexte, il importe plus de savoir que le troisième mari de la femme en question était infirmier dans cet hôpital que de savoir où il se trouvait. D'où le remplacement alors du nom de la ville par l'expression: *chez les fous.*

Il y a des cas où les périphrases définitionnelles ne correspondent pas pleinement à l'idée exprimée par l'original:
- *MIT (Massachussets Institute of Technology) → Toutes les facultés de New York*
La version française ne correspond pas au sigle américain. Seule demeure l'idée d'institution de l'enseignement supérieur.

En généralisant, nous pouvons dire que l'emprunt d'un terme ou d'une notion à la langue de départ ne permet souvent pas de transférer en même temps tous les sèmes que cette notion renferme. Dans la majorité des cas, une explication supplémentaire est nécessaire. La contrainte de concision limite cette possibilité.

3.4 Equivalence

Un autre procédé de traduction, à propos des éléments culturels, consiste à trouver certains équivalents terminologiques. C'est la conversion. Elle peut avoir des formes différentes, mais en principe, il s'agit de déclencher, dans la tête du récepteur, le même type d'associations qu'évoque l'original. On peut distinguer divers types d'équivalents.

3.4.1 Equivalence dans la langue de départ

On peut essayer de trouver un équivalent dans la langue de départ, supposé mieux connu par les spectateurs étrangers que le terme premier original, par exemple:

- Radcliffe → Harvard
Harvard est une université plus réputée dans le monde entier que *Radcliffe.*

3.4.2 Equivalence dans la langue d'arrivée
Il s'agit de trouver dans la culture d'arrivée une réalité qui serait comparable à celle de la culture de départ. Cette réalité peut être envisagée de plusieurs points de vue.

- Equivalence terminologique
On essaie de trouver, dans le contexte socio-culturel de la langue d'arrivée, une institution, un diplôme, une fonction, un organisme correspondants à l'original:
Merril Lynch - Bourse et Valeurs - die Börse
Chutes and Ladder - Jeu de l'oie - Mensch ärgere dich nicht
Ces notions renvoient à des réalités sociales comparables: institution, jeu.

- Equivalence fonctionnelle
Ce type d'équivalence consiste à souligner la fonction d'un objet, ou d'un phénomène, dans un contexte déterminé, pour trouver un autre objet ou phénomène dans la langue d'arrivée, qui pourrait remplir la même fonction:
rice krispies cookies - macarons maison - ciasteczka domowe (gâteaux faits à la maison), les équivalents français et polonais ne précisent pas comment se présentent les gâteaux en question mais soulignent qu'il s'agit de gâteaux faits à la maison, d'une autre valeur sociale donc que les gâteaux achetés. Autre exemple:

- *Wzorowe* ***zachowanie***. (Conduite exemplaire.) - *Tak jak obiecałem* ***same piątki***. (Comme j'ai promis seulement les cinq.)	-**Prix d'excellence**, dis donc! - Je t'avais promis **de bonnes notes.**

Il s'agit d'un dialogue entre un enfant et sa mère, après la remise des bulletins, à la fin de l'année scolaire. En Pologne, il y a deux éléments qui comptent dans ces bulletins: *la conduite* (zachowanie) et les notes de différentes matières. Le garçon a eu une note de conduite *excellente* et *cinq* dans toutes les matières, *cinq* étant la meilleure note dans le système scolaire polonais. Dans les deux cas, on a cherché une équivalence fonctionnelle dans le système français (*prix d'excellence* et *bonnes notes.*)

- Equivalence contextuelle
Dans le film déjà cité: *Peggy Sue got married*, le terme *graduation* est traduit, en fonction du contexte par trois équivalents différents:

-They married right after *graduation.*	- Il se sont mariés après *l'examen.*
- After *graduation*	- On finit *les études secondaires.*
- Past *graduation*	- Après *les oraux.*

En généralisant, on peut dire que la conversion cherche à susciter les mêmes idées ou associations sémantiques chez le récepteur étranger que chez le récepteur natif de la culture de départ.

3.5 Adaptation

La frontière entre la catégorie d'équivalence et celle d'adaptation n'est pas toujours nette. On peut même dire que l'adaptation est un cas extrême d'équivalence, qui gomme la couleur locale de l'original. Cornu (1983) cite une adaptation de nom propre:
- *Willie Mays → Pélé le footballeur*
Il s'agit d'éveiller les mêmes connotations dans l'original et dans sa traduction.

3.6 Substitution par la référence énonciative

Souvent la nécessité de condenser le texte original dans le sous-titrage ne permet pas de préciser certaines réalités ou de développer certains sigles, bien connus par les récepteurs de l'original, mais obscurs pour les récepteurs étrangers. Dans certains de ces cas, on peut remplacer la référence culturelle par une référence contextuelle:

- Vous êtes ingénieur? - Oui, à l'**EDF**.	- *Pan jest in żynierem?* - *Tak, pracuję* ***tutaj***. (Oui, je travaille **ici**.)
- Viking	**- Mon éditeur**

Dans le premier exemple, le traducteur n'avait ni la possibilité de développer le sigle *EDF,* ni de le rendre par un sigle correspondant en polonais, ce qui aurait été possible par contre en allemand: *Ich bin Ingenieur bei der AEG.* Par conséquent, il l'a remplacé par une référence énonciative: *ici*, solution d'autant plus plausible que le locuteur a accompagné sa réplique d'un geste d'ostension.

Dans le deuxième exemple, le nom de la maison d'édition est remplacé par une spécification, renvoyant au *je* de l'énonciation.

3.7 Allusions au "déjà connu"

Un autre groupe de problèmes concerne la traduction de fragments de textes qui font allusion à un autre texte connu, à certains événements historiques, à tout un savoir culturel qui peut être ignoré par les membres d'une autre société. Wojtasiewicz (1992: 77) remarque que souvent on distingue entre allusions historiques d'une part et allusions littéraires de l'autre, tout en affirmant qu'il y a des allusions littéraires qui en même temps peuvent être fondées sur certains événements historiques. En plus, il existe des allusions qui font référence à d'autres phénomènes relevant de la culture, comme les arts plastiques, la musique etc. Il propose donc de les appeler les "allusions érudites". Pour les comprendre, le récepteur doit disposer d'un savoir supplémentaire par rapport à la stricte connaissance linguistique. Lederer (1994: 35) les appelle les *compléments cognitifs*.

Or, Wojtasiewicz constate que parmi ces compléments cognitifs, il y en a qui dépassent les frontières linguistiques, par exemple les allusions à la culture antique ou à la tradition chrétienne; il y en a d'autres par contre qui sont strictement liés à la culture et à la tradition d'une société donnée. Même si l'on arrive à les traduire au niveau linguistique, souvent elles ne peuvent déclencher les mêmes associations ou souvenirs chez les récepteurs de l'original et chez ceux de la traduction.

Dans le film *Kochankowie mojej mamy*, à un certain moment on chante un cantique près de l'arbre de Noël.

- *Wśród nocnej ciszy głos się rozchodzi,* *wstańcie pasterze, Bóg się wam rodzi...*	- Dans le silence de la nuit une voix se répend. Levez-vous bergers endormis, Dieu vous attend.

Au niveau linguistique, ces deux textes sont équivalents, mais comment signaler l'importance qu'on attache en Pologne à la Fête de Noël et à ces cantiques chantés dans toutes les familles, la veille?

Dans certains cas, les traducteurs omettent les allusions:

- *To od kiedy pani handluje wódka?* (Depuis quand vous vendez de la vodka?) - *Wódką? Co pan mówi?!* ***Za Niemca to się handlowało tym i owym, ale wódką?*** *Jak Boga kocham nigdy w życiu.* (De la vodka? Qu'est-ce que vous dites? Pendant le temps des Allemands on vendait	- J'ai un mandat de perquisition pour un trafic illicite d'alcool. Vous vous en occupez depuis longtemps? - Je ne me suis jamais occupée de vendre de la vodka.

ceci ou cela, mais de la vodka? Jamais de ma vie. Je le jure, Dieu m'en est témoin.)	

Toute la situation présentée dans le film peut paraître bizarre pour un récepteur étranger: une femme cache des bouteilles de vodka dans son lit et les vend illégalement, au moment où les magasins sont fermés, à une époque de rationnement (années 80). En s'expliquant devant la police, elle réfère à la deuxième guerre mondiale et à l'occupation nazie. Le trafic illicite d'alcool ou d'autres produits n'était pas alors perçu comme un comportement contre la loi, car c'était la loi de l'occupant. Le passage est condensé, sans aucune de ces allusions.

4. En guise de conclusion

Quelles soient les distances entre les langues et les cultures, un texte à traduire sert toujours une intention, est employé dans une situation précise. Il y a donc toujours la possibilité d'expliquer au récepteur étranger les fragments de la réalité de l'original qui lui sont inconnus.

Il n'empêche, les contraintes techniques du sous-titrage rendent sûrement cette tâche plus difficile. L'impossibilité de développer certaines idées, d'introduire des explications ou des reformulations paraphrastiques, oblige le traducteur à manipuler le texte et à renoncer à certains éléments, relevant de la couleur locale. Toutefois, beaucoup de ces éléments sont fournis aussi par l'image.

Sources primaires

Les exemples cités proviennent des films suivants:

- **Bohater roku** de F.Falk; **Le héros de l'année**, en version française.
- **Kochankowie mojej mamy** de R.Piwowarski; **Les amants de ma mère**, en version française.
- **L'ami de mon amie** de E.Rohmer; **Przyjaciel mojej przyjaciółki**, en version polonaise.
- **Peggy Sue got married** de F.Coppola; **Peggy Sue wyszła za mąż**, en version polonaise et **Peggy Sue s'est mariée**, en version française.

ANGLICISMS AND TV SUBTITLES IN AN ANGLIFIED WORLD

Henrik Gottlieb
University of Copenhagen, Denmark

1. Different translation strategies

An increasing part of the language in the media worldwide is translated from English: best-selling books as well as more "anonymous" material (news items in newspapers and on the radio, advertisements, manuals, etc.), and - of special interest here – innumerable "international" films and TV programmes. Such Anglophone sources influence practically all the world's languages. How is the situation in minor speech communities where English is becoming more than just a "foreign" language, and what language policies are recommendable in the media industries of such countries?

As part of an answer to these questions, this paper looks at Anglicisms in the Danish subtitling of English-language TV programmes. Every time a subtitle is created, the subtitler may, consciously or not, choose:

(a) total surrender (non-translation of for instance cursing and puns in English), thus generating *overt Anglicisms,*
(b) the use of unnatural-sounding English-flavored Danish constructions - displaying what could be labeled *covert Anglicisms*,
(c) the use of commonly accepted English loans, *adoptions,*
(d) or fully translated dialogue in idiomatic Danish.

Strictly speaking, strategies a, b and c all involve Anglicisms, either direct loans (*weekend, computer, lease, grand old man*) or indirect ones (*kernefamilie* = *nuclear family*, *speedbåd* = *speed boat*). However, in the 'quality in translation'-context of this paper, integrated and accepted English loans will not be considered Anglicisms. This means that the uncontroversial (c) strategy will not receive any critical comments here. Below, each strategy is illustrated by one authentic example:

A. *Overt Anglicisms (non-translated items; unidiomatic Danish)*

In Joel Schumacher's *Falling Down* (featuring Michael Douglas as disillusioned citizen-turned-desperado), one of the main characters, a retiring police sergeant (Robert Duvall), now somewhat frustrated, tells his boss: "Fuck you, Captain Yardley! Fuck you very much" after having received a slightly condescending compliment for his hard work in tracking madman Douglas down. On Danish TV (Danmarks Radio, April 6. 1996) these lines were rendered:

Fuck you, kaptajn Yardley.
Fuck you, very much.

This verbatim copying of the English allusion to the polite "Thank you very much" is unprecedented, even in modern colloquial Danish; an obvious example of the "hard-core"' category of overt Anglicisms. (A less obvious Anglicism – a covert one – is at play here, too: an American police captain is not a *kaptajn* in Danish, but a *kommissær*. Military titles are not used in the Danish police hierarchy.)

B. *Covert Anglicisms (words or constructions copied from English; unidiomatic Danish)*

As seen in the *kaptajn* example, covert Anglicisms do not stand out to the uninitiated, since no English words or word elements are used in the translation. However, the English pattern is transferred even when a Danish model does exist. Often, such Anglicisms owe their existence to carelessness; at other times media-specific factors are at play. Although the meaning may get through, stylistic violations are common; in some cases the message itself is distorted, making subtitle readers confused.

In the following example (*Beverly Hills 90210*, episode 3; TV2 Jan. 22, 1994), the initial subtitle distorts the semantic content. Luckily, the picture - and the following subtitle – will probably get the message across, i.e. the fact that the young rich girl speaking – and just caught shoplifting – is indeed willing to pay for her goods:

"Listen, why don't I just pay like I always do, like
I intended, and you and I will just delete this whole thing.
Your choice." [she shows her credit cards to the shop assistant]

In Danish, the *why don't* plus *pronoun and finite verb* construction is usually to be taken as an earnest question, not a statement. Still, the subtitler copies this misleading construction, cf. my idiomatic English back-translation of the two subtitles:

Hvorfor betaler jeg ikke bare, som jeg altid gør, og *ville* have gjort	[How come that I don't pay, as I always do, and would have done,]
-og så slår vi en streg over det hele ... Vælg selv	[- and then we will wipe out the whole thing ... You choose.]

C. *Adoptions (accepted, identifiable loans; idiomatic Danish)*

Many such loans refer to technical or cultural entities originating in the Anglo-American world. Often these are fully integrated in Danish, although they may be less known or less easily understood by Danes than by native English speakers.

On March 15, 1997, Danish TV2 showed the American thriller *Rising Sun* from 1993, featuring Sean Connery and Wesley Snipes. In this film, based on a Michael Crichton best-seller and set in a Japanese business milieu in California, the dialogue contains a large number of Japanese loan words. These are all retained in the Danish subtitles, as are several English terms. In the following sequence, our Black American detective (Snipes) refers sarcastically to the surveillance system in a Japanese-owned office building: "Maybe they got instant replay?". In the Danish subtitles, this is rendered as:

Med replay i slow-motion?	[With replay in slow motion?]

Here, the term *replay*, internationally used in televised spectator sports, is reinforced by another (accepted) English lexical item so that nobody should be unaware of what is meant.

D. *All-Danish constructions (fully rephrased; idiomatic Danish)*

In a comforting majority of instances, common English constructions like the above-mentioned *why don't* etc. are rendered in a fully idiomatic way in Danish TV subtitles. One of several all-Danish translation options is the *hvad med* (literally: "what with") plus *infinite verb* construction found below. (Source: *The Good Family* (featuring Tony Curtis); TV2, Jan. 23, 1994.)

"Oh, by the way, you know, the Crandalls don't like turkey, so why don't you make them one of your roast beefs, huh?"

Crandalls kan ikke lide kalkun, så hvad med at lave roastbeef?	[The Crandalls don't like turkey, so how about making roast beef?]

Notice that in isolation, the Danish "roastbeef", now a fully integrated loan word, would place this subtitle in the other acceptable category, i.e. (C).

2. Feedback from the soundtrack: Generator of Anglicisms?

In point 21 of the *Code of Good Subtitling Practice* (Ivarsson & Carroll 1998: 158), it is stated that "There must be a close correlation between film dialogue and subtitle content; source language and target language should be synchronised as far as possible."

At first sight, one can only agree: with the auditive feedback from the original soundtrack, subtitles should be in sync with the dialogue. However, as subtitling is a supplementary (additive) type of translation, the subtitler is faced with an interesting problem: unlike books, for instance, where the foreign reader either buys a translated version or goes for the original, subtitled TV is (still today) a one-size-fits-all enterprise; we all get the same translated version – plus the original at the same time (cf. Gottlieb 1997: 95-99 & 127-129).

This means that in subtitling from English in countries where large segments of the viewers understand English, subtitlers sometimes censor themselves, sacrificing idiomatic translation for "close correlation" with the dialogue. (cf. Sajavaara 1991: 388). Subtitlers' fears of departing from the word order of the original dialogue often lead to unnatural-sounding clones of English phrases and constructions. In both the Scandinavian, the Dutch, and even the Slovene literature on subtitling, I have found mention of the following prototypical situation:

After a dramatic sequence, the main character, wiping the dust off his jacket, answers the question from his worried female counterpart "Are you all right?" with a calm "Yes". In the subtitles, this exchange is very often rendered unidiomatically (by repeating the "optimistic" question plus "yes"-sequence), where a "pessimistic" question plus "no" would sound more natural in several languages other than English. In Danish guise, this standard Anglicism looks as follows:

- Er du uskadt? - Ja.	[-Are you unscathed? - Yes.]

Afraid of colliding with the dialogue, the Danish subtitler often settles for the police-report-sounding and totally uncolloquial *uskadt* in the first line, simply to avoid a "Yes" being rendered as a "No", as in the more idiomatic:

- Skete der noget?	[- Did anything (serious) happen?
- Nej.	- No.]

This subtitling strategy misjudges what could be phrased the minimal translational unit. Instead of considering the entity "question + answer" a pragmatic whole, these elements are rendered separately. Had the source language been anything but English, subtitlers might have felt free to express themselves in their true national idiom.

3. Falling Down and *Ghostbusters*: Two American films, two kinds of Anglicisms

In this section, we will take a systematic look at the types and frequencies of Anglicisms found in two contemporary American films subtitled for Danish public-service TV, and compare the "Anglicism profiles" of the two films in question.

While *Falling Down*, a scathing critique of modern America, was chosen for its blatant use of American swearwords in the subtitles, *Ghostbusters*, more good-natured and mainstream, was believed to be a neutral point of comparison as far as Anglicisms are concerned. However, as we shall see, the difference between these films lies not so much at the quantitative level – both films display Anglicisms in five percent of their subtitles – but at the qualitative level. Whereas the subtitles for *Falling Down* contain a large number of unintegrated Anglicisms, *Ghostbusters* – with its less obscene dialogue – unleash a similarly great number of less offensive, auditively induced Anglicisms in its Danish version.

Below, all overt and covert Anglicisms found in the two films are listed, with back-translations in square brackets, and – when needed – the original dialogue in curly brackets:

	GHOSTBUSTERS	**FALLING DOWN**
Film data	Dir. Ivan Reitman 1984: 107 minutes	Dir. Joel Schumacher 1993: 115 minutes
Broadcast data	Danmarks Radio January 14, 1994 Subtitler: Niels Søndergaard 818 subtitles	Danmarks Radio April 6, 1996 Subtitler: Jørgen Christiansen 1035 subtitles

	ANGLICISMS OVERT TYPES	
	Wow!	Er du min *fair lady?* (2 tokens) [are you my fair lady]
	ektoplasma-entiteter [ectoplasmic entities]	*London Bridge is falling down* (2 tokens)
	torb (2 tokens) (invented sci-fi word)	drive-by-skyderiet (4 tokens) [the drive-by shooting]
	sloar (2 tokens) (ditto)	yard (cf. meter)
	all right (4 tokens) (outdated in Danish) mr. (+ name) miss (+ name) (3 tokens),	Det er ikke vores *policy* [this is not our policy] mr. (+ name) (6 tokens) miss (+ name) (2 tokens)
	sir.	High school-skønhedsdronning [high school beauty queen] {homecoming queen} Cool, mand. [cool, man] Det må vaere en *groundkeeper* {He must be the groundskeeper} *Fore!* (2 tokens) *Five!* Shit ... (3 tokens) Det er ikke fucking graffiti (7 tokens) [this is no fucking graffiti] sin fuckede taske [his fucking briefcase] motherfucker (3 tokens) Fuck så ud af bilen! [get the fuck out of the car] Fuck it! Fuck you! (4 tokens) Fuck dig og din frihed! [fuck you and your freedom] Fuck dem! [fuck them] Svanse-fucker![queer fucker] Du bliver fucket i røven [you are fucked in the ass] Fuck you, very much
Total: All overt Anglicisms	8 types; 15 tokens	24 types; 49 tokens

	GHOSTBUSTERS	**FALLING DOWN**
	COVERT TYPES	
Time & space induced	stab (idiomatic: personale) {staff}	[none found]
Visually induced	GHOSTBUSTERS SUPER-DIÆT {GHOSTBUSTERS' SUPER DIET}	[none found]
Auditorily induced: "exotic" terms of address	dr. (+ name) (7 tokens) , doktor (titles rarely used in Danish) Barrett. Dana Barrett. (idiomatic: Dana Barrett)	kaptajn (2 tokens) [captain] (correct: kommissær)
Auditorily induced unidiomatic lexemes:	mineralvand (2 tokens) [mineral water] (idiomatic: danskvand) bygningen [the building] (idiomatic: ejendommen / huset)	diskriminerende! [discriminating] (correct: sans for detaljer) etablissement [establishment] (idiomatic: forretning)
Auditorily induced: unidiomatic phrases	det magiske ord (2 tokens) [the magic word] (idiomatic: trylleformularen) Der må være en vej ind. [there must be a way in] (idiomatic: ... en indgang) Ifølge kørekortet er han Louis Tully fra Central Park West. [according to the driver's license he is etc.] (idiomatic: ... hedder han Louis Tully ...) Jeg er [I am] (+ name) (3 tokens) (idiomatic: Mit navn er ...) Jeg kan dårligt vente! [I can hardly wait] (idiomatic: Det glæder jeg mig til) Er du uskadt? (+ answer) (5 tokens) {are you all right?} / {are you okay?} (idiomatic: skete der noget? / kan du klare det?)	én, der aldrig fyrer noget *shit* eller *fuck* af [one who never comes up with any fuck or shit]
Total: Covert Anglicisms	13 types; 27 tokens	4 types; 5 tokens

All Anglicisms	21 types; 42 tokens	28 types; 54 tokens
Frequency of Anglicisms:	5.1% of all subtitles	5.2% of all subtitles

Distribution of Anglicisms in the two films

	Ghostbusters	***Falling Down***
Covert Anglicisms	27 tokens: 64% of all Anglicisms	5 tokens: 9% of all Anglicisms
Overt Anglicisms	15 tokens: 36% of all Anglicisms	49 tokens: 91% of all Anglicisms

4. Same frequency, different distribution: two opposite profiles

My hypothesis concerning the differences in Anglicism frequencies between the two films is clearly falsified by the data: surprisingly, in both films five percent of the subtitles contain Anglicisms.

Concerning the types of Anglicisms, however, there are significant differences between the two sets of subtitles, as can be seen in the table above: whereas almost two thirds of the Anglicisms found in *Ghostbusters* are covert types, more than ninety percent of the Anglicisms in *Falling Down* are overt types.

This almost complementary distribution in the two subtitled films is partly due to the different cinematographic styles, and hence the different language, found in these two Hollywood productions. Most importantly, however, the two subtitlers seem to adapt different strategies in their work. In *Falling Down*, the subtitler has adopted the American four-letter lingo without idiomatic scruples, whereas the subtitler of *Ghostbusters*, avoiding such blatant US imports, displays a more latent stock of Anglicisms. Thus, the stylistic differences between the two films are accentuated in their Danish versions.

5. The ubiquity of Anglicisms

Whereas the number and relative predominance of overt Anglicisms in *Falling Down* may constitute an extreme in Danish subtitling practices so far, the profile of *Ghostbusters* – with its high percentage of (auditorily induced) English-sounding Danish constructions – is expected to be quite typical of the state of the art in Scandinavian television.

But also in non-subtitling countries are English-language imports likely to produce a high number of non-idiomatic elements in translations: in Germany, dubbed versions of American films often have an unnatural ring to them. In his excellent works on English-German dubbing (Herbst 1994 & 1995), Thomas Herbst lists a large number of such cases, as for example this calque-type translation of the utterance "My life was in danger" by "Mein Leben war in Gefahr" instead of the more idiomatic *Ich war in Lebensgefahr* (Herbst 1995: 263).

In Spain, another dubbing country, critical observers talk about "the effect that English is having on the Spanish speaker at home as a result of the vast quantities of badly translated material flooding the spheres of journalism, radio, television and advertising" (Lorenzo 1996: 18, quoting A. Gooch: *Spanish and the Onslaught of the Anglicism*).

Similar vehicles for the introduction of Anglicisms are pointed out by Danish pioneer in Anglicism research, Knud Sørensen:

> There is no doubt that Anglicisms occur with the greatest frequency in the media. Thus journalists, who often draw on English-language sources, are chiefly responsible for the English infiltration of the Danish language. (Sørensen 1986: 45)

A totally different potential cause of Anglicisms in non-English speaking cultures is the undeniable brevity of certain English words and expressions. This is particularly relevant in Finland, partly because, for morphosyntactic reasons, the average Finnish word takes up more spaces in a subtitle row than its English counterpart, and partly because in Finnish cinema subtitling, only one line is available for the translation – the other line renders the dialog in Swedish, Finland's other official language. Against this background, this statement by a Finnish linguist is hardly surprising:

> In addition to direct lexical borrowings of the *cowboy* or *big band* type, where the concepts designated by the words have been adopted simultaneously with the words to the effect that the words and concepts have become an integral part of Finnish, the English influence consists of a large amount of non-Finnish expressions which have been adopted through translation, partly under severe restrictions of space in contexts such as television subtitles, comic strips, or advertisements. (Sajavaara 1986: 71)

In Sweden, in one of the most thorough empirical studies of Anglicisms worldwide, Martin Gellerstam compared the vocabulary in 27 novels translated from English with 29 "native" Swedish novels. On the vocabulary differences between these two text corpora, Gellerstam concludes (1986: 91): "Many English words seem to trigger a standard translation in Swedish although the Swedish translation differs stylistically from the English original." Even more interesting than his demonstration of the inevitable presence of such covert Anglicisms in (quality) translations is Gellerstam's advice– in discussing semantic changes in existing words due to English influence – to future Anglicism hunters:

> (...) fiction is probably not the best domain for studying this group of words especially if your aim is to study the phenomenon as such rather than to find instances of translationese. A normal Swedish newspaper (leading articles, book reviews or political comments) will probably be an even better source (...) *The English language is there all the same, somewhere in the back of the journalist's mind*, in the shape of telegrams and foreign magazines and newspapers. (Gellerstam 1986:93; my emphasis)

So even if we disregard translation(s), the English language will continue to exert its influence on other languages; the most dramatic effect being their loss of domains, as when for instance translations are no longer economically viable. As Danish novelist and translator Annette Lindegaard observes:

> The tendency is clear: a rapidly growing number of Danes read English almost as well as they do Danish. This phenomenon is also reflected in sales figures for literature. Danes have long since discovered that it is cheaper to buy English paperbacks than Danish translations, much to the chagrin of Danish publishers. (Lindegaard 1996: 154)

The English influence is so strong that even in texts with no English original, existing morphological and syntactic patterns in non-English speech communities are being contested these years. In language, as in human behavior in general, motivated and repeated violations of norms, undertaken by persons – in casu subtitlers, dubbers and journalists – who communicate with mass audiences, eventually become new norms. As the prestige norm is, has long been, and will continue to be English, domestic languages may expect attacks on all linguistic features that do not correspond with modern English usage. This brings us back to the "dangers" of the inconspicuous covert Anglicisms, so abundantly represented in the Danish version of *Ghostbusters*. In the words of a Danish linguist:

> While the battle – the losing battle – is being fought over the overt loans, there are subtler processes at work which *readjust the vocabulary in accordance with the dominant language*. This is happening elsewhere, too, but the close family relationship between English and Danish facilitates some of the less overt processes. The outcome for the recipient language may be quite dramatic in the end: it may be reduced to the status of an alternative code adapted to give expression to the culture associated with the dominant language. (Larsen 1994: 35; my emphasis)

For future subtitling, the consequences of this international discussion could be that in several minor speech communities, we would not have to waste time subtitling from English. Most viewers would simply argue: "All the people who can read subtitles know English anyway, and besides, our language is not that different from English anymore, so why bother?"

INCIDENTAL FOREIGN-LANGUAGE ACQUISITION BY CHILDREN WATCHING SUBTITLED TELEVISION PROGRAMS*

Marijke Van de Poel
Géry d'Ydewalle
Katholieke Universiteit Leuven,
Leuven, Belgium

Watching television has become a common way of receiving information worldwide. Moreover, many of the television programs from some countries are available in many other countries. Accordingly, one often has to view television programs with languages other than the native language. Because of the larger costs of dubbing, subtitling has become a popular way of dealing with the language problem; this is especially true in smaller speech communities (larger speech communities often have the financial resources for dubbing). Subtitling in the native language is an expedient and relatively inexpensive procedure relative to the cost of dubbing voices in the language of the country receiving the television programs.

Subtitling is particularly informative because it supplies the viewer with the following three different channels of information: the pictorial information, the original sound-track, and the translation of the text in the subtitles. Though the information is somewhat redundant, it is of interest to ask whether the three sources of information can be processed simultaneously and if so, to what extent can they be processed, and what implication these sources of information have for the viewer. For an extended discussion, see d'Ydewalle and Gielen (1992). Of primary importance is whether viewing subtitled programs increases the viewers' comprehension and knowledge of a second language.

To allow for foreign-language acquisition, at least the channel in which the foreign language is presented should be processed. The presence of the native language should facilitate the foreign-language acquisition. Additionally, the pictorial information may also support the processing of the two available languages but the primary question remains: Is there evidence that the subtitles are indeed read and that the sound-track is being processed?

Several studies of eye-movement recordings indicate that reading of subtitles is an automatic process and takes place independently of familiarity with subtitling, knowledge of the foreign language spoken, and the availability of a sound- track (for a review of the available studies, see d'Ydewalle & Gielen, 1992). Subtitles are not only read mandatorily, but are also processed in detail and remembered quite well: Participants are able to recognize surprisingly well the precise formulation of subtitles (M. Gielen, 1988).

Sohl (1989) and Van de Poel and d'Ydewalle (in preparation) used the double-task technique to investigate whether children and adults follow the foreign language in the sound-track while viewing a subtitled movie. Reaction times to the second task (light flashes and beeps) were slower in the conditions with sound-track and subtitles or sound-track alone than in the conditions with subtitles alone or when just the image was provided, suggesting that both children and adults made an effort to process the foreign language in the sound-track.

Since both subtitles (in the native language) and sound-track (in the foreign language) are processed almost in parallel, there may be language acquisition in such a context. Simultaneous viewing of the subtitles and listening to the soundtrack may be a factor in language acquisition. Can watching (and enjoying) subtitled television programs incidentally lead to foreign-language acquisition?

There is already evidence available (see Winitz, 1996) about superior acquisition of a second language when the input and process of learning are implicit; moreover, incidental learning through the use of pictures has been shown to be very effective, and under these conditions retention is extremely high (Postovsky, 1981). Pavakanun and d'Ydewalle (1992) and d'Ydewalle and Pavakanun (1995, 1996, 1997) investigated incidental foreign-language acquisition in the context of watching subtitled television programs. Adult participants were shown subtitled cartoons (about 15 minutes long); immediately thereafter, foreign-language acquisition was tested. Results indicated substantial acquisition effects on vocabulary tests for both normal (foreign language in sound-track and native language in subtitles) and reversed subtitling conditions (foreign language in subtitles and native language in sound-track), regardless of the (dis)similarity between the native and foreign languages. However, performance in tests on syntax and grammar acquisition remained relatively poor.

Several authors explicitly point to differences in language acquisition between adults and children, both neuropsychologically (Lenneberg, 1967), and culturally and affective (Lambert, Gardner, Olton, & Tunstall, 1970; Lambert & Klineberg, 1967; Larsen & Smalley, 1972; MacNamara, 1973), leading to the conclusion that especially children are successful in acquiring a language by being exposed to the language in an informal context, whereas the effect of such an informal contact is usually more limited in adults. In the context of first-language acquisition the notion *critical period* is applied (Lenneberg, 1967), suggesting that children who do not start to acquire a language by the age of 12 will never succeed in achieving normal language proficiency afterwards, even with extensive language training. (Admittedly, Lenneberg mostly used the critical-period hypothesis to emphasize that particularly pronunciation after puberty would not be native-like.) For second- or foreign-language acquisition, preference is given to the more moderate notion of a *sensitive* period, which implies that after that period foreign-language acquisition can still take place to some degree, though not in the same way and/or not to the same extent as before the age of 12.

Although some authors favor adults in foreign-language acquisition by pointing to their higher capacity for planning, coordinating and controlling the learning in an explicit learning/teaching environment (Ervin-Tripp, 1981; McLaughlin, 1981), everyone seems to agree that children are more sensitive to foreign-language acquisition in a natural context of implicit learning.

Eye-movement research with children indicates similar patterns of attention allocation when watching subtitled television as were found for adults: From age 8 on, children read subtitles in a similar way as adults (d'Ydewalle & Van Rensbergen, 1989). Further evidence suggests that children also make an effort to process the sound-track (Lorch, Anderson, & Levin, 1979; Pezdek & Hartman, 1983; Pezdek & Stevens, 1984). Therefore, it can be expected that they will acquire a foreign language as adults, or even better than them.

The major points of interest of the present study** are the following. By extending the findings of d'Ydewalle and Pavakanun (1995, 1996, 1997) and Pavakanun and d'Ydewalle (1992), we investigated implicit foreign-language acquisition in children. To determine not only the possibilities but also the boundaries and limits of foreign-language acquisition in a context like watching subtitled television, the tests involved vocabulary, morphology, and syntax. The first step in foreign-language acquisition is mastering new words, and this should be apparent in tests on vocabulary. Further steps involve the acquisition of the morphology and syntax of the foreign language; we expect such an acquisition only to occur after some formal learning of the foreign language. Therefore, the study included children before and after formal learning of the first foreign language (French) was started at school. By choosing French and Danish as foreign languages (whereas the first language for all participants was Dutch), the effect of first- and foreign-language similarity could be investigated at the same time (Danish being more similar to Dutch). Finally, using different age groups may give insight into the development of children's implicit language-acquisition capacities and could contribute to our understanding of the existence of a sensitive period for foreign-language acquisition.

1. Method

1.1 Participants

A total of 327 children in the third, fourth, fifth and sixth grades of a primary school in Dutch-speaking Belgium participated in the experiment. In order to be at Grade 3 of the primary school, children in Belgium need to be fluent in speaking, reading, and writing the native language. Considering the typical Belgian situation, it is fair to assume that all children in the present study have incidentally been facing spoken and written French to various extents; formal teaching of French starts at Grade 5, but even at Grade 6, the children are not yet able to speak French. All children were between the ages of 8 and 12 years, native speakers of Dutch, and not informed of the purpose of the experiment. Except for the French language learning from Grade 5 on, all children were monolingual.

1.2 Stimuli

A 10-min. long movie with successive static pictures (i.e., a still-motion movie) was selected in order for the participants to give full attention to the story and the text, and to keep attention constant across different film events (and by consequence, different text parts). The selected film was entitled *Young Deer*.

Because there is considerable discussion in the literature about facilitation versus inhibition of foreign-language acquisition for similar and dissimilar languages (Dato, 1975; Dulay & Burt, 1972, 1973, 1974, 1975; Hakuta, 1975; Titone & Danesi, 1985), two foreign languages were chosen: Danish and French. The two languages differ not only with regard to the amount of similarity with the native language (Dutch), but also in the likelihood of finding prior foreign-language knowledge among the participants of our study: Danish and Dutch are Germanic languages, and therefore more similar to each other than French, a Romance language.

From the original version of the Dutch text, a French and a Danish translation were constructed by native speakers of those two languages. Because children generally pay more attention to a women's voice (Anderson & Lorch, 1983), dubbing of the sound-track was done by female native speakers. The use of a still-motion movie implied that several subtitles were presented in combination with a single picture. To assure nevertheless equal attention across the different sentences, each picture alteration was followed by a pause of 3 seconds, in which no text was presented and which allowed the children to screen the picture first before shifting to the text. The onset time of all subtitles was synchronized with the beginning of the same text part in the sound-track. The presentation time of all subtitles was defined according to the 6-seconds construction rule, which proved to be the most convenient for the viewer (d'Ydewalle, Van Rensbergen, & Pollet, 1987). The 6-seconds construction rule implies a presentation of the subtitle during 6 seconds when it contains 64 characters and spaces; the presentation rate is made proportionally shorter as a function of the number of characters and spaces in the subtitle.

Four different versions of the film were constructed, one for each experimental condition, depending on the foreign language used (French versus Danish) and whether it was presented in the sound-track or in the subtitles: Dutch subtitles and French sound-track, French subtitles and Dutch sound-track, Dutch subtitles and Danish sound-track, and Danish subtitles and Dutch sound-track. The control condition received a fifth version with Dutch in both sound-track and subtitles. Brightness and sound were kept as constant as possible across the different versions.

To assess language acquisition, three different tests were constructed. The Vocabulary Test contained 20 words (10 for the visual part and 10 for the auditory part; see further) for which the correct translation in the foreign language had to be picked out from a list of three alternatives which all appeared in the film (e.g., *bed* with the three French alternatives: *nom, lait, lit*; and Danish alternatives: *hegn, navn, seng*). All target words occurred at least four times during the whole film and all words were content words. In the Syntax Test, the correct construction of a sentence had to be picked out from three alternatives which differed only in word order (e.g., in Danish: "Johdy havde ikke glemt den lille hjort, Johdy ikke havde den lille hjort glemt, Johdy havde den lille hjort ikke glemt"; and in French: "maintenant Jody devait faire aussi le travail de papa, maintenant Jody aussi devait le travail de faire papa, maintenant devait Jody aussi faire le travail de papa"). The 10 sentences (5 for the visual part and 5 for the auditory part; see further) occurred literally in the movie and the alternatives were chosen to differ substantially from the correct sentence. The Morphology Test presented 10 sentences (5 for the visual part and 5 for the auditory part; see further) in which only a few marked words differed among the three alternatives and the correct form had to be picked out (e.g., "Jody, shoot Flag down!" in Danish: "Jody, *skød* Flag ned!; Jody, *skyd* Flag ned!; Jody, *skødte* Flag ned!", and "Father and Jody went to the forest" in French: "Papa et Jody sont *allés* au bois, Papa et Jody sont *allé* au bois, Papa et Jody sont *aller* au bois"). For this test only elementary structures of the particular foreign language with high occurrence in the film were used.

Since not all language components are equally salient in the auditory and the visual mode, all tests had different visual and auditory subtests, containing different visually versus auditory salient test items of the respective languages. This implies that performances for both the visual and auditory subtests cannot be compared directly; the performance can only be compared with the performance in the same subtests in the control condition. Visual subtests were presented on paper; auditory subtests were recorded on a videotape and played on the same recorder as the movie.

1.3 Procedure

In each of the four grades, there were five experimental groups, one for each condition. In each condition for each grade, there were about an equal number of boys and girls. Testing was done in groups of about 20 children, defining each time one condition. The experiment took place in the same room using the same equipment for all groups.

The children were told that the experimenter was interested in the way in which people watch television. No attention was drawn to the language and the children were instructed to watch the movie as they do at home, in anticipation of "a few questions". In order to keep the purpose of the experiment hidden, the reference to "a few questions" was deliberately kept vague.

A Panasonic video recorder and a Philips television set were used to play the video. Luminance and sound were adjusted at the beginning of the experiment and remained constant across sessions. All groups were shown one version of the movie according to the experimental condition and were tested immediately afterwards. Children to which the foreign language had been presented in the subtitles received the visual subtests of all tests for the respective foreign language only, whereas children who heard the foreign language in the sound-track received the auditory subtests only. Though this implies that children in the visual and auditory conditions are not directly comparable, we kept the number of subtests limited in order to reduce the total duration of the experiment within a reasonable amount of time (less than one hour). Only for the Vocabulary Test both subtests were given to all groups: In the Vocabulary Test, the children were indeed able to respond quickly. Children in the control condition received all subtests for both foreign languages. Test order was kept constant across groups: first, the Vocabulary Test, followed by the Syntax Test, and finally, the Morphology Test.

In addition, preliminary testing showed that the Syntax and Morphology Tests were very hard to perform for the third graders, resulting in substantial frustration and considerable guessing behavior. Therefore, these tests were only administered for the fourth, fifth and sixth graders, whereas the third graders only received the Vocabulary Test.

After the completion of the test, any possible knowledge of the foreign language was checked individually. Fifteen children who were acquainted with the language used in any other way than the courses given at school (for French, Grade 5 and 6) were excluded from further analyses.

At the end of each session the children were informed about the intent of the experiment and were explicitly told not to say anything about the whole session to their classmates and siblings at the same school. This demand was well acted upon and was taken as a rather pleasant "secret".

2. Results

2.1 Vocabulary Test

An analysis of variance on the Danish Vocabulary Test shows significant main effects for the foreign language presentation [$F(2, 177) = 12.926$, $MSE = 2.567$, $p < .0001$] and for the nature of the test [$F(1, 177) = 9.278$, $MSE = 2.069$, $p < .003$]. There was also a significant interaction between the foreign language presentation and the nature of the test [$F(2, 177) = 3.537$, $MSE = 2.069$, $p < .04$]. A posteriori Tukey tests were carried out to test simple effects; as the visual and auditory tests have other items, the a posteriori analysis was done separately on the two tests. On the visual test, providing the foreign language either in the subtitles or in the sound-track significantly improves performance (M = 51% and 50% correct) as compared with the performance in the control condition (M = 41% correct); the difference between the two ways of presenting the foreign language was not significant. On the auditory test, the foreign language in the sound-track significantly improved performance (M = 58% correct) as compared to the control condition (M = 48% correct); the performance difference between the control condition (M = 48% correct) and the condition with the foreign language in the subtitles (M = 50%) is not significant. Accordingly, the visual test displays clear acquisition effects, independently from the presentation mode of the foreign language (subtitles and sound-track); in the auditory test, acquisition is only apparent when the foreign language is in the sound-track. Thus presenting the foreign language in the sound-track improves acquisition in the visual and auditory tests, while the foreign language in the subtitles only improves performance in the visual test.

From Figures 1a (Visual Test) and 1b (Auditory Test), it is worth noting of the absence of any systematic effect of grade levels. Grade did not produce a significant main effect; it was also not involved in a significant interaction with the other variables.

Figure 1. *Percentage correct performance in the Danish Vocabulary Test*

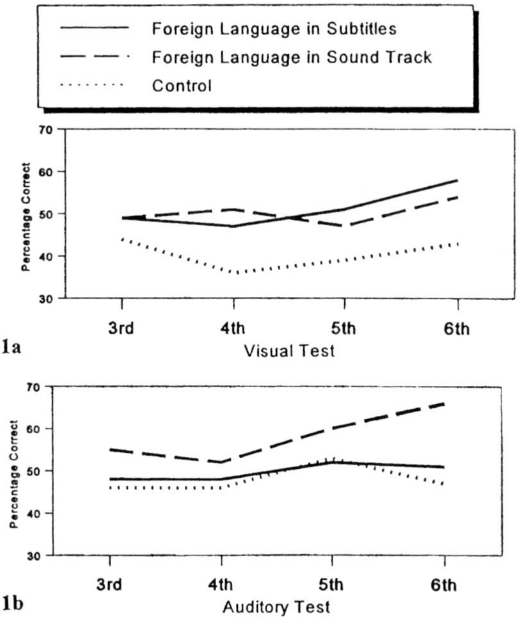

Figure 1a

Figure 1b

For French, there is a main effect of age [F(3, 171) = 189.227, MSE = 1.966, p < .0001]: As can be expected from the French-language teaching at school in Grades 5 and 6, Grade 6 performed best (M = 81% correct), followed by Grade 5 (M = 69% correct), whereas there is no significant difference between Grades 4 and 3 (M = 43% and 39% correct). The nature of the test also produces a significant main effect [F(1, 171) = 6.615, MSE = 2.088, p < .02], with a better performance on the visual test (M = 60% correct) than on the auditory test (M = 56% correct). The significant interaction between both main effects [F(3, 171) = 4.447, MSE = 2.088, p < .005] is involved in a significant second-order interaction between age, the nature of the test, and the nature of availability of the foreign language [F(6, 171) = 3.483, MSE = 2.088, p < .003]. Looking at Figures 2a and 2b, it appears that in almost all grades, the availability of the foreign language (either in the sound-track or in the subtitles) does not significantly increase performance above the one of the control condition. Only for Grade 6, performance in the auditory test for children receiving the foreign language in the sound-track is significantly better (M =

Figure 2. *Percentage correct performance in the French Vocabulary Test*

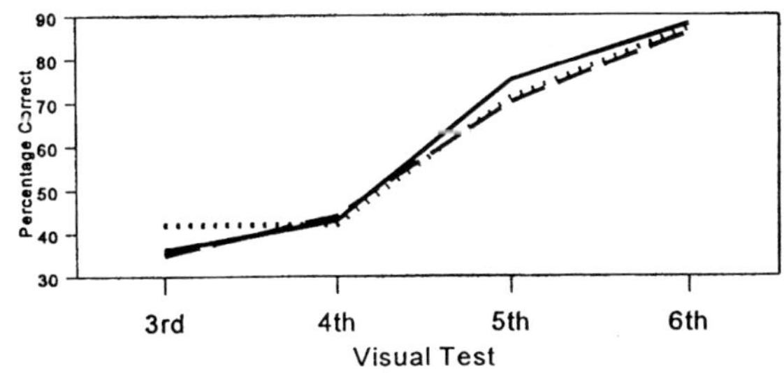

Figure 2a

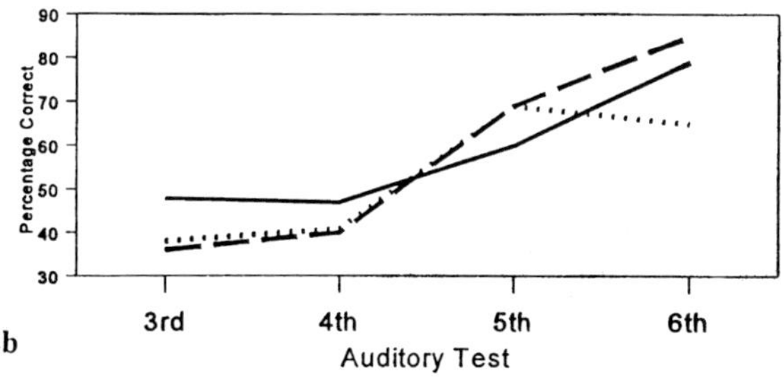

Figure 2b

85% correct) than the performance in the control condition ($\underline{M}$ = 65% correct). These results can be taken to conclude that no acquisition effects due to the movie occurred for French.

2.2 Syntax Test

The analysis of variance on the Danish Syntax Test shows neither significant main nor significant interaction effects at all. For French, there is only a significant effect of the nature of the test [$\underline{F}(1, 176) = 6.441$, $\underline{MSE} = 1.563$, $\underline{p} < .02$], scores being higher on the auditory test ($\underline{M}$ = 44% correct) than on the visual test ($\underline{M}$ = 38% correct); as different items are included in the two tests, nothing important can be concluded from this difference. Since performances in neither experimental conditions are better than in the control condition, there is no evidence for acquisition of foreign language due to its availability in the film.

Figure 3. *Percentage correct performance in the Danish Morphology Test*

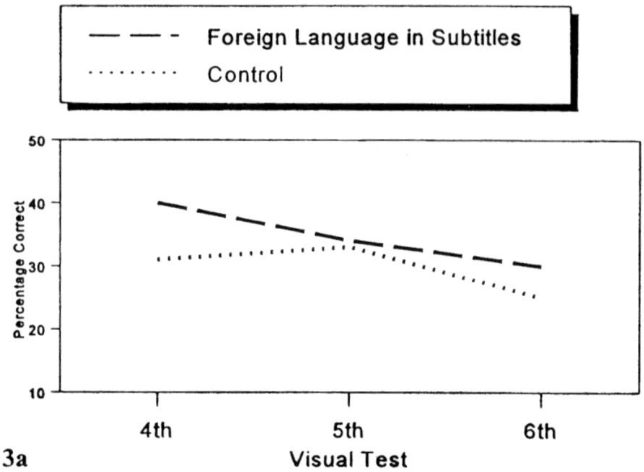

Figure 3a

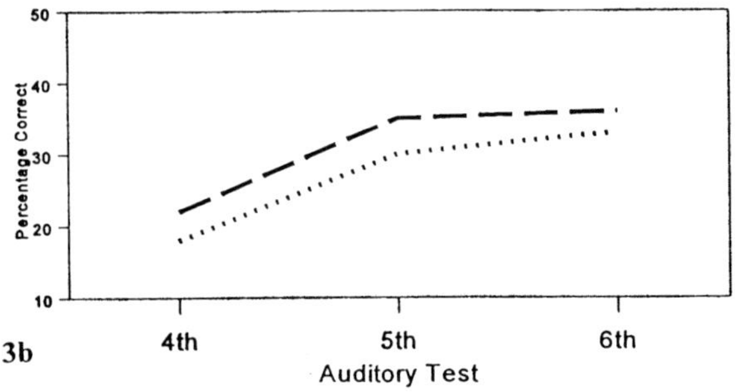

Figure 3b

2.3 Morphology Test

In the Danish Morphology Test, there is a significant interaction between age and the nature of the test [$\underline{F}(2, 182) = 7.225$, $\underline{MSE} = .923$, $\underline{p} < .001$]. A posteriori Tukey tests provide only one significant difference: In the auditory test, there is a significant increase of performance from Grade 4 ($\underline{M} = 22\%$ correct) to Grade 5 ($\underline{M} = 35\%$ correct; see Figure 3b). Although Figure 3a and particularly Figure 3b suggest a superior performance when the foreign language is available in the film, the differences are not significant.

For French (see Figures 4a and 4b), a significant main effect of the nature of the test is present [$\underline{F}(1, 176) = 6.425$, $\underline{MSE} = 1.073$, $\underline{p} < .02$]: Scores on the auditory test are higher ($\underline{M} = 43\%$ correct) than on the visual test ($\underline{M} = 31\%$ correct). As the effect appears in the experimental conditions as well as in the control conditions, it only suggests that the items in the auditory test are easier.

An analysis of the auditory testing alone reveals a significant main effect of condition: Performance in the auditory test is higher when the foreign language is available in the sound-track (M = 43% correct) than in the control condition [M = 34% correct; $F(1, 87) = 4.107$, $MSE = 1.386$, $p < .05$; see Figure 4b].

Figure 4. *Percentage correct performance in the French Morphology Test*

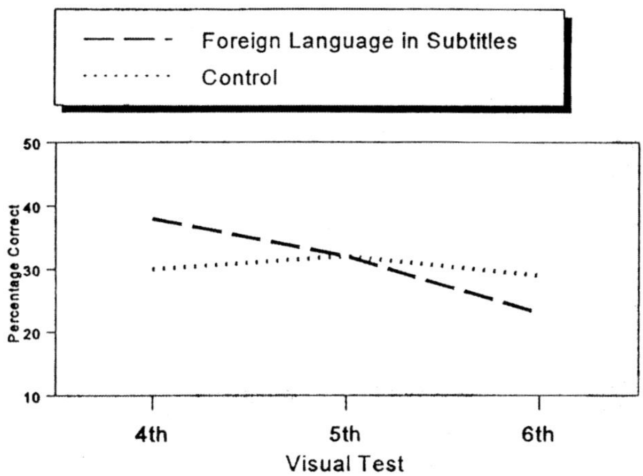

Figure 4a

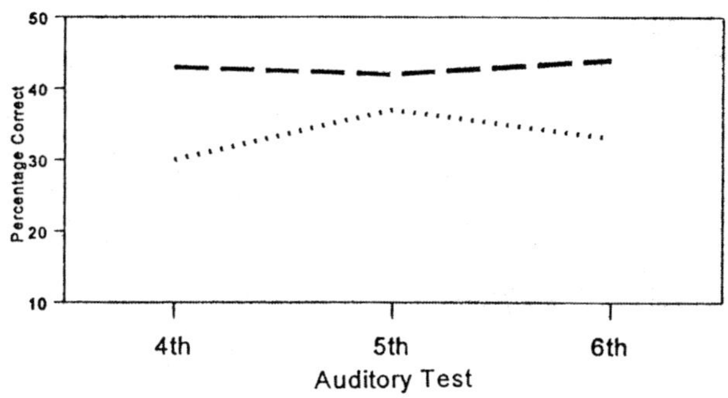

Figure 4b

3. Discussion

In summary, it appears that in both the visual and auditory parts of the Vocabulary Test, acquisition effects emerge when Danish is available in the sound-track available; when Danish is provided in the subtitles, there is only acquisition in the visual part of the Vocabulary Test. In the French Vocabulary Test, no acquisition is apparent, except in the auditory test when the sound-track contains the French language. If we subtract the performance score of the appropriate control condition from the score of the several experimental conditions in the Vocabulary Test and we divide the difference score by the score of the control condition (for convenience, then to be multiplied by 100 to get a percentage), we obtain an acquisition index. Table 1 gives the acquisition index for the several conditions. It then appears that, from the movie, more Danish than French is acquired (with one exception). As Danish is more similar to Dutch than French is, similarity between the first and second language affects acquisition scores.

Table 1. *Acquisition Index in the Vocabulary Test as a Function of the experimental Conditions*

	Foreign language	
	in Subtitle	in Sound-Track
Danish Vocabulary Test		
Visual Test	24.9	23.2
Auditory Test	3.5	21.7
French Vocabulary Test		
Visual Test	0.1	-2.5
Auditory Test	9.1	7.6

Availability of the foreign language does not affect scores on the Syntax Test. The same was found for the Morphology Test, except in the auditory test when French is available in the sound-track.

The results on all tests provide no evidence for more acquisition of French in the movie, following French teaching at school (Grades 5 and 6).

Previously we have reported similar findings; the present study is the first with children Grades 3 to 6. Pavakanun and d'Ydewalle (1992, Experiments 1 and 2; see also d'Ydewalle & Pavakanun, 1996) with High School and University students obtained strong acquisition effects on a similar Vocabulary Test while no acquisition effects appeared in a similar Syntax Test. d'Ydewalle and Pavakanun (1997), with students finishing their secondary school, obtained acquisition effects on all tests, but this was particularly evident in the Vocabulary Test. In the present study, the strongest (if not exclusive) evidence of language acquisition also emerges in the Vocabulary Test. The exception is d'Ydewalle and Pavakanun (1995; University and Grade 9 students) where no effects at all were obtained. Words, particularly nouns, are indeed the easiest building blocks in acquiring a new language; accordingly, it is not too surprising to find the first signs of language acquisition in the Vocabulary Test. It is of course also possible that the other tests were not sensitive enough to detect acquisition effects. At least one effect appeared in the present study: When French was available in the sound-track, children performed better in the auditory version of the French Morphology Test.

An attempt to make a direct comparison between the acquisition index in the present study, involving children, and the ones in the former studies with adolescents and adults is not possible, because of a large number of small methodological differences as well as differences in native and foreign languages used. Also, a single experiment comparing the performance of children and adults is difficult because no movie can be used which will attract similar interest and attention of both groups. Suffice to state that on the whole, children here did not show stronger acquisition effects; in fact, most comparisons suggest stronger effects with adults. Evidence for a sensitive period for second-language acquisition is not supported by the findings.

Similarity with the native language may cause interference in acquiring a foreign language; however, the similarity could also rather facilitate the acquisition process. The present study used Danish and French as foreign languages, Danish being linguistically closer to Dutch than French. The effects obtained are typically stronger for the Danish conditions than for French (except for the Morphology Test). Therefore, the results seem to favor the facilitation hypothesis. Interference is rather to be expected when there is explicit learning; interference largely operates when rules are taught.

Our study does not enable a decision regarding whether the facilitation effect is due to attentional factors (a similar language could be easier to attend to), to the acquisition process itself (linguistically closer structures are easier to retain) or to an interaction of both.

Dulay and Burt (1974, 1975) stated that the order of acquisition of linguistic structures depends upon the structure of the language to be acquired. The precise order of acquisition for one language is then determined by the relative complexity of the different structures, easy structures being acquired before the more complex ones. Based on this theory, one could predict that children with some teaching of French at school will acquire more complex structures than children without such a prior knowledge. However, no evidence is obtained for this view as performances in the experimental conditions involving French were not better than in the control condition with regard to syntax and morphology tests, in Grades 5 and 6.

With adults, the reversed subtitling mode (with foreign language in the subtitles and the native language in the sound-track) results in more vocabulary acquisition than does the normal subtitling mode (foreign language in sound-track and native language in subtitles; see d'Ydewalle & Pavakanun, 1996, 1997; Pavakanun & d'Ydewalle, 1992; but d'Ydewalle & Pavakanun, 1995, for one exception): More new words are acquired when they are presented visually than auditorily, independently of the visual or auditory nature of the test. Consistent with former research showing that reading subtitles is automatic and mandatory (for a summary, see d'Ydewalle & Gielen, 1992), d'Ydewalle and Pavakanun (1997) stated that the processing of the subtitles is the major activity, explaining the better processing of the foreign language in the reversed subtitling mode.

The present study with children gives another picture: When there is a significant difference between the experimental conditions, it is always to the advantage of the condition with the foreign language in the sound-track (i.e., the normal subtitling mode). In the auditory Danish Vocabulary Test, children perform better with Danish in the sound-track; at Grade 6 in the auditory French Vocabulary Test, again a better performance is obtained when French is in the sound-track; and finally, the auditory Morphology Test shows superior performance for children receiving French in the sound-track. In general, younger children perform better in the auditory presentation mode, whereas adults seem to perform better with visual presentation of the foreign language.

If there is indeed a shift in the ways to process the information, this could be because there is a shift in preference of channel of information, a shift in relative efficiency of information processing linked to cognitive growth, or both. Evidence for the first view comes from d'Ydewalle and Van Rensbergen (1989) who found that younger children preferred watching dubbed movies in their own language, contrary to older children and adults who preferred the original foreign movie with subtitles in the native language. Another possibility, however, could simply be that young children are not provided with sufficient reading capacities to allow reading foreign-language subtitles presented with the 6-seconds rule. Although d'Ydewalle and Van Rensbergen (1989) demonstrated adult-like reading of subtitles in children from age 8 on, the study only investigated reading subtitles in the native language (i.e., there was no reversed-subtitling condition). Reading in a foreign language takes much more time through the lack of contextual (verbal) information (Cziko, 1978) and through the lack of sufficiently developed phonologically recoding processes (Van Orden, Johnston, & Hale, 1988). As both general cognitive ability and reading capacity increase with age, older children will succeed better in reading foreign language subtitles, which is a necessary condition to attain language acquisition in the reversed subtitling mode.

In conclusion, the present study shows real but limited foreign-language acquisition by children watching a subtitled movie, despite the short exposure time (10 minutes). For the practical purpose of language acquisition with subtitles, further studies need to use longitudinal exposures in order to assess cumulative effects. Moreover, it is also important to delay the time of the language-acquisition assessment; in the present study with children and in the former studies with adults, the assessment followed immediately after the exposure of the movie.

At a more theoretical level, we do not find evidence for a sensitive language-acquisition period: There was not more acquisition by the children in the present study than by the adults in the former studies. The acquisition here did not profit from the more formal language learning at school (Grades 5 and 6). Contrary to the adults, the children tended to acquire more when the foreign language was in the sound-track than in the subtitles.

* Paper first presented as a report in *Psychological Reports*, Katholieke Universiteit Leuven, n° 221 (September 1997) and previously published in *Journal of Psycholinguistic Research* 1999: 28, 227-244 (Kluwer Academic / Plenum Publishers), and here reprinted by permission of the authors and the publisher.

** The reporting of this work has been made possible by a grant from the Dutch Government of Belgium (CAW 96/06). We thank the primary school "De Kraal", Herent, Belgium, for participating in this study. We also thank Harris Winitz whose comments on an early version of the paper helped considerably to improve the quality.

EPILOGUE

FOUR REMARKS ON TRANSLATION RESEARCH AND MULTIMEDIA*

Anthony Pym
Universitat Rovira i Virgili
Tarragona, Spain

The Misano conference (September 1997) has been, for me, an occasion to learn about "multimedia", in inverted commas because it is not yet a term I use with any confidence. Inevitably one listens, reflects and responds, theorizing for want of any more practical way to make sense. A general impression, from this position of relative externality and perhaps ignorance:

(1) Much of the research I see in this field remains on the level of isolated descriptions, incurring the risk of intellectual fragmentation. My further points are perhaps no more than speculative echoes of that gut reaction: I want to suggest that

(2) such fragmentation might ensue from some of the current tenets of Descriptive Translation Studies itself, which should not remain unperturbed by application to what is still a passably new object; then, as a tenuous consequence, that

(3) research in this particular field cannot and should not pretend to any sublime neutrality, as if we were all not already involved; and finally, now more clearly on the level of my own drum-beating, that

(4) such involvement could concern changing power relations, particularly the power newly accrued to groups of mediators (ourselves included) able to manipulate the complexity at the core of transcultural media (a term I feel happier with). I'll elaborate on my remarks one by one.

1. Fragmentation?

There can be little doubt that the long-term project we know as Descriptive Translation Studies has achieved much, most usefully by challenging the narrowly linguistic source-based prescriptions that still inform many of our teaching practices.

In proclaiming the need for broadly systemic target-based descriptions, the project has enabled us to accumulate knowledge about the diversity of translational behaviour and its role within cultures. In doing so, however, Descriptive Translation Studies has encouraged research in the humanities to look and sound like the work of lab-coated scientists somehow entirely disinterested in their object: we would have nothing to strive for save a systematic description or the odd abstract law, and the latter is still rarely in evidence or recognized as a collective goal. Let me concede that the edifice thus raised is in many respects a fine and beautiful thing. But let me ask if the people should be expected to leave behind all personal involvement when choosing to work within those confines rather than others. Further, let me suggest, as a temporary answer, that the research we do in this field is necessarily marked by our own position and potential agency, that the claim to neutrality is a double-edged professional fiction, and that our work may achieve greater importance if we unloosen the lab coats a little and grapple more directly with the issues involved.

There is research and research. If we take the work presented in this conference as a small cross-section of descriptive translation studies, we observe several quite different levels of involvement. On the one hand there are contributions that aim to be purely taxonomic, postulating categories about which little debate would seem called for. Others aspire to similar neutrality through a more informative mode of discourse: Catalans tell us about Catalan television, Italians compare this with Italian television, and the exchange produced is no doubt quite comforting for all concerned. Still further attitudes are also present: relatively uncirculated information about translation programmes operative on the internet, for example, can at once fondle popular indignation at the dominance of English and arouse slightly more optimistic visions of a multilingual future, and to envisage a future is surely to manifest one's own involvement. Then again, on a more critical tack, research can do things like take official institutions to task for not elaborating, or simply not applying, practicable policies in the field of language and media (an example of which would be the critical statistics reported by Reine Meylarts in this volume).

All these modes of research are descriptive, yet some researchers seem more involved than others. Note that the difference doesn't map onto any neat distinction between some people expressing objective truths and others mouthing off mere opinions. Instead, I suggest, a broad watershed lies in the selection and formation of fields that somehow connect with actual social problems, the kinds of things that people experience and are worried about (internet English) or the kinds of white lies that people are told and consume every day (national language policies). The more the object is formulated in terms of socially lived problems in need of solution, the more likely the resulting research is to question endemic beliefs, arouse interest in a field, make the researcher feel involved, and perhaps even be of importance to the people who ultimately finance our labours. What some want to term "multimedia" may indeed be such a field. But not all approaches are likely to grasp its socially problematic aspects; not everyone is prepared to risk conflict by upsetting their objectified world; not all research aspires to the kind of involvement and importance I admire.

The key steps are thus taken when one forms an object of study, on the level of field formation. There are then good reasons to expect that a relatively undefined and unruly term like "multimedia" will create trouble for any attempt to handle it with methodological precepts developed for other objects (bear in mind that the tools of Descriptive Translation Studies have been handed down most directly from a structuralist moment in comparative literature). To be sure, one can apply certain current doctrines (priority of target side, systemic conditioning of reception, exclusion of evaluation, patterning of translational behaviour) and a piece of research will result and will probably win approval from the theorists. But nothing can guarantee that the work thus done will be of social importance. Worse, nothing can stop that process from producing just one piece of research destined to sit alongside many others, building up no more than accumulative weight on the bookshelf of theses and proceedings, remaining an ultimately fragmentary contribution to a storehouse of fragments, powerless in its subservience to the principles it applied. For as long as descriptive methods fail to address critically the issues of field formation, an object like "multimedia" can perhaps do no more than this: adding pieces of empirical knowledge to the stockpile so far accumulated, for reasons that only a privileged few are able to formulate (the search for "laws" and the like).

Happily, this is not quite what I have found. As noted, there are degrees of involvement within descriptivism. And "multimedia" is indeed a term sufficiently unkempt to mess up the aesthetics of those clean white lab-coats. I will now consider what that term could be doing to one of our dominant principles.

2. Target-side conditioning?

In reaction against source-text linguistics, the front-line brand of descriptivism associated with Gideon Toury insists that the real games are played out on the target side. This tenet has produced results of the kind seen in this conference: television documentaries on Brazil are products of the systems receiving the documentaries; Portuguese and Catalan television systems conform, grosso modo, to the language policies of Portugal and Catalonia. Fair enough: the research thus produced is interesting and useful, indeed as interesting and useful as the principles applied. Yet there is little sign of our researchers asking about possible conditioning from other quarters. I'm thinking here of wide transcultural movements, the stuff of ideologies and markets: perhaps the evangelical churches that have spread their influence in Brazil and have major correlatives in some parts of Europe; perhaps consortia of regional television stations; certainly the international markets for media products, technologies and economies that inevitably condition product costs and indeed possibilities in any local market;

and with equal certainty the transcultural ebbs and flows of nationalist sentiment, since each local mode of belonging, in seeking to define and defend identity, inevitably takes and learns from the many alter egos in similar cultures. We have no reason to suppose that such things are automatically dominant factors, as if international power relations of one kind or another were all that really mattered. Yet we should regret, I believe, that a doctrinal approach to target-side conditioning invites us to obviate research hypotheses incorporating such factors.

The problem has been recognized from within Descriptive Translation Studies. For some time now, José Lambert has been pointing out the ways in which international media make it difficult to say exactly who the sender and the receiver are (for those who still believe in simple communication models) and, by extension, which system is sending and which is receiving. The problem is not hard to find: for example, semantics worry me when German broadcasters (which do indeed call themselves Sender) transmit a series of programmes (Sendungen) but in fact do little more than select, order and (yes!) translate a series of international products, beaming the result via satellite all over Europe to people like myself who, although quite happy to watch and listen from places like my little Spanish mountain, would not willingly call themselves parts of a German cultural system. This is where target-side doctrines create more problems than they solve. This is where other analytical tools are needed. And this is where, of course, José Lambert quite correctly points out that we have to redefine our notion of what a culture (or system) is. Agreed. So let's start doing it. Two suggestions:

What is a culture? For me, at the moment, it is a set of factors creating resistance to the movement of information; or more exactly, sets of factors that alter the status of information as it is moved. Or something like that. The basic point is that cultures are what you always thought they were, but now we can approach them from the perspective of texts and text-bearers that are in movement, crossing time and space; we don't have to start from those zero-degree time-and-space entities that would be sedentary cultures as absolute senders and receivers. This is not the place to pursue the problems thus raised. But this is one of the more theoretical questions I would like to have dealt with in the frame of the conference.

My second suggestion responds to the question to where the determinants on media translation might actually lie. In terms of my little cultural epistemology, we would look first not at the target culture but at the particular people involved in actually moving the texts (cultural products, whatever) and responding to the changes brought about in the status of the information (by translating, but also selecting, arranging, programming, and constructing metatexts). Where are these people to be found? Well, they might be paid by target-side entities, but they themselves are necessarily operating between at least two cultures, in what I like to call intercultural space (inter- in the sense of an intersection, an overlap of cultures and/or languages). If we looked more closely at those people and the configuration of that space, we might find rather more than target-system determinism. But to do so, we would have to revise at least this part of Descriptive Translation Studies.

Again, these are theoretical questions that I would like to have discussed. They are certainly parts of my own political agenda, which broadly seeks to weaken the epistemological role of national cultures and correspondingly heighten the importance of operative intercultures. They are also questions that should, I suggest, intimately concern our own involvement as researchers: If we are in a position to study translational phenomena, surely we ourselves are by definition straddling at least one cultural border? Are we not already operating on the edges of intercultural space? Is our position, indeed our potential agency, not then formally similar to that of the intermediaries we are studying? But such questions, again, are effectively quashed by the reigning tenet of target-side domination.

3. Subjectless research?

Let me now ask the same questions of a concrete piece of research, a paper I was asked to ventriloquize at the conference and of which a version appears in this volume. ("Incidental foreign-language acquisition by children while watching subtitled television programs" by M. Van de Poel and G. D'Ydewalle). The paper was published in Psychological Reports, Katholieke Universiteit Leuven, no. 221, September 1997, which means it was hot off the press at the time of the conference. How did it get to the conference? Through instant globalization thanks to the English language? Through my avid regular reading of KU Psychological Reports? Not at all. What we have here is a small piece of networking: from one university department to another, to José Lambert, to myself, to the conference, and now to you. The text has been moved. Conceivably, its status has changed with each jump. It was, for example, introduced to me as proof that children learn foreign languages through subtitles, and thus, implicitly, that subtitling is socially more beneficial than dubbing. Indeed, such might be its real contribution to this conference. And yet, read closely, the conclusions are not quite so simple: we certainly find there is "real but limited foreign-language acquisition by children watching a subtitled movie", but also that "there was not more acquisition by the children in the present study than by adults in the former studies", countering the hypothesis of a sensitive language-acquisition period. Further, "younger children perform better in the auditory presentation mode [when the foreign language is in the soundtrack], whereas adults seem to perform better with visual presentation of the foreign language", which is surely what one would expect, since younger children have more trouble reading. But then, since this study was carried out with Dutch as L1 and French and Danish as L2s, "more Danish than French is acquired" and there is "no evidence for more acquisition of French [...] following French teaching at school", suggesting, as might be expected, that "[a]s Danish is more similar to Dutch than French is, similarity between the first and second language affects acquisition scores". And so on into the fine details, since the research and its results are in fact complex, or at least more complex than any bald claim that subtitling is more educational than dubbing.

So what? Well, this research is likely to be important to anyone who, like me, has television-watching children who are supposed to be learning foreign languages. In fact, my daughter is downstairs right now, plugged into Ted Turner's Cartoon Network, as usual, taking in hours of images and sounds without the slightest hint of a subtitle. If only the Belgian research had been applied here! Give us more subtitles so we can learn more languages! My daughter can receive many of those cartoons in French, English or Spanish (we don't insist on the Swedish or Dutch) simply by changing the sound channel (we get *The Flintstones* in superb Quebecker French!) and she is surely learning something as a result. So can the Belgians' research, valid and complex as it is, really be used to proclaim the social benefits of dubbing over subtitling? No, technology gives us more possibilities than those included in the field of research; multimedia is even more complex than our humble science.

Consider, now, the possible involvement of the researchers in this project. One might ask, for example, why a Dutch-speaking university in Belgium would select Danish and French as rival L2s. Could it have something to do with the fact that the research was funded by "the Dutch government of Belgium" Personally I would have expected the government to be dubbed "Flemish" in English. What are the implications of finding that Flemish children pick up Danish more easily than French, even "following French teaching at school"? What might that mean in the context of the Katholieke Universiteit Leuven, which split with what is now the Université de Louvain la Neuve, precisely along the French-Flemish divide? Or within the uneasy union of Belgium itself? Surely some political position balances research suggesting that Belgian children could have more to do with Danish than with French? And that position, if indeed it is there (but I am changing the status of the information!), is inscribed in the very formation of the field itself.

Don't get me wrong: I think this is a good piece of research; it is by no means compromised by the possible position and involvement of the researchers. My simple point is that the researchers might be playing much the same intercultural games as those involved in formulating and applying translation policies (to dub or to subtitle, etc.). The complexity of their findings may help them appear neutral (as Bourdieu says, scientists have an active interest in appearing to be disinterested), but that is simply to say that complexity helps shield their strategic power.

4. Intercultural power?

What we call "multimedia" is similarly complex. That's why the "multi-" is there. And this complexity, which is really the only level of the field I want to deal with here, perhaps functions in ways similar to the complexity of scientific research. It means that not everyone can enter the domain where such cultural products are produced, distributed and transformed. Not everyone can translate them, decide whether they should be translated, determine how this should be done, or do research on the process. The complexity of the "multi" perhaps acts as a field-forming device, at least in the sociological sense of producing and maintaining professional boundaries. On the inside of our boundaries would be the people who know about the media, who can receive and work on their numerous codes, and who are not shaken by the corresponding plurality of their languages. On the outside would be those who consume, as best they can, the products ensuing from that complexity, receiving rather than producing translations. The inside would tend to be intercultural (in the sense outlined above); the outside would be a series of source and target systems (in the sense familiar to descriptivists). And we, along with translators and those who most actively inform their work, would be more on the inside than the outside of the field thus configured.

I want to suggest that the complexity of multimedia might also be the condition for a potential shift of power within this intercultural field. If I were a slightly politicized target-side descriptivist, I might believe that effective power lay in the hands of the governments owning or legislatively controlling television networks, ultimately representing the social systems of end receivers. If I were a Marxist millenarian, I might improve on this belief by finding control in the owners of multinational networks, at best guided by purely commercial ends, relatively unrestrained by national legislation. The nature of complexity, however, and of the intercultural space that it might configure, allows us to imagine a kind of power only loosely constrained by social reception or transnational ownership. The codes are so complex, their variety so vast, the cultures so intertwined, that only the technicians, the linguists, the market-researchers, the geeks, the media specialists, can effectively make decisions on an informed basis. A Rupert Murdoch is clever not because he knows about the intricacies of newspaper and television networks but because he employs people who do, and he is prepared to trust their judgement in many cases. Similarly, those who employ translators in multimedia situations need not know about the difficulties of translation (clients' briefs typically say little) but must employ and trust translators who do. To pretend otherwise would be to make everyone an expert in intercultural complexity.

Now, where might the effective power lie? If what I have described is more than a pipe dream, decision-making power over difficult questions like translation decisions must first lie with translators and those who formally share their intercultural space: complexity means that the financial piper need not always call the tune. More generally, this kind of power potentially lies not with target cultures, nor with fat-cat owners, but with the technicians, the people skilled at handling complex codes, and the people like us who believe we are skilled enough to talk about those skills. This is one good reason why multimedia research can rarely pretend to be neutral. But might it also be a reason why much of our research seems so fragmented, so unprogrammatic, and so paradoxically powerless?

There is something tragic in this analysis. The intellectuals, to use an unfashionable term for people skilled in the handling of complex codes, after a century or so of complaining about the classes who held power and manipulated society, now find themselves (ourselves) in position of more than chimerical power. And yet we don't know what to do with it. At least, not in any coordinated way, not as a coherent social group, not as a virtual community, certainly not as a new social class. Why not? Among the many possible answers, let me paraphrase just one: John Frow, in the last chapter of *Cultural Studies and Cultural Value* (1995), suggests that complexity could also be the condition of our disunity. This is basically for two reasons. First, since our power comes from relative specialization, we tend to remain specialist technicians even among ourselves: translators are not interpreters; dubbers are not subtitlers; researchers are not practitioners; and no one seems to be like those strangely anonymous people who decide translation policies. Second, since our power comes from handling complex codes, we are professionally given to criticize and even mistrust the kind of relatively simple language that can foster belonging and map out collective goals. If you like, we become too specialized and too smart for any unifying ideology. The outcome, on this analysis, must be professional fragmentation, a vision limited to technical aspects and short-term goals, and glib satisfaction with the authoritative strategies of neutral science. Which is precisely what I seem to have found.

* A. Pym was asked to act as one of the discussants at the Misano international seminar (September 1997). He spoke after the last round table on "Charting a future for multimedia translation research". The editors have retained as much as possible the orality and interactivity of the speech.

References

AALTONEN, Outi. 1995. "Subtitling as Culture-Bound Meaning Production". In GAMBIER, Y. (ed.), 384-387.

AGB Hellas (ed.). 1995. *TV Yearbook 94-95*. Athens: Organopublica A.E.

AGB Hellas (eds). 1996. *TV Yearbook 95-96*. Athens: Organopublica A.E.

ALCANDRE, Jean Jacques. 1995. "Une formation universitaire pour la traduction audiovisuelle". In GAMBIER, Y. (ed.), 443-445.

ALEXIEVA, Bistra. 1986. "Proyavi na asimetria v prevoda na uslovni izrechenia ot angliyski na bulgarski" (Asymmetry in translating conditionals from English into Bulgarian). In VASEVA, I., IVANOVA , M. & ALEXIEVA, B. (eds), *Proyavi na mezhduezikova asimetria pri prevod ot chuzhd ezik na bulgarski* (Interlingual asymmetry in translating from a foreign language into Bulgarian). Sofia: BAN, 188-267.

ALEXIEVA, Bistra. 1997a. "A Typology of Interpreter-Mediated Events". *The Translator* 3 (2): 153-174.

ALEXIEVA, Bistra. 1997b. "The Polysemiotic Text in Multimedia Communication and Its Translation and Interpreting". Manuscript. Seminar in Misano Adriatico, on *Multimedia Translation*, September 1997.

ALEXIEVA, Bistra. 1997c. "Interpreting Mediated TV Events". In KLAUDY, K. & KOHN, J. (eds), *Transferre Necesse Est.* Proceedings of the 2nd International Conference on Current Trends in Studies of Translation and Interpreting, Budapest, 5-7 September 1996. Budapest: Scholastica Publishers, 171-174.

ALLEN, Woody. 1993. *Manhattan Murder Mystery. Combined Continuity*. Los Angeles: Gelula & Co., Inc. 1995. *Misterioso asesinato en Manhattan*. Barcelona: Fábula Tusquets Editores. [Translated by Claudio López Lamadrid].

ANDERSON, Benedict. 1983. *Imagined communities*. London: Verso.

ANDERSON, Daniel R., & LORCH, E. P. 1983. Looking at television: Action or reaction? In BRYANT, J. & ANDERSON, D. (eds), *Children's understanding of television: Research on attention and comprehension.* New York: Academic Press, 1-33.

ANDERSON, J. 1997. "Never a sure thing". *Sight & Sound* 7 (9): 22-27.

ANG, Ien. 1996. *Living room wars: rethinking the media audiences for a post-modern world.* London: Routledge.

AUMONT, Jacques, GAUDREAULT, André & MARIE, Michel (eds). 1989. *Histoire du cinéma. Nouvelles approches*. Paris: Publications de la Sorbonne. Série Langue et langages.

ÁVILA, Alejandro. 1997. *El doblaje*. Madrid: Cátedra Signo e Imagen.

BAKER, Mona 1997. "Non-Cognitive Constraints and Interpreter Strategies Political Interviews". In SIMMS, K. (ed.), *Translating Sensitive Texts. Linguistic Aspects*. Amsterdam: Rodopi, 113-131.

BAKER, W. & FAULKNER, R.R. 1991. "Role as resource in the Hollywood Film Industry". *American Journal of Sociology* 7: 279-309.

BALASUBRAMANIAN, V. 1994. *State of the Art Review on Hypermedia issues and applications* <http://isg.sfu.ca/_duchier/misc/hypertext_review>

BALESTRIERI, L. 1984. *L'informazione audiovisiva. Problemi di linguaggio*. Torino: ERI Edizioni Rai Radiotelevisione Italiana.

BALIO, Tino. 1976. *The American Film Industry*. Madison: University of Wisconsin Press.

BALIO, Tino. 1998. "The art film market in the new Hollywood". In NOWELL-SMITH, G. & RICCI, R. (eds), *Hollywood & Europe*. London: BFI.

BARRY, S. Dec. 1995-Jan.1996. "Review of *La Haine*." *Film Ireland* 50: 37-38.

BLANE, Sandra. 1996. "Interlingual Subtitling in the Languages Degree". In SEWELL & HIGGINS (eds), *Teaching Translation in Universities: Present and Future Perspecives.* London: CILT, 183-207.

BLOCH, M. 1991. "Language, anthropology and cognitive practice". *Man* 26: 183-97.

BOLINGER, D. & SEARS, D. A. 1981. *Aspects of language*. New York: Harcourt Brace, Jovanovitch.

BORDWELL, David. 1985. "The Classical Hollywood Style". In BORDWELL, David, STAIGER Janet & THOMPSON, Kristin, *The Classical Hollywood Cinema. Film Style and Mode of Production to 1960*. London: Routledge & Kegan Paul, 1-84.

BROS-BRANN, Eliane. 1993. "Simultaneous Interpretation and the Media: Interpreting Live for Television". In PICKEN, C. (ed.), *Translation - the Vital Link. La traduction au coeur de la communication*. Proceedings of the XIII FIT World Congress, Brighton, August 1993. Vol.2. London: Institute of Translation and Interpreting, 267-271.

BRYSON, Norman. 1983. *Vision and Painting. The Logic of the Gaze*. New Haven & London: Yale University Press.

BSAC/MBS Seminar Report. 1992. *The Challenge of Language in European Film*. Madrid: Media Business School.

BURLING, Robbins. 1992. *Patterns of language: Structure, Variation, Change*. San Diego, California: Academic Press.

CATTRYSSE, Patrick. 1991. "Vertaling, Adaptatic en Intertekstualiteit". *Communicative* 21 (1): 38-47.

CATTRYSSE, Patrick. 1992. *Pour une théorie de l'adaptation filmique. Le film noir américain*. Bern: Peter Lang.

CATTRYSSE, Patrick. 1995. "Audio-visual translation and new media", Brussels, KUB [unpublished paper; appeared in a slightly different form in *Koninklijke Zuidnederlandse Maatschappij voor Taalen, Letterkunde en Geschiedenis* (1995)]

CATTRYSSE, Patrick. 1997. "Audio-visual Translation and New Media". In HODGSON,R. & SOUKUP,P.A. (eds), 67-89.

CATTRYSSE, Patrick. 1998. "Translation in the New Media Age: Implications for Research and Training". In GAMBIER, Y. (ed.), 7-12.

CHALIER, Chantal & MUELLER, Felicity. 1998. "Subtitling for Australian Television: The SBS Endeavour". In GAMBIER, Y. (ed.), 97-101.

CHION, Michel. 1988. *La Toile Trouée. La Parole au Cinéma*. Paris: Editions de l'etoile.

CHION, Michel. 1990. *L'Audiovision*. Paris: Nathan.

CORMACK, M. 1998. "Minority Language Media in Western Europe". *European Journal of Communication* 13 (1): 33-52.

CORNU, Jean-François. 1983. *Traduction et cinéma. Remarques sur la traduction d'un dialogue de film*. Mémoire de maîtrise, Université de Nantes.

COULMAS, Florian. 1991. "European integration and the idea of the national language". In COULMAS, F. (ed.), *A Language Policy for the European Community*. New York: Mouton de Gruyter.

CUNNINGHAM, Stuart & JACKA, Elizabeth (eds) 1996. *Australian Television and International Mediascapes*. Cambridge: University Press.

CZIKO, G. A. 1978. "Differences in first- and second-language reading: The use of syntactic, semantic and discourse constraints". *Canadian Modern Language Review*, 34: 473-489.

DALY, A. F. 1985. "Interpreting for International Satellite Television". *Meta* 30 (1): 91-96.

DANAN, Martine. 1995. "Le sous-titrage: Stratégie culturelle et commericale". In GAMBIER, Y. (ed.), 272-281

DATO, Daniel P. 1975. "On psycholinguistic universals in children's learning of Spanish". In DATO, D. P. (ed.), 235-254.

DATO, Daniel P. (ed.). 1975. *Developmental psycholinguistics: Theory and applications*. Washington, DC: Georgetown University Press.

DAVIES MESSENGER, Máire. 1989. *Television is Good for your Kids*. London: Hilary Shipman.

DAYAN, Daniel & KATZ, Elihu. 1992. *Media Events, the Live Broadcasting of History*. Cambridge, Mass.: Harvard University Press.

DE WAARD, J & NIDA, Eugene .A. 1986. *From One Language to Another. Functional Equivalence in Bible Translating.* Nashville, Tennessee: Nelson.

DEEMER, Charles. 1994. *What is Hypertext?* http://www.teleport.com/~cdeemer/essay.html

DELABASTITA, Dirk. 1989. "Translation and Mass-Communication: Film and TV Translation as Evidence of Cultural Dynamics". *Babel 35 (4)*: 193-218.

DELABASTITA, Dirk. 1990. "Translation and the Mass Media". In BASSNETT, S. & LEFEVERE, A. *Translation History and Culture*. London: Pinter Publishers Ltd , 97-109.

DESROCHES, Yves. 1984. "Le doublage, cet inconnu". *Circuit* 7: 6-8.

DÍAZ-CINTAZ, Jorge. 1997. *El subtitulado en tanto que modalidad de traducción filmica dentro del marco teórico de los Estudios sobre Traducción.* (Misterioso asesinato en Manhattan, *Woody Allen, 1993*). Valencia: Universitat de València. PhD Thesis.

DITMARS, H. 1996. "Algiers in Paris". *Sight & Sound* 6 (1): 14-17.

DMOCH, Thomas. 1996. "Internationale Werbung". In MECKEL, M., & KRIENER, M. (eds), 179-200.

DRIES, Josephine. 1994. "Training Language Transfer Professionals in Europe". *Libri e Riviste d'Italia. La Traduzione. Saggi e Documenti (II)*. Roma: Ministero per i beni culturali e ambientali, 281-287.

DRIES, Josephine. 1995. *Dubbing and Subtitling. Guidelines for Production and Distribution.* Düsseldorf: European Institute for the Media.

DULAY, H. C., & BURT, M. K. 1972. "Goofing: An indicator of children's second language learning strategies". *Language Learning*, 22: 235-252.

DULAY, H. C., & BURT, M. K. 1973. "Should we teach children syntax?" *Language Learning,* 23: 245-258.

DULAY, H. C., & BURT, M. K. 1974. "Natural sequences in child second language acquisition". *Language Learning*, 24: 37-53.

DULAY, H. C., & BURT, M. K. 1975. "A new approach to discovering universal strategies of child second language acquisition". In DATO, D. P. (ed.), 209-234.

D'YDEWALLE, Géry., & GIELEN, I. 1992. Attention allocation with overlapping sound, image, and text. In RAYNER, K. (ed.), *Eye movements and visual cognition: Scene perception and reading.* New York: Springer-Verlag, 415-427.

D'YDEWALLE, Géry, & PAVAKANUN, Ubowanna. 1995. Acquisition of a second/foreign language by viewing a television program. In WINTERHOFF-SPURK, P. (ed.), *Psychology of media in Europe: The state of the art - perspectives for the future.* Opladen, Westdeutscher Verlag GmbH, 51-64.

D'YDEWALLE, Géry, & PAVAKANUN, Ubowanna. 1996. "Le sous-titrage à la télévision facilite-t-il l'acquisition des langues?" In GAMBIER, Y. (ed.), 217-223.

D'YDEWALLE, Géry, & PAVAKANUN, Ubowanna. 1997. Could enjoying a movie lead to language acquisition? In WINTERHOFF-SPURK, P. & VAN DER VOORT, T. (eds), *New horizons in media psychology*. Opladen, Westdeutscher Verlag GmbH, 145-155.

D'YDEWALLE, Géry, PRAET, C. & VAN RENSBERGEN, J. 1991. "Watching Subtitled Television: Automatic Reading Behaviour". *Communication Research 18 (5), October 1991*: 650-666.

D'YDEWALLE, Géry, & VAN RENSBERGEN, J. 1989. "Developmental studies of text-picture interactions in the perception of animated cartoons with text". In MANDL, H. & LEVIN, J. R. (eds), *Knowledge acquisition from text and pictures.* Amsterdam: Elsevier Science Publishers B.V., 223-248.

D'YDEWALLE, Géry., VAN RENSBERGEN, J., & POLLET, J. 1987. Reading a message when the same message is available auditorily in another language: The case of subtitling. In O'REGAN, J. K. & LÉVY-SCHOEN, A. (eds), *Eye movement: From physiology to cognition*. Amsterdam: Elsevier Science Publishers B.V., 313-321.

ECO, Umberto. 1968. *La struttura assente. La ricerca semiotica e il metodo strutturale.* Milano: Bompiani.

ERVIN-TRIPP, Susan. 1981. "Social process in first- and second-language learning". In WINITZ, H. (ed.), *Native language and foreign language acquisition*. New York: The New York Academy of Sciences, 33-47.

EVANS, G. 1996. "Gramercy levels *Hate* at young Americans". *Variety*, Feb. 23: 11-20. *Évènement du Jeudi* 18-24 May, 1995. "Review of *La Haine*".

FALCON, R. 1998. "V for Video". *Sight & Sound* 8 (3): 24-28.

FAWCETT, Peter. 1983. "Translation modes and constraints". *The Incorporated Linguist* 22 (4): 186-190.

FAWCETT, Peter 1995. "Translation and Power Play". *The Translator* 1 (2): 177-192.

FERGUSON, M. 1992. "The mythology about globalization". *European Journal of Communication* 7 (1): 69-93.

FLINT, M. 1996. "International Film Distribution". *International Media Law* 14 (4): 2-3.

FODOR, István. 1976. *Film Dubbing: Phonetic, Semiotic, Esthetic and Psychological Aspects*. Hamburg: Helmut Buske Verlag.

FRATER, P. 1996. "Language Lessons". *Screen International* 16 February 1996: 14-16.

GAMBIER, Yves. 1994. "Audiovisual Communication: Typological Detour". In DOLLERUP, C. & LINDEGAARD, A. (eds), *Teaching Translation and Interpreting 2: Insights, Aims, Visions*. Selected papers from the Second 'Language International' Conference, Elsinore, Denmark, 4-6 June 1993. Amsterdam & Philadelphia: John Benjamins, 275-283.

GAMBIER, Yves. (ed.) 1995. *Communication audiovisuelle et transferts linguistiques / Audiovisual Communication and Language Transfer*. International Forum. Strasbourg, 22-24.6.1995. *Translatio* 14 (3-4) (Special Issue of the FIT Newsletter).

GAMBIER, Yves. (ed.). 1996. *Les transferts linguistiques dans les médias audiovisuels*. Villeneuve d'Ascq: Presses Universitaires du Septentrion.

GAMBIER, Yves (ed.). 1998. *Translating for the Media. Papers from the International Conference "Languages & the Media", Berlin, November 22-23, 1996*. University of Turku: Centre for Translation and Interpreting.

GAMBIER, Yves. & GILE, Daniel. & TAYLOR, Christopher (eds). 1997. *Conference Interpreting: Current Trends in Research. Proceedings of the International Conference on Interpreting: What Do We Know and How?*, Turku, August 1994. Amsterdam & Philadelphia: John Benjamins.

GAMBIER, Yves & SUOMELA-SALMI, Eija. 1994. "Audiovisual communication. Problems and issues at stake in subtitling". In PÜRCHEL, Heiner et al.: *Intercultural Communication, Proceedings of the 17th LAUD Symposium,* Duisburg 23-27 March 1992. Frankfurt a.M / Berlin / Bern / New York / Paris / Wien: Peter Lang, 369-392.

GANZ-BLÄTTLER, Ursula. 1994. "Angelsächsische Krimiserien und ihre deutsche Bearbeitung" *SPIEL. Siegener Periodicum zur internationalen empirischen Literaturwissenschaft* 13 (2): 231-255.

GARCIA LANDA, Mariano 1990. "A General Theory of Translation (and of Language)". *Meta* 35 (3): 476-488.

GELLERSTAM, Martin. 1986. "Translationese in Swedish novels translated from English". In WOLLIN, L. & LINDQUIST, H. (eds.), *Translation Studies in Scandinavia*. Lund: Lund University Press, 88-95.

GIELEN, M. 1988. *Perceptie en ondertitels: De parafoveale en perifere informatieverwerking van ondertitels* [Perception and subtitles: The Parafoveal and peripheral information processing of subtitles]. Unpublished license thesis, University of Leuven, Belgium.

GILBEY, R. 1995. "Review of *La Haine*". *Premiere* 161 (Dec. 1995): 10-11.

GILE, Daniel 1995. *Basic Concepts and Models for Interpreter and Translator Training*. Amsterdam & Philadelphia: John Benjamins.

GOTTLIEB, Henrik. 1994a. "Subtitling: Diagonal Translation". *Perspectives: Studies in Translatology* 2 (1): 101-112.

GOTTLIEB, Henrik. 1994b. "Subtitling: people translating people". In DOLLERUP, Cay & LINDEGAARD, Annette (eds), *Teaching Translation and Interpreting 2*. Amsterdam & Philadelphia: John Benjamins, 261-274.

GOTTLIEB, Henrik. 1997. *Subtitles, Translation & Idioms*. University of Copenhagen: Center for Translation Studies.

GRAMSCI, Antonio. 1985. "Selections from Cultural Writings". In FORGAES, D. & NOWELL-SMITH, G. (eds). Translated by Boelhower, W. Cambridge, Mass.: Harvard University Press.

GREEN, Fred Pratt. 1982. *The Hymns and Ballads of Fred Pratt Green*. Carol Stream, Illinois: Hope Publishing Co.

GRICE, Herbert Paul. 1975. "Logic and Conversation". In COLE, P. & MORGAN, J.L. (eds), *Syntax and Semantics,* Vol.3: *Speech Acts*. New York: Academic Press, 41-58.

GRONBECK, B., FARRELL, J., SOUKUP, P. (eds). 1991. *Consciousness and culture.* Newberry Park, California: Sage.

GUNTER, Barrie. 1982. *The Effects of Subtitles on the Appreciation of TV Programmes Among the Hearing Audience.* Audience Research Department. London: Independent Broadcasting Authority.

GUNTER, Barrie & SVENNEVIG, Michael. 1987. *Behind and in Front of the Screen: Television's Involvement with Family Life.* London & Paris: John Libbey.

HAKUTA, K. (1975). "Learning to speak a second language: What exactly does the child learn?" In DATO, D. P. (ed.), 193-208.

HALL, S. July 22 1992. "Our mongrel selves". *New Statesman* (Special Issue: Borderlands): 6-7.

HALLIDAY, M.A.K & RUQAIYA, Hasan 1976. *Cohesion in English.* London & New York: Longman.

HARRIS, Brian. 1990. "Norms in Interpretation". *Target* 2 (1): 115-119.

HAYLES, Katherine. 1992. "The materiality of Informatics". *Configurations* 1 (1): 147-170.

HEMPEN, Frans. 1998. "Introducing the VVFT, the Dutch Union of Translators for the Media". In GAMBIER, Y. (ed.), 51-56.

HERBST, Thomas. 1994. *Linguistische Aspekte der Synchronisation von Fernsehserien.* Tübingen: Niemeyer.

HERBST, Thomas. 1995. "People do not Talk in Sentences: Dubbing and the Idiom Principle". In GAMBIER, Y. (ed.), 257-271.

HINDMARSH, R. & LUYKEN, G.-M. 1986. "Overcoming Language Barriers in European Television". *Multilingua* 5 (2): 101-107.

HODGSON Jr., Robert & SOUKUP P.A. (eds). 1997. *From One Medium to Another. Basic Issues for Communicating the Bible in New Media.* Kansas City: Sheed & Ward and American Bible Society.

HOSKINS, C., MIRUS, R. & ROZENBOOM W. 1989. "US television programs in the international market: unfair pricing?" *Journal of Communication* 39 (2): 55-74.

HOUSE, Juliane. 1986. "Acquiring translational competence in interaction". In HOUSE, J. & S. BLUM-KULKA (eds) *Interlingual and Intercultural Communication. Discourse and Cognition in Translation and Second Language Studies*. Tübingen: Gunter Narr, 179-194.

HUBERT-LACOMBE, Patricia. 1996. *Le cinéma français dans la guerre froide*. Paris: L'Harmattan.

HUNSTON, Susan. 1993. "Projecting a sub-culture: the construction of shared worlds by projecting clauses in two registers". *Language & Culture*. 2: 98-112. *The Independent.* Nov. 16, 1995. "Review of *La Haine*".

ITC (Independent Television Commission) (ed.). 1996. *Television: Ethnic Minorities' Views.* London. England: ITC.

IVARSSON, Jan. 1992. *Subtitling for the Media: a Handbook of an Art*. Stockholm. Transedit.

IVARSSON, Jan & CARROLL, Mary. 1998. *Subtitling*. Simrishamn: TransEdit.

IZARD, Natàlia. 1992. *La traducció cinematogràfica*. Barcelona: Centre d'Investigació de la Comunicació.

JAKOBSON, Roman. 1959. "On linguistic aspects of translation". In BROWER, R: *On translation*. New York: Oxford University Press, 232-239.

JAMES, Heulwen, ROFFE, Ian & THORNE, David. 1996. "Assessment and skills in screen translation". In DOLLERUP, C. & APPEL, V. (eds), *Teaching Translation and Interpreting 3*. Amsterdam & Philadelphia: John Benjamins, 177-186. *Jeune Cinema*. June 1995. "Review of *La Haine*".

JOHNSON, Marguerite. 1992. "Read their lips. In Germany, putting words into the mouths of actors from abroad is a major specialized industry". *Time*, 14th September: 1992: 62.

KAINDL, Klaus 1998. "Die Übersetzung als Inszenierung: Ein interdisziplinärer Rahmen zur Analyse von Opernübersetzung". *Target* 9 (2): 271-287.

KANAVAKIS, Emmanuel. 1977. *I Thesi tis Tileoraseos stin Elliniki Ikogenia* [*The Place of Greek Television in the Greek Family*] (PhD Thesis). Athens: Iatriki Sholi.

KARAMITROGLOU, Fotios. 1996. *Translation Theory and Screen/Film Translation: An Evaluative Overview*. MSc Dissertation submitted to the University of Manchester Institute of Science and Technology, Dept. of Language Engineering.

KARAMITROGLOU, Fotios. 1998. *Towards a Methodology for the Investigation of Norms in Audiovisual Translation: The Choice Between Subtitling and Revoicing in Greece*. PhD Thesis submitted to the University of Manchester Institute of Science and Technology, Dept. of Language Engineering.

KARLIN, S. 1998. "We've never had it so good". *The Times* 31 July 1998: 40.

KAUFMANN, Francine. 1995. "Formation à la traduction et à l'interprétation pour les médias audiovisuels". In GAMBIER, Y. (ed.), 431-442.

KEMP, S. 1998. "Some Others' Tongue". *Screen International* 27 February 1998: 26-29.

KILBORN, Richard. 1993. "'Speak my Language': Current Attitudes to Television Subtitling and Dubbing". *Media, Culture and Society*, 15 (4), October 1993: 641-660.

KORONAIOU, Alexandra. 1992. *Neoi kai Mesa Mazikis Enimerosis*. [*Youth and Mass Media*]. Athens: Odysseas.

KRESS, Gunther. 1997. *Before Writing. Rethinking the Paths to Literacy*. London: Routledge.

KRESS, Gunther & VAN LEEUWEN, Theo. 1996. *Reading Images. The Grammar of Visual Design*. London: Routledge.

KROEBER-RIEL, Werner. 1992. "Die Globalisierung der Euro-Werbung. Ein konzeptioneller Ansatz der Konsumentenforschung". *Marketing* 4: 261-266.

KROGSTAD, Morten. 1998. "Subtitling for cinema films and video/television". In GAMBIER, Y. (ed.), 57-64.

KURZ, Ingrid. 1986. "Simultaneous Interpretation of a Panel Discussion with Jeane Kirkpatrick on Austrian TV". In KUMMER, K. (ed.), *Building Bridges. Proceedings of the 27th Annual Conference of ATA*. Medford, N.J.: Learned Information Inc., 379-384.

KURZ, Ingrid. 1990. "Overcoming Language Barriers in European Television". In BOWEN, D. & BOWEN, M. (eds), *Interpreting - Yesterday, Today, and Tomorrow* (ATA Series vol. IV). Binghamton, New York: State University of New York Press, 168-175.

KURZ, Ingrid. 1991. "Live Interpreting Via Satellite Transmission". *The Jerome Quarterly* 6 (3): 9-10.

KURZ, Ingrid. 1993. "The 1992 U.S. Presidential Elections: Interpreting the "American Debatathon" for Austrian Television". In PICKEN, C. (ed.), *Translation – the Vital Link. La traduction au coeur de la communication*. Proceedings of the XIII FIT World Congress, Brighton, August 1993. Vol.1. London: Institute of Translation and Interpreting, 441-445.

KURZ, Ingrid. 1996. "Special Features of Media Interpreting as Seen by Interpreters and Users". In *New Horizons. Horizons nouveaux*. Proceedings of the XIVth FIT World Congress, Melbourne, February 1996. Vol.2. Melbourne: AUSIT, 957-965.

KURZ Ingrid & BROS-BRANN, E. 1996. "L'interprétation en direct pour la télévision". In GAMBIER, Y. (ed.), 207-216.

KURZ, Ingrid & PÖCHHACKER, F. 1995. "Quality in TV Interpreting". In GAMBIER, Y. (ed.), 350-358.

LAKOFF, Robin Tolmach. 1982. "Some of my favourite writers are literate: the mingling of oral and literate strategies in written communication". In TANNEN, Deborah (ed.), *Spoken and Written Language. Exploring Orality and Literacy*. Norwood & New Jersey: Ablex, 239-260.

LAMBERT, José. 1990 "Le sous-titrage et la question des traductions. Rapport sur une enquête In ARNTZ, R. & THOME, G. (eds), *Übersetzungswissenschaft. Ergebnisse und Perspektiven*, Tübingen: Narr, 228-238.

LAMBERT, José. 1997. "Problems and Challenges of Translation in an Age of New Media and Competing Models". In HODGSON, R. & SOUKUP, P. A. (eds), 51-65.

LAMBERT, José & DELABASTITA, Dirk 1996. "La traduction des textes audiovisuels: modes et enjeux culturels". In GAMBIER, Y. (ed.), 33-58.

LAMBERT, Wallace, E., GARDNER, R. C., OLTON, R., & TUNSTALL, K. 1970. "A study of the roles of attitudes and motivation in second-language learning". In FISHMAN, J. A (ed.), *Readings in the sociology of language*. The Hague: Mouton, 473-491.

LAMBERT, Wallace, E., & KLINEBERG, Otto. 1967. *Children's views of foreign peoples: A cross-national study*. New York: Appleton.

LANDOW, George. 1992. *Hypertext: the convergence of contemporary critical theory and technology*. Baltimore & London: Johns Hopkins University Press.

LAPLACE, Colette. 1997. "L'interprétation simultanée à la télévision: aspects culturels". *Terminologie et Traduction* 3: 121-141.

LARSEN, Fritz. 1994. "More than loan-words. English influence on Danish". *RASK. Internationalt Tidsskrift for Sprog og Kommunikation* 1: 21-46. Odense University: Institute for Languages and Communication.

LARSEN, D. N., & SMALLEY, William, Allen. 1972. *Becoming Bilingual: A Guide to Language Learning*. New Canadian, CT: Practical Anthropology.

LARUE, Jan. 1970. *Guidelines for Style Analysis*. New York: W.W. Norton & Co.

LEDERER, Marianne. 1994. *La traduction aujourd'hui. Le modèle interprétatif*. Paris: Hachette.

LEFEVERE, André 1992. *Translation, History, Culture: a Sourcebook*. London & New York: Routledge.

LEFKOWITZ, Natalie. 1991. *Talking backwards, looking forwards: the French language game verlan*. Tübingen: Narr.

LENNEBERG, Eric, H. 1967. *Biological foundations of language*. New York: Wiley.

LEV, Peter. 1993. *The Euro-American Cinema*. Austin: University of Texas Press.

LIEBES, Tamar 1990. *The export of meaning: Cross-cultural readings of Dallas*. New York: Oxford University Press.

LINDEGAARD, Annette. 1996. "Translations: originals in dialogue". *Perspectives. Studies in Translatology* 4 (1): 153-162.

LÓPEZ ESCOBAR, E. (1993): "Valores vulnerables en la televisión multicanal española". In BLUMLER, J.G., *Televisión e interés público*, Barcelona: Bosch.

LORCH, P. E., ANDERSON, D. R., & LEVIN, R. S. 1979. "The relationship of visual attention to children's comprehension of television". *Child Development*, 50: 722-727.

LORENZO, Emilio. 1996. *Anglicismos Hispánicos*. Madrid: Editorial Gredos, Biblioteca Románica Hispánica.

LUYKEN, Georg-Michael & al. 1991. *Overcoming Language Barriers in Television. Dubbing and Subtitling for the European Audience* (Media Monographs 13). Manchester: The European Institute for the Media.

MACAULAY, Marcia 1996. "Asking to ask: The strategic function of indirect requests for information in interviews". *Pragmatics*, 6(4): 491-509.

MACNAMARA, John. 1973. Nurseries, streets, and classrooms: Some comparisons and deductions. *Modern Language Journal*, 57: 250-254.

MANDERBACH, Jochen. 1988. *Das Remake - Studien zu seiner Theorie und Praxis.* Siegen: Universität-Gesamthochschule.
MAYORAL, Roberto, KELLY, Dorothy & GALLARDO, Natividad 1988. "The Concept of Constrained Translation. Non-Linguistic Perspectives on Translation". M*eta* 33 (3), 356-367.
MCCORMICK, A. 1997. *Writ small: Subtitling for SBS Television:* Address to "Language and the Media", Style Council Sydney 97, 21-23 November 1997: 5.
MCLAUGHLIN, Barry. 1981. Differences and similarities between first- and second-language learning. In WINITZ, H. (ed.), *Native language and foreign language acquisition.* New York: The New York Academy of Sciences, 23-32.
MCQUAIL, Denis. 1997. *Audience analysis.* London: Sage.
MEAUX SAINT-MARC, F. 1998. "The Rogue Element". *Screen International.* 27 February 1998.
MECKEL, Miriam. 1996. "Die vernetzte Welt". In MECKEL, M. & KRIENER, M. (eds), 299-322.
MECKEL, Miriam & KRIENER, M. (eds). 1996. *Internationale Kommunikation.* Opladen: Westdeutcher Verlag.
METZ, Christian 1971. *Langage et cinéma.* Paris: éditions Klincksieck.
MINCHINTON, John. 1986. *Booklet on Subtitling.* Unpublished manuscript.
MINCHINTON, John. 1993. *Subtitling.* Hertfordshire, England: J. Minchinton.
MIZUNO, Akira. 1997. "Broadcast Interpreting in Japan. Some Theoretical and Practical Aspects". In GAMBIER, Y. & GILE, D. & TAYLOR, C. (eds), 192-194.
MONA, Tiziana. 1995. "La choix et l'impact politico-culturels de la traduction simultanée d'émissions de télévision en Suisse". In GAMBIER, Y. (ed.), 329-336.
Le Monde Feb. 14, 1996. "Review of *La Haine*".
Le Monde Aug. 4, 1996, "Report of Speech by the French Minister of Culture": 16.
MOREAU, Hubert. 1995. "Interprétation simultanée sur chaîne bilingue". In GAMBIER, Y. (ed.), 359-362.
MORLEY, David & ROBINS, Kevin. Autumn 1989. "Spaces of identity: communication technologies and the reconfiguration of Europe". *Screen* 30 (4): 4-19.
MOULTHROP, Stuart. 1995. *Getting over the Edge* <http://raven.ubalt.edu/Moulthrop/sam_home.html>
MULHOLLAND, Joan 1991. *The Language of Negotiation.* London & New York: Routledge.
NIDA, Eugene A. 1964. *Toward a Science of Translating.* Leiden: Brill.
NISHIYAMA, Sen. 1988. "Simultaneous Interpreting in Japan and the Role of Television: A Personal Narration". *Meta* 33(1): 64-69.
NOWELL-SMITH, Geoffrey & RICCI, Steven. (eds.) 1998. *Hollywood & Europe.* London: BFI Publishing.
O'CONNELL, Eithne. 1998. "Choices and Constraints in Film Translation". In BOWKER, L., CRONIN, M., KENNY, D. & PEARSON, J. (eds), *Unity in Diversity: Current Trends in Translation Studies.* Manchester: St. Jerome Publishing, 61-67.
ODIN, Jaishree. 1996. "Postcolonialism, Hypertextuality and Network Culture". Paper presented at Vassar College, New York.
PALMER, Patricia. 1988. "The Social Nature of Children's Television Viewing". In DRUMMOND & PATERSON (eds), *Television and its Audience: International Research Perspectives.* London: BFI Publishing, 139-153.
PANOFSKY, Erwin. 1955. *Meaning in the Visual Arts.* Garden City, New York: Doubleday.
PAPAGEORGIOU, Ioannis. 1981. *Tileorasi kai Paidi* [*Television and the Child*]. Athens: Epitheorisi Horofylakis.
PAVAKANUN, Ubowanna., & D'YDEWALLE, Géry. 1992. Watching foreign television programs and language learning. In ENGEL, F. L., BOUWHUIS, D. G., BÖSSER, T. & D'YDEWALLE, G. (eds), *Cognitive modelling and interactive environments in language learning.* Berlin: Springer, 193-198.

PEZDEK, Kathy, & HARTMAN, E. F. 1983. "Children's television viewing: Attention and comprehension of auditory versus visual information". *Child Development*, 54: 1015-1023.

PEZDEK, Kathy, & STEVENS, E. 1984. "Children's memory for auditory and visual information on television". *Developmental Psychology*: 20, 212-218.

PINHAS, R. 1972. "Les retombées scientifiques des opérations Apollo sur l'interprétation simultanée". *La linguistique* 8 (1): 143-147.

PISEK, Gerhard. 1994. *Die grosse Illusion. Probleme und Möglichkeiten der Filmsynchronisation. Dargestellt an Woody Allens "Annie Hall", "Manhattan" und "Hannah and Her Sisters".* Trier: WVT.

POSTER, Mark. 1995. *The Second Media Age.* Cambridge: Basil Blackwell.

POSTER, Mark. 1997. "Cyberdemocracy: Internet and the Public Sphere". In PORTER, D. (ed.), *Internet Culture.* London & New York: Routledge, 201-217.

POSTOVSKY, V. A. 1981. "The priority of aural comprehension in the language acquisition process". In WINITZ, H. (ed.), *The comprehension approach.* Rowley, MA: Newbury House. 170-186.

REDDMANN, H. 1984. "Status Report of the Working Party *Radio and Television*". *AIIC Bulletin* 12 (2): 9-41.

REEVE, Barry. 1995. "Report on the workshop". In GAMBIER, Y. (ed.), 418-421.

REMAEL, Aline. 1995-96. "From the BBC's *Voices from the Island* to the Briton's *De President van Robbeneilan.* A case study in TV translation." *Linguistica Antverpiensia*, XXIX-XXX, 107-128.

RIDING, A. Feb. 4 1996. "A raw French film survives translation". *The New York Times:* 20.

ROBBINS, Vernon K. 1984. *Jesus the teacher. A socio-rhetorical interpretation of Mark.* Philadelphia: Fortress.

ROSA, Alexandra Assis 1999. "The Centre and the Edges. Linguistic Variation and Subtitling *Pygmalion* into Portuguese". In VANDAELE, Jeroen (ed.), *Translation and the (Re)location of Meaning*. Selected Papers of the CETRA Research Seminars in Translation Studies 1994-1996. Leuven: KUL, 317-338.

ROSCHKE, R. 1994. "Scholarship, Research, and Decision-Making in an Electronic Environment". Paper delivered to American Bible Society Research Team.

ROSS, Nigel. 1995. "Dubbing American in Italy". *English Today 41 11(1)*: 45-48.

ROZAT, Jean. 1995. "ARTE et le bilinguisme". *Traduire* 163/164: 23-28.

RYAN, Marie-Laure. 1994. "Immersion vs. Interactivity: Virtual Reality and Literary Theory". *Postmodern culture* 5 (1).

SAARIO, Marjatta & OKSANEN, Susanna 1996. *Le sur-titrage des opéras à l'Opéra national de Finlande.* In GAMBIER, Y. (éd.), 185-196.

SAJAVAARA, Kari. 1986. "Aspects of English influence on Finnish". In VIERECK, W. & BALD W.D. (eds.), 65-78.

SAJAVAARA, Kari. 1991. "English in Finnish: Television subtitles". In IVIR, Vladimir & KALOGJERA, Damir (eds), *Languages in Contact and Contrast.* Berlin & New York: Mouton de Gruyter, 381-390.

SÁNCHEZ-MESA MARTÍNEZ, Domingo. 1997. "Multilinguism and Language Transfer in ODL: New communicative patterns in virtual society". In SÁNCHEZ-MESA, D., LAMBERT J., APOLLON, D. & VAN DEN BRANDEN, J. (eds), *Crosscultural and Linguistic Perspectives in European ODL,* Granada: Universidad de Granada/Transcult, 29-66.

SCOTTO, M. 1998. "Au Forum de Strasbourg, les professionnels changent de stratégie face à l'AMI". *Le Monde* 17 September 1998: 24.

SELS, Chris & VAN DEN BRANDEN, Jeff. 1995. "Cultural factors influencing learning within TLEs". In VAN DEN BRANDEN, J. et al., *Handbook of Cultural Factors in use of TLE*. Heverlee: EuroPACE 2000 (EOUN-EuroPace 2000).

SEREN-ROSSO, M. L. 1989. "Dubbing: le doublage made in France". *Language International* 1(5): 31-33.

SHLESINGER, Miriam 1989. *Simultaneous Interpretation as a Factor in Effecting Shifts in the Position of Texts on the Oral-Literate Continuum*. Unpublished MA Thesis. Tel Aviv University.

SHLESINGER, Miriam 1995. "Shifts in Cohesion in Simultaneous Interpreting". *The Translator* 1 (2): 193-214.

SHONE, T. 1998. "Why can't our films talk the talk?". *The Sunday Times* 9 August 1998: 2-3.

SHREVE, Gregory M. 1997. "From Scriptural to Virtual: Bible Translation, Hypercommunication, and Virtual Reality". In HODGSON, R. & SOUKUP, S.J. (eds), 263-290.

SMITH, Stephen. 1998. "The language of subtitling". In GAMBIER, Y. (ed.), 139-149.

SOHL, G. 1989. *Het verwerken van de vreemdtalige gesproken tekst in een ondertiteld TV-programma* [Processing of spoken foreign language in a subtitled television programme]. Unpublished license thesis, University of Leuven, Belgium.

SØRENSEN, Knud. 1986. "On Anglicisms in Danish". In VIERECK, W. & BALD W.D. (eds), 31-50.

SPERBER, Dan & WILSON, Deirdre 1986/1995. *Relevance. Communication and Cognition*. Oxford / Cambridge: Blackwell.

STIPP, Horst. 1993. "The Challenge to Improve Television for Children: A New Perspective". In BERRY, Gordon & ASAMEN, Joy Keiko (eds), *Children & Television: Images in a Changing Sociocultural World*. Newbury Park, London & New Delhi: Sage, 296-302.

STRANIERO, Sergio. F. 1999 "The Interpreter on the (Talk)show: Analyzing Interaction and Participation Framework". *The Translator* 5 (2): 303-326. Special Issue on Dialogue Interpreting.

STREET, Brian V. 1993. "Culture is a Verb: Anthropological aspects of language and cultural process". In GRADDOL, D., THOMPSON, L. & BYRAM, M. *Language and Culture*. Clevedon: BAAL & Multilingual Matters.

STROLZ, Birgit. 1997. "Quality in Media Interpreting - A Case Study". In GAMBIER, Y. & GILE, D.& TAYLOR, C. (eds), 194-197.

STYAN, D. Autumn/Winter 1995. "Review of *La Haine". Vertigo* 5: 45-47

SULER, John. 1996. "A Revue of *The Internet Regression* by N. Holland" *The Psychology of Cyberspace* <http://www1.rider.edu/~suler/psycyber/psycyber.html>.

SVERRISSON, A. 1998. "Iceland". *Variety International Film Guide:* 191-93.

SZCYPIORSKI, A. 1990. *Amerykańskie whisky i inne opowiadania,* Poznań: SAWW. Traduit en français en 1995: *Whisky américain.* Paris: Ed. de Fallois.

TALENS, Jenaro. 1995. "Writing against Simulacrum: The Place of Literature and Literary Theory in the Electronic Age". *Boundary* 2, 22 (1): 1-21.

TAYLOR, I. 1993."Putting words in their mouths". *Moving Pictures International* 10 June 1993.

TELEVISIÓ DE CATALUNYA 1997: *Criteris lingüístics sobre traducció i doblatge*. Barcelona: Edicions 62.

THOMAS, N. 1993. "Unofficial Babel". *Borderlands*.

TITONE, Renzo & DANESI, Marcel. 1985. *Applied psycholinguistics: An introduction to the psychology of language learning and teaching*. Toronto: University of Toronto Press.

TOMASZKIEWICZ, Teresa. 1993. *Les opérations linguistiques qui sous-tendent le processus de sous-titrage des films.* Poznań: Wydawnictwo Naukowe UAM.

TOMASZKIEWICZ, Teresa. 1997. "Dialogues de films sous-titrés: code oral ou code écrit ?" In LUZZATI, D.et al. (eds), *Le Dialogique*. Bern: Peter Lang, 183-195.

TOMASZKIEWICZ, Teresa. 1998. "Traduction dans les mass-médias". In PUPPEL, S. (ed.), *Scripta Manent*, Poznań: Wydzial Neofilologii UAM: 229-242.

TOOLAN, Michael 1996. *Total Speech. An Integrational Linguistic Approach to Language.* Durham & London: Duke University Press.

TORREGROSA, Carmen. 1996. "Subtítulos: traducir los márgenes de la imagen". *Sendebar* (Revista de la Facultad de Traducción e Interpretación de Granada) 7:73-88.

TOURY, Gideon. 1980. "The Translator as a Nonconformist-To-Be, or: How to Train Translators So As to Violate Translational Norms". In POULSEN, S.-O. & WILSS, W. (eds), *Angewandte Übersetzungswissenschaft. Internationales übersetzungswissenschaftliches Kolloquium an der Wirtschaftsuniversität Arhus/Danemark,* 19-21 Juni 1980. Århus, 180-194.

TOURY, Gideon 1995. *Descriptive Translation Studies and Beyond.* Amsterdam & Philadelphia: John Benjamins.

VAN DEN BRANDEN, J., & LAMBERT, J. 1999. "Cultural and Linguistic Diversity, Threat or Challenge for Virtual Instruction". In FEYTEN, C. & NUTTA, J. (eds), *Virtual Instruction, Issues and Insights from an International Perspective.* Tampa: Libraries Unlimited, Teacher Ideas Press.

VAN ORDEN, G. C., JOHNSTON, J. C., & HALE, B. L. 1988. "Word identification in reading proceeds from spelling to sound to meaning". *Journal of Experimental Psychology: Learning, Memory and Cognition* 14: 371-386. *Variety International Film Guide.* 1998. Spanish Cinema Now, 45-66.

VIAGGIO, Sergio 1997. "Do Interpreters Have the Right to Improve Upon the Original? The Eternal Tug-of-War Between Professional and Expectancy Norms". In *The IIIrd Meeting of Interpreters and Translators from the Countries of Central and Eastern Europe.* Budmerice 97. Prague: JTP, 69-73.

VIAGGIO, Sergio. 1998. "The Landa+Viaggio general theory and models of translation and interlingual intercultural mediation". *TEXTconTEXT* 12=NF 2:177-211.

VIAGGIO, Sergio. 1999. "The Teacher As Setter of Professional Norms. Some Thoughts on Quality in Simultaneous Interpretation". In VIEZZI, Maurizio (ed.), *Quality Forum 1997. Esperienze, problemi, prospettive.* Atti della giornata di studi sulla qualità in interpretazione, Trieste, 14 novembre 1997. Trieste: Scuola Superiore di Lingue Moderne per Interpreti e Traduttori, Università degli Studi di Trieste, 101-119.

VIERECK, Wolfgang & BALD, Wolf-Dietrich (eds). 1986. *English in Contact with Other Languages.* Budapest: Akadémiai Kiadó.

VINCENDEAU, Ginette. 1989. "Films en versions multiples". In AUMONT et al. (eds), 101-117.

VITKUS, Inesse. 1995. "Film and Programme Translation Policy and Techniques in Latvia: Latvian Television, Cinemas and Private TV Stations". In GAMBIER, Y. (ed.), 316-320.

VOLMAR, Victor. 1950. "Foreign Versions". *Journal of the Society of Motion Picture.* 55, November 1950: 536-546.

WHITE, H. C. 1981. "Where do markets come from?". *American Journal of Sociology* 81: 730-80.

WHITMAN-LINSEN, Candace. 1992. *Through the Dubbing Glass: The Synchronization of American Motion Pictures into German, French and Spanish.* Frankfurt am Main: Peter Lang.

WINITZ, Harris. 1996. "Grammaticality judgment as a function of explicit and implicit instruction in Spanish". *Modern Language Journal* 80: 32-46.

WOJTASIEWICZ, O. 1992. *Wstęp de teorii tłumaczenia.* Warszawa: Tepis (2nd edition).

Index

Only comprehensive key concepts, individual languages, and some TV broadcasting companies are indexed below.

List of films, TV programmes, videos cited

Benjamins Translation Library

A complete list of titles in this series can be found on *www.benjamins.com*

88 **GILE, Daniel, Gyde HANSEN and Nike K. POKORN (eds.):** Why Translation Studies Matters. 2010. xi, 269 pp. **[EST Subseries 5]**

87 **HALE, Sandra Beatriz, Uldis OZOLINS and Ludmila STERN (eds.):** The Critical Link 5. Quality in interpreting – a shared responsibility. 2009. vii, 255 pp.

86 **WAKABAYASHI, Judy and Rita KOTHARI (eds.):** Decentering Translation Studies. India and beyond. 2009. xi, 219 pp.

85 **BRAGA RIERA, Jorge:** Classical Spanish Drama in Restoration English (1660–1700). 2009. xv, 330 pp.

84 **MONACELLI, Claudia:** Self-Preservation in Simultaneous Interpreting. Surviving the role. 2009. xxi, 182 pp.

83 **TORIKAI, Kumiko:** Voices of the Invisible Presence. Diplomatic interpreters in post-World War II Japan. 2009. x, 197 pp.

82 **BEEBY, Allison, Patricia RODRÍGUEZ INÉS and Pilar SÁNCHEZ-GIJÓN (eds.):** Corpus Use and Translating. Corpus use for learning to translate and learning corpus use to translate. 2009. x, 151 pp.

81 **MILTON, John and Paul BANDIA (eds.):** Agents of Translation. 2009. vi, 337 pp.

80 **HANSEN, Gyde, Andrew CHESTERMAN and Heidrun GERZYMISCH-ARBOGAST (eds.):** Efforts and Models in Interpreting and Translation Research. A tribute to Daniel Gile. 2009. ix, 302 pp.

79 **YUSTE RODRIGO, Elia (ed.):** Topics in Language Resources for Translation and Localisation. 2008. xii, 220 pp.

78 **CHIARO, Delia, Christine HEISS and Chiara BUCARIA (eds.):** Between Text and Image. Updating research in screen translation. 2008. x, 292 pp.

77 **DÍAZ CINTAS, Jorge (ed.):** The Didactics of Audiovisual Translation. 2008. xii, 263 pp. (incl. CD-Rom).

76 **VALERO-GARCÉS, Carmen and Anne MARTIN (eds.):** Crossing Borders in Community Interpreting. Definitions and dilemmas. 2008. xii, 291 pp.

75 **PYM, Anthony, Miriam SHLESINGER and Daniel SIMEONI (eds.):** Beyond Descriptive Translation Studies. Investigations in homage to Gideon Toury. 2008. xii, 417 pp.

74 **WOLF, Michaela and Alexandra FUKARI (eds.):** Constructing a Sociology of Translation. 2007. vi, 226 pp.

73 **GOUADEC, Daniel:** Translation as a Profession. 2007. xvi, 396 pp.

72 **GAMBIER, Yves, Miriam SHLESINGER and Radegundis STOLZE (eds.):** Doubts and Directions in Translation Studies. Selected contributions from the EST Congress, Lisbon 2004. 2007. xii, 362 pp. **[EST Subseries 4]**

71 **ST-PIERRE, Paul and Prafulla C. KAR (eds.):** In Translation – Reflections, Refractions, Transformations. 2007. xvi, 313 pp.

70 **WADENSJÖ, Cecilia, Birgitta ENGLUND DIMITROVA and Anna-Lena NILSSON (eds.):** The Critical Link 4. Professionalisation of interpreting in the community. Selected papers from the 4th International Conference on Interpreting in Legal, Health and Social Service Settings, Stockholm, Sweden, 20-23 May 2004. 2007. x, 314 pp.

69 **DELABASTITA, Dirk, Lieven D'HULST and Reine MEYLAERTS (eds.):** Functional Approaches to Culture and Translation. Selected papers by José Lambert. 2006. xxviii, 226 pp.

68 **DUARTE, João Ferreira, Alexandra ASSIS ROSA and Teresa SERUYA (eds.):** Translation Studies at the Interface of Disciplines. 2006. vi, 207 pp.

67 **PYM, Anthony, Miriam SHLESINGER and Zuzana JETTMAROVÁ (eds.):** Sociocultural Aspects of Translating and Interpreting. 2006. viii, 255 pp.

66 **SNELL-HORNBY, Mary:** The Turns of Translation Studies. New paradigms or shifting viewpoints? 2006. xi, 205 pp.

65 **DOHERTY, Monika:** Structural Propensities. Translating nominal word groups from English into German. 2006. xxii, 196 pp.

64 **ENGLUND DIMITROVA, Birgitta:** Expertise and Explicitation in the Translation Process. 2005. xx, 295 pp.

63 **JANZEN, Terry (ed.):** Topics in Signed Language Interpreting. Theory and practice. 2005. xii, 362 pp.

62 **POKORN, Nike K.:** Challenging the Traditional Axioms. Translation into a non-mother tongue. 2005. xii, 166 pp. **[EST Subseries 3]**

61 **HUNG, Eva (ed.):** Translation and Cultural Change. Studies in history, norms and image-projection. 2005. xvi, 195 pp.

60 **TENNENT, Martha (ed.):** Training for the New Millennium. Pedagogies for translation and interpreting. 2005. xxvi, 276 pp.

59 **MALMKJAER, Kirsten (ed.):** Translation in Undergraduate Degree Programmes. 2004. vi, 202 pp.

58 **BRANCHADELL, Albert and Lovell Margaret WEST (eds.):** Less Translated Languages. 2005. viii, 416 pp.

57 **CHERNOV, Ghelly V.:** Inference and Anticipation in Simultaneous Interpreting. A probability-prediction model. Edited with a critical foreword by Robin Setton and Adelina Hild. 2004. xxx, 268 pp. **[EST Subseries 2]**

56 **ORERO, Pilar (ed.):** Topics in Audiovisual Translation. 2004. xiv, 227 pp.

55 **ANGELELLI, Claudia V.:** Revisiting the Interpreter's Role. A study of conference, court, and medical interpreters in Canada, Mexico, and the United States. 2004. xvi, 127 pp.

54 **GONZÁLEZ DAVIES, Maria:** Multiple Voices in the Translation Classroom. Activities, tasks and projects. 2004. x, 262 pp.

53 **DIRIKER, Ebru:** De-/Re-Contextualizing Conference Interpreting. Interpreters in the Ivory Tower? 2004. x, 223 pp.

52 **HALE, Sandra Beatriz:** The Discourse of Court Interpreting. Discourse practices of the law, the witness and the interpreter. 2004. xviii, 267 pp.

51 **CHAN, Leo Tak-hung:** Twentieth-Century Chinese Translation Theory. Modes, issues and debates. 2004. xvi, 277 pp.

50 **HANSEN, Gyde, Kirsten MALMKJAER and Daniel GILE (eds.):** Claims, Changes and Challenges in Translation Studies. Selected contributions from the EST Congress, Copenhagen 2001. 2004. xiv, 320 pp. **[EST Subseries 1]**

49 **PYM, Anthony:** The Moving Text. Localization, translation, and distribution. 2004. xviii, 223 pp.

48 **MAURANEN, Anna and Pekka KUJAMÄKI (eds.):** Translation Universals. Do they exist? 2004. vi, 224 pp.

47 **SAWYER, David B.:** Fundamental Aspects of Interpreter Education. Curriculum and Assessment. 2004. xviii, 312 pp.

46 **BRUNETTE, Louise, Georges L. BASTIN, Isabelle HEMLIN and Heather CLARKE (eds.):** The Critical Link 3. Interpreters in the Community. Selected papers from the Third International Conference on Interpreting in Legal, Health and Social Service Settings, Montréal, Quebec, Canada 22–26 May 2001. 2003. xii, 359 pp.

45 **ALVES, Fabio (ed.):** Triangulating Translation. Perspectives in process oriented research. 2003. x, 165 pp.

44 **SINGERMAN, Robert:** Jewish Translation History. A bibliography of bibliographies and studies. With an introductory essay by Gideon Toury. 2002. xxxvi, 420 pp.

43 **GARZONE, Giuliana and Maurizio VIEZZI (eds.):** Interpreting in the 21st Century. Challenges and opportunities. 2002. x, 337 pp.

42 **HUNG, Eva (ed.):** Teaching Translation and Interpreting 4. Building bridges. 2002. xii, 243 pp.

41 **NIDA, Eugene A.:** Contexts in Translating. 2002. x, 127 pp.

40 **ENGLUND DIMITROVA, Birgitta and Kenneth HYLTENSTAM (eds.):** Language Processing and Simultaneous Interpreting. Interdisciplinary perspectives. 2000. xvi, 164 pp.

39 **CHESTERMAN, Andrew, Natividad GALLARDO SAN SALVADOR and Yves GAMBIER (eds.):** Translation in Context. Selected papers from the EST Congress, Granada 1998. 2000. x, 393 pp.

38 **SCHÄFFNER, Christina and Beverly ADAB (eds.):** Developing Translation Competence. 2000. xvi, 244 pp.

37 **TIRKKONEN-CONDIT, Sonja and Riitta JÄÄSKELÄINEN (eds.):** Tapping and Mapping the Processes of Translation and Interpreting. Outlooks on empirical research. 2000. x, 176 pp.

36 **SCHMID, Monika S.:** Translating the Elusive. Marked word order and subjectivity in English-German translation. 1999. xii, 174 pp.

35 **SOMERS, Harold (ed.):** Computers and Translation. A translator's guide. 2003. xvi, 351 pp.

34 **GAMBIER, Yves and Henrik GOTTLIEB (eds.):** (Multi) Media Translation. Concepts, practices, and research. 2001. xx, 300 pp.

33 **GILE, Daniel, Helle V. DAM, Friedel DUBSLAFF, Bodil MARTINSEN and Anne SCHJOLDAGER (eds.):** Getting Started in Interpreting Research. Methodological reflections, personal accounts and advice for beginners. 2001. xiv, 255 pp.

32 **BEEBY, Allison, Doris ENSINGER and Marisa PRESAS (eds.):** Investigating Translation. Selected papers from the 4th International Congress on Translation, Barcelona, 1998. 2000. xiv, 296 pp.

31 **ROBERTS, Roda P., Silvana E. CARR, Diana ABRAHAM and Aideen DUFOUR (eds.):** The Critical Link 2: Interpreters in the Community. Selected papers from the Second International Conference on Interpreting in legal, health and social service settings, Vancouver, BC, Canada, 19–23 May 1998. 2000. vii, 316 pp.

30 **DOLLERUP, Cay:** Tales and Translation. The Grimm Tales from Pan-Germanic narratives to shared international fairytales. 1999. xiv, 384 pp.

29 **WILSS, Wolfram:** Translation and Interpreting in the 20th Century. Focus on German. 1999. xiii, 256 pp.

28 **SETTON, Robin:** Simultaneous Interpretation. A cognitive-pragmatic analysis. 1999. xv, 397 pp.

27 **BEYLARD-OZEROFF, Ann, Jana KRÁLOVÁ and Barbara MOSER-MERCER (eds.):** Translators' Strategies and Creativity. Selected Papers from the 9th International Conference on Translation and Interpreting, Prague, September 1995. In honor of Jiří Levý and Anton Popovič. 1998. xiv, 230 pp.

26 **TROSBORG, Anna (ed.):** Text Typology and Translation. 1997. xvi, 342 pp.

25 **POLLARD, David E. (ed.):** Translation and Creation. Readings of Western Literature in Early Modern China, 1840–1918. 1998. vi, 336 pp.

24 **ORERO, Pilar and Juan C. SAGER (eds.):** The Translator's Dialogue. Giovanni Pontiero. 1997. xiv, 252 pp.

23 **GAMBIER, Yves, Daniel GILE and Christopher TAYLOR (eds.):** Conference Interpreting: Current Trends in Research. Proceedings of the International Conference on Interpreting: What do we know and how? 1997. iv, 246 pp.

22 **CHESTERMAN, Andrew:** Memes of Translation. The spread of ideas in translation theory. 1997. vii, 219 pp.

21 **BUSH, Peter and Kirsten MALMKJAER (eds.):** Rimbaud's Rainbow. Literary translation in higher education. 1998. x, 200 pp.

20 **SNELL-HORNBY, Mary, Zuzana JETTMAROVÁ and Klaus KAINDL (eds.):** Translation as Intercultural Communication. Selected papers from the EST Congress, Prague 1995. 1997. x, 354 pp.

19 **CARR, Silvana E., Roda P. ROBERTS, Aideen DUFOUR and Dini STEYN (eds.):** The Critical Link: Interpreters in the Community. Papers from the 1st international conference on interpreting in legal, health and social service settings, Geneva Park, Canada, 1–4 June 1995. 1997. viii, 322 pp.

18 **SOMERS, Harold (ed.):** Terminology, LSP and Translation. Studies in language engineering in honour of Juan C. Sager. 1996. xii, 250 pp.

17 **POYATOS, Fernando (ed.):** Nonverbal Communication and Translation. New perspectives and challenges in literature, interpretation and the media. 1997. xii, 361 pp.

16 **DOLLERUP, Cay and Vibeke APPEL (eds.):** Teaching Translation and Interpreting 3. New Horizons. Papers from the Third Language International Conference, Elsinore, Denmark, 1995. 1996. viii, 338 pp.

15 **WILSS, Wolfram:** Knowledge and Skills in Translator Behavior. 1996. xiii, 259 pp.

14 **MELBY, Alan K. and Terry WARNER:** The Possibility of Language. A discussion of the nature of language, with implications for human and machine translation. 1995. xxvi, 276 pp.

13 **DELISLE, Jean and Judith WOODSWORTH (eds.):** Translators through History. 1995. xvi, 346 pp.

12 **BERGENHOLTZ, Henning and Sven TARP (eds.):** Manual of Specialised Lexicography. The preparation of specialised dictionaries. 1995. 256 pp.

11 **VINAY, Jean-Paul and Jean DARBELNET:** Comparative Stylistics of French and English. A methodology for translation. Translated and edited by Juan C. Sager and M.-J. Hamel. 1995. xx, 359 pp.

10 **KUSSMAUL, Paul:** Training the Translator. 1995. x, 178 pp.

9 **REY, Alain:** Essays on Terminology. Translated by Juan C. Sager. With an introduction by Bruno de Bessé. 1995. xiv, 223 pp.

8 (1st) **GILE, Daniel:** Basic Concepts and Models for Interpreter and Translator Training. 1995. xvi, 278 pp.

8 **GILE, Daniel:** Basic Concepts and Models for Interpreter and Translator Training. **Revised edition.** 2009. xv, 283 pp.

7 **BEAUGRANDE, Robert de, Abdullah SHUNNAQ and Mohamed Helmy HELIEL (eds.):** Language, Discourse and Translation in the West and Middle East. 1994. xii, 256 pp.

6 **EDWARDS, Alicia B.:** The Practice of Court Interpreting. 1995. xiii, 192 pp.

5 **DOLLERUP, Cay and Annette LINDEGAARD (eds.):** Teaching Translation and Interpreting 2. Insights, aims and visions. Papers from the Second Language International Conference Elsinore, 1993. 1994. viii, 358 pp.

4 **TOURY, Gideon:** Descriptive Translation Studies – and beyond. 1995. viii, 312 pp.

3 **LAMBERT, Sylvie and Barbara MOSER-MERCER (eds.):** Bridging the Gap. Empirical research in simultaneous interpretation. 1994. 362 pp.

2 **SNELL-HORNBY, Mary, Franz PÖCHHACKER and Klaus KAINDL (eds.):** Translation Studies: An Interdiscipline. Selected papers from the Translation Studies Congress, Vienna, 1992. 1994. xii, 438 pp.

1 **SAGER, Juan C.:** Language Engineering and Translation. Consequences of automation. 1994. xx, 345 pp.